CW00607127

English Tourism Council

2 0 0 0

Somewhere Special

THE PERFECT SOURCE FOR THE VERY BEST IN ENGLISH HOSPITALITY

To Begin

All you need to know about the guide and how to use it

5 Welcome...

6 How to use the guide

8 England at a glance

9 The new National Rating Scheme

Contents

13 England's North Country

63 England's Heartland

125 England's West Country

171 South & South East England

Plus... Useful Information

215 General information and advice

220 Index

'Somewhere Special' 2000

Published by: **Jarrold Publishing,** Whitefriars, Norwich NR3 1TR, *in association with the* **English Tourism Council,** Thames Tower, Black's Road, Hammersmith, London W6 9EL *and* **Celsius,** St Thomas House, St Thomas Street, Winchester SO23 9HE.

Managing Editor, ETC: Lara Maiklem
Design, compilation and production: Celsius
Editorial contributors: Tessa Lecomber, Hugh Chevallier
Cartography: Colin Earl
Printed and bound in Great Britain

© English Tourist Board (except where stated), 1999

ISBN 0-7117-1091-0

Important:

The English Tourism Council
The English Tourism Council is the national body for English tourism. The ETC is funded by the Department for Culture, Media and Sport and was launched in July 1999 as a radical transformation of the existing English Tourist Board. Its role is to support the business of tourism and to drive forward a long-term vision for the industry. It will do this by working to improve the quality of England's tourism experience – for example, by working to increase standards in accommodation and service quality across the industry – to strengthen competitiveness and to encourage the wise growth of tourism. The ETC is a strategic body brokering partnerships, setting standards, developing policy, providing research and forecasts and championing issues at the highest level

Front cover: The Swan Hotel (page 94)
Back cover: Cross Lanes Guest House (page 182), Skiddaw Hotel (page 23) and Tye Rock Country House Hotel (page 141)

Somewhere Special is the guide for the discerning traveller, featuring hundreds of hotels, B&Bs, inns, farmhouses and guest accommodation all offering their guests that little bit extra. The format is easy to use, with attractive, detailed entries cross-referenced to full-colour maps, plus articles and features as well as helpful hints. Whatever your budget, and whether you want a short get-away or a longer break, **Somewhere Special** offers a choice of accommodation that promises a warm welcome and a stay that's special.

Welcome...

Your sure signs of where to stay

As in other English Tourism Council guides, all accommodation included in this invaluable title has been assessed under the Council's new National Rating Scheme (see page 9). In **Somewhere Special**, however, you are promised something extra, for every single entry has achieved a top quality rating of Four or Five Diamonds, or a Star or Diamond rating with a Gold or Silver Award (see page 9). This means that whatever range of facilities are on offer, they are presented with exceptional care, individuality and quality of service.

Quality first

Whether you're looking for no-holds-barred luxury on a grand scale, a short break in a small hotel with character or an intimate bed and breakfast that gives personal attention to perhaps only three or four guests, you're looking in the right guide. The criterion for inclusion in **Somewhere Special** is excellence rather than the range of facilities available – though of course you'll be able to see at a glance exactly what's on offer.

How to use the guide

Somewhere Special will enable you to find that special place to stay – whichever part of the country you are planning to visit. Even if you only have a rough idea of where you wish to go, you can easily use this guide to locate a quality place to stay.

The guide is divided into four distinct sections: England's North Country, England's Heartland, England's West Country, and South & South East England. Overleaf you will find a break-down of which county is in which region, together with an accompanying 'England-at-a-glance' map.

Regional maps

At the start of each section is a full-colour regional map which clearly plots by number the location of all the **Somewhere Special** entries, as well as the positions of major roads, towns, stations and airports. If you know the area you want to visit, first locate the possible establishments on the regional map and then turn to the appropriate pages in the regional section.

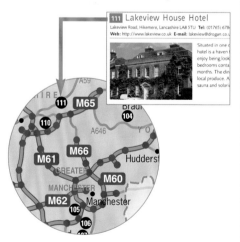

The entries are listed by their geographical position, so you'll find that the places you're interested in are usually close to each other in the listing.

Other features of the guide

As well as the entries – 453 in all – you'll find many interesting and informative features on a wide variety of subjects scattered throughout the book. The four comprehensive introductions to the regions start on pages 13, 63, 125 and 171. At the back of the book (starting on page 215) you will find more detailed information about booking accommodation. You are strongly recommended to read this before committing yourself to any firm arrangements, bearing in mind the fact that all details have been supplied by proprietors themselves. Finally, you will find a complete alphabetical index to all the establishments featured in the guide, cross-referenced to the page number on which they appear.

The entries in more detail

The entries are designed to convey as much information as possible in a clear, attractive and easy-to-read format. A fictional sample entry is shown below, together with an explanation of the layout of information.

Each entry shows the establishment's Star or Diamond rating. In **Somewhere Special**, of course, every entry will have a rating of either Four or Five Diamonds, or a Star or Diamond rating with a Gold or Silver Award.

1   Entries cross-referenced by number to full-colour maps at the beginning of each regional section

2   Establishment name plus Star or Diamond rating

3   Address and full contact details

4   Full description of establishment

5   Prices per **room** per night for bed & breakfast (double room prices are for two people)

6   Prices per **person** per night for dinner, bed & breakfast (half board) and any minimum booking requirement

7   Lunch and evening meal times (if available)

8   Number of bedrooms and bathrooms

9   Number of parking spaces

10 Months open (only shown if establishment is **not** open all year)

11 Credit and charge cards accepted

12 Symbols showing the full range of facilities and services available (see the back cover flap for a key)

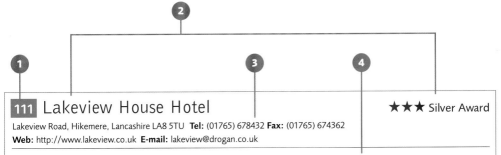

2

1   **3**   **4**

111 Lakeview House Hotel

★ ★ ★ Silver Award

Lakeview Road, Hikemere, Lancashire LA8 5TU **Tel:** (01765) 678432 **Fax:** (01765) 674362
Web: http://www.lakeview.co.uk **E-mail:** lakeview@drogan.co.uk

Situated in one of the most superb locations, right on the lake shore, our hotel is a haven for those who appreciate the finer things in life and who enjoy being looked after with care and courtesy. The public rooms and master bedrooms contain antique furniture. Log fire in public rooms in the winter months. The dining room offers the best of English cooking using the pick of local produce. A cedarwood lodge in the grounds contains a swimming pool, sauna and solarium for the exclusive use of our guests.

Bed & Breakfast per night: single room from £40.00–£51.00; double room from £74.00–£96.00
Dinner, Bed & Breakfast per person, per night: £98.00–£120.00 (min 2 nights)
Lunch available: 1200–1430
Evening meal: 1800 (last orders 2200)

Bedrooms: 7 single, 14 double, 11 twin, 8 triple
Bathrooms: 40 en-suite
Parking: 38 spaces
Open: All year except Christmas
Cards accepted: Mastercard, Visa, Switch/Delta, Amex, JCB, Visa Electron, Solo

5 6 7   **8 9 10 11**   **12**

England at a glance

This guide is divided into four main regional sections. A map of the area, showing each entry and its nearest town or city, as well as nearby major roads or motorways, can be found after the regional introduction.

England's North Country
Cheshire, Cumbria, Durham, East Riding of Yorkshire, Greater Manchester, Lancashire, Merseyside, North & North East Lincolnshire, North, South & West Yorkshire, Northumberland, Tees Valley, Tyne & Wear and York.

England's Heartland
Bedfordshire, Cambridgeshire, Derbyshire, Essex, Gloucestershire, Herefordshire, Hertfordshire, Leicestershire, Lincolnshire, Norfolk, Northamptonshire, Nottinghamshire, Rutland, Shropshire, Staffordshire, Suffolk, Warwickshire, West Midlands, and Worcestershire.

England's West Country
Bath & North East Somerset, Bristol, Cornwall, Devon, Isles of Scilly, North Somerset, Somerset, South Gloucestershire, Western Dorset and Wiltshire.

South & South East England
Berkshire, Buckinghamshire, East & West Sussex, Eastern Dorset, Hampshire, Isle of Wight, Kent, London, Oxfordshire and Surrey.

England's
North Country

England's
Heartland

South &
South East
England

England's
West Country

The Lansdown Grove (page 167)

The new National Rating Scheme

Pinkhill Cottage (page 180)

The English Tourism Council, in response to consumer demand, has created a new rating scheme for Hotels and Guest Accommodation, using Stars for Hotels and Diamonds for Guest Accommodation (which embraces B&Bs, farmhouses and inns). The new scheme puts greater emphasis on quality, particularly in areas of cleanliness and guest care. Now, when you see one of our signs showing Stars or Diamonds, you'll know that the hotel or guest accommodation has been visited overnight anonymously by our qualified assessors. It's that simple and that easy to find quality accommodation to meet your expectations.

Gold and Silver Awards

Look out for the Gold and Silver Awards which are exclusive to the English Tourism Council. They are awarded to those establishments which not only achieve the overall quality required for their Star or Diamond rating, but also reach the highest level of quality in those specific areas which guests identify as being really important for them. They will reflect the quality of comfort and cleanliness you will find in the bedrooms and bathrooms and the quality of service you'll enjoy throughout your stay.

The Grand Hotel (page 201)

An assessor calls

Before a quality grading is awarded, one of our qualified assessors visits the guesthouse, B&B, farmhouse, inn or hotel for an assessment.

The assessor books in advance, but does not reveal his or her identity on arrival. Sadly for those contemplating a career move, the assessor does not have a lazy time; he or she is busy noting the standard of décor, the state of the grounds, the quality of the food and the courtesy of the staff. Once the bill has been paid the next morning, the assessor announces his or her identity to the management and tours the building.

At the end of the tour, they discuss the conclusions, with the assessor making suggestions where helpful. Only after the visit does the assessor arrive at a conclusion for the quality grade – so the assessment is 100% independent and reliable.

Tylney Hall Hotel (page 184)

Danesfield House (page 183)

Stars for Hotels

These new ratings are your sign of quality assurance, giving you the confidence to book the accommodation that meets your expectations. Based on the internationally recognised rating of one to five Stars, the new system puts greater emphasis on quality and is based on research which shows exactly what consumers are looking for when choosing a hotel. Ratings are awarded from one to five Stars – the more Stars, the higher the quality and the greater the range of facilities and level of services provided.

> Remember that only Star rated hotels with a Gold or Silver Award qualify for entry in Somewhere Special.

The Star ratings explained

At a ★ hotel you will find:
Practical accommodation with a limited range of facilities and services, and a high standard of cleanliness throughout. Friendly and courteous staff to give you the help and information you need to enjoy your stay.
Restaurant/eating area open to you and your guests for breakfast and dinner. Alcoholic drinks will be served in a bar or lounge. 75% of bedrooms will have en-suite or private facilities.

At a ★★ hotel you will find:
In addition to what is provided at ★
Good overnight accommodation with more comfortable bedrooms, better equipped – all with en-suite or private facilities and colour television. A relatively straightforward range of services, including food and drink and a personal style of service. A restaurant/dining room for breakfast and dinner. A lift is normally available.

At a ★★★ hotel you will find:
In addition to what is provided at ★ and ★★
Possibly larger establishments, but all offering significantly greater quality and range of facilities and services, and usually more spacious public areas and bedrooms. A more formal style of service with a receptionist on duty and staff responding well to your needs and requests. Room service of continental breakfast. Laundry service available. A wide selection of drinks, light lunch and snacks served in a bar or lounge.

At a ★★★★ hotel you will find:
In addition to what is provided at ★, ★★ and ★★★
Accommodation offering superior comfort and quality; all bedrooms with en-suite bath, fitted overhead shower and WC. The hotel will have spacious and very well appointed public areas and will put a strong emphasis on food and drink. Staff will have very good technical and social skills, anticipating and responding to your needs and requests. Room service of all meals and 24 hour drinks, refreshments and snacks. Dry cleaning service available.

At a ★★★★★ hotel you will find:
In addition to what is provided at ★, ★★, ★★★ and ★★★★
A spacious, luxurious establishment offering you the highest international quality of accommodation, facilities, services and cuisine. It will have striking accommodation throughout, with a range of extra facilities. You will feel very well cared for by professional, attentive staff providing flawless guest services. A hotel that fits the highest international standards for the industry, with an air of luxury, exceptional comfort and a sophisticated ambience.

Grapevine Hotel (page 97)

Diamonds for Guest Accommodation

The Diamond ratings for Guest Accommodation reflect visitor expectations of this sector – a wide variety of serviced accommodation, embracing B&Bs, inns, farmhouses and guest accommodation, for which England is renowned.

The quality of what is provided is more important to visitors than a wide range of facilities and services. Therefore, the same minimum requirement for facilities and services applies to all Guest Accommodation from one to five Diamonds, while progressively higher levels of quality and customer care must be provided for each rating.

In Somewhere Special, only those establishments with a Four or Five Diamond rating, or a Diamond rated property with a Gold or Silver Award, qualify for entry in the guide.

The Great House Restaurant and Hotel (page 120)

The Diamond ratings explained

At ◆◆◆ guest accommodation you will find:
A good overall level of quality. For example, good quality, comfortable bedrooms; well maintained, practical décor; a good choice of quality items available for breakfast; other meals, where provided, will be freshly cooked from good quality ingredients. A good degree of comfort provided for you, with good levels of customer care. A comfortable bed, with clean bed linen and towels and fresh soap. Adequate heating and hot water available at reasonable times for baths or showers at no extra charge. A sound overall level of quality and customer care in all areas.

At ◆◆◆◆ guest accommodation you will find:
In addition to what is provided at ◆◆◆
A very good overall level of quality in all areas and customer care showing very good levels of attention to your needs.

At ◆◆◆◆◆ guest accommodation you will find:
In addition to what is provided at ◆◆◆ and ◆◆◆◆
An excellent overall level of quality. For example, ample space with a degree of luxury, an excellent quality bed, high quality furniture, excellent interior design. Breakfast offering a wide choice of high quality fresh ingredients; other meals, where provided, featuring fresh, seasonal local ingredients. Excellent levels of customer care, anticipating your needs.

The Acer Hotel (page 53)

Home Farm (page 83)

Note: Somewhere Special only features establishments with three, four or five Diamonds.

Accessibility

It's all very well deciding exactly where you'd like to stay, but if you find difficulty in walking or are a wheelchair user, then you also need to know how accessible a particular establishment is. If you book your accommodation at an establishment displaying the Accessible symbol, there's no longer any guesswork involved. The National Accessible Scheme forms part of the *Tourism for All* campaign that is being promoted by all National and Regional Tourist Boards throughout Britain. There are three categories of accessibility, based upon what are considered to be the practical needs of wheelchair users:

 Category 1: accessible to all wheelchair users including those travelling independently

 Category 2: accessible to a wheelchair user with assistance

 Category 3: accessible to a wheelchair user able to walk short distances and up at least three steps.

Additional help and guidance for those with special needs can be obtained from:

Holiday Care Service
2nd Floor, Imperial Buildings
Victoria Road
Horley
Surrey
RH6 7PZ
Telephone (01293) 774535
Fax (01293) 784647
Minicom (01293) 776943

Choose Quality Assessed Accommodation

...from the English Tourism Council's official range of Accommodation Guides

Whether it's a hotel, B&B, self-catering holiday home, or working farm you can be assured that each property has been quality graded to meet your expectations.

Available from all good bookshops

England's North Country

▶ Grace Darling

Few women have attracted such uninvited public adulation as Grace Darling. Daughter of a lighthouse keeper, Grace lived a lonely life on the Farne Islands, off the Northumberland coast. On 7 September 1838 she and her father risked their lives to rescue nine survivors from the wrecked steamer *Forfarshire*, putting out in heavy seas in a tiny rowing-boat. The newspapers made her a national heroine overnight. At Bamburgh are the Grace Darling Museum and the cottage where she was born. Weather permitting, a boat trip around the Farne Islands is an unforgettable experience (tel: 01665 720884).

▶ Humber Bridge

`Parliament approved construction of a Humber bridge in 1959, but it took 22 years to open, and cost £98 million, almost four times the original estimate. The result, however, is impressive. With a central span of almost a mile (4,626ft - 1,410m), the Humber Bridge was until very recently the longest unsupported section of bridge in the world. Visitor facilities include viewing areas at both ends; the northern side also has a tourist information centre and country park; views of and from the bridge are magnificent.

Peak after peak

The soul of England's North Country lies in the Pennines, England's mountainous backbone stretching from the borders of Scotland to the borders of the Midlands. The North boasts the Lake District, two glorious coastlines, countless imposing castles and, in York, one of the most perfect cities one could ever wish for, but somehow the sheer scale of the Pennine ridge dominates. The mountains run for around 200 miles (322km), the peaks rising above 2,000ft (610m), too many to count.

Exploring on foot

The most famous way to savour the Pennine experience, fitness and time permitting, is to walk Britain's oldest long-distance path. About 10,000 people each year complete the 268 miles (431km) of the Pennine Way, though many more – perhaps 300,000 – join it for a mile or two from one of 535 separate access points. Two of these are intersections with other waymarked paths. The Coast-to-Coast Walk, as its name suggests, links the Irish Sea with the North Sea, traversing the Lake District, Yorkshire Dales and North York Moors national parks on its 190-mile (306km) route, while the Dales Way (81 miles - 130km) is a low-level path along the banks of the Wharfe, Dee, Lune and Kent rivers. The Cumbria Way (Ulverston to Carlisle) guides you through Lakeland grandeur. The Cleveland Way falls almost entirely within the North York Moors national park, but still extends over 100 miles (161km). Roughly following the river from its source high in the Dales to the sea, from near Preston, the wise walker tackles the Ribble Way in a downhill direction. Altogether quieter and less dramatic is the Wolds Way, wending from near Hull to Filey, where it joins the Cleveland Way. Needless to say, all these – as well as Hadrian's Wall, which can be walked for its entire length – explore scenery of the utmost beauty. All make an ideal starting point for shorter strolls, too.

Mills to museums

Towards the southern end of the Pennines the valleys become more populated. The fast-flowing rivers that long ago powered the mills are lined with the characterful small houses built for the workers. Once reviled, but now revered, towns such as Holmforth and Hebden Bridge have justly become visitor attractions in their own right. And the factories have in many instances been turned into imaginative museums and galleries. The Armley Mills Industrial Museum, Leeds, occupies what was once the largest woollen mill in the world; Saddleworth Museum and Art Gallery houses working woollen textile machinery; much of Salts Mill, near Bradford is devoted to the works of the artist, David Hockney; and, at Macclesfield, Paradise Mill produced silk until the 1980s. At Sheffield, those with an interest in industrial archaeology can indulge themselves at either the Abbeydale Industrial Hamlet or Kelham Island

Industrial Museum. If you prefer more modern scientific endeavour, then try the Jodrell Bank Science Centre & Arboretum, south of Manchester, home of a massive steerable radio telescope.

On a grand scale

A few miles from Jodrell Bank lies Tatton Park, one of the finest country houses of the North and on a decidedly grand scale. Other lesser-known properties to explore include: medieval Raby Castle with its nine towers (near Staindrop, County Durham); the very Victorian Lady Waterford Hall, decorated with murals depicting familiar Bible stories (Ford, Northumberland); Dalemain, a stately home intriguingly adapted from the original pele tower, now home of the Westmorland and Cumberland Yeomanry Museum (Penwith, Cumbria); Burton Constable Hall, an Elizabethan setting for a remarkable collection of scientific instruments (Sproatley, East Riding of Yorkshire); Croxteth Hall, where visitors can join an Edwardian house party or look at an extensive collection of rare breed animals (Liverpool, Merseyside); and Browsholme Hall, full of unusual objects squirrelled by the Parker family, owners of the hall for over 400 years (near Whitewell, Lancashire).

For art's sake

The North Country has a range of arts and music festivals to rival the rest of England. As always, the breadth of entertainment is prodigious. For concerts devoted to early music – and played in some of England's most glorious medieval churches – visit either the York Early Music Festival (July) or, 25 or so miles (40km) further east, the Beverley and East Riding Early Music Festival (May). At the other end of the spectrum, go south to Huddersfield in November for the Contemporary Music Festival. The Lake District hosts jazz, orchestral and chamber concerts at a number of venues as part of its Summer Music festivities (August), while Chester does broadly the same – as well as adding a fringe element, too – in July. Bradford (late June and early July) and Harrogate (late July and early August) both add comedy and street theatre to a range of musical concerts. Manchester, meanwhile, devotes three weeks in May to its Streets Ahead festival. Circus events and fireworks provide alternatives to the music, dance and theatre – and everything is free. And, if you thought the Aldborough Festival was exclusive to Suffolk, look closely at the spelling. A village near Boroughbridge, North Yorkshire, holds the Northern Aldborough (not Aldeburgh) Festival each July; classical music is once again the subject.

Fishing villages and golden sands

The coastline of Northumberland, England's north-eastern extremity, bears intriguing resemblance to Cornwall, in the extreme south-west. Fine sandy beaches, a history peopled by saints and martyrs, and

▶ **Grizedale Sculpture Trail**

A walk through Grizedale Forest offers an intriguing trail of discovery in the hunt for 80 or so large-scale sculptures dotted along its pathways. The Sculpture Trail began as an opportunity for sculptors to develop diverse works on the theme of the Forest, and the sculptures are inspired by the materials and forms which naturally occur there: wildlife, rock formations, drystone walls, and, of course, trees. Most are sited on the Silurian Way, a 9½-mile (15km) circular walk starting at the Visitor Centre (tel: 01229 860010) where maps (that include short-cuts) may be purchased.

▶ **Lawnmowers on Display**

The British Lawnmower Museum (tel: 01704 501336) is based in the seaside resort of Southport, Merseyside. Prized exhibits include some of the first machines dating from the early 19th century, mowers once belonging to Nicholas Parsons and to Prince Charles, another capable of cutting a 2-inch (5cm) wide strip, and what is believed to be the only hand-powered rotary lawnmower in existence. Also on view is the world's largest collection of toy mowers and one of the oldest surviving racing lawnmowers (built by the curator).

▶ Bowes Museum

In the entrance hall, on the stroke of every hour, a large silver swan whirrs into action, slowly bending its articulated silver neck to swallow a silver fish. This bizarre mechanical toy is one of many valuable treasures

amassed by John Bowes, Earl of Strathmore, who in 1869 began building this outrageously inappropriate French château-style mansion to house his possessions. The imposing rooms contain paintings by El Greco, Goya, Boucher and Courbet, together with superb displays of furniture, ceramics and tapestries (tel: 01833 690606).

▶ Gondola

Gondola is the National Trust's only steam yacht, and plies up and down Coniston Water in the Lake District for around seven months each year. Described as 'a perfect combination of the Venetian Gondola and the English Steam Yacht', she was launched at Coniston in 1859, remaining in service until 1937, when her hull became a houseboat and her boiler was used for the cutting of timber in a saw mill. In 1977 she was bought by the National Trust, and, restored to former glory, once more ferries visitors the length of the lake.

a rural interior characterise both. In Northumberland, it is never difficult to escape the throng, but take a trip to the Farne Islands, and you will be outnumbered by both birds and seals. The golden shores south of Bamburgh and north of Dunstanburgh, two glorious beaches that never seem busy, have the added attraction of offering views of their respective castles. Further south, into the North York Moors national park, the coastline is more for the fossil hunter and the walker – the Cleveland Way here follows the sea – than the sun-seeker. Many of the picturesque villages, such as Ravenscar, Runswick Bay, Staithes and Robin Hood's Bay, tumble down cliffs that yield an array of fossils. Then come the famous resorts of Scarborough, Filey and Bridlington, each with magnificent sandy beaches ideal for family outings. Southport, on the southern Lancashire shores, has endless sand, as does its illustrious neighbour, Blackpool, over the Ribble Estuary. North again is Morecambe Bay, at low tide around 150 square miles (38,850 hectares) of gleaming but potentially treacherous sand. Away from the bustle of Blackpool and the teaming birdlife of Morecambe Bay, try Annaside or Gutterby Spa, two of the region's remoter beaches.

Former glories

Hidden away on Cumbria's westernmost point is an elegant port that, 250 years ago, was busier than Liverpool. Retaining many 17th- and 18th-century buildings, and with pleasure craft bobbing up and down in the old harbour, Whitehaven makes an unusual excursion from the Lake District. The North has countless towns that invite unhurried exploration. One is Hexham, whose focal point is the magnificent abbey, dating largely from the 12th-century, but it also has Georgian streets surrounding the Shambles, the shelter for the lively Tuesday market. Others to consider are: Rothbury, also in Northumberland, an attractive small market town with a medieval bridge; Barnard Castle (County Durham), where visitors can marvel at the exhibits in the Bowes Museum then clamber over the ruins of the lofty castle to admire the views of the River Tees; Beverley (East Riding of Yorkshire), a superb mixture of medieval and Georgian architecture; Pickering (North Yorkshire), whose ancient coaching inns reflect its heyday as an important stop on the way to Scarborough and Whitby; Clitheroe (Lancashire), where a diminutive Norman castle watches over the stone-built houses; and Macclesfield (Cheshire), a former weaving centre in the shadow of the southern Pennines with fine 18th-century townhouses.

North Country fare

The region produces a number of edible specialities, confectionery and cheeses in particular. Cumbria, renowned for its coiled, smoky sausage, also produces Cumberland rum butter – originally eaten to celebrate the arrival of a newborn child and still made in Whitehaven – as well as Kendal mint cake, famously taken on expeditions to Mount Everest. Pontefract was once the centre of liquorice cultivation and, although the plant is no longer grown, Pontefract cakes are manufactured in the town. Nantwich Museum devotes a room to Cheshire cheese, while three Yorkshire Dales – Swaledale, Wensleydale and Coverdale – give their names to crumbly cheeses made within the national park. The finest kippers are traditionally sold on the quayside at Whitby.

A Northern miscellany

The North Country can also offer many other curiosities. Around Ingleton are a number of cave systems, of which the vast Gaping Ghyll cavern is one of the most impressive. Also in North Yorkshire, but west of Masham, is the Druid's Temple, a 19th-century folly built in imitation of a miniature Stonehenge. Hale, just over the Mersey from Runcorn, boasts the grave of John Middleton, a local giant reputedly 9 ft 3 inches (2.8m) tall, while at Lower Heysham, near Morecambe, on a promontory above the sandy beach, are some strange rock 'coffins', perhaps carved by 9th-century missionaries from Ireland. And in one of England's furthest-flung spots, high up in the Pennines where Cumbria and Durham meet, is Cauldron Snout, a magnificent waterfall and series of cataracts.

Contact numbers
Lake District National Park Visitors' Centre (tel: 01539 446601)
Yorkshire Dales National Park (tel: 01756 752774)
North York Moors National Park (tel: 01439 770657)
Hadrian's Wall (tel: 01434 344363)
The Armley Mills Industrial Museum, Leeds (tel: 0113 263 7861)
Saddleworth Museum and Art Gallery, Uppermill (tel: 01457 874093)
Salts Mill, Bradford (tel: 01274 531163)
Paradise Mill, Macclesfield (tel: 01625 618228)
Abbeydale Industrial Hamlet, Sheffield (tel: 0114 236 7731)
Kelham Island Museum, Sheffield (tel: 0114 272 2106)
Jodrell Bank Science Centre & Arboretum (tel: 01477 571339)
Tatton Park, Knutsford (tel: 01565 654822)
Raby Castle, Staindrop (tel: 01833 660202)
Lady Waterford Hall, Ford (tel: 01890 820224)
Dalemain, Penwith (tel: 01768 486450)
Burton Constable Hall, Sproatley (tel: 01964 562400)
Croxteth Hall, Liverpool (tel: 0151 228 5311)
Browsholme Hall, Whitewell (tel: 01254 826719)
York Early Music Festival (tel: 01904 645738)
Beverley and East Riding Early Music Festival (tel: 01904 645738)
Huddersfield Contemporary Music Festival (tel: 01484 472103)
Lake District Summer Music (tel: 01539 733411)
Chester Summer Festival (tel: 01244 320722)
Bradford Festival (tel: 01274 309199)
Harrogate International Festival (tel: 01423 562303)
Manchester Streets Ahead (tel: 0161 238 4500)
Northern Aldborough Festival (tel: 01423 324899)
Nantwich Museum (tel: 01270 627104)

► Abbeys of the Dales and Moors

When Cistercian monks from Normandy established the foundations of Rievaulx, Fountains, Jervaulx and Byland, they were given some of the poorest tracts of wasteland to farm by the Norman lords. But, by recruiting large numbers of lay-brethren and using efficient farming methods, they turned moorland into a productive asset. In this they were emulated by other religious orders: the Augustinians at Kirkham, Guisborough and Bolton, and the Benedictines at York and Whitby. Today, of these great communities, only hauntingly beautiful ruins remain, many gracing some of England's most ravishing countryside.

► Berwick-upon-Tweed

Berwick-upon-Tweed, though still in England, is further north than much of the Hebridean island of Islay. Oddly, it is cut off from the county which bears its name, for Berwickshire lies in Scotland. Not surprisingly, Berwick's history is intractably bound up with the struggle between the English and the Scots; between 1147 and 1482, the town changed hands 13 times. The 16th century saw the town walls comprehensively fortified against a Scots-French attack which never materialised, hence their amazing state of preservation. A two-mile (3km) walk around these ramparts gives spectacular views of the historic town.

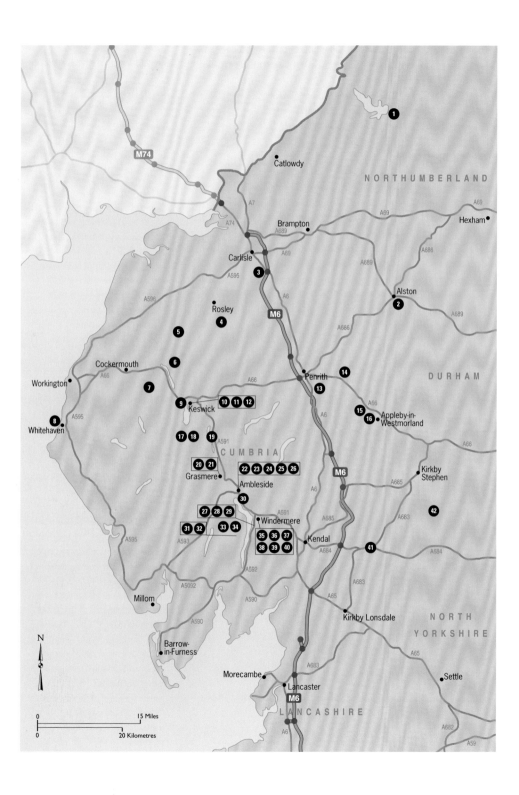

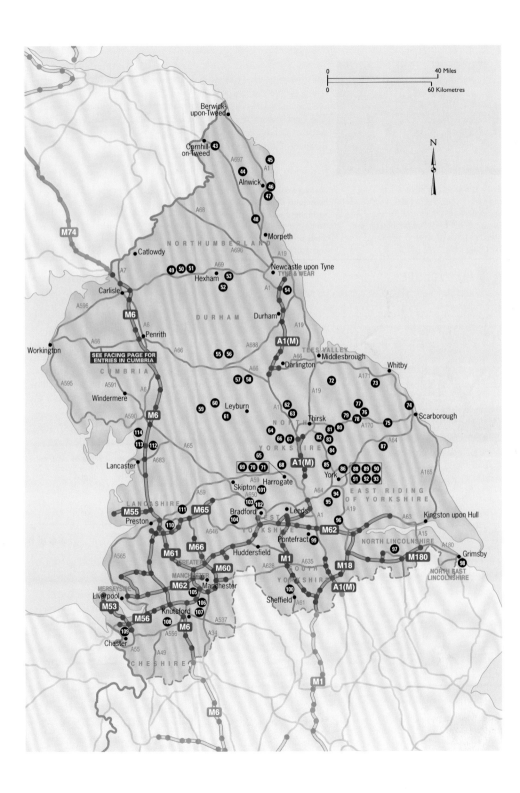

0 _____ 40 Miles
0 _____ 60 Kilometres

N

Berwick-upon-Tweed

Cornhill-on-Tweed **43**

A697
45
A1
44
Alnwick **46**
47

A68
48
Morpeth

A19
NORTHUMBERLAND
A696

Catlowdy
A7
A69
Newcastle upon Tyne
TYNE & WEAR
49 **50** **51**
Hexham **53**
52
A1
54

Carlisle
A6
DURHAM
Durham

M6
A66
Penrith
A19

Workington
A596
A66
A688
A1(M)
TEES VALLEY
55 **56**
A66
Middlesbrough
Whitby
A595
A591
CUMBRIA
A66
Darlington
A171
72
73

Windermere
A6
57 **58**
A19
74
Scarborough
M6
60 Leyburn
59
61
62
77
76
A170
75
Thirsk
63
79 **78**
NORTH
64
81 **80**
66 **67**
82 **83**
A64
YORKSHIRE
84
87
114
65
85
86 **88** **89** **90**
113 **112**
69 **70** **71**
68 A1(M)
York
91 **92** **93**
Lancaster
A65
A683
Harrogate
EAST RIDING
A59
Skipton
A64
OF YORKSHIRE
101
A650
94
A165
LANCASHIRE
111 M65
103 **102**
95
A19
Kingston upon Hull
M55
110
Bradford
A63
Preston
104
Leeds
A646
WEST
M62
96
A15
YORKSHIRE
Pontefract **99**
M61 M66
Huddersfield
97
M180
Grimsby
60
M1 A635
M18
98
M62
105 Manchester
A628
SOUTH
A1(M)
NORTH EAST
MERSEYSIDE
106
YORKSHIRE
LINCOLNSHIRE
Liverpool
GREATER
100
MANCHESTER
M53
Knutsford **107**
Sheffield
A61
M56
108 M6
Chester **109**
A556
A537
A55
A49
A34
CHESHIRE

M74

SEE FACING PAGE FOR
ENTRIES IN CUMBRIA

M1

M6

1 The Pheasant Inn (by Kielder Water) ◆◆◆◆

Stannersburn, Falstone, Hexham, Northumberland NE48 1DD **Tel:** (01434) 240382 **Fax:** (01434) 240382
E-mail: thepheasantinn@kielderwater.demon.co.uk

Traditional 17th-century inn, 375 years old, run by the Kershaw family for the last 15 years. Beamed ceilings, exposed stone walls, centrally heated, open fires provide its cosy atmosphere. An emphasis is maintained on home cooking, using carefully prepared local produce. Eight en-suite bedrooms offer comfortable accommodation with all the modern conveniences you would expect. An ideal location for visiting Kielder Water, Hadrian's Wall, Rothbury (Cragside) and the Scottish Border country.

Bed & Breakfast per night: single occupancy from £35.00–£45.00; double room from £60.00–£65.00
Dinner, Bed & Breakfast per person, per night: £45.00–£50.00 (min 2 nights)
Lunch available: 1200–1430

Evening meal: 1900 (last orders 2100)
Bedrooms: 4 double, 3 twin, 1 family
Bathrooms: 8 en-suite
Parking: 30 spaces
Cards accepted: Mastercard, Visa, Switch/Delta, Eurocard, JCB

2 Greycroft ◆◆◆◆ Silver Award

Middle Park, The Raise, Alston, Cumbria CA9 3AR **Tel:** (01434) 381383

Come! Enjoy our home in a small hamlet one mile from the historical town of Alston, the setting for the television series of Jane Eyre and Oliver Twist. Start the day with a good, hearty breakfast, dinner optional. Ideal for walking or touring. Many footpaths criss-cross these hills; woodland and riverside walks, the most famous being the Pennine Way. The Lakes, Hadrian's Wall, Scottish Borders and rural Northumbria are all within easy reach.

Bed & Breakfast per night: single occupancy from £19.00–£23.00; double room from £38.00–£42.00
Dinner, Bed & Breakfast per person, per night: £29.00–£32.00
Evening meal: 1800 (last bookings 1600)

Bedrooms: 1 double, 1 triple
Bathrooms: 2 en-suite
Parking: 2 spaces
Open: All year except April

3 Staggs Cottage ◆◆◆◆

Brisco, Carlisle, Cumbria CA4 0QS **Tel:** (01228) 547419

Enjoy a warm welcome in this 18th-century converted barn situated in a pretty, quiet, rural area easily reached from junction 42 of the M6. Carlisle is convenient – approximately 3.5 miles away. A short drive from the Northern fells and lakes, Hadrian's Wall and the Scottish Border towns. The racecourse and the Carlisle/Settle Railway are close by. The open views are interesting in all seasons. A home of artwork and music. Full English breakfasts, with winter log fires to start the day.

Bed & Breakfast per night: single occupancy from £23.00–£28.00; double room from £40.00–£54.00

Bedrooms: 2 twin
Bathrooms: 1 en-suite, 1 public
Parking: 2 spaces

Entries are cross referenced by number to the maps on pages 18–19

4 Swaledale Watch ◆◆◆◆

Whelpo, Caldbeck, Wigton, Cumbria CA7 8HQ **Tel:** (016974) 78409 **Fax:** (016974) 78409

Swaledale Watch is a busy sheep farm just outside picturesque Caldbeck and within the Lake District National Park. Enjoy great comfort, excellent food, a warm welcome and peaceful, unspoilt surroundings. A central location for touring, walking or exploring the rolling Northern Fells. All rooms are beautifully decorated, homely, and have private facilities. Chilly evenings mean open fires in the lounges with books for every interest. A magical, memorable walk lies within 150 yards of the house. Your happiness is our priority.

Bed & Breakfast per night: single occupancy from £19.00–£22.00; double room from £36.00–£42.00
Dinner, Bed & Breakfast per person, per night: £31.00–£34.00
Evening meal: 1900 (last bookings 1400)

Bedrooms: 2 double, 2 triple
Bathrooms: 4 en-suite
Parking: 10 spaces

5 Woodlands Country House ◆◆◆◆

Ireby, Cumbria CA5 1EX **Tel:** (016973) 71791 **Fax:** (016973) 71482
Web: http://www.woodlnd.u-net.com **E-mail:** hj@woodlnd.u-net.com

Woodlands is a most elegant Victorian house, tastefully refurbished throughout to reflect the period. It enjoys fine views and is set within carefully maintained and spacious grounds. Ireby, a truly unspoilt Cumbrian village, is an ideal base for exploring the Northern Lakes. John and Helen Payne have established a reputation for fine food, affordable wines, the warmest of welcomes and a highly personal service. Residential licence. Non-smoking. Vegetarian alternatives. Pets welcome. Suitable for wheelchair users.
♿ **Category 2**

Bed & Breakfast per night: single occupancy from £28.00–£35.00; double room from £56.00–£65.00
Dinner, Bed & Breakfast per person, per night: £44.50–£49.00
Evening meal: 1930 (last bookings 1600)

Bedrooms: 3 double, 2 twin, 2 triple
Bathrooms: 7 en-suite
Parking: 12 spaces
Open: All year except January
Cards accepted: Mastercard, Visa, Switch/Delta, Eurocard

6 Ravenstone Lodge ◆◆◆◆

Bassenthwaite, Keswick, Cumbria CA12 4QG **Tel:** (017687) 76629 or (017687) 76638 **Fax:** (017687) 76629
E-mail: ravenstone.lodge@talk21.com

A warm and friendly welcome awaits you at Ravenstone Lodge, our 19th-century stone-built property nestling at the foot of Ullock Pike, just four miles north of Keswick on the A591. The lodge is set in five acres of spectacular countryside with a private terrace, a large walled garden and ample off-the-road parking space. Enjoy the relaxed atmosphere of our stable dining room, bar and large Victorian-style conservatory.

Bed & Breakfast per night: single occupancy from £32.50–£34.50; double room from £61.00–£65.00
Dinner, Bed & Breakfast per person, per night: £47.00–£49.00
Evening meal: 1900 (last bookings 1800)

Bedrooms: 6 double, 2 twin, 1 family
Bathrooms: 9 en-suite
Parking: 12 spaces
Cards accepted: Mastercard, Visa, Switch/Delta, Eurocard, JCB, Visa Electron, Solo

At-a-glance symbols are explained on the flap inside the back cover

7 The Old Vicarage ♦♦♦♦

Church Lane, Lorton, Cumbria CA13 9UN **Tel:** (01900) 85656 **Fax:** (01900) 85656
Web: http://www.oldvicarage.co.uk **E-mail:** enquiries@oldvicarage.co.uk

Lake District country guest house surrounded by fields yet lying in the charming village of Lorton, a hidden gem with historic connections. Elegant Victorian property of character with stunning views, lovely wooded grounds of more than an acre, and log fires. Tastefully refurbished rooms including four-poster, ground floor and superb family suite. Excellent four-course dinners, good wine list and abundant fresh flowers. Local pub just five minutes' walk.

Bed & Breakfast per night: single occupancy from £25.00–£30.00; double room from £50.00–£60.00
Dinner, Bed & Breakfast per person, per night: £40.00–£45.00
Evening meal: 1930 (last bookings 1000)

Bedrooms: 5 double, 3 twin
Bathrooms: 7 en-suite, 1 public
Parking: 12 spaces
Open: All year except January
Cards accepted: Mastercard, Visa, Switch/Delta, Eurocard, JCB, Solo

8 Corkickle Guest House ♦♦♦♦

1 Corkickle, Whitehaven, Cumbria CA28 8AA **Tel:** (01946) 692073 **Fax:** (01946) 692073

A small but elegant Grade II listed Regency house built in 1819 and close to the centre of the Georgian town and harbour of Whitehaven. Well situated for exploring the delights of the Western Lake District and coast. All six bedrooms are well appointed and decorated with guests' comfort in mind, and all have en-suite or private facilities. There is a comfortable dining room and lounge ideal for a quiet read or a friendly chat. You can be assured of a warm welcome.

Bed & Breakfast per night: single room from £22.50–£31.00; double room £45.00
Dinner, Bed & Breakfast per person, per night: £32.50–£41.00
Evening meal: 1900

Bedrooms: 2 single, 3 double, 1 twin
Bathrooms: 4 en-suite, 1 private, 1 room with private shower, 1 public
Parking: 2 spaces

9 Derwent Cottage ♦♦♦♦♦ Gold Award

Portinscale, Keswick, Cumbria CA12 5RF **Tel:** (017687) 74838
E-mail: dercott@btinternet.com

Gleaming silver, cut glass, spacious en-suite bedrooms and elegant furnishings are all to be found at Derwent Cottage. This Lakeland house, dating from the 18th century, stands in an acre of secluded gardens in the quiet village of Portinscale, one mile from Keswick. A four-course, candle light table d'hôte is served at 1900 each evening with classical music in the background. A residential licence is held, and drinks and wine are available throughout the evening. We are a totally non-smoking establishment.

Bed & Breakfast per night: double room from £52.00–£78.00
Dinner, Bed & Breakfast per person, per night: £40.00–£53.00
Evening meal: 1900 (last orders 1900)

Bedrooms: 4 double, 2 twin
Bathrooms: 6 en-suite
Parking: 10 spaces
Open: March-October
Cards accepted: Mastercard, Visa, JCB

Entries are cross referenced by number to the maps on pages 18–19

10 Skiddaw Hotel

★★★ Silver Award

Market Square, Keswick, Cumbria CA12 5BN **Tel:** (017687) 72071 **Fax:** (017687) 74850

Overlooking Keswick's historic market square, the Skiddaw Hotel provides the perfect location in the heart of the English Lake District for that special break. Try one of our 'Summit' rooms for that extra touch of luxury and dine in our new restaurant '31 The Square'. Complimentary facilities exclusive to our residents include in-house saunas, mid-week golf, and access to a nearby (eight miles outside Keswick) leisure club with fully equipped gym and swimming pool.

Bed & Breakfast per night: single room from £40.00–£51.00; double room from £74.00–£96.00
Dinner, Bed & Breakfast per person, per night: £98.00–£120.00 (min 2 nights)
Lunch available: 1200–1430
Evening meal: 1800 (last orders 2200)

Bedrooms: 7 single, 14 double, 11 twin, 8 triple
Bathrooms: 40 en-suite
Parking: 8 spaces
Cards accepted: Mastercard, Visa, Switch/Delta, Amex, JCB, Visa Electron, Solo

11 Hunters Way Guest House

◆◆◆◆

4 Eskin Street, Keswick, Cumbria CA12 4DH **Tel:** (017687) 72324

Michael and Moira Smith invite you to their comfortable Victorian home, which is quietly situated near wonderful scenery, yet only five minutes' easy walk from the centre of Keswick. This beautiful Grade II listed building, recently attractively refurbished throughout, has spacious en-suite rooms. Enjoy our home-made bread and jams with a super breakfast. Imaginative dinner menus, using local produce, are our speciality. Relax on arrival with a welcoming cup of tea in the lounge. Totally non-smoking.

Bed & Breakfast per night: single room from £18.00–£20.00; double room from £42.00–£46.00
Dinner, Bed & Breakfast per person, per night: £29.00–£34.00
Evening meal: 1830

Bedrooms: 2 single, 3 double, 1 twin
Bathrooms: 4 en-suite, 1 public

12 Lynwood House

◆◆◆◆ Silver Award

35 Helvellyn Street, Keswick, Cumbria CA12 4EP **Tel:** (017687) 72398 **Fax:** (017687) 74090
E-mail: lynwoodho@aol.com

Built in the 1890s, our family-run guest house is situated in a quiet, residential area of Keswick. The town centre is five minutes' level walk away, while Derwentwater can be reached within ten minutes. Our breakfast menu includes traditional and vegetarian/organic options and our home is non-smoking throughout, with secure storage for bicycles. An ideal base for touring or walking within some of the most beautiful landscapes in Britain.

Bed & Breakfast per night: single room from £17.50–£18.00; double room from £32.00–£40.00

Bedrooms: 1 single, 2 double, 1 triple
Bathrooms: 1 en-suite, 1 public

At-a-glance symbols are explained on the flap inside the back cover

13 The White House

Clifton, Penrith, Cumbria CA10 2EL **Tel:** (01768) 865115

A guesthouse where non-smokers are thoroughly spoilt! This converted 18th-century farmhouse is in a rural area close to Ullswater, Haweswater and the Eden Valley. Our comfortable home, which has attractive gardens, is centrally heated and double glazed throughout. There are three double/twin en-suite rooms and one single with private bathroom. We have a full licence and provide excellent home-cooked food with a high standard of imaginative meals. A car is essential and we have ample off-road parking.

Bed & Breakfast per night: single room £21.00; double room £46.00
Dinner, Bed & Breakfast per person, per night: £35.00–£37.00
Evening meal: 1900 (last orders 1900)

Bedrooms: 1 single, 1 double, 1 twin, 1 triple
Bathrooms: 3 en-suite, 1 private
Parking: 8 spaces
Open: March–October

14 The Black Swan Inn

Culgaith, Penrith, Cumbria CA10 1QW **Tel:** (01768) 88223 **Fax:** (01768) 88223

Chris and Dawn Pollard invite you to their inn which is situated in the Eden Valley, seven miles west of Appleby and close to the River Eden and the Settle to Carlisle Railway. The Black Swan is a traditional 17th-century Cumbrian inn with oak beams, an open fire in winter and a beer garden for summer. You will find the finest quality in food, real ale and accommodation. Shooting, fishing, golf, swimming and walking are all to hand.

Bed & Breakfast per night: single occupancy from £37.50–£42.50; double room from £55.00–£65.00
Dinner, Bed & Breakfast per person, per night: £37.50–£42.50
Lunch available: 1200–1430

Evening meal: 1800 (last orders 2130)
Bedrooms: 4 double, 3 twin
Bathrooms: 6 en-suite, 1 public
Parking: 12 spaces
Cards accepted: Mastercard, Visa, Switch/Delta, Diners, Visa Electron, Solo

15 Eden Grove House

♦♦♦♦ Silver Award

Bolton, Appleby-in-Westmorland, Cumbria CA16 6AL **Tel:** (017683) 62321

Eden Grove is a friendly non-smoking house situated in the beautiful Eden Valley, with en-suite bedrooms which have colour television and many extras for your comfort. This is a superb location for visiting the Lakes, Dales and North Pennines, and a trip on the Settle–Carlisle railway is a must. Locally produced food is used whenever possible, together with home-made bread and preserves. Delicious three-course dinners, with old fashioned puddings such as treacle tart, sticky toffee etc, are cooked in the Aga and served in the conservatory overlooking the garden. Phone Jeanette for a brochure.

Bed & Breakfast per night: single occupancy from £20.00–£22.00; double room from £44.00–£46.00
Dinner, Bed & Breakfast per person, per night: £34.00–£36.00
Evening meal: 1830

Bedrooms: 1 double, 1 twin
Bathrooms: 2 en-suite
Parking: 3 spaces

Entries are cross referenced by number to the maps on pages 18–19

16 Appleby Manor Country House Hotel

★★★ Silver Award

Roman Road, Appleby-in-Westmorland, Cumbria CA16 6JB **Tel:** (017683) 51571 or (017683) 51570 **Fax:** (017683) 52888
Web: http://www.applebymanor.co.uk **E-mail:** reception@applebymanor.co.uk

Probably the most relaxing and friendly hotel you'll choose. Set amidst breathtaking beauty, you'll find spotlessly clean bedrooms; satellite television and video films; sunny conservatory and terraces; magnificent lounges; log fires; a splendid indoor leisure club with small pool, jacuzzi, steam room, sauna and sunbed; and great food in the award-winning restaurant. With an 18-hole golf course, the mountains and valleys of the Lake District, and the Yorkshire Dales and North Pennine Fells close by, you're certain to enjoy yourselves.

Bed & Breakfast per night: single occupancy from £72.00–£78.00; double room from £104.00–£116.00
Dinner, Bed & Breakfast per person, per night: £62.00–£89.00 (min 2 nights)
Lunch available: 1100–1500

Evening meal: 1900 (last orders 2100)
Bedrooms: 13 double, 8 twin, 1 triple, 8 family
Bathrooms: 30 en-suite **Parking:** 51 spaces
Cards accepted: Mastercard, Visa, Switch/Delta, Amex, Diners, Eurocard, JCB, Maestro, Visa Elect

Settle – Carlisle Railway

By any sensible reckoning this railway line should never have been built. Its very existence is due to a combination of a commercial row and Victorian over-confidence. The disagreement was between two rival railway companies, the hubris on the part of the surveyors who believed that civil engineering could overcome all the problematic terrain lying between Settle and Carlisle. In the end, of course, the surveyors were not entirely wrong: the most audacious and dramatically scenic line in England was built, but it almost bankrupted its owners.

In the 1850s and 1860s, keen to pocket a share of the lucrative traffic bound for Scotland, the Midland Railway hoped to purchase, from its great rival, the London and North-Western Railway, the right to use the Lancaster–Carlisle stretch. The two companies couldn't agree and in 1866 Parliament passed a bill allowing the construction of a new line involving, among other things, surmounting Ais Gill summit (1,169ft high - 356m). It was estimated to cost £2.2 million – an astronomical sum. Closer inspection by the Midland's surveyors soon brought home the folly of their plans, and in 1868 the two companies belatedly agreed terms for co-operation. Parliament, however, demanded that the railway be built.

From that day on the problems seemed endless: bedrock on which to secure viaduct arches lay far deeper than anticipated; cuttings became tunnels; embankments became viaducts; one bog, near Ais Gill, swallowed up 'fill' for 12 months without the embankment proceeding a single yard; floods drowned men in the tunnels.

Railway building in the Victorian age was a labour-intensive business. Up to 6,500 navvies worked for 6½ years for good wages to compensate for the appalling conditions. The graveyards at both Chapel-le-Dale and Cowgill had to enlarge their plots, with, on average, one navvy dying each week. The human cost is unknown, but the financial cost mounted to over £3.5 million.

In 1876 the line opened and, despite regular gloomy predictions, it continues to be open, affording passengers views of enormous beauty. Progress along this line, however, is not rapid – ageing structures such as Ribblehead Viaduct cannot withstand speeding rolling-stock. Not such a bad thing, really, as passengers have more time to marvel at the lunatic nature of this civil engineering miracle.

Excursions are available; call the Settle–Carlisle information line on 0660 660607 (premium rate).

At-a-glance symbols are explained on the flap inside the back cover

17 Greenbank

Borrowdale, Keswick, Cumbria CA12 5UY **Tel:** (017687) 77215 **Fax:** (017687) 77215

Greenbank is a lovely Victorian house in a peaceful setting. Here you can enjoy magnificent views of Derwentwater and the Borrowdale Valley. There are ten comfortable well-appointed bedrooms, each with an en-suite bathroom. Log fires, honesty bar, newspapers to browse through. We particularly enjoy providing imaginatively presented meals, with interesting menus using lots of local fresh produce.

Bed & Breakfast per night: single room from £28.00–£34.00; double room from £56.00–£68.00
Dinner, Bed & Breakfast per person, per night: £40.00–£46.00
Evening meal: 1900 (last bookings 1700)

Bedrooms: 1 single, 6 double, 2 twin, 1 triple
Bathrooms: 10 en-suite
Parking: 15 spaces
Open: All year except January
Cards accepted: Mastercard, Visa, Switch/Delta, Eurocard

18 Hazel Bank

Rosthwaite, Borrowdale, Keswick, Cumbria CA12 5XB **Tel:** (017687) 77248 **Fax:** (017678) 77373
Web: http://www.hazelbankhotel.demon.co.uk **E-mail:** enquiries@hazelbankhotel.demon.co.uk

Standing on an elevated site overlooking the village of Rosthwaite, there are unsurpassed views of the Borrowdale Valley and central Lakeland Peaks. The peaceful location makes Hazel Bank an ideal base for walkers, birdwatchers and lovers of the countryside, with direct access to many mountain and valley walks. The Victorian residence has been carefully and sympathetically converted to provide quality country house accommodation. Non-smokers only. Vegetarians welcome.

Dinner, Bed & Breakfast per person, per night: £43.00–£59.50 (depending on length of stay and booking notice)
Evening meal: 1900 (last orders 1900)

Bedrooms: 5 double, 4 twin
Bathrooms: 9 en-suite
Parking: 12 spaces
Cards accepted: Mastercard, Visa, Switch/Delta, Eurocard, JCB, Solo

19 Dale Head Hall Lakeside Hotel

★★★ Silver Award

Thirlmere, Keswick, Cumbria CA12 4TN **Tel:** (017687) 72478 **Fax:** (017687) 71070
Web: http://www.dale-head-hall.co.uk **E-mail:** enquiry@dale-head-hall.co.uk

With Helvellyn rising majestically behind, the hotel stands alone on the shores of Lake Thirlmere. At Dale Head Hall we offer a friendly home, a place of relaxation and beauty, set apart from the increasing pace of the modern world. Little can compare to a delicious dinner, prepared with love and care, particularly when wholesome ingredients come from the hotel's walled garden. AA 2 Rosettes, RAC Restaurant Award.

Bed & Breakfast per night: double room from £67.00–£100.00
Dinner, Bed & Breakfast per person, per night: £61.00–£77.50
Evening meal: 1930 (last orders 2000)

Bedrooms: 6 double, 2 twin, 1 triple
Bathrooms: 9 en-suite **Parking:** 20 spaces
Open: All year except January
Cards accepted: Mastercard, Visa, Switch/Delta, Amex, Eurocard, Maestro, Visa Electron

Entries are cross referenced by number to the maps on pages 18–19

20 Craigside House ◆◆◆◆

Grasmere, Ambleside, Cumbria LA22 9SG **Tel:** (015394) 35292

Craigside House is the ideal place to stay if you want peace and quiet. It is situated in grounds of 1.5 acres with delightful views and there is ample parking. There are three large bedrooms, all with en-suite facilities (bath and shower in each) and two have lake views. Grasmere village is a 15-minute walk away and has a plentiful choice of restaurants. There are many beautiful walks direct from the house.

Bed & Breakfast per night: single occupancy from £38.00–£66.00; double room from £56.00–£72.00

Bedrooms: 2 double, 1 twin
Bathrooms: 3 en-suite
Parking: 6 spaces

21 Woodland Crag Guest House ◆◆◆◆

Howe Head Lane, Grasmere, Ambleside, Cumbria LA22 9SG **Tel:** (015394) 35351 **Fax:** (015394) 35351

A warm welcome and an informal atmosphere are found in this delightful house, situated on the edge of Grasmere near Dove Cottage. Secluded but with easy access to all facilities, the accommodation has fine tastefully-decorated bedrooms, all with individual character and wonderful views of the Lake, Fells or gardens. Ideal for walking and centrally placed for the motorist (enclosed parking). All major outdoor activities are catered for nearby, including sailing, fishing, wind surfing and pony trekking. Totally non-smoking.

Bed & Breakfast per night: single room from £25.00–£28.00; double room from £54.00–£60.00

Bedrooms: 2 single, 2 double, 1 twin
Bathrooms: 3 en-suite, 1 public
Parking: 5 spaces

22 Riverside Lodge ◆◆◆◆

Rothay Bridge, Ambleside, Cumbria LA22 0EH **Tel:** (015394) 34208 **Fax:** (015394) 31884
Web: http://www.riversidelodge.co.uk **E-mail:** alanrhone@riversidelodge.co.uk

Riverside Lodge is a house of immense charm and character in an idyllic riverside setting, just 500 yards from the centre of Ambleside and a similar distance from the head of Lake Windermere. The atmosphere is very relaxed and informal with just five en-suite bedrooms accommodating a total of ten guests. The house also contains a fully equipped luxury self-catering cottage to accommodate a discerning couple.

Bed & Breakfast per night: double room from £50.00–£65.00

Bedrooms: 4 double, 1 triple
Bathrooms: 5 en-suite
Parking: 6 spaces
Cards accepted: Mastercard, Visa

At-a-glance symbols are explained on the flap inside the back cover

23 Highfield House Country Hotel
★★ Silver Award

Hawkshead Hill, Ambleside, Cumbria LA22 0PN **Tel:** (015394) 36344 **Fax:** (015394) 36793
E-mail: Highfield.Hawkshead@btinternet.com

In picturesque setting with magnificent views, here is a tranquil and beautiful holiday location near to charming Hawkshead village. Dinner is the day's highlight, the daily changing menu of traditional and modern British influence is all freshly prepared, accompanied by a wide choice of select wines. 11 en-suite bedrooms with every comfort, an elegant lounge and cosy residents' bar. We hope you come and enjoy the friendly and relaxed ambience of Highfield: a warm welcome awaits you. AA Rosette.

Bed & Breakfast per night: single room from £43.50–£45.00; double room from £83.00–£94.00
Dinner, Bed & Breakfast per person, per night: £59.00–£65.00
Evening meal: 1900 (last orders 2030)

Bedrooms: 2 single, 6 double, 3 twin
Bathrooms: 11 en-suite
Parking: 15 spaces
Open: All year except January
Cards accepted: Mastercard, Visa, Switch/Delta, Eurocard, JCB

24 Grey Friar Lodge Country House Hotel
◆◆◆◆

Clappersgate, Ambleside, Cumbria LA22 9NE **Tel:** (015394) 33158 **Fax:** (015394) 33158
Web: http://www.cumbria-hotels.co.uk **E-mail:** greyfriar@veen.freeserve.co.uk

A beautiful, lakeland-stone country house, ideally set in the heart of the Lake District between Ambleside and the Langdales, with superb river and mountain views and tasteful, well-appointed rooms. A warm, friendly and informal atmosphere is achieved by Pamela and David Veen, complemented by exceptional hospitality and imaginative home cooking. Recommended by leading guides.

Bed & Breakfast per night: single occupancy from £36.50–£60.00; double room from £53.00–£85.00
Dinner, Bed & Breakfast per person, per night: £44.00–£60.00
Evening meal: 1930

Bedrooms: 6 double, 2 twin
Bathrooms: 7 en-suite, 1 private
Parking: 12 spaces
Open: mid February – mid December
Cards accepted: Mastercard, Visa, Switch/Delta, Eurocard, JCB

25 Ambleside Lodge
◆◆◆◆

Rothay Road, Ambleside, Cumbria LA22 0EJ **Tel:** (015394) 31681 **Fax:** (015394) 34547
Web: http://www.ambleside-lodge.com **E-mail:** cherryho@globalnet.co.uk

Ambleside Lodge is an elegant Lakeland home situated just a minute's walk from the village centre and 3–4 minutes' stroll from Lake Windermere. Set in 2.5 acres of peaceful grounds, Ambleside Lodge provides a fine blend of high quality accommodation and excellent value for money. The Lodge offers a choice of beautifully furnished double rooms, king size four-posters with jacuzzi spa baths and complimentary private leisure club facilities.

Bed & Breakfast per night: single room from £30.00–£45.00; double room from £50.00–£150.00

Bedrooms: 2 single, 16 double, 1 twin
Bathrooms: 19 en-suite
Parking: 25 spaces
Cards accepted: Mastercard, Visa, Switch/Delta, Eurocard, Solo

Entries are cross referenced by number to the maps on pages 18–19

26 The Drunken Duck Inn   ◆◆◆◆

Barngates, Ambleside, Cumbria LA22 0NG **Tel:** (015394) 36347 **Fax:** (015394) 36781
Web: http://www.drunkenduckinn.co.uk **E-mail:** info@drunkenduckinn.co.uk

Situated in 60 acres, at a crossroads in the middle of nothing but magnificent scenery. Although set apart it is literally within minutes of most of what Lakeland has to offer. Award-winning accommodation and food. Visit Barngates Brewery and sample the three real ales brewed on site. Family run for over 25 years, we know how to look after our guests.

Bed & Breakfast per night: single occupancy from £55.00–£60.00; double room from £80.00–£140.00
Lunch available: 1200–1430
Evening meal: 1800 (last orders 2100)

Bedrooms: 8 double, 1 twin
Bathrooms: 9 en-suite
Parking: 60 spaces
Cards accepted: Mastercard, Visa, Switch/Delta, Amex, JCB

27 Oakbank House   ◆◆◆◆

Helm Road, Bowness-on-Windermere, Windermere, Cumbria LA23 3BU **Tel:** (015394) 43386 **Fax:** (015394) 47965
E-mail: oakbank@netuk.com

Join us at Oakbank House and enjoy stylish, comfortable, well-appointed accommodation. All our rooms are en-suite and most have views over Lake Windermere and Bowness village. All have tea trays, television and video with in-house complimentary video library and even irons and boards. We are only five minutes' stroll from the lake, shops and restaurants. Also free membership to luxury leisure club. Guaranteed high standards and warm welcome. Private parking.

Bed & Breakfast per night: single occupancy from £35.00–£60.00; double room from £57.00–£80.00
Dinner, Bed & Breakfast per person, per night: £43.50–£55.00
Evening meal: 1800 (last orders 2000)

Bedrooms: 4 double, 2 twin, 6 triple
Bathrooms: 11 en-suite, 1 private
Parking: 12 spaces
Cards accepted: Mastercard, Visa, Switch/Delta, Eurocard

28 Lowfell   ◆◆◆◆

Ferney Green, Bowness-on-Windermere, Windermere, Cumbria LA23 3ES **Tel:** (015394) 45612 or (015394) 48411 **Fax:** (015394) 48411
Web: http://www.lakes-pages.co.uk **E-mail:** louise@lakes-pages.co.uk

Guests have loved this house – full of light, beautifully decorated and immaculately maintained – yet relaxed and unpretentious, much like the family who live here. Arrive in the winter to find cosy fires, squashy sofas and glowing lamps, and in the summer to a gloriously secluded acre of garden. In the morning walk off a scrumptious breakfast – the village, Lake and Fells are a five minute stroll away. Pretty bedrooms have supremely comfortable beds (one king size) and lots of nice touches. The 'family and friends suite' is a charming hide-away in the loft.

Bed & Breakfast per night: double room £50.00

Bedrooms: 1 double, 2 twin
Bathrooms: 3 en-suite
Parking: 4 spaces
Cards accepted: Mastercard, Visa, Switch/Delta, Amex

At-a-glance symbols are explained on the flap inside the back cover

29 Linthwaite House Hotel

★★★ Gold Award

Crook Road, Windermere, Cumbria LA23 3JA **Tel:** (015394) 88600 **Fax:** (015394) 88601
Web: http://www.linthwaite.com **E-mail:** admin@linthwaite.com

Country house hotel, 20 minutes from the M6, situated in 14 acres of peaceful hilltop grounds, overlooking Lake Windermere and with breathtaking sunsets. The 26 rooms have en-suite bathrooms, satellite television, radio, telephone and tea/coffee making facilities. The AA 2 Rosette restaurant serves modern British food using local produce complemented by fine wines. There is a tarn for fly-fishing, croquet, golf practice hole and free use of nearby leisure spa. Romantic breaks feature a king-size double bed with canopy, champagne, chocolates and flowers. English Tourist Board 'Hotel of the Year' 1994. ⚹ **Category 3**

Bed & Breakfast per night: single room from £90.00–£110.00; double room from £90.00–£250.00
Dinner, Bed & Breakfast per person, per night: £59.00–£140.00
Lunch available: 1230–1330

Evening meal: 1915 (last orders 2045)
Bedrooms: 1 single, 21 double, 4 twin
Bathrooms: 26 en-suite
Parking: 30 spaces
Cards accepted: Mastercard, Visa, Switch/Delta, Amex, Eurocard

30 Wateredge Hotel

★★★ Silver Award

Waterhead Bay, Ambleside, Cumbria LA22 0EP **Tel:** (015394) 32332 **Fax:** (015394) 31878
E-mail: reception@wateredgehotel.co.uk

Wateredge is a delightfully situated family-run hotel on the shores of Windermere, with gardens leading to the lake edge. It was developed from two 17th-century fishermen's cottages which are still part of the charm of the whole building. Relax in comfortable lounges overlooking the lake, or on our lakeside patio where teas and light lunches are served. In the evening, dine under oak beams and enjoy exquisitely cooked food. Cosy bar, pretty bedrooms and relaxed friendly service.

Bed & Breakfast per night: single room from £48.00–£64.00; double room from £74.00–£156.00
Dinner, Bed & Breakfast per person, per night: £57.00–£98.00
Lunch available: 1215–1400 (light lunches in lounges or lakeside patio)

Evening meal: 1900 (last orders 2030)
Bedrooms: 3 single, 12 double, 8 twin
Bathrooms: 23 en-suite
Parking: 25 spaces
Cards accepted: Mastercard, Visa, Switch/Delta, Amex, Eurocard, JCB

31 Buckle Yeat Guest House

◆◆◆◆

Near Sawrey, Ambleside, Cumbria LA22 0LF **Tel:** (015394) 36446 or (015394) 36538 **Fax:** (015394) 36446
Web: http://www.buckle-yeat.co.uk **E-mail:** info@buckle-yeat.co.uk

Buckle Yeat is situated in Near Sawrey which is centrally located in the heart of the beautiful English Lakes. A 16th-century Lakeland cottage with open fires and oak beams which has been tastefully renovated and decorated to the highest standards, providing a warm and relaxing atmosphere in which to enjoy a break. Breakfast consists of a wide choice to suit all diets and everything is prepared to order.

Bed & Breakfast per night: single room from £25.00–£27.00; double room from £50.00–£54.00

Bedrooms: 1 single, 4 double, 2 twin
Bathrooms: 6 en-suite, 1 private
Parking: 9 spaces
Cards accepted: Mastercard, Visa, Switch/Delta, Amex, JCB

Entries are cross referenced by number to the maps on pages 18–19

32 Sawrey House Country Hotel ◆◆◆◆◆

Near Sawrey, Ambleside, Cumbria LA22 0LF **Tel:** (015394) 36387 **Fax:** (015394) 36010
Web: http://www.sawrey-house.com **E-mail:** enquiries@sawrey-house.com

Situated in three acres of grounds in the centre of the Lake District National Park, this family-run hotel offers a very special combination of elegance and comfort. It directly overlooks both Grizedale Forest and Esthwaite Water, nestling in the peaceful conservation hamlet which won the heart of Beatrix Potter, whose house 'Hilltop' lies nearby. We place special emphasis on our delicious five-course dinners, complemented with a well-stocked cellar offering reasonably priced wines. AA 2 Rosettes.

Bed & Breakfast per night: single room from £45.00; double room from £90.00–£112.00
Dinner, Bed & Breakfast per person, per night: £60.00–£75.00
Evening meal: 1900 (last orders 2000)

Bedrooms: 1 single, 5 double, 4 twin, 1 triple
Bathrooms: 11 en-suite
Parking: 20 spaces
Open: All year except January
Cards accepted: Mastercard, Visa, Switch/Delta

33 Yewfield Vegetarian Guest House ◆◆◆◆

Yewfield, Hawkshead Hill, Ambleside, Cumbria LA22 0PR **Tel:** (015394) 36765 **Fax:** (015394) 36765
Web: http://www.yewfield.co.uk

A peaceful and quiet retreat, ideally situated for walking and enjoying this exquisite region of rare natural beauty. The house is set in 25 acres of private grounds where a ten minute stroll leads you to a magnificent viewpoint overlooking Tarn Hows. All rooms are individually appointed to a very high standard with en-suite bath and shower, colour television, radio and tea-making facilities.

Bed & Breakfast per night: single occupancy from £25.00–£40.00; double room from £40.00–£70.00

Bedrooms: 2 double, 1 twin
Bathrooms: 3 en-suite
Parking: 10 spaces
Open: February–October

34 Borwick Lodge ◆◆◆◆ Silver Award

Outgate, Hawkshead, Ambleside, Cumbria LA22 0PU **Tel:** (015394) 36332 **Fax:** (015394) 36332

1998 and 1999 winner of the AWARD for 'Accommodation of the Highest Standards'. A leafy driveway entices you to a rather special 17th-century country house with magnificent panoramic lake and mountain views, quietly secluded in the heart of the Lakes. The beautiful en-suite bedrooms include 'Special Occasions' and 'Romantic Breaks' with king-size four-poster beds. Rosemary and Colin Haskell welcome you to this most beautiful corner of England. TOTALLY NON-SMOKING.

Bed & Breakfast per night: single occupancy from £40.00–£60.00; double room from £50.00–£100.00

Bedrooms: 5 double, 1 family
Bathrooms: 6 en-suite
Parking: 8 spaces
Open: All year except January and February

At-a-glance symbols are explained on the flap inside the back cover

35 Holbeck Ghyll Country House Hotel

★★★ Gold Award

Holbeck Lane, Windermere, Cumbria LA23 1LU **Tel:** (015394) 32375 **Fax:** (015394) 34743
Web: http://www.holbeck-ghyll.co.uk **E-mail:** accommodation@holbeck-ghyll.co.uk

Peacefully located in eight acres of grounds with breathtaking views across Lake Windermere. 19th-century hunting lodge, former home of Lord Lonsdale, with log fires and intimate candlelit oak-panelled restaurant serving AA 3 Rosette food. Luxurious bedrooms with vases of fresh flowers, decanters of sherry and fluffy bathrobes. Young, caring staff offering genuine hospitality. Holbeck Ghyll is 'Something Special' for that eagerly-awaited important anniversary or birthday celebration. Rated by all guide books in their highest category. Central Lakes location. Luxury health spa and tennis court. Cumbria Tourist Board 'Hotel of the Year' 1998–99.

Dinner, Bed & Breakfast per person, per night: £75.00–£150.00
Lunch available: 1200–1400
Evening meal: 1900 (last orders 2115)

Bedrooms: 11 double, 8 twin, 1 triple
Bathrooms: 20 en-suite
Parking: 26 spaces
Cards accepted: Mastercard, Visa, Switch/Delta, Amex, Diners, JCB

Piel Island

Just offshore from Barrow in Furness is Piel Island, a small rocky outcrop in the sea surmounted by the brooding ruins of a castle. Tiny and unimportant it may be, but it still has its ferry service, pub – even its own king.

The island has a colourful history. It is separated from the mainland yet remains fairly accessible, so making it a useful haven in troubled times. From the 14th century it was the centre of a lively smuggling trade largely orchestrated by the monks of Furness Abbey. They built the impressive castle as a fortified warehouse to keep their cargoes safe from raiders, and to keep the King's customs men at bay.

The island's most historic moment arrived in June 1487, when Lambert Simnel, pretender to the English throne, landed at Piel with 8,000 men. Simnel was an impostor, a baker's son claiming to be the Earl of Warwick (then imprisoned in the Tower of London) who, backed by Margaret of Burgundy, gathered a force of German mercenaries and Irish recruits, intending to take the throne by force. Leaving Piel, he set off across Furness towards London, but was defeated at the Battle of Stoke on June 16th. In contrast, the 18th century brought more prosperous and settled times to the island, with Piel's busy harbour servicing Furness's thriving shipping and iron industries. The island's pub and its few houses were built at this time.

The Ship Inn continues to flourish, a useful watering-hole for sailors and day trippers from the mainland. The landlord is traditionally known as the 'King of Piel', a reference, it is supposed, to Lambert Simnel's claim to the throne. Anyone who sits in a particular old wooden chair in the pub, becomes a 'Knight of Piel', and must carry out certain gallant duties – such as buying everyone a drink, being a moderate smoker, a lover of the opposite sex, and generally of good character. If shipwrecked, a Knight of Piel has the right to free board and lodging in the pub.

The ferry from Roa runs from April to October, 11am–5pm weather permitting (telephone in advance: 01229 835809), making the island an easy day trip. Facilities are minimal (the island has neither electricity nor telephone) but for those wishing to stay longer, camping is permitted anywhere on the island by arrangement, on arrival, with the Ship Inn.

Entries are cross referenced by number to the maps on pages 18–19

36 Gilpin Lodge Country House Hotel and Restaurant ★★★ Gold Award

Crook Road, Windermere, Cumbria LA23 3NE **Tel:** (015394) 88818 **Fax:** (015394) 88058
Web: http://www.gilpin-lodge.co.uk **E-mail:** hotel@gilpin-lodge.co.uk

A friendly, elegant, relaxing hotel in twenty acres of woodlands, moors and delightful country gardens. Twelve miles from the M6, two miles from Lake Windermere and almost opposite Windermere golf course. Sumptuous bedrooms – many with jacuzzi baths, split-level sitting areas and four-poster beds. Exquisite cuisine (AA 3 Rosettes). Guests have free use of nearby leisure club. Year-round breaks.

Bed & Breakfast per night: single occupancy from £60.00–£110.00; double room from £80.00–£180.00
Dinner, Bed & Breakfast per person, per night: £55.00–£110.00
Lunch available: 1200–1430

Evening meal: 1900 (last orders 2100)
Bedrooms: 9 double, 5 twin
Bathrooms: 14 en-suite **Parking:** 40 spaces
Cards accepted: Mastercard, Visa, Switch/Delta, Amex, Diners, Eurocard, JCB, Maestro, Visa Elect

37 Lindeth Fell Country House Hotel ★★ Silver Award

Windermere, Cumbria LA23 3JP **Tel:** (015394) 43286 or (015394) 44287 **Fax:** (015394) 47455
Web: http://www.lindethfell.co.uk **E-mail:** kennedy@lindethfell.co.uk

'One of the most beautifully situated hotels in Lakeland'. In a magnificent garden setting above Lake Windermere, Lindeth Fell offers brilliant lake views, peaceful surroundings and superb modern English cooking (AA Rosette and RAC Merits) – at highly competitive prices. Lawns are laid for croquet and putting, and Windermere Golf Club is one mile away. Good fishing is available free and interesting walks start from the door. Call for a brochure from the resident owners. Special breaks available in low season.

Bed & Breakfast per night: single room from £49.00; double room from £98.00
Dinner, Bed & Breakfast per person, per night: £70.00–£85.00
Lunch available: 1230–1400
Evening meal: 1930 (last orders 2030)

Bedrooms: 2 single, 5 double, 5 twin, 2 triple
Bathrooms: 14 en-suite
Parking: 20 spaces
Cards accepted: Mastercard, Visa, Switch/Delta

38 Holly Park House ◆◆◆◆

1 Park Road, Windermere, Cumbria LA23 2AW **Tel:** (015394) 42107 **Fax:** (015394) 48997
Web: http://www.s-h-systems.co.uk/hotels/hollypk.html

An elegant stone-built house dating back to 1880 and standing in a quiet position, just a short walk from Windermere centre and about one mile from bustling Bowness. Noted for its spacious, well-furnished bedrooms and lounge, which is a charming room with a lovely marble fireplace – just the place to relax with a drink after an enjoyable day's activities. The resident proprietors offer a warm welcome and try to ensure a pleasant and memorable stay.

Bed & Breakfast per night: single occupancy from £28.00–£33.00; double room from £40.00–£52.00

Bedrooms: 3 double, 1 triple, 2 family
Bathrooms: 6 en-suite
Parking: 4 spaces
Cards accepted: Mastercard, Visa, Switch/Delta, Amex, Diners, Visa Electron, Solo

At-a-glance symbols are explained on the flap inside the back cover

39 Beaumont ◆◆◆◆

Thornbarrow Road, Windermere, Cumbria LA23 2DG **Tel:** (015394) 45521 **Fax:** (015394) 46267
Web: http://www.beaumont-holidays.co.uk **E-mail:** ss2000@beaumont-holidays.co.uk

Beaumont is a gracious Victorian house with a friendly, informal atmosphere. Ideally located midway between Windermere and Bowness, set in an elevated position in one acre of beautiful landscaped gardens, with panoramic views of the surrounding fells. There are five en-suite bedrooms, all with colour television, radio and tea/coffee making facilities. There is a comfortable lounge and dining room with a log fire. Guests have free use of a local swimming/leisure club. ⚡ **Category 3**

Bed & Breakfast per night: double room from £46.00–£74.00

Bedrooms: 3 double, 1 twin, 1 family
Bathrooms: 5 en-suite
Parking: 10 spaces
Cards accepted: Mastercard, Visa, Switch/Delta, Amex, Eurocard, JCB, Solo

40 Fir Trees ◆◆◆◆

Lake Road, Windermere, Cumbria LA23 2EQ **Tel:** (015394) 42272 **Fax:** (015394) 42272
Web: http://www.fir-trees.com **E-mail:** firtreeshotel@email.msn.com

Ideally situated midway between Windermere and Bowness villages, Fir Trees offers luxurious bed and breakfast in a Victorian guest house of considerable character and charm. Antiques and beautiful prints abound in the public areas, while the bedrooms are immaculately furnished and decorated. Breakfasts are simply delicious and the hospitality genuinely warm and friendly. As one might expect, Fir Trees is enthusiastically recommended by leading guides while providing exceptional value for money. We have excellent off-street parking and are exclusively a non-smoking establishment.

Bed & Breakfast per night: single occupancy from £30.00–£40.00; double room from £44.00–£64.00

Bedrooms: 6 double, 1 twin, 1 triple
Bathrooms: 8 en-suite
Parking: 9 spaces
Cards accepted: Mastercard, Visa, Switch/Delta, Amex, Eurocard, JCB

41 Bridge House ◆◆◆◆

Brigflatts, Sedbergh, Cumbria LA10 5HN **Tel:** (015396) 21820 **Fax:** (015396) 21820

Situated amidst the beauty of the Yorkshire Dales, in rural surroundings with open views over the Fells. Two miles from the old market town of Sedbergh along the Dales Way and within easy reach of the Lakes. The 17th-century stone barn offers good home cooking with local produce. A warm welcome in comfortable accommodation which comprises a private wing of two bedrooms, one twin, one double, with vanity units and shared bath/shower room with separate toilet.

Bed & Breakfast per night: single occupancy from £20.00–£22.00; double room from £37.00–£40.00
Dinner, Bed & Breakfast per person, per night: £29.00–£32.50

Bedrooms: 1 double, 1 twin
Bathrooms: 1 public
Parking: 3 spaces

Entries are cross referenced by number to the maps on pages 18–19

42 Ing Hill Lodge ◆◆◆◆

Mallerstang Dale, Kirkby Stephen, Cumbria CA17 4JT **Tel:** (017683) 71153
E-mail: IngHill@FSBDial.co.uk

Unwind in peace and comfort at this small Georgian house in Mallerstang, a little known dale on the fringe of the National Park. Superb views with peace and quiet for your preferred relaxation. Excellent en-suite shower rooms, comfortable bedrooms with television, a 'butler's pantry' for tea and coffee making and your choice of breakfast. Lounge with books, maps, open fire and central heating throughout for your comfort. We also have our own field for dogs to run off-lead.

Bed & Breakfast per night: double room from £40.00–£50.00

Bedrooms: 2 double, 1 twin
Bathrooms: 3 en-suite
Parking: 5 spaces
Open: All year except January and February

43 The Coach House ◆◆◆◆

Crookham, Cornhill-on-Tweed, Northumberland TD12 4TD **Tel:** (01890) 820293 **Fax:** (01890) 820284
Web: http://www.secretkingdom.com/coach/house.htm

The Coach House offers warm, spacious bedrooms surrounding a sunlit courtyard. The large lounge, with peach leather furniture and fine pictures, overlooks a west-facing terrace. A flock of Soay sheep graze beneath the damson trees. Food is fresh and varied, reflecting modern ideas on healthy eating, with some Mediterranean influence. Local fish, game and meat are used, organically-reared where possible. Special diets catered for. Excellent facilities for disabled guests. Lovingly renovated to a high standard.
♿ **Category 1**

Bed & Breakfast per night: single room from £25.00–£39.00; double room from £50.00–£78.00
Dinner, Bed & Breakfast per person, per night: £42.50–£56.50
Evening meal: 1930 (last orders 1930)

Bedrooms: 2 single, 2 double, 5 twin
Bathrooms: 7 en-suite, 2 public
Parking: 12 spaces
Open: Easter–October
Cards accepted: Mastercard, Visa, Eurocard

44 The Old Manse ◆◆◆◆◆ Silver Award

New Road, Chatton, Alnwick, Northumberland NE66 5PU **Tel:** (01668) 215343 or 07885 540567
Web: http://www.oldmansechatton.ntb.org.uk **E-mail:** chattonbb@aol.com

The Old Manse, winner of Pride of Northumbria Bed & Breakfast of the Year 1999, is a lovingly restored Victorian family home. We offer a romantic four-poster or ground floor suite, an open log fire and excellent home cooking which will make your visit memorable. Set in large grounds with a fishpond, the Old Manse is central for Northumberland's beaches, castles and hills. We invite you to share our 'special' home with us.

Bed & Breakfast per night: single occupancy from £26.00–£42.00; double room from £52.00–£60.00

Bedrooms: 1 double, 1 twin
Bathrooms: 2 en-suite
Parking: 4 spaces

At-a-glance symbols are explained on the flap inside the back cover

45 | Low Dover Beadnell Bay

Harbour Road, Beadnell, Chathill, Northumberland NE67 5BJ **Tel:** (01665) 720291 or 07971 444070 **Fax:** (01665) 720291
Web: http://www.lowdover.demon.co.uk **E-mail:** kathandbob@lowdover.demon.co.uk

Kath and Bob warmly invite you to relax in our luxurious beachside home which has an atmosphere of serene peace and tranquillity. Feel special in our superior, elegant, ground-floor suites, each with patio doors and lounges. Enjoy a hearty home-cooked breakfast with panoramic views across Beadnell Bay and over to the Cheviot Hills. Sit in our beautiful gardens, admire the many hanging baskets or stroll fifty yards down to the golden beach and beyond. Spectacular scenery surrounds us, surrender to the charm of Northumberland. Three miles to the Farne Islands. Private parking. Free brochure.

Bed & Breakfast per night: double room from £52.00–£58.00

Bedrooms: 1 double, 1 triple
Bathrooms: 2 en-suite
Parking: 4 spaces

46 | Hawkhill Farmhouse

Lesbury, Alnwick, Northumberland NE66 3PG **Tel:** (01665) 830380

Relax and enjoy the friendly atmosphere of our spacious farmhouse with its magnificent views over lovely countryside. Only two miles from the coast and glorious sandy beaches. Elegant dining room and large sitting room with access to lawns and grounds. All bedrooms are en-suite with central heating, television and tea/coffee making facilities. Ideal for relaxing, birdwatching, walking, golfing and visiting castles and other historic sites. Secluded private parking.

Bed & Breakfast per night: double room from £45.00–£50.00

Bedrooms: 1 double, 2 twin
Bathrooms: 3 en-suite
Parking: 10 spaces
Open: April–October

47 | High Buston Hall

 ♦♦♦♦ Silver Award

High Buston, Alnmouth, Alnwick, Northumberland NE66 3QH **Tel:** (01665) 830606 or 07050 041774 **Fax:** (01665) 830707
Web: http://members.aol.com/highbuston

High Buston Hall is a Grade II listed Georgian villa, standing on a rocky promontory overlooking Northumberland's heritage coastline, lying between Alnmouth and Warkworth and seven miles from Alnwick. Here you can enjoy the tranquillity of the Northumbrian countryside and stunning sea views. The Hall is tastefully furnished with many French and English antiques. It has extensive gardens and is non-smoking.

Bed & Breakfast per night: single occupancy £45.00; double room £75.00

Bedrooms: 3 double
Bathrooms: 2 en-suite, 1 private
Parking: 9 spaces

Entries are cross referenced by number to the maps on pages 18–19

48 Linden Hall Hotel, Health Spa & Golf Course ★★★★ Silver Award

Longhorsley, Morpeth, Northumberland NE65 8XF **Tel:** (01670) 516611 **Fax:** (01670) 788544
Web: http://www.lindenhall.co.uk

Linden Hall is a superb Georgian Country House set in four-hundred-and-fifty acres just twenty minutes north of Newcastle-upon-Tyne. All fifty bedrooms are individually furnished, some with four-poster beds. The award-winning Dobson Restaurant uses the finest of local produce, with the Linden Tree Bar and Grill offering a more relaxed alternative. Leisure facilities include an 18-hole golf course, indoor swimming pool, fitness room, beauty spa, steam room, snooker, croquet and putting.

Bed & Breakfast per night: single room from £97.50–£127.50; double room from £125.00–£195.00
Dinner, Bed & Breakfast per person, per night: £69.50–£93.50 (min 2 nights, 2 sharing)
Evening meal: 1900 (last orders 2145)

Bedrooms: 2 single, 33 double, 15 twin
Bathrooms: 50 en-suite
Parking: 300 spaces
Cards accepted: Mastercard, Visa, Switch/Delta, Amex, Diners, Eurocard, JCB

49 Holmhead Guest House ◆◆◆◆

on Thirlwall Castle Farm, Hadrian's Wall, Greenhead, via Carlisle CA6 7HY **Tel:** (016977) 47402 **Fax:** (016977) 47402
E-mail: Holmhead@hadrianswall.freeserve.co.uk

Holmhead Farm Guest House is a 200-year-old farmhouse built of stone from Hadrian's Wall and situated near spectacular Roman remains, museums and excavations. Your host, Pauline Staff, is a qualified tour guide and a expert on Hadrian's Wall and is happy to help plan your itinery or arrange personally guided tours. Offering cosy en-suite bedrooms with lovely views, award-winning breakfasts and, by arrangement, candlelit dinner parties using fresh local produce. Every effort is made to ensure you get the very best combination of local historical interest, comfort and catering from your holiday. Licenced. Non-smoking. AA 3 Egg Cups.

Bed & Breakfast per night: double room from £54.00–£55.00
Dinner, Bed & Breakfast per person, per night: £46.00–£47.00 (min 2 nights, except walkers)
Lunch available: packed lunches £2–£5

Evening meal: 1930 (last bookings 1600)
Bedrooms: 1 double, 2 twin, 1 triple
Bathrooms: 4 en-suite
Parking: 6 spaces
Cards accepted: Mastercard, Visa, Eurocard

50 Broomshaw Hill Farm ◆◆◆◆◆ Gold Award

Willia Road, Haltwhistle, Northumberland NE49 9NP **Tel:** (01434) 320866 **Fax:** (01434) 320866
Web: http://www.broomshawhill.ntb.org.uk **E-mail:** broomshaw@msn.com

For visitors looking for luxury and value. An 18th-century farmhouse enlarged and modernised to very high standards, but still retaining its old world charm. The house is set on the side of a wooded valley through which runs the Haltwhistle Burn. It stands on the conjunction of a footpath and bridleway, both leading to Hadrian's Wall. You can be assured of a warm welcome, with every effort made to ensure your stay is enjoyable.

Bed & Breakfast per night: double room from £44.00–£45.00

Bedrooms: 2 double, 1 twin
Bathrooms: 2 en-suite, 1 private
Parking: 8 spaces
Open: March–October

At-a-glance symbols are explained on the flap inside the back cover

51 Ashcroft

◆◆◆◆ Silver Award

Lantys Lonnen, Haltwhistle, Northumberland NE49 0DA **Tel:** (01434) 320213 **Fax:** (01434) 320213

Elegantly furnished former vicarage, set in large award-winning, terraced gardens. Ample private parking within grounds. Warm, friendly welcome with expert local knowledge. Extensive breakfast choice served in our beautiful dining room overlooking the garden and the hills beyond. Conveniently situated on the southern edge of our small market town, yet only 200 yards from the market square. The perfect base from which to explore Hadrian's Wall and surrounding area. Non-smoking throughout. Colour brochure available.

Bed & Breakfast per night: single room from £22.50–£30.00; double room from £45.00–£50.00

Bedrooms: 1 single, 2 double, 1 twin, 1 triple, 2 family
Bathrooms: 6 en-suite, 1 private
Parking: 14 spaces
Cards accepted: Mastercard, Visa, Eurocard

52 Rye Hill Farm

◆◆◆◆

Slaley, Hexham, Northumberland NE47 0AH **Tel:** (01434) 673259 **Fax:** (01434) 673259
E-mail: enquiries@consult-courage.co.uk

The farm dates back some 300 years and is a traditional small livestock holding set in beautiful, unspoilt countryside with fantastic panoramic views. The accommodation is in specially converted barns adjoining the farmhouse. All bedrooms are en-suite with tea/coffee making facilities, television and large bathtowels. Meals are taken around two pine tables in the dining room that overlooks the garden. Evening meals are a speciality not to be missed!

Bed & Breakfast per night: single occupancy £25.00; double room £40.00
Dinner, Bed & Breakfast per person, per night: £32.00–£37.00
Evening meal: 1930 (last bookings 1700)

Bedrooms: 3 double, 1 twin, 2 family
Bathrooms: 6 en-suite
Parking: 6 spaces
Cards accepted: Mastercard, Visa, Switch/Delta, Visa Electron

53 Clive House

◆◆◆◆

Appletree Lane, Corbridge, Northumberland NE45 5DN **Tel:** (01434) 632617

Originally built in 1840 as part of Corbridge Village School, Clive House has been tastefully converted to provide four lovely en-suite bedrooms, one of which has a four-poster. The village centre, with many speciality shops and eating places, is a few minutes' walk away. At the centre of Hadrian's Wall country, historic Corbridge is an ideal base for exploring Northumberland, and a convenient break between York and Edinburgh. A warm, personal welcome awaits.

Bed & Breakfast per night: single room from £34.00–£38.00; double room £48.00

Bedrooms: 1 single, 3 double
Bathrooms: 4 en-suite
Parking: 3 spaces

Entries are cross referenced by number to the maps on pages 18–19

54 Ye Olde Cop Shop

◆◆◆◆

6 The Green, Washington Village, District 4, Sunderland, Tyne and Wear NE38 7AB **Tel:** (0191) 416 5333 **Fax:** (0191) 416 5333
Web: http://www.users.globalnet.co.uk/ **E-mail:** yeoldecopshop@btinternet.com

This detached stone building is a former police station in the heart of a village steeped in history and close to the ancestral home of George Washington. The house is enthusiastically run by its friendly owners, where cleanliness, comfort and hospitality are of an excellent standard. All rooms have en-suite facilities and are decorated to a very high standard. Secured car parking with surveillance cameras, full fire certificate, food hygiene, Welcome Host and Welcome Host International certificate holders. Strictly no smoking. Directions: turn off district 4 and follow signs for Washington Village/Washington Old Hall. Over crossroads 20 yards, turn left next to library.

Bed & Breakfast per night: single room from £26.00; double room from £40.00
Evening meal: 1800

Bedrooms: 1 single, 2 double, 2 twin
Bathrooms: 5 en-suite
Parking: 8 spaces
Cards accepted: Mastercard, Visa, Switch/Delta, Eurocard, JCB, Visa Electron

The Angel of the North

In February 1998, something remarkable happened on the southern edge of Gateshead, one of England's erstwhile industrial centres. Here, on a hilltop visible from both the A1 and the main London–Newcastle railway, a winged figure was sighted. No ordinary angel, this, for reports spoke of it being as high as four double-decker buses and with a span as wide as a jumbo jet. It stood with wings outstretched, suggesting welcome and embrace. Word got out, cameras arrived and a website was devoted to it. More remarkable still, all these reports turned out to be entirely true.

The Angel of the North, to give it its full name, is almost certainly England's most high-profile work of art. The creation of sculptor Antony Gormley, it towers 65ft (20m) above its site at the head of the Team Valley – and is set to become as much a symbol of the North-East as the Tyne Bridge. Its history, though, begins back in 1989, when the former bath block at the Team Colliery was reclaimed. This, Gateshead Council decided, would be an ideal location for a 'landmark sculpture'. Once the site had been landscaped, the council asked a shortlist of international artists to pitch for the commission, a competition won in January 1994 by Gormley.

The scale of the design clearly called for considerable funding, but the expense – about £800,000 all told – was met without any

contributions from the local council tax. Both the size and the exposed position meant that the 200-ton angel would have to be enormously strong to cope with winds of up to 100mph (160kph). The engineering firm of Ove Arup was called in to advise and, after close consultation with the sculptor, fabrication began at nearby Hartlepool. By September 1997, vast sections of the sculpture, made from a weather-resistant steel designed to mellow to a rich red-brown, were arriving at Team Valley under police escort.

Thanks to its lofty position – it reminds the sculptor of a megalithic mound – more than one person every second will see the angel. This, in theory, works out at 33 million a year. Given that it is thought it will have a life of a hundred years or more, a lot of people are going to witness this arresting apparition.

55 Brunswick House

55 Market Place, Middleton-in-Teesdale, Barnard Castle, County Durham DL12 0QH **Tel:** (01833) 640393 **Fax:** (01833) 640393
Web: http://www.brunswickhouse.ntb.org.uk **E-mail:** brunswick@teesdaleonline.co.uk

Situated in unspoilt Teesdale, our guest house provides the perfect centre for those seeking to enjoy the delights of unspoilt countryside, quiet roads, flower-filled meadows and gentle strolls through the breathtaking scenery of the North Pennines. Our reputation is built on outstanding home cooking using, wherever possible, only fresh and local produce. The house, dating from 1760, retains great charm with beamed ceilings and original fireplaces, thoughtfully combined with all modern comforts.

Bed & Breakfast per night: single occupancy from £22.50–£30.00; double room from £38.00–£45.00
Dinner, Bed & Breakfast per person, per night: £32.00–£38.50
Evening meal: 1930 (last bookings 1900)

Bedrooms: 3 double, 2 twin
Bathrooms: 5 en-suite
Parking: 5 spaces
Cards accepted: Mastercard, Visa, Switch/Delta, Amex, Diners, Eurocard, JCB, Maestro, Visa Elect

56 Cloud High 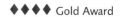 Gold Award

Eggleston, Barnard Castle, County Durham DL12 0AU **Tel:** (01833) 650644 **Fax:** (01833) 650644

Idyllically situated at 1000 feet in peaceful, secluded countryside, Cloud High commands magnificent, unrivalled views of Teesdale and surrounding Dales. Here the emphasis is on comfort, luxury and relaxation, with every amenity in the lovely en-suite bedrooms and private lounge. Breakfasts taken in the conservatory overlooking the garden and with a backdrop of the Pennines are our speciality. The perfect base for exploring this historical, cultural and scenic area. Come and be pampered!

Bed & Breakfast per night: single occupancy from £27.50–£32.00; double room from £43.00–£49.00

Bedrooms: 2 double, 1 twin
Bathrooms: 3 en-suite
Parking: 4 spaces

57 Throstle Gill Farm

Dalton, Richmond, North Yorkshire DL11 7HZ **Tel:** (01833) 621363 **Fax:** (01833) 621363

Nestling in a secluded hollow beside a tumbling stream, Throstle Gill provides spacious en-suite rooms overlooking a lovely garden in a tranquil setting. Mid-way between London and Edinburgh, it is an excellent base to stop over and tour the North Yorkshire Moors and Dales, particularly Herriot country. The historic town of Richmond is nearby, and there are many pleasant walks and bird-watching opportunities. A warm and friendly welcome awaits you. Brochure on request.

Bed & Breakfast per night: single occupancy from £18.00–£25.00; double room from £36.00–£40.00

Bedrooms: 1 double, 1 twin
Bathrooms: 2 en-suite
Parking: 10 spaces
Open: April–October

Entries are cross referenced by number to the maps on pages 18–19

58 Dalton Hall ◆◆◆◆

Dalton, Richmond, North Yorkshire DL11 7HU **Tel:** (01833) 621339

If it's peace and relaxation you are after you will be coming to the right place. We are perched halfway up a hill, surrounded by fields, overlooking a small lake, midway between the historic market towns of Richmond and Barnard Castle. The Hall (mentioned by Sir Walter Scott in his epic poem 'Rokeby') is a mixture of medieval and Georgian styles, but is all you would expect of a modern Bed & Breakfast - welcoming, warm and comfortable.

Bed & Breakfast per night: single occupancy from £22.50; double room £36.00

Bedrooms: 2 double, 1 twin
Bathrooms: 3 en-suite
Parking: 4 spaces

59 Rookhurst Country House Hotel ◆◆◆◆

West End, Gayle, Hawes, North Yorkshire DL8 3RT **Tel:** (01969) 667454 **Fax:** (01969) 667128
E-mail: rookhurst@lineone.net

At Wensleydale's heart, Rookhurst fronts the Pennine Way, ten minutes' walk from Hawes. With 17th, 18th and 19th-century architectures, the hotel offers contrasting styles and a varied content of four-poster beds, antique furniture, porcelain and needlework. Memories are jogged with set dinner menus containing such evocative dishes as beef casseroles with dumplings and apple crumbles, while dry-cure bacon, free-range eggs, our local butcher's sausages, along with Judith's home-made breads, set you up for the day!

Bed & Breakfast per night: double room from £64.00–£94.00
Dinner, Bed & Breakfast per person, per night: £42.00–£65.00
Evening meal: 1930

Bedrooms: 4 double, 1 twin
Bathrooms: 4 en-suite, 1 private
Parking: 6 spaces
Cards accepted: Mastercard, Visa, Switch/Delta, Visa Electron, Solo

60 Helm ◆◆◆◆ Silver Award

Askrigg, Leyburn, North Yorkshire DL8 3JF **Tel:** (01969) 650443 **Fax:** (01969) 650443
Web: http://www.helmyorkshire.com **E-mail:** holiday@helmyorkshire.com

Idyllically situated with 'the finest view in Wensleydale'. Experience the comfort, peace and quiet of our 17th-century hillside Dales farmhouse. Each charmingly furnished bedroom has en-suite facilities and many special little touches. Period furniture, oak beams and log fires create the ideal atmosphere in which to relax and share our passion for really good food. We offer a superb choice of breakfasts, home-made bread and preserves, exceptionally good dinners and an inspired selection of wines. Totally non-smoking.

Bed & Breakfast per night: double room from £62.00–£76.00
Dinner, Bed & Breakfast per person, per night: £49.50–£56.50
Evening meal: 1900 (last orders 1900)

Bedrooms: 2 double, 1 twin
Bathrooms: 3 en-suite
Parking: 5 spaces
Open: All year except December
Cards accepted: Mastercard, Visa, Switch/Delta, Eurocard

At-a-glance symbols are explained on the flap inside the back cover

61 The Grange

West Burton, Leyburn, North Yorkshire DL8 4JR **Tel:** (01969) 663348

The Grange is a private country house set in its own landscaped gardens. It offers quality bed and breakfast with optional evening meal. All the bedrooms are en-suite and furnished to the highest standard. The public rooms contain fine antique furniture and log fires in winter months. There is a large river frontage area for summer months. No smoking in bedrooms.

Bed & Breakfast per night: single occupancy from £30.00–£35.00; double room from £50.00–£60.00
Dinner, Bed & Breakfast per person, per night: £40.00–£48.00
Evening meal: 1900 (last orders 2000)

Bedrooms: 2 double, 1 twin
Bathrooms: 2 en-suite, 1 private
Parking: 10 spaces

Swaledale Sheep

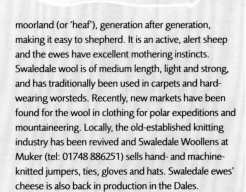

Visitors exploring the fells of the Yorkshire Dales will soon appreciate the National Park's choice of emblem – the Swaledale tup, or adult male sheep. With its characteristic black face, white nose and the curly horns that are carried by both sexes of the breed it is a distinctive sight. One of Britain's most popular breeds for wool, meat and crossing with other types of sheep, the Swaledale began life in the Pennine hills, being bred to survive some of the harshest winter conditions in the country, and has since played a significant part in trimming the Dales landscape. It is sometimes seen on the fells with a newer breed, the Dalesbred, originally a cross between the Swaledale and the Scottish blackface and easily confused with the Swaledale (look at the faces: the Swaledale is black with an all-white nose, the Dalesbred has two white patches).

The Yorkshire Dales have a tradition of sheep-farming that goes back to the monastic houses of the Middle Ages. Today's sheep farmers distinguish between hardy breeds, such as the Swaledale and Dalesbred, which graze the impoverished uplands, and the more productive and weightier halfbreeds such as Mashams (distinguished by their long, crinkly fleece), raised in the lusher valleys. One characteristic of the Swaledale that farmers appreciate, apart from its ability to look after itself on the high fells, is its habit of returning to and staying on the same area of

moorland (or 'heaf'), generation after generation, making it easy to shepherd. It is an active, alert sheep and the ewes have excellent mothering instincts. Swaledale wool is of medium length, light and strong, and has traditionally been used in carpets and hard-wearing worsteds. Recently, new markets have been found for the wool in clothing for polar expeditions and mountaineering. Locally, the old-established knitting industry has been revived and Swaledale Woollens at Muker (tel: 01748 886251) sells hand- and machine-knitted jumpers, ties, gloves and hats. Swaledale ewes' cheese is also back in production in the Dales.

In March and April visitors to Hazelbrow Farm, Low Row, may see lambs being born and can also try their hand at bottle-feeding – as well as holding chicks, feeding hens and watching cows being milked (tel: 01748 886224). Alternatively, to see some particularly fine specimens, visit one of the agricultural shows in the area, Reeth in late August, Muker early September, or the May Fair at Tan Hill Inn. (Phone the Dales National Park office on 01756 752748 for details.)

Entries are cross referenced by number to the maps on pages 18–19

62 Little Holtby ◆◆◆◆

Leeming Bar, Northallerton, North Yorkshire DL7 9LH **Tel:** (01609) 748762 **Fax:** (01609) 748822

Today's discerning traveller is looking for somewhere special, where the warmth of welcome and attention to your comfort will remain a treasured memory. Beams, polished wood floors, log fires and antiques all add to the charm of an old farmhouse. All guest rooms have wonderful views. Treat yourself to a really memorable stay.

Bed & Breakfast per night: single occupancy £25.00; double room from £40.00–£45.00
Dinner, Bed & Breakfast per person, per night: £32.50–£35.00
Evening meal: 1930 (last orders 2100)

Bedrooms: 2 double, 1 twin
Bathrooms: 1 en-suite, 1 public
Parking: 10 spaces

63 Milton House ◆◆◆◆◆ Silver Award

Londonderry, Northallerton, North Yorkshire DL7 9NE **Tel:** (01677) 423142 **Fax:** (01677) 423142
E-mail: rachel@miltonhouse79.co.uk

An attractive Arts & Crafts house, standing in five acres of gardens and tree-lined paddocks, offering welcoming and comfortable accommodation. Elegant period bedrooms with contemporary en-suite facilities, a pretty, private sitting room and a hearty breakfast create the country house atmosphere our guests remember. Convenient for the A1, north/south travel, or as a base for exploring North Yorkshire, the Dales, Moors and heritage coast. Secure illuminated car parking. A no smoking home.

Bed & Breakfast per night: single occupancy from £25.00–£28.00; double room from £50.00–£56.00

Bedrooms: 1 double, 1 twin
Bathrooms: 2 en-suite
Parking: 6 spaces
Cards accepted: Mastercard, Visa

64 Limetree Farm ◆◆◆◆

Hutts Lane, Grewelthorpe, Ripon, North Yorkshire HG4 3DA **Tel:** (01765) 658450

Old Dales farmhouse in woodland setting on nature reserve. While horses graze the wild flower meadows, all kinds of poultry wander freely around the farmyard. We are central for touring or walking, with Fountains Abbey nearby. The farmhouse has oak panelling, exposed beams and stonework and open fires. Furnished with antiques to a high standard, the bedrooms all have their own private facilities with tea/coffee making facilities, colour television and central heating. Colour brochure 01765 658450.

Bed & Breakfast per night: single occupancy from £25.00–£28.00; double room from £40.00–£46.00
Dinner, Bed & Breakfast per person, per night: £32.00–£35.00
Evening meal: 1800 (last orders 1900)

Bedrooms: 2 double, 1 twin
Bathrooms: 2 en-suite, 1 private
Parking: 10 spaces

At-a-glance symbols are explained on the flap inside the back cover

65 Knottside Farm ◆◆◆◆◆

The Knott, Pateley Bridge, Harrogate, North Yorkshire HG3 5DQ **Tel:** (01423) 712927 **Fax:** (01423) 712927

Situated within easy reach of York, Harrogate, Dales and North York Moors, this lovingly refurbished house, which nestles into the hillside, has panoramic views over Nidderdale. A very special experience awaits the visitor. An atmosphere of comfort and relaxation pervades the delightful accommodation where attention to detail is second to none. However, what really sets this place apart is the amazing quality of the cuisine. Nigel is Cordon Bleu trained and cooking is obviously the love of his life.

Bed & Breakfast per night: double room from £50.00–£53.00
Dinner, Bed & Breakfast per person, per night: £42.50–£44.00
Evening meal: 1930 (last orders 2000)

Bedrooms: 2 double
Bathrooms: 1 en-suite, 1 private
Parking: 4 spaces

66 Mallard Grange ◆◆◆◆ Silver Award

Aldfield, nr Fountains Abbey, Ripon, North Yorkshire HG4 3BE **Tel:** (01765) 620242

Rambling, 16th-century farmhouse full of character and charm in glorious countryside near Fountains Abbey. Offering superb quality and comfort, spacious rooms furnished with care and some lovely antique pieces. En-suite bedrooms have large comfortable beds, warm towels, colour television, hair dryer and refreshments tray. Delicious breakfasts! Pretty walled garden. Safe parking. Ideally placed for Harrogate, York, Yorkshire Dales, North York Moors and a wealth of historic houses, castles and gardens. Excellent evening meals locally.

Bed & Breakfast per night: single occupancy from £30.00; double room from £45.00–£50.00

Bedrooms: 2 double, 2 twin
Bathrooms: 3 en-suite, 1 private
Parking: 2 spaces

67 The Old Deanery ◆◆◆◆

Minster Road, Ripon, North Yorkshire HG4 1QS **Tel:** (01765) 603518 **Fax:** (01765) 692798
Web: http://www.theolddeanery.co.uk

The Old Deanery, which is Grade II listed, was built in 1604 and is adjacent to Ripon Cathedral. The Minster Drawing Room is oak panelled and has a log fire. Choose from either the Cardinal or Georgian restaurant, ideal for a romantic dinner or dinner party. Our menu provides a wide choice of cuisine and an extensive wine list. Lunch is available in the Garden Room Café. All en-suite bedrooms with television, tea and coffee, hair dryer. Civil marriages, wedding receptions and conferences. Our mission is to give quality personal individual service.

Bed & Breakfast per night: single occupancy from £55.00–£65.00; double room from £78.00–£110.00
Dinner, Bed & Breakfast per person, per night: £55.00–£70.00
Evening meal: 1830 (last orders 2130)

Bedrooms: 2 double, 1 twin
Bathrooms: 3 en-suite
Parking: 20 spaces
Open: All year except January
Cards accepted: Mastercard, Visa, Switch/Delta, JCB, Solo

68 The Boar's Head Country Hotel

★★★ Silver Award

Ripley Castle Estate, Harrogate, North Yorkshire HG3 3AY **Tel:** (01423) 771888 **Fax:** (01423) 771509
Web: http://www.ripleycastle.co.uk/boarsheadhotel **E-mail:** boarshead@ripleycastle.co.uk

Overlooking the cobbled village square, this elegant country hotel is at the heart of the historic Ripley Estate. De luxe bedrooms with king-size beds are individually designed and decorated, and the award-winning restaurant offers the best English cuisine and a fine wine selection. The bistro and pub specialise in bar meals and serve a range of hand-pulled Yorkshire and guest beers. 'Somewhere Special' guests enjoy admission to the glorious walled gardens and grounds of Ripley Castle. ⚡ **Category 3**

Bed & Breakfast per night: single occupancy from £95.00–£115.00; double room from £115.00–£135.00
Dinner, Bed & Breakfast per person, per night: £75.00–£95.00 (min 2 nights)
Lunch available: 1200–1430

Evening meal: 1900 (last orders 2130)
Bedrooms: 5 double, 20 twin
Bathrooms: 25 en-suite
Parking: 43 spaces
Cards accepted: Mastercard, Visa, Switch/Delta, Amex, Diners, Eurocard

69 Valley Hotel

◆◆◆◆

93-95 Valley Drive, Harrogate, North Yorkshire HG2 0JP **Tel:** (01423) 504868 **Fax:** (01423) 531940
Web: http://www.harrogate.com/valley **E-mail:** valley@harrogate.com

The Valley Hotel has an enviable position overlooking the famous Valley Gardens and is a family-owned hotel offering a warm welcome to both tourists and business guests. We are dedicated to providing a personal, friendly, enthusiastic service. Genuine home-cooked breakfasts for all tastes, including vegetarian. All rooms are en-suite with colour television, hairdryer, telephone and beverage tray. Lift to all floors. Licensed bar and lounge. Easy walking for town centre, shops and restaurants. Free permits for parking.

Bed & Breakfast per night: single room from £35.00–£45.00; double room from £55.00–£65.00

Bedrooms: 4 single, 3 double, 5 twin, 2 triple, 2 family
Bathrooms: 16 en-suite
Parking: 3 spaces
Cards accepted: Mastercard, Visa, Switch/Delta, Amex, Diners, Solo

70 Britannia Lodge Hotel

◆◆◆◆

16 Swan Road, Harrogate, North Yorkshire HG1 2SA **Tel:** (01423) 508482 **Fax:** (01423) 526840

Centrally located in one of Harrogate's most peaceful and select conservation areas, the Britannia Lodge Hotel is a charming 19th-century town house set in delightful gardens and with private off-road parking. Nigel and Julia Macdonald offer an elegant, cosy lounge and bar with an open fire on chilly days, and 12 pretty bedrooms, many with antique furniture, but not sacrificing creature comfort. Personal service and attention to detail come as standard. For further details please contact us for our colour brochure.

Bed & Breakfast per night: single room from £39.00–£50.00; double room from £59.00–£90.00

Bedrooms: 4 single, 6 double/twin, 2 triple
Bathrooms: 12 en-suite
Parking: 7 spaces
Cards accepted: Mastercard, Visa, Switch/Delta, Amex, Diners, Eurocard, Solo

At-a-glance symbols are explained on the flap inside the back cover

71 Ruskin Hotel and Restaurant

◆◆◆◆◆ Silver Award

1 Swan Road, Harrogate, North Yorkshire HG1 2SS **Tel:** (01423) 502045 **Fax:** (01423) 506131
Web: http://www.smoothhound.co.uk/hotels/ruskin.html **E-mail:** ruskin.hotel@virgin.net

A truly outstanding small Victorian hotel set in lovely mature gardens in a quiet conservation area, only five minutes' stroll from the town, magnificent gardens and conference/exhibition halls. Beautifully appointed and decorated, antique furnished en-suite bedrooms, including a four-poster room. Gracious and relaxing drawing room with fine antiques, open fire and interesting books. Renowned for superb breakfasts and excellent English cuisine served in the delightful Victorian-style restaurant with bar. Private floodlit car park. Award winners for the highest standards and real quality.

Bed & Breakfast per night: single room from £55.00–£75.00; double room from £80.00–£120.00
Dinner, Bed & Breakfast per person, per night: £50.00–£70.00 (min 2 nights)
Evening meal: 1900 (last orders 2030)

Bedrooms: 2 single, 3 double, 1 triple
Bathrooms: 6 en-suite
Parking: 10 spaces
Cards accepted: Mastercard, Visa, Switch/Delta, Amex, Eurocard, JCB, Maestro, Visa Electron, Solo

Wade's Causeway

Wade, legend has it, was a giant, a Saxon King who lived in Mulgrave Castle, Lythe. Legend also decrees that he lies buried near by, stretched out between two standing stones a mile or so apart, the one near Goldsborough, the other at East Barnby. His giantess wife, Bell, kept cows at Pickering Castle and so had to cross 20 miles (32km) of moorland each day to milk them. To make things easier, Wade built her a footpath. He scooped out earth, creating the Hole of Horcum near Saltersgate, and what was left over he threw across the moors, making Blakey Topping or, some say, Roseberry Topping. Bell helped in the construction work by carrying stones for the surface in her apron, dropping some now and then and leaving great mounds dotted about the moors.

Wade's Causeway is, if the truth be told, Britain's best-preserved stretch of Roman road. Under the governorship of Agricola, the Romans built a network of roads and forts north of York in about 80AD. One of these roads ran 25 miles (40km) north from Malton, entering the North York Moors at Cawthorne, north of Pickering, where four camps were built in about 100AD, and running on across to a signal station and landing point on the coast at Goldsborough. After the Romans left, the road lay uncared for on the bleak and boggy moor, with heather gradually creeping over it, until it was rediscovered in 1914. A section about 1¼ miles (2km) long was cleared.

Like any other Roman road, or stratum (from which our word 'street' derives), Wade's Causeway was constructed with a foundation of large stones that were then covered with pebbles or gravel. About 16ft (4.8m) wide, it is cambered, allowing drainage into gutters at either side. The gravel top-surface is lost, but foundation slabs, some kerb stones and a few drainage culverts at the northern end survive. Only a century ago most of our roads were unsurfaced tracks, so it is nothing but amazing, and a tribute to the engineering skills of the Romans, that a length of road constructed some 2,000 years ago should have survived in such remarkably good condition.

Wade's Causeway is on Wheeldale Moor, south-west of the village of Goathland, parallel to and west of Wheeldale Beck. It is best approached either from Goathland (it is close to Wheeldale Lodge Youth Hostel, 2 miles (3.2km) south of the village) or from the minor road between Stape and Egton Bridge at National Grid ref. SE 805 975.

Entries are cross referenced by number to the maps on pages 18–19

72 Manor House Farm ◆◆◆◆

Ingleby Greenhow, Great Ayton, Cleveland TS9 6RB **Tel:** (01642) 722384
E-mail: mbloom@globalnet.co.uk

A charming old farm (part c1760) set idyllically in 168 acres of parkland and woodland at the foot of the Cleveland Hills in the North York Moors National Park. Wildlife surrounds the farmhouse. The environment is tranquil and secluded, and the accommodation is warm and welcoming. Guests have their own entrance, dining room and lounge with library. Evening dinners are prepared meticulously and the hosts are proud of their reputation for fine food and wines. Brochure available.

Dinner, Bed & Breakfast per person, per night: £42.50–£50.00
Evening meal: 1900 (last bookings 1600)

Bedrooms: 1 double, 2 twin
Bathrooms: 1 en-suite, 2 private
Parking: 66 spaces
Open: All year except Christmas
Cards accepted: Mastercard, Visa, Switch/Delta, Eurocard, JCB, Visa Electron, Solo

73 Broom House ◆◆◆◆

Broom House Lane, Egton Bridge, Whitby, North Yorkshire YO21 1XD **Tel:** (01947) 895279 **Fax:** (01947) 895657
E-mail: welcome@BroomHouseEgtonBridge.freeserve.co.uk

Broom House – an excellent place to stay. We provide comfortable en-suite rooms in old country farmhouse style, log fires in public rooms in winter, first class meals prepared by our resident chef and an idyllic setting with views over the Esk Valley. Egton Bridge is considered to be one of the prettiest villages in Yorkshire, situated in Eskdale with many fascinating corners to explore. A peaceful haven located within beautiful countryside yet close to Whitby and the east coast.

Bed & Breakfast per night: single occupancy £25.00; double room £39.00
Dinner, Bed & Breakfast per person, per night: £31.45
Evening meal: 1830 (last orders 2000)

Bedrooms: 3 double, 1 twin, 1 triple
Bathrooms: 5 en-suite
Parking: 5 spaces

74 Harmony Country Lodge ◆◆◆◆

80 Limestone Road, Burniston, Scarborough, North Yorkshire YO13 0DG **Tel:** 0800 298 5841 or 07971 421430 **Fax:** 0800 298 5841
Web: http://www.spiderweb.co.uk/Harmony **E-mail:** harmonylodge@cwcom.net

Unique in design and three miles from Scarborough, Harmony offers a peaceful and relaxing smoke-free retreat within 1.5 acres of private grounds. Set in an elevated position with superb 360 degree panoramic views of the sea and National Park. The rooms, including the attractive dining room, guest lounge and conservatory, are tastefully decorated with attention to detail and all have superb views. You can spoil yourself with a relaxing fragrant massage during your stay.

Bed & Breakfast per night: single room from £20.00–£28.00; double room from £40.00–£50.00
Dinner, Bed & Breakfast per person, per night: £32.00–£40.00
Evening meal: 1830

Bedrooms: 2 single, 4 double, 1 twin
Bathrooms: 4 en-suite, 2 rooms with private wc, 1 public
Parking: 11 spaces

75 Littlegarth ◆◆◆◆

High Street, Ebberston, Scarborough, North Yorkshire YO13 9PA **Tel:** (01723) 850045 or (01723) 850151 **Fax:** (01723) 850151

Located in an idyllic and secluded setting between York and the coast, Littlegarth is an attractive and spacious 1920s country house offering warm, attentive but unobtrusive hospitality and high standards of comfort. Many of Yorkshire's major attractions are within easy reach: historic York, the heritage coast, the North York Moors and Dales National Parks, Whitby and the Captain Cook Trail, besides numerous museums, abbeys, castles, stately homes and gardens. We offer our own professionally qualified guided tours. Brochure available.

Bed & Breakfast per night: single occupancy from £30.00–£35.00; double room from £40.00–£50.00

Bedrooms: 1 double, 1 twin
Bathrooms: 2 en-suite
Parking: 5 spaces
Open: March–October

76 High Farm ◆◆◆◆

Cropton, Pickering, North Yorkshire YO18 8HL **Tel:** (01751) 417461

High Farm is an elegant Victorian farmhouse located at the edge of a quiet, unspoilt village, with fine views over the North York Moors National Park. Relax and unwind in the old world charm and sample home baking over an open fire. Enjoy the beautiful one acre garden planted with trees, shrubs and roses. Ideal base for walkers and nature lovers. Visit nearby Castle Howard, Rievaulx Abbey and Moors Railway. Private parking. A short stroll from the village inn and brewery.

Bed & Breakfast per night: single occupancy £24.99; double room £40.00

Bedrooms: 3 double
Bathrooms: 3 en-suite
Parking: 10 spaces

77 Sevenford House ◆◆◆◆

Thorgill, Rosedale Abbey, Pickering, North Yorkshire YO18 8SE **Tel:** (01751) 417283 **Fax:** (01751) 417505

Originally a vicarage, and built from the stones of Rosedale Abbey, Sevenford House stands in four acres of lovely gardens in the heart of the beautiful Yorkshire Moors National Park. Three tastefully furnished en-suite bedrooms with television, radio, and tea/coffee making facilities, offer wonderful views of the surrounding valley and moorland. A relaxing guests' lounge/library with open fire. This is an excellent base for exploring the region. Riding and golf locally. Ruined abbeys, Roman roads, steam railways, beautiful coastline and pretty fishing towns are all within easy reach.

Bed & Breakfast per night: double room £45.00

Bedrooms: 2 double, 1 triple
Bathrooms: 3 en-suite
Parking: 6 spaces

Entries are cross referenced by number to the maps on pages 18–19

78 Red Lion House ◆◆◆◆

Crown Square, Kirkbymoorside, York, North Yorkshire YO62 6AY **Tel:** (01751) 431815

Situated in a quiet square in the centre of this small market town, Red Lion House is the perfect base from which to explore this lovely area. The generous-sized bedrooms have crisp cotton bedding, colour television and many little extras to make your stay more comfortable. Enjoy an excellent breakfast in front of the old range in our flagstoned dining room. There are good local pubs within easy walking distance for evening meals.

Bed & Breakfast per night: single occupancy £25.00; double room from £35.00–£40.00

Bedrooms: 2 double, 1 twin
Bathrooms: 1 en-suite, 1 public
Parking: 2 spaces

79 The Cornmill ◆◆◆◆

Kirby Mills, Kirkbymoorside, York, North Yorkshire YO62 6NP **Tel:** (01751) 432000 **Fax:** (01751) 432300
Web: http://www.kirbymills.demon.co.uk **E-mail:** cornmill@kirbymills.demon.co.uk

An 18th-century watermill and Victorian farmhouse have been converted to provide luxury bed and breakfast accommodation with gardens and paddock on the River Dove, ten minutes from the beautiful North York Moors. Bedrooms, sitting room, honesty bar, wood-burning stove and bootroom for walkers' gear are in the farmhouse. One room is wheelchair friendly and two have four-posters. The old milling floor is now the dining room with glass floor over the millrace. Sumptuous breakfasts and tranquillity bring guests back time and again. Sorry, no children. ♿ **Category 3**

Bed & Breakfast per night: double room from £54.00–£65.00
Dinner, Bed & Breakfast per person, per night: £52.50 (groups of 4+, weekends only, pre-booked)
Evening meal: 1900

Bedrooms: 3 double, 2 twin
Bathrooms: 5 en-suite
Parking: 12 spaces
Open: April-October
Cards accepted: Mastercard, Visa

80 Sproxton Hall ◆◆◆◆

Sproxton, Helmsley, North Yorkshire YO62 5EQ **Tel:** (01439) 770225 **Fax:** (01439) 771373
E-mail: info@sproxtonhall.demon.co.uk

Relax in the tranquil atmosphere and comfort of our 17th-century Grade II listed farmhouse. Magnificent views over idyllic countryside on a 300 acre working farm, one mile south of the market town of Helmsley. Lovingly and tastefully furnished, giving the cosy elegance of a country home. Restful, oak-beamed drawing room with log fire. Enjoy a hearty breakfast in a most attractive dining room. Extremely comfortable, centrally heated double and twin bedrooms. En-suite or private bathrooms, tea-making facilities, remote control colour television. Guests' laundry facilities. Delightful country garden to relax in. No smoking.

Bed & Breakfast per night: double room from £44.00–£54.00

Bedrooms: 1 double, 2 twin
Bathrooms: 2 en-suite, 1 private
Parking: 10 spaces
Cards accepted: Mastercard, Visa, Eurocard

At-a-glance symbols are explained on the flap inside the back cover

81 Shallowdale House

♦♦♦♦♦ **Silver Award**

West End, Ampleforth, York, North Yorkshire YO62 4DY **Tel:** (01439) 788325 **Fax:** (01439) 788885

Shallowdale House is stunningly situated, in extensive hillside gardens, on the southern edge of the North York Moors National Park (20 miles north of York). Phillip Gill and Anton van der Horst have carefully created a distinctively elegant and restful place to stay, where good food matters and the service is always friendly and attentive. All the rooms enjoy exceptional panoramic views of gorgeous countryside and this is an excellent base for exploring a beautiful area.

Bed & Breakfast per night: single occupancy from £40.00–£50.00; double room from £60.00–£75.00
Dinner, Bed & Breakfast per person, per night: £50.00–£57.50 (min 2 sharing)
Evening meal: 1930

Bedrooms: 1 double, 2 twin
Bathrooms: 2 en-suite, 1 private
Parking: 3 spaces
Cards accepted: Mastercard, Visa

82 Burtree House Farm

♦♦♦♦

Burtree House, York Road, Hutton Sessay, Thirsk, North Yorkshire YO7 3AY **Tel:** (01845) 501333 or (01845) 501562 **Fax:** (01845) 501596

A relaxing, peaceful country house in private grounds with views over the Hambleton Hills and White Horse of Kilburn. Close to the A19 and within easy access of the A1. Rooms include a spacious lounge with log fire, a large conservatory and a luxury en-suite bedroom with king-size four-poster bed, private balcony, mirrored dressing room, satellite television and video. All rooms have television, radio alarm and tea/coffee making facilities. A trouser press is available.

Bed & Breakfast per night: double room from £60.00–£75.00

Bedrooms: 1 single, 2 double
Bathrooms: 2 en-suite, 1 private
Parking: 8 spaces

83 Oldstead Grange

♦♦♦♦♦

Oldstead, Coxwold, York, North Yorkshire YO61 4BJ **Tel:** (01347) 868634 **Fax:** (01347) 868634
Web: http://www.yorkshireuk.com **E-mail:** oldsteadgrange@yorkshireuk.com

Beautiful, quiet situation amidst our fields, woods and valleys near Byland Abbey in the North York Moors National Park. Oldstead Grange blends traditional 17th-century features with superb comfort and luxury. Spacious en-suite bedrooms include large, comfortable beds, colour television, warm towels and robes, fresh flowers and refreshment tray with home-made chocolates and biscuits. Speciality breakfast dishes. Light suppers on request or good evening meals locally. Telephone us for best terms, more details and colour brochure.

Bed & Breakfast per night: single occupancy from £30.00–£40.00; double room from £50.00–£60.00

Bedrooms: 1 double, 1 twin, 1 family
Bathrooms: 3 en-suite
Parking: 3 spaces
Cards accepted: Mastercard, Visa, Delta, Eurocard

Entries are cross referenced by number to the maps on pages 18–19

84 The Old Vicarage ◆◆◆◆

Market Place, Easingwold, York, North Yorkshire YO61 3AL **Tel:** (01347) 821015 **Fax:** (01347) 823465

Standing in the market square, yet surrounded by half an acre of gardens with croquet lawn and ample parking, our 18th-century home provides a tranquil haven easily accessible to York, the Moors and Dales. Tastefully furnished, well-appointed bedrooms are complemented with patchwork quilts and little unexpected extra touches. A traditional English breakfast using local produce is served in the east-facing dining room and the drawing room, with its grand piano, is exclusively for guests' enjoyment.

Bed & Breakfast per night: double room from £50.00–£60.00

Bedrooms: 2 double, 2 twin
Bathrooms: 4 en-suite
Parking: 5 spaces
Open: All year except January and December
Cards accepted: Mastercard, Visa

85 Village Farm Holidays ◆◆◆◆

Cherry Tree Avenue, Newton-on-Ouse, York, North Yorkshire YO30 2BN **Tel:** (01347) 848064 **Fax:** (01347) 848065
Web: http://www.yorkshire.co.uk/stayat/villagefarm **E-mail:** vfholidays@cs.com

Situated between York and Easingwold, in a peaceful location close to Beningborough Hall, Village Farm Holidays is the perfect retreat for those who appreciate the tranquillity of rural life in accommodation that offers guests an irresistible combination of discreet hospitality, antique tradition and modern comforts in a 200-year-old former Georgian farmhouse. There is a guest snooker room and, for the more energetic, the Yoredale Way Walk and National Cycle Route No. 65 pass through the village, which has two excellent public houses offering fine cuisine. This is the ideal place for the discerning guest to stay.

Bed & Breakfast per night: single occupancy from £20.00–£25.00; double room from £40.00–£50.00

Bedrooms: 1 double, 1 twin
Bathrooms: 2 en-suite
Parking: 12 spaces

86 Southlands Bed and Breakfast ◆◆◆◆

Huntington Road, Huntington, York YO3 9PX **Tel:** (01904) 766796 **Fax:** (01904) 764536
E-mail: SouthlandsBandB.York@btinternet.com

Avoid the hustle and bustle of York and stay in Southlands – a large detached house, with private parking, in attractive gardens on the edge of the city. A regular five-minute bus journey takes you to the city centre two miles away. Convenient for visiting all of Yorkshire, with superb scenery and other attractions. From Huntington/Strensall roundabout on the A1237, head for York/Huntington, and the house is 1.25 miles on the left.

Bed & Breakfast per night: single occupancy £28.00; double room from £38.00–£40.00

Bedrooms: 1 double, 2 twin
Bathrooms: 3 en-suite
Parking: 4 spaces
Cards accepted: Mastercard, Visa, Switch/Delta

87 Scagglethorpe Manor ◆◆◆◆

Main Street, Scagglethorpe, Malton, North Yorkshire YO17 8DT **Tel:** (01944) 758909 **Fax:** (01944) 758909
Web: http://www.visityorkshire.com

Scagglethorpe is a small unspoilt village, with pub, situated amid glorious countryside at the foot of the Wolds with moors, dales, east coast and York easily accessible. Our Grade II listed 17th-century farmhouse provides the perfect combination of generous and attentive hospitality with the privacy of your own home. You will be welcomed with tea/coffee and home baking. Breakfasts are delicious and substantial. Come and go as you please and enjoy our lovely gardens in summer or relax beside log fires in winter.

Bed & Breakfast per night: single occupancy from £27.00–£29.00; double room from £44.00–£48.00

Bedrooms: 2 double, 1 twin
Bathrooms: 2 en-suite, 1 private
Parking: 10+ spaces

88 Ashbourne House Hotel ◆◆◆◆

139 Fulford Road, York YO10 4HG **Tel:** (01904) 639912 **Fax:** (01904) 631332
E-mail: ashbourneh@aol.com

Just a short distance from the city, on the southerly A19 approach road. Aileen and David Minns await to welcome you to their friendly family home. The bedrooms are well equipped, offering comfort and modern facilities. A lounge with a small bar where guests can relax. Flower fairies adorn the walls in the dining room, along with the craftsman-made furniture, where freshly prepared meals are served.

Bed & Breakfast per night: double room from £40.00–£60.00
Dinner, Bed & Breakfast per person, per night: £37.50–£47.50
Evening meal: 1900 (last bookings 1800)

Bedrooms: 1 single, 3 double, 2 twin, 1 family
Bathrooms: 6 en-suite, 1 private
Parking: 6 spaces
Cards accepted: Mastercard, Visa, Amex, Diners, Eurocard

89 City Guest House ◆◆◆◆

68 Monkgate, York YO31 7PF **Tel:** (01904) 622483

'Arrive as guests, leave as friends.' A non-smoking, family-run Victorian guest house situated only two minutes' walk from the Minster, shops and restaurants. All bedrooms are en-suite and well equipped with tea/coffee making facilities and colour television. A good choice of breakfast is available with attentive and friendly service.

Bed & Breakfast per night: single room from £22.00–£30.00; double room from £42.00–£54.00

Bedrooms: 1 single, 4 double, 1 twin, 1 family
Bathrooms: 6 en-suite, 1 room with private shower
Parking: 5 spaces
Cards accepted: Mastercard, Visa, Switch/Delta, Eurocard

Entries are cross referenced by number to the maps on pages 18–19

90 The Hazelwood ◆◆◆◆

24-25 Portland Street, York YO31 7EH **Tel:** (01904) 626548 **Fax:** (01904) 628032
Web: http://www.thehazelwoodyork.com **E-mail:** reservations@thehazelwoodyork.com

Luxury and elegance in the very heart of York. The Hazelwood is situated only 400 yards from York Minster yet in an extremely quiet side street and has its own car park. The bedrooms in our elegant Victorian townhouse are individually styled and have recently been refurbished to the highest standards using designer fabrics. We offer a wide choice of high quality breakfasts, including vegetarian, ranging from traditional English to croissants and Danish pastries. We operate a non-smoking policy throughout.

Bed & Breakfast per night: single room from £40.00–£65.00; double room from £55.00–£80.00

Bedrooms: 1 single, 7 double, 4 twin, 2 triple
Bathrooms: 14 en-suite
Parking: 11 spaces
Cards accepted: Mastercard, Visa, Switch/Delta, JCB, Visa Electron, Solo

91 Bishops Hotel ◆◆◆◆

135 Holgate Road, Holgate, York YO24 4DF **Tel:** (01904) 628000 **Fax:** (01904) 628181

Relax at the award-winning 'Bishops' where we have created a refreshingly individual bed & breakfast hotel offering excellent service in comfortable surroundings. Our traditional Victorian villa has been beautifully restored throughout with individually designed en-suite bedrooms. Enjoy garden views from our sunny dining room where a delicious choice of breakfast is served. We are ideally situated within walking distance of the city's main attractions and provide an excellent base for exploring Yorkshire's magnificent countryside. Non-smoking.

Bed & Breakfast per night: single room from £27.00–£40.00; double room from £54.00–£80.00
Lunch available: (snacks) 1200–2100

Bedrooms: 2 single, 3 double, 2 triple, 2 family
Bathrooms: 9 en-suite
Parking: 9 spaces
Cards accepted: Mastercard, Visa, Switch/Delta

92 The Acer Hotel ◆◆◆◆ Silver Award

52 Scarcroft Hill, York YO24 1DE **Tel:** (01904) 653839 **Fax:** (01904) 677017
Web: http://www.acerhotel.co.uk **E-mail:** info@acerhotel.co.uk

Are you looking for somewhere special to stay? Then look no further. A warm welcome awaits you at our elegantly restored and refurbished licensed hotel. We offer superior accommodation, housekeeping of the highest standard and friendly service to create a relaxed atmosphere for our guests. Quietly situated, a short walk from the railway station, racecourse and attractions, the hotel is ideal for a short stay or longer break any time of year. A non-smoking establishment.

Bed & Breakfast per night: single occupancy £35.00; double room from £50.00–£60.00

Bedrooms: 2 double, 1 family
Bathrooms: 3 en-suite
Cards accepted: Mastercard, Visa, Delta

93 Holmwood House Hotel ◆◆◆◆

112-114 Holgate Road, York YO2 4BB **Tel:** (01904) 626183 **Fax:** (01904) 670899
Web: http://www.holmwoodhousehotel.co.uk **E-mail:** holmwood.house@dial.pipex.com

Close to the city walls, an elegant listed Victorian town house offering a feeling of home with a touch of luxury. All the en-suite bedrooms are different in size and decoration, some with four-poster beds and one has a spa bath; all rooms are non-smoking. Imaginative breakfasts are served to the sound of gentle classical music. The inviting sitting room, with its open fire, highlights the period style of the house. Car park. On the A59.

Bed & Breakfast per night: single occupancy from £55.00–£70.00; double room from £65.00–£90.00

Bedrooms: 10 double, 3 twin, 1 triple
Bathrooms: 14 en-suite
Parking: 9 spaces
Cards accepted: Mastercard, Visa, Switch/Delta, Amex, Eurocard, Visa Electron, Solo

94 The Manor Country House ◆◆◆◆

Acaster Malbis, York YO23 2UL **Tel:** (01904) 706723 **Fax:** (01904) 706723
Web: http://www.mywebpage.net/manor.house **E-mail:** manorhouse@selcom.co.uk

Family-run manor house in rural tranquillity, with private lake, set in five and a half acres of beautiful mature grounds on the banks of the River Ouse. Fish in the lake, cycle or walk. Close to racecourse and only a 10 minute car journey from the city – or take the leisurely river bus (Easter to October). Conveniently situated to take advantage of the Dales, Moors, Wolds and splendid coastline. Cosy lounge and licensed lounge bar with open fire. Conservatory breakfast room with Aga-cooked food.

Bed & Breakfast per night: single room from £38.00–£45.00; double room from £50.00–£68.00

Bedrooms: 1 single, 4 double, 2 twin, 3 triple
Bathrooms: 10 en-suite
Parking: 15 spaces
Cards accepted: Mastercard, Visa, Delta, Eurocard

95 Glebe Farm ◆◆◆◆

Bolton Percy, York, North Yorkshire YO23 7AL **Tel:** (01904) 744228

An elegant family-run Victorian farmhouse on a working farm. Offering excellent accommodation within easy reach of York city. The Moors, Dales and coast can be reached within an hour. Self-contained en-suite annexe, conservatory, garden and ample parking. The farm is in a quiet village with an exceptional 15th-century church. Bolton Percy is four miles from Tadcaster and nine miles from York.

Bed & Breakfast per night: single occupancy from £22.00–£26.00; double room from £40.00–£48.00

Bedrooms: 1 twin
Bathrooms: 1 en-suite
Parking: 2 spaces
Open: April–October

Entries are cross referenced by number to the maps on pages 18–19

96 Barff Lodge ◆◆◆◆

Mill Lane, Brayton, Selby, North Yorkshire YO8 9LB **Tel:** (01757) 213030 **Fax:** (01757) 212313
E-mail: barfflodge@aol.com

Spectacularly positioned and featuring a central courtyard. Pleasingly-priced accommodation with private access to all the rooms, offers the discerning guest unequalled quality and the personal attention of the owners. The peaceful countryside location belies the easy accessibility to major roads (M62 is six miles and the A19 Selby/Doncaster is half-a-mile away). Adjacent to Selby Golf Club, there are excellent modestly-priced places to eat nearby. Totally non-smoking.

Bed & Breakfast per night: single occupancy £28.00; double room £40.00

Bedrooms: 4 double, 1 twin
Bathrooms: 5 en-suite
Parking: 5 spaces
Cards accepted: Mastercard, Visa, Eurocard

97 Forest Pines Hotel ★★★★ Silver Award

Ermine Street, Broughton, Brigg, Scunthorpe, South Humberside DN20 0NQ **Tel:** (01652) 650770 or (01652) 650756 **Fax:** (01652) 650495
Web: http://www.forestpines.co.uk **E-mail:** enquiries@forestpines.co.uk

Superbly located for all business and pleasure needs. Nestling amid an idyllic landscape of wooded parkland, the hotel is a haven for those who enjoy being pampered. Easily accessible from the motorway system, Lincoln, Hull and York are within easy reach. International cuisine is served in the elegant Beech Tree Restaurant. Extensive table d'hôte and à la carte menus are available daily. For more casual dining, the Buttery and Grill is open all day, every day. Forest Pines, a 27 hole championship golf course provides the perfect venue for golfing breaks. The luxurious leisure club and beauty spa make this an ideal venue for a relaxed break.

Bed & Breakfast per night: single occupancy from £61.00–£86.00; double room from £72.00–£94.00
Dinner, Bed & Breakfast per person, per night: £55.50–£123.00
Lunch available: all day

Evening meal: 1900 (last orders 2200)
Bedrooms: 37 double, 49 twin
Bathrooms: 86 en-suite
Parking: 300 spaces
Cards accepted: Mastercard, Visa, Switch/Delta, Amex, Diners, Eurocard

98 Tudor Terrace Guest House ◆◆◆◆

11 Bradford Avenue, Cleethorpes, North East Lincolnshire DN35 0BB **Tel:** (01472) 600800 **Fax:** (01472) 501395
Web: http://www.web-marketing.co.uk/tudor-terrace **E-mail:** tudor.terrace@btinternet.com

'Somewhere special' for guests who deserve that little extra comfort and attention. Located close to the Winter Gardens, Leisure Centre and Boating Lake. Hosted by David and Janice, this very large Victorian house is situated within a conservation area. All rooms are decorated to an extremely high standard including a ground floor room for disabled visitors. Private gardens with patio area, off/on-street parking. A no smoking establishment. A colour brochure is available.

Bed & Breakfast per night: single room from £16.00–£24.00; double room from £30.00–£36.00
Dinner, Bed & Breakfast per person, per night: £22.50–£24.50 (pre-booked only)
Evening meal: 1800 (last orders 2000)

Bedrooms: 2 single, 3 double, 1 twin
Bathrooms: 4 en-suite, 1 room with private shower, 1 public
Parking: 3 spaces

At-a-glance symbols are explained on the flap inside the back cover

99 Wentbridge House Hotel

★★★ Silver Award

Wentbridge, Pontefract, West Yorkshire WF8 3JJ **Tel:** (01977) 620444 **Fax:** (01977) 620148

Dating from 1700 and situated in twenty acres of the beautiful Went Valley among century-old trees, Wentbridge House is within easy reach of the M62 and A1. A traditional open fireplace and a fine collection of Meissen porcelain welcome you to the cocktail bar. The Fleur de Lys Restaurant, with its international ambience and many awards including an AA Rosette and RAC Dining Award Level 2, attracts cosmopolitan lovers of food and wine. Individually furnished bedrooms include the Oakroom with its Mouseman four-poster bed.

Bed & Breakfast per night: single room from £60.00–£98.00; double room from £70.00–£108.00
Dinner, Bed & Breakfast per person, per night: £58.00–£77.00
Lunch available: 1200–1400
Evening meal: 1930 (last orders 2130)

Bedrooms: 1 single, 14 double, 4 twin
Bathrooms: 19 en-suite
Parking: 100 spaces
Cards accepted: Mastercard, Visa, Switch/Delta, Amex, Diners, Eurocard, Visa Electron, Solo

100 Whitley Hall Hotel

★★★ Silver Award

Elliott Lane, Grenoside, Sheffield S35 8NR **Tel:** (0114) 245 4444 **Fax:** (0114) 245 5414

Whitley Hall dates from the 16th century and is a lovely country house standing in its own thirty acres of gardens, woodland and lakes. Privately owned as a hotel for over twenty five years, we offer accommodation, food and service of the highest quality and in the best English tradition. This popular country hotel is ideally situated between the Yorkshire Dales and Derbyshire Peak District and only a few minutes from Sheffield's theatres, sports facilities and magnificent Meadowhall shopping complex.

Bed & Breakfast per night: single room from £57.50–£80.50; double room from £74.00–£102.00
Lunch available: 1145–1400
Evening meal: 1900 (last orders 2130)

Bedrooms: 2 single, 10 double, 6 twin, 1 family
Bathrooms: 19 en-suite
Parking: 100 spaces
Cards accepted: Mastercard, Visa, Switch/Delta, Amex, Diners, Visa Electron, Solo

101 Rombalds Hotel and Restaurant

★★★ Silver Award

West View, Wells Road, Ilkley, West Yorkshire LS29 9JG **Tel:** (01943) 603201 **Fax:** (01943) 816586
Web: http://www.rombalds.co.uk **E-mail:** reception@rombalds.demon.co.uk

Located on the edge of the famous Ilkley Moor, yet within walking distance of the centre of the beautiful Victorian spa town of Ilkley, this elegant Georgian hotel is run by the resident proprietors, Jo and Colin Clarkson. The AA 2 Rosette award-winning restaurant is well known for its cuisine and friendly service. The hotel is the ideal location for touring the North of England, with York, the Lakes and Peak District all approximately one hour's drive away.

Bed & Breakfast per night: single room from £55.00–£99.50; double room from £80.00–£119.00
Dinner, Bed & Breakfast per person, per night: £52.75–£64.50 (min 2 nights, 2 sharing)
Lunch available: 1200–1400

Evening meal: 1830 (last orders 2130)
Bedrooms: 1 single, 11 double, 2 twin, 1 triple
Bathrooms: 15 en-suite
Parking: 22 spaces
Cards accepted: Mastercard, Visa, Switch/Delta, Amex, Diners, Eurocard, JCB, Solo

Entries are cross referenced by number to the maps on pages 18–19

102 Marriott Hollins Hall Hotel & Country Club ★★★★ Silver Award

Hollins Hill, Baildon, Shipley, West Yorkshire BD17 7QW **Tel:** (01274) 530053 **Fax:** (01274) 530187

Set in over 200 acres of glorious countryside, our hotel provides the ideal base from which to explore the Yorkshire Moors, Brontë Country and Salts Mill, as well as the shopping and leisure attractions of Leeds and Bradford. Relax in one of our 122 spacious, well-appointed bedrooms and dine in our stylish Heathcliff's Restaurant. Facilities also include an 18-hole golf course, fully equipped leisure club with indoor swimming pool and health and beauty spa.

Bed & Breakfast per night: single occupancy from £64.00–£74.00; double room from £78.00–£98.00
Dinner, Bed & Breakfast per person, per night: £59.00–£69.00
Evening meal: 1900 (last orders 2200)

Bedrooms: 76 double, 46 twin
Bathrooms: 122 en-suite
Parking: 250 spaces
Cards accepted: Mastercard, Visa, Switch/Delta, Amex, Diners, Eurocard

Salts Mill

A marvel of its age and pre-eminent among Bradford's textile mills until its closure in the 1980s, Salts Mill was built in 1853 by Titus Salt for his worsted manufacturing business. Now the vast Italianate-style mill is a Grade II listed building, still surrounded by the terraced sandstone houses and community buildings of the village that the visionary Salt planned to cater for his workers' every need. In 1987 it was bought by locally-born Jonathan Silver and since then has been undergoing creative but sympathetic restoration. It is now home to several businesses (employing some 1,400 people in fields such as electronics and manufacturing) and a clutch of cultural enterprises. Of the latter, the most notable are the galleries devoted to the work of artist David Hockney, another of Bradford's sons, a schoolmate of Jonathan Silver and a regular visitor to the mill.

The 1853 Gallery, on the ground floor of the main spinning block, was the first of the three Hockney galleries to open. On its walls hang 350 original works, a permanent exhibition of cartoons, prints, paintings and computer-generated images from Hockney's childhood years to recent times. Here, too, a bookshop displays its wares not on conventional shelves but on tables, chairs and other pieces of furniture, between vases of flowers and local pottery. The mood is set for browsing with

strains of Hockney's favourite pieces of music, often from opera, playing in the background. A second gallery is to be found in an old wool-sorting room, next to Salts Diner on the second floor. This is an experimental space and exhibitions change regularly: the past few years have, for example, seen pictures of Hockney's dachshunds and his opera sets. The third and newest gallery, above the Diner, is a more intimate space, displaying images that have a particular meaning for David Hockney personally.

Apart from the galleries, Salts Mill has some fairly upmarket shops, whose goods range from contemporary furniture and high-quality household objects to top designer label clothes. The civilised, relaxed atmosphere that pervades the galleries carries through to Salts Diner, where you can pick up a newspaper to read while you enjoy good, reasonably priced food and drink. Salts Mill (tel: 01274 531163, fax 01274 531184) is open daily 10am–6pm, admission free. Frequent trains link Saltaire with Bradford and Leeds.

103 Five Rise Locks Hotel ◆◆◆◆

Beck Lane, Bingley, West Yorkshire BD16 4DD **Tel:** (01274) 565296 **Fax:** (01274) 568828
E-mail: 101731.2134@compuserve.com

Built for a wealthy Victorian mill owner, the house stands in mature gardens overlooking the Aire valley, yet is only a few minutes' walk away from the Five Rise Locks and Bingley town centre. Each en-suite bedroom has a unique view and has been individually designed and furnished. Enjoy home cooking prepared with intelligence and imagination and wines from a well-chosen list in elegant, yet comfortable, surroundings. Experience Haworth – the Brontës, Esholt village, steam trains, museums and tranquil, vast open spaces.

Bed & Breakfast per night: single room from £35.00–£48.00; double room from £55.00–£60.00
Dinner, Bed & Breakfast per person, per night: £42.00–£62.00
Evening meal: 1930 (last orders 2100)

Bedrooms: 1 single, 5 double, 3 twin
Bathrooms: 9 en-suite
Parking: 15 spaces
Cards accepted: Mastercard, Visa, Switch/Delta, Eurocard, JCB, Maestro, Visa Electron, Solo

104 Bankfield Bed and Breakfast ◆◆◆◆

Danny Lane, Luddendenfoot, Halifax, West Yorkshire HX2 6AW **Tel:** (01422) 883147

If you are looking for peace, tranquillity and good value for money, let us welcome you to our Georgian home. Bankfield is surrounded by a large secluded walled garden, situated between Halifax and Hebden Bridge. Comfortable spacious bedrooms are fully equipped. A wholesome breakfast is served in the conservatory watching the garden's morning visitors. Lovely walking area, good pubs and restaurants. Also an ideal retreat for business people working in the area. Non-smoking, private parking.

Bed & Breakfast per night: single occupancy from £20.00–£25.00; double room from £36.00–£44.00

Bedrooms: 1 double, 1 twin
Bathrooms: 1 en-suite, 1 private
Parking: 4 spaces

105 Cornerstones ◆◆◆◆

230 Washway Road, Sale, Cheshire M33 4RA **Tel:** (0161) 283 6909 or (0161) 283 1753 **Fax:** (0161) 283 6909
E-mail: tcasey@cwcom.net

Cornerstones is located on the main A56 road into the city centre. The building is Victorian – built by Sir William Cunliff Brooks, Lord of the Manor. A total refurbishment was carried out in 1985, reproducing the splendour of the Victorian era. Brookland Metro station is less than five minutes' walk away, and on the fifteen minute journey into the city you will pass Manchester United Football Club, Lancashire County Cricket Club and the G-Mex. At your journey's end you will find an abundance of shops, theatres, museums and art galleries.

Bed & Breakfast per night: single room from £25.00–£35.00; double room £50.00
Dinner, Bed & Breakfast per person, per night: £45.00–£55.00
Evening meal: 1930

Bedrooms: 3 single, 3 double, 3 twin
Bathrooms: 5 en-suite, 2 rooms with private shower, 1 public
Parking: 10 spaces
Cards accepted: Mastercard, Visa, JCB

Entries are cross referenced by number to the maps on pages 18–19

106 Stanneylands Hotel

★★★ Silver Award

Stanneylands Road, Wilmslow, Cheshire SK9 4EY **Tel:** (01625) 525225 **Fax:** (01625) 537282
E-mail: gordonbeech@thestanneylandshotel.co.uk

A strikingly handsome country house hotel set in beautiful gardens. With open fires and oak-panelled dining rooms, hospitality abounds on every hand. Stanneylands offers the very finest of English and International cuisine, prepared and served with pride and care. Ideally located for visiting Styal Mill, Jodrell Bank, Tatton Park and Bramall Hall, and within easy reach of the motorway network and Manchester International Airport.

Bed & Breakfast per night: single room from £60.50–£98.50; double room from £96.00–£119.00
Lunch available: 1200–1445
Evening meal: 1900 (last orders 2200)

Bedrooms: 7 single, 11 double, 13 twin
Bathrooms: 31 en-suite
Parking: 80 spaces
Cards accepted: Mastercard, Visa, Switch/Delta, Amex, Diners

107 The Alderley Edge Hotel

★★★ Silver Award

Macclesfield Road, Alderley Edge, Cheshire SK9 7BJ **Tel:** (01625) 583033 **Fax:** (01625) 586343
Web: http://www.alderley-edge-hotel.co.uk **E-mail:** sales@alderley-edge-hotel.co.uk

Originally a mill owner's private residence, this country house hotel is set in its own grounds with breathtaking views over the surrounding Cheshire countryside, yet just a matter of minutes from major air, road and rail links. The most recent additions, following extensive refurbishment, are a further 12 bedrooms, bringing the total to 44, plus the bridal and presidential suites. Deservedly recognised for excellent food, service and beautifully appointed facilities. ↑ **Category 3**

Bed & Breakfast per night: single occupancy from £40.00–£108.00; double room from £80.00–£155.00
Lunch available: 1200–1400
Evening meal: 1900 (last orders 2200)

Bedrooms: 31 double, 11 twin, 4 suites
Bathrooms: 46 en-suite
Parking: 90 spaces
Cards accepted: Mastercard, Visa, Switch/Delta, Amex, Diners

108 Manor Farm

◆◆◆◆

Cliff Road, Acton Bridge, Northwich, Cheshire CW8 3QP **Tel:** (01606) 853181 **Fax:** (01606) 853181

Peaceful, rural, elegantly-furnished traditional country house with open views from all rooms. Situated away from roads down a long private drive, above the banks of the River Weaver. A large garden provides access to a private path through our woodland into the picturesque valley. In the heart of Cheshire, we are an ideal location for business or pleasure, within easy reach of Chester, Merseyside and the motorway network. Ample safe parking.

Bed & Breakfast per night: single room from £20.00–£25.00; double room from £40.00–£50.00

Bedrooms: 1 single, 2 twin
Bathrooms: 1 en-suite, 2 private
Parking: 14 spaces

At-a-glance symbols are explained on the flap inside the back cover

109 Crabwall Manor Hotel and Restaurant

★★★ Silver Award

Parkgate Road, Mollington, Chester, Cheshire CH1 6NE **Tel:** (01244) 851666 **Fax:** (01244) 851400
Web: http://www.crabwall.com **E-mail:** sales@crabwall.com

Crabwall Manor is a country house hotel situated just 1.5 miles away from Chester. Set in its own private grounds with 48 individually designed, luxurious bedrooms. Crabwall Manor can also boast an AA 3 Rosette and RAC Blue Ribbon award-winning restaurant. The 'Spa at Crabwall' is a new £2 million development at the hotel and includes an 18 metre swimming pool, gymnasium, aerobic studio, spa pool, sauna, steam room, juice bar and three beauty treatment rooms.

Bed & Breakfast per night: single occupancy from £90.00–£120.00; double room from £120.00–£145.00
Lunch available: 1200–1400
Evening meal: 1900 (last orders 2130)

Bedrooms: 48 double/twin
Bathrooms: 48 en-suite
Parking: 120 spaces
Cards accepted: Mastercard, Visa, Switch/Delta, Amex, Diners, JCB

Port Sunlight

'It is my hope... to build houses in which our work-people will be able to live and be comfortable – semi-detached houses, with gardens back and front.' So said Lord Leverhulme on 3 March 1888 at the opening of Port Sunlight – 3 miles (4.8km) south-east of Birkenhead on the Wirral peninsula. The name the soap manufacturer chose for his garden village was appropriate; Sunlight Soap was Lever Brothers' leading brand, while the opportunity for all workers to live their lives away from the dark and shady back-to-backs so prevalent in Victorian Britain was central to his beliefs.

As well as providing quality houses for his workers, Leverhulme paid generously for shorter hours. A late-19th-century working man would have considered himself most fortunate to receive a wage of 25 shillings (£1.25) for a 48-hour week. There was a small rent to pay, but the maintenance of the garden village was funded by Lever Brothers' profits – and few other workers could have afforded such comfortable accommodation. A reasonable wage, secure job and subsidised housing were important to the industrialist, but Leverhulme felt there was more to life than simply work and the home. He ran several educational initiatives, built a cottage hospital and encouraged a range of clubs and societies that fostered an appreciation of music, science and the arts. By the time the hospital was finished in 1907, the benefits for the 3,600 population were clear: those living in Port Sunlight enjoyed an average death rate and a level of infant mortality half that in nearby Liverpool.

Very much a family man, Lord Leverhulme (born William Hesketh Lever in 1851) was devastated at the death of his wife, Lady Lever, in 1913. She had shared his vision of a just and equitable society and his love of the arts, and so in her memory he created the Lady Lever Art Gallery in which to exhibit their extensive collection. Perhaps the main focus of a visit to Port Sunlight is the gallery's magnificent works of art. Foremost are the pre-Raphaelite paintings of Burne-Jones, Lord Leighton and Sargent, but also on display are canvases by Turner, Constable, Gainsborough and Reynolds – as well as notable collections of English furniture and Wedgwood china. Equally fascinating is to wander through the garden village itself, with its varying architectural styles. Leverhulme took a personal interest in the development and amongst the 30 or so architects he employed was a young Edwin Lutyens (17–23 Corniche Road). Further details about all aspects of Port Sunlight are available from the Heritage Centre (95 Greendale Road, Port Sunlight, tel: 0151 644 6466).

Entries are cross referenced by number to the maps on pages 18–19

110 Alden Cottage ◆◆◆◆

Kemple End, Birdy Brow, Stonyhurst, Clitheroe, Lancashire BB7 9QY **Tel:** (01254) 826468

Luxury accommodation in an idyllic 17th-century beamed cottage, situated in an area of outstanding natural beauty overlooking the Ribble and Hodder valleys. Four miles west of Clitheroe, one mile north of Stonyhurst College and the village of Hurst Green. Charming, individually furnished rooms with all modern comforts and fresh flowers. Private facilities, including jacuzzi bath. Perfect for a peaceful and relaxing stay away from it all. Ribble Valley Civic Design and Conservation award winner.

Bed & Breakfast per night: single occupancy from £22.00–£23.50; double room from £44.00–£47.00

Bedrooms: 2 double, 1 twin
Bathrooms: 1 public
Parking: 6 spaces

111 Northcote Manor ★★★ Gold Award

Northcote Road, Langho, Blackburn, Lancashire BB6 8BE **Tel:** (01254) 240555 **Fax:** (01254) 246568
Web: http://www.ncotemanor.demon.co.uk **E-mail:** admin@ncotemanor.demon.co.uk

Northcote Manor is a privately owned, 14 bedroom country house hotel situated in the beautiful Ribble Valley in the heart of north-west England. In the capable hands of Craig Bancroft and award-winning chef Nigel Haworth, the Manor is best known for its excellent restaurant and friendly hospitality, awarded a Michelin Star and, in 1999, an independent hotel of the year award. Gourmet one-night breaks available from £150 per couple which include champagne, a five-course gourmet dinner and stunning Lancashire breakfast.

Bed & Breakfast per night: single occupancy from £90.00–£100.00; double room from £110.00–£130.00
Dinner, Bed & Breakfast per person, per night: £150.00–£175.00
Lunch available: 1200–1330

Evening meal: 1900 (last orders 2130)
Bedrooms: 10 double, 4 twin
Bathrooms: 14 en-suite
Parking: 50 spaces
Cards accepted: Mastercard, Visa, Switch/Delta, Amex, Diners

112 New Capernwray Farm ◆◆◆◆◆

Capernwray, Carnforth, Lancashire LA6 1AD **Tel:** (01524) 734284 **Fax:** (01524) 734284
Web: http://www.newcapfarm.co.uk **E-mail:** newcapfarm@aol.com

Ideal London to Scotland stop, just three miles from junction 35 of the M6. Ideal for Lake District and Yorkshire Dales. Welcoming, wonderfully relaxed, friendly atmosphere. Superb, award-winning accommodation in 17th-century former farmhouse, full of character in beautiful countryside. Luxuriously-equipped, king, queen and twin bedrooms with en-suite or private facilities. Renowned for warmth, comfort and excellent, four-course, candlelit dinners (unlicensed, please bring your own wines). Maps, guide books and personal help given on local sightseeing and onward routes.

Bed & Breakfast per night: single occupancy from £40.00–£45.00; double room from £60.00–£70.00
Dinner, Bed & Breakfast per person, per night: £52.50–£57.50
Evening meal: 1930

Bedrooms: 2 double, 1 twin
Bathrooms: 2 en-suite, 1 private
Parking: 4 spaces
Open: March–October
Cards accepted: Mastercard, Visa, Eurocard, JCB

At-a-glance symbols are explained on the flap inside the back cover

113 Ferncliffe Country Guest House

55 Main Street, Ingleton, via Carnforth, North Yorkshire LA6 3HJ **Tel:** (015242) 42405

Susan and Peter Ring offer a warm welcome to their typical Dales guest house. Built in 1897, the house retains some Victorian features whilst providing all modern facilities. Ideally situated for those who wish to explore the Yorkshire Dales or the Lake District, either by car, on foot or bicycle. We pride ourselves on offering comfortable accommodation, a hearty English breakfast and all the amenities you would expect.

Bed & Breakfast per night: single occupancy £29.00; double room £46.00

Bedrooms: 1 double, 4 twin
Bathrooms: 5 en-suite
Parking: 5 spaces
Open: February-October
Cards accepted: Mastercard, Visa, Delta

114 Willowfield Hotel

The Promenade, Arnside, Cumbria LA5 0AD **Tel:** (01524) 761354
Web: http://www.smoothhound.co.uk/hotels/willowfi.html **E-mail:** kerr@willowfield.net1.co.uk

Quietly situated in a superb estuary-side location, with stunning views to the Lakeland hills, this small family-run Victorian private hotel for non-smokers offers relaxation, good traditional English food (with table licence) and well-equipped comfortable rooms. The view from the conservatory is just wonderful - we believe we have something quite special in this picturesque village, one of South Lakeland's best kept secrets and all within just 7.5 miles of the M6 (junction 36).

Bed & Breakfast per night: single room from £24.00; double room from £50.00–£56.00
Dinner, Bed & Breakfast per person, per night: £37.00–£41.00
Evening meal: 1900

Bedrooms: 2 single, 3 double, 3 twin, 2 triple
Bathrooms: 7 en-suite, 2 public
Parking: 8 spaces
Cards accepted: Mastercard, Visa

Key to Symbols

For ease of use, the key to symbols appears on the back of the cover flap and can be folded out while consulting individual entries. The symbols are designed to enable you to see at a glance what's on offer, and whether any particular requirements you have can be met. Most of the symbols are clear, simple icons and few require any further explanation, but the following points may be useful:

Alcoholic drinks: Alcoholic drinks are available at all types of accommodation listed in the guide unless the symbol [UL] (unlicensed) appears. However, even in licensed premises there may be some restrictions on the serving of drinks, such as being available to diners only.

Smoking: Some establishments prefer not to accommodate smokers, and if this is the case it will be indicated by the symbol ⚲. Other establishments may offer facilities for non-smokers such as no smoking bedrooms and parts of communal rooms set aside for non-smokers. Please check at the time of booking if the non-smoking symbol does not appear.

Pets: The symbol 🐕 is used to show that dogs are not accepted in any circumstances. Some establishments will accept pets, but we advise you to check this at the time of booking and to enquire as to whether any additional charge will be made to accommodate them.

Entries are cross referenced by number to the maps on pages 18–19

England's Heartland

▶ The Malvern Hills

Looking from the east, the Malverns, rising from the Severn Plain, seem to belie their modest height. What they lack in altitude, however, they more than make up for in age, beauty and the panoramas they offer. On a clear day the views from the top stretch to far-distant horizons. The best way to explore these glorious hills – they stretch roughly 8 miles (13km) in a north–south direction – is on foot, but several roads cross the Malverns affording magnificent views for the less mobile.

▶ Eyam and the Plague

In September 1665 a journeyman tailor lodging in the village of Eyam in the Derbyshire Peak opened a parcel of cloth sent from London where bubonic plague was then raging. Within four days he was dead – and plague had descended on Eyam. The young rector, William Mompesson, persuaded the whole village to make a courageous act of self-sacrifice and Eyam was sealed off from the outside world for a year. But Eyam paid dearly for its bravery: out of an estimated population of 350, some 250 died. An exhibition in Eyam church recounts the full story.

Away from the throng

From East Anglia's fertile plains to the rugged border country of the Welsh Marches, from the Home Counties' prosperous market towns to the dark, stone-built communities of the Peaks, the great swathe of counties that forms England's heartlands has it all. And for the most part you can have the elegance, the raw beauty, the culture and the history to yourself. Yes, the Peak District National Park is deservedly popular and yes, Stratford-upon-Avon is rightly a stop on most visitors' itineraries, but choose your moment wisely and even these can be enjoyed at a leisurely pace, the madding crowd left far behind.

In the steps of literary giants

Whatever your particular bent, there's ample opportunity to indulge it. Keen to follow in the footsteps of the famous? Try Lichfield, whose sons include three major figures from the 18th-century flowering of the arts: Joseph Addison, David Garrick and Dr Johnson. The last has his own museum, based in the house of his birth in Breadmarket Street. Other places of literary pilgrimage are D H Lawrence's Eastwood and Lord Byron's gothic Newstead Abbey (both Nottinghamshire, though at opposite ends of the social scale), Shaw's comfortable Corner in Ayot St Lawrence (Hertfordshire), A E Housman's much wilder Wenlock Edge (Shropshire) and Samuel Pepys's urbane Brampton (Cambridgeshire).

Lanes for walking, cycling or pootling

But if meandering lazily along English backwaters on a limpid afternoon is more your taste, consider a few of the following. Add a couple more ingredients – a half-decent road map and nothing to hurry back for – and you are guaranteed some perfect pootling. Almost anywhere away from the big towns will reward an adventurous spirit, but these are an eclectic assortment of suggested starting points. Try the warren of lanes switchbacking around the Golden Valley in the shadow of the Black Mountains. Or the northern reaches of the Cotswolds, whose vistas stretch to the Malverns, the Vale of Evesham and Stratford-upon-Avon. There's the little-known but savagely beautiful countryside around the Clee Hills south and west of Bridgnorth, or the gentler, undulating farmland of Suffolk between Diss and Southwold. Norfolk's north coast offers sleepy villages – a pair are appropriately called Little and Great Snoring – and unspoilt coastline. And there are the Lincolnshire Wolds west of Louth, where few visitors discover the distinct charms of Bag Enderby or Normanby le Wold.

Striking out

But if the narrowest of lanes still has too much of the hurly-burly, swap the car for a pair of boots, the road atlas for a walking map. Strike out along the footpaths and bridleways. A good place to start is on one of England's many long-distance paths. Almost all have circular walks of anything from two to 20 miles (3–32km) sharing their waymarks, so don't be put off by the "long-distance" bit.

Running down the western edge of the region, and criss-crossing in and out of Wales is Offa's Dyke Path, which roughly follows the route of the 8th-century earthwork constructed by the Mercian king to keep the Welsh at bay. Also oriented north–south but stretching from Staffordshire to the Cotswolds is the Heart of England Way. Rural in character for most of its length, it follows the Birmingham and Fazeley Canal to the east of the city, before dropping down to Chipping Campden (where it joins the Cotswold Way) and skirting the oriental splendour of Sezincote (see next page). Two more long-distance paths explore East Anglia's many sandy beaches. The first, the Peddars Way and Norfolk Coast Path, was, as its name suggests, once two separate routes. It starts in the flinty fields near Thetford and follows the course of a Roman road (the Peddars Way) till it reaches the coast near Holme. From here until Cromer – the Norfolk Coast Path – you will have as company the varied birdlife that throngs the dunes and marshes. The Suffolk Coast Path between Lowestoft and Felixstowe involves a couple of ferries, and skirts the cliffs that once supported the lost medieval village of Dunwich.

Art for all

One highlight of the Suffolk Coast path is Snape Maltings, home of the Aldeburgh Festival (June), devoted in part to the music of Sir Benjamin Britten. The welcome proliferation of literary and musical festivals ensures a huge number of events, catering for every taste. By way of a small sample, you can now choose your venue from: Cheltenham (jazz in April, music – and cricket – in July, literature in October), Chelmsford Cathedral (jazz, classical and art exhibitions, May), Solihull (folk music, May), Thaxted (classical and jazz, weekends in June and July), Ludlow (music, drama and dance, June), Warwick and Leamington Spa (classical music, July), Ledbury (poetry, July), Oundle (organ recitals, July), Buxton (opera, July), Three Choirs Festival (August) and Ross-on-Wye (dance, comedy and theatre, August).

Narrow streets and imposing townhouses

Most such events are understandably based in attractive, historical market towns, the sort of town that specialises in medieval higgledy-piggledyness, Elizabethan and Jacobean sturdiness, Georgian elegance or a combination of these and countless other architectural styles. Some are well-known, others less so. Tewkesbury, for example, is a fine medieval town that has long been blessed by – and suffered from – its position at the confluence of the rivers Severn and Avon. A magnificent row of 15th-century shops and the intriguingly named House of the Nodding Gables are a couple of venerable survivors of the regular flooding. Bewdley is a thoroughly gracious former river port higher up the Severn. Since 1798, the centrepiece has been Thomas Telford's elegant bridge, but as well as the myriad streets ideal for strolling, there is a station on the scenic Severn Valley Railway. Bromyard, by contrast, has a striking hill setting, two old coaching inns and a clutch of timber-framed houses, not to mention sweeping

▶ Birmingham Pre-Raphaelites

Birmingham's City Museum and Art Gallery (tel: 0121 303 2834) houses the largest (and arguably finest) collection of Pre-Raphaelite art in the world, including Holman Hunt's The Last of England, The Blind Girl by Millais and Rossetti's Beata Beatrix, together with a vast number of other paintings, drawings and crafts. Near by, Wightwick Manor, just outside Wolverhampton (tel: 01902 761108) is entirely furnished and decorated by some of the most prominent Pre-Raphaelite artists, while in Birmingham Cathedral may be found some superb stained-glass designed by Edward Burne-Jones, Pre-Raphaelite and native of the city.

▶ Kilpeck

At Kilpeck, eight miles (13km) south-west of Hereford, is the tiny sandstone church of Sts Mary and David. Its size may be modest, but its stone-carvings are the most glorious example of the exuberant work of the 12th-century Herefordshire School of stonemasons. The south door in particular, long protected by a wooden porch, displays a magnificent array of carvings – of beasts, fishes, foliage, fruit – in an almost pristine state. Similar work may be found in churches at Fownhope and Rowlstone (both in Herefordshire) and at Ruardean in the Forest of Dean, all set in glorious countryside.

► Slimbridge

When the naturalist and painter Peter Scott founded the Wildfowl & Wetlands Trust at Slimbridge, Gloucestershire, in 1946, he operated from two derelict cottages and used wartime pill-boxes as hides. Today the organisation is internationally recognised for its research into wetland conservation, and, at Slimbridge, offers visitors a superb opportunity to watch a vast range of birds. In winter up to 8,000 migrants fly in to the 800-acre (323-hectare) reserve, forming possibly the world's largest collection of ducks, geese and swans. Slimbridge is also the only place in Europe where all six species of flamingo can be seen!

► Bakewell Puddings

The story of Bakewell's famous puddings is one of triumph over adversity. In 1860 a cook at the White Horse Inn (now the Rutland Arms) preparing a strawberry tart for some dignitaries mistakenly placed egg mixture intended for the pastry base on top of the jam. The resulting 'disaster' was nevertheless cooked up and promptly declared a culinary masterpiece. The puddings (those in the know never call them 'tarts') have been served in the town ever since.

views from the nearby Bromyard Downs. Uppingham is crammed full of 17th-, 18th- and 19th-century buildings all made from the glorious, mellow Rutland stone of the area. Southwold has the pleasing air of a town ignored by most aspects of the 20th century. The Suffolk port enjoyed something of a renaissance when it became fashionable with Victorian holidaymakers, but otherwise just the right amount of nothing has entertained locals and visitors ever since the bustling medieval harbour silted up. Melton Mowbray's cattle market was established over 900 years ago. Not much in the town is quite as old, but 14th-century Anne of Cleves' House is about to see its eighth century.

Pies and produce

Melton's real fame derives from its associations with pork pies and Stilton cheese, both of which are still made and sold here. Bakewell, in Derbyshire, is synonymous with a delicious upside-down jam tart, widely available in the area, but the town is also worth visiting for an agricultural show in August and its fine stone architecture. Heacham, in Norfolk, has long been the English headquarters of lavender growing; tours are available. Spalding, over the border into Lincolnshire, draws thousands in early May to its annual flower parade, while asparagus takes centre stage at the Fleece Inn at Bretforton in Worcestershire. The ancient pub, owned by the National Trust, runs an auction devoted to asparagus on the evening of the last Sunday in May.

Homes and gardens

The Trust owns and manages a vast range of properties throughout the region, from Mr Straw's House in Worksop – a modest turn-of-the-century semi – to the working Theatre Royal in Bury St Edmunds. A random sample of other historic houses – most still privately owned – includes: Weston Park (Palladian mansion with gardens by 'Capability' Brown, Staffordshire); Eastnor Castle (Georgian castle with Gothic interiors, Ledbury, Herefordshire); Woburn Abbey (18th-century mansion with considerable art collection, Bedfordshire); Audley End (17th-century house with Adam touches, Essex); Stanford Hall (riverside William and Mary house with notable ballroom, Swinford, Leicestershire); Sezincote (reputedly the inspiration for the Indian-style Brighton Pavilion, Moreton-in-Marsh, Gloucestershire); Burghley House (Elizabethan palace with baroque interiors, Stamford, Lincolnshire); Kentwell Hall (Tudor mansion with garden maze, Long Melford, Suffolk); and Sulgrave Manor (ancestral home of George Washington, Northamptonshire). All these properties run special events of one form or another in high season.

Look East

The region's coastline runs from Essex to Lincolnshire. Essex has a mixture of lonely marsh and fine beach, while Suffolk alternates sand and shingle. Norfolk's golden shores, though, stretch for mile after mile, and Lincolnshire – after a marshy section around the Wash – boasts more excellent beaches. Naturally, there are the famous seaside resorts, with their quintessentially

English attractions and their cheerful brashness, but there is another side to the coastline. For a quieter maritime excursion try Frinton (Essex), Covehithe (Suffolk), Happisburgh – pronounced 'Haysborough' – Holkham and Hunstanton (all Norfolk) and Anderby Creek (Lincolnshire). Unique amongst east-coast resorts, Hunstanton has the distinction of facing west. Watch the sun go down over the waves in the knowledge that no one else within 150 or so miles (240km) is doing the same...

Divine inspiration

And, of course, there are the region's countless churches. The medieval stone-carvers of Herefordshire honed their skills to perfection at Kilpeck. Distinctive round towers stand out against the gentle Norfolk landscape, as at Sedgeford. The warm, honey-coloured stone that characterises so many of the unsung Northamptonshire villages was used on consecrated ground, too; Brixworth is a marvellous Saxon church in an imposing setting. In Suffolk and northern Essex, the locally abundant flint was the main material in such opulent churches as Long Melford and Dedham, both villages of remarkable beauty aside from their churches.

Contact numbers

Samuel Johnson Birthplace Museum, Lichfield (tel: 01543 264972)
D H Lawrence Birthplace, Eastwood (tel: 01773 763312)
Newstead Abbey, Newstead (tel: 01623 455900)
Shaw's Corner, Ayot St Lawrence (tel: 01438 820307)
Aldeburgh Festival of Music and the Arts (tel: 01728 452935)
Cheltenham International Jazz Festival (tel: 01242 237377)
Cheltenham Festival of Literature (tel: 01242 521621)
Cheltenham International Festival of Music (tel: 01242 521621)
Solihull Festival (tel: 01676 535818)
Thaxted Festival (tel: 01371 831421)
Warwick and Leamington Festival (tel: 01926 410747)
Ledbury Poetry Festival (tel: 01531 634156)
Oundle International Festival (tel: 01832 272026)
Buxton Festival (tel: 01298 70395)
Three Choirs Festival (tel: 01905 616200)
Ross-on-Wye Festival (tel: 01594 544446)
Bakewell Agricultural Show (tel: 01629 813227)
Norfolk Lavender, Heacham (tel: 01485 570384)
Spalding Flower Parade (tel: 01775 724843)
Fleece Inn, Bretforton (tel: 01386 831173)
Mr Straw's House, Worksop (tel: 01909 482380)
Theatre Royal, Bury St Edmunds (tel: 01284 755127)
Weston Park, Shifnal (tel: 01952 852100)
Eastnor Castle, Ledbury (tel: 01531 633160)
Woburn Abbey (tel: 01525 290666)
Audley End (tel: 01799 522399)
Stanford Hall, Swinford (tel: 01788 860250)
Burghley House, Stamford (tel: 01780 752451)
Kentwell Hall, Long Melford (tel: 01787 310207)
Sulgrave Manor (tel: 01295 760205)

► **Garman Ryan Collection**

Ask where you can see works by Van Gogh, Turner, Picasso, Constable, Cézanne, Gainsborough, Titian, Reynolds and Gauguin outside London, and few would suggest Walsall. But the Garman Ryan collection at the Walsall Museum and Art Gallery boasts some 353 works by these and other artists. Their presence here is due to Kathleen Garman, wife of the renowned English sculptor,

Sir Jacob Epstein, who, together with American sculptress Sally Ryan, Epstein's lifelong admirer, amassed this superb collection. After Ryan's death, Garman, who was born at Wednesbury, near Walsall, donated the collection to the town.

► **Dunmow Flitch**

The once-common phrase 'to eat Dunmow bacon' means to live in conjugal bliss, and refers to an ancient custom still practised in Great Dunmow, near Bishop's Stortford in Essex. In order to win a flitch (or side) of bacon, a couple must prove that in the first twelve months and a day of their marriage they have not exchanged a word of anger, and certainly never repented of the day they wed. The trial, held every four years before a bewigged judge, is conducted with the utmost (mock) seriousness.

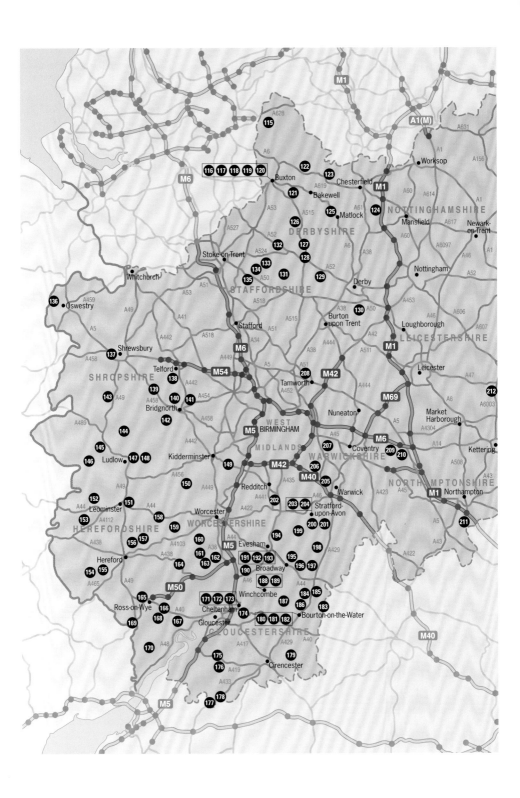

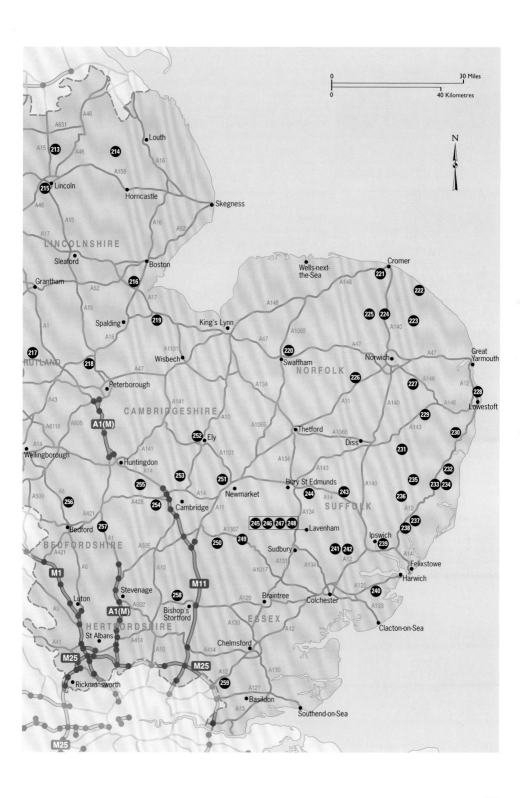

115 Wind in the Willows Hotel

★★ Silver Award

Derbyshire Level, off Sheffield Road (A57), Glossop, Derbyshire SK13 7PT **Tel:** (01457) 868001 **Fax:** (01457) 853354
Web: http://www.windinthewillows.co.uk **E-mail:** info@windinthewillows.co.uk

Situated on the edge of the Pennines with unspoilt views of the Peak District National Park. "Not so much an hotel, more a delightful experience" as someone said. A delightful combination of antiques, wood panelling, log fires and homely atmosphere, but with true professionalism. All rooms are individual and have en-suite facilities of the highest standard. Some half-tester beds, four-poster and brass beds, all of which are antiques. The dining room offers fine English food, all freshly prepared.

Bed & Breakfast per night: single occupancy from £72.00–£90.00; double room from £99.00–£117.00
Evening meal: 1930 (last orders 1945)

Bedrooms: 9 double, 3 twin
Bathrooms: 12 en-suite
Parking: 20 spaces
Cards accepted: Mastercard, Visa, Switch/Delta, Amex, Diners, Eurocard

---

116 Grendon Guesthouse

◆◆◆◆ Silver Award

Bishops Lane, Buxton, Derbyshire SK17 6UN **Tel:** (01298) 78831
Web: http://www.beyond-the-net.ndirect.co.uk/grendon

A warm welcome awaits you at our beautiful Edwardian home with far-reaching hill views, within one mile of Buxton's historic centre. Our very spacious bed sitting rooms provide the ultimate in comfort, with king-size beds equipped with superior mattresses and duvets; one room having a four-poster bed and dressing room. Delicious breakfasts include all the favourites plus fresh fruit salad and home-made bread. Evening meals available. Remembered and revisited by many.

Bed & Breakfast per night: single occupancy from £33.00–£40.00; double room from £42.00–£60.00
Dinner, Bed & Breakfast per person, per night: £33.00–£40.00 (min 2 sharing)
Evening meal: 1900 (last bookings 1600)

Bedrooms: 2 double, 1 twin
Bathrooms: 3 en-suite
Parking: 8 spaces
Cards accepted: Mastercard, Visa, Delta

---

117 Ford Side House

◆◆◆◆

125 Lightwood Road, Buxton, Derbyshire SK17 6RW **Tel:** (01298) 72842

Peaceful, elegant Edwardian house for non-smokers, situated in a premier residential area, yet very close to the town's attractions, the Peaks and Dales. All guest rooms are en-suite with full amenities. Drying facilities for walkers. Private parking. Full fire certificate. We are licensed to supply wines and spirits to complement our delicious food (prepared to order in early and late season).

Bed & Breakfast per night: double room from £38.00–£42.00
Dinner, Bed & Breakfast per person, per night: £31.50–£33.50
Evening meal: 1900

Bedrooms: 2 double, 1 twin
Bathrooms: 3 en-suite
Parking: 3 spaces
Open: March–October

Entries are cross referenced by number to the maps on pages 68–69

118 Cressbrook Hall ◆◆◆◆

Cressbrook, Buxton, Derbyshire SK17 8SY **Tel:** (01298) 871289 or 0800 358 3003 **Fax:** (01298) 871845
Web: http://www.aseweb.co.uk/cressbrookhall/index.htm **E-mail:** stay@cressbrook-hall.swinternet.co.uk

A period piece with pedigree! Cressbrook Hall is a fine William IV residence, built 1835 and enjoying a spectacular hillside location. The formal gardens designed by Edward Kemp are currently under restoration. Self-catering cottages, together with elegant serviced accommodation in the Hall are available for weekends or longer visits and ideal for reunions, management training/team building and special family celebrations. Hall 'home catering' gives you more free time to enjoy this idyllic place. Accommodation which is decidedly, delightfully different! ↑ **Category 3**

Bed & Breakfast per night: single occupancy from £45.00–£60.00; double room from £65.00–£95.00
Dinner, Bed & Breakfast per person, per night: £63.00–£113.00
Evening meal: 1830 (last orders 1930)

Bedrooms: 2 double, 1 twin
Bathrooms: 3 en-suite
Parking: 10 spaces
Cards accepted: Mastercard, Visa, Switch/Delta, Eurocard

119 Buxton View ◆◆◆◆

74 Corbar Road, Buxton, Derbyshire SK17 6RJ **Tel:** (01298) 79222

Stone-built guest house offering a 'home from home' atmosphere. Set in a quiet area with views of the scenery around, only a few minutes from lovely Buxton town with its very impressive buildings and parks and interesting shops. Open all year round. Parking. Baby equipment available on request.

Bed & Breakfast per night: single room from £21.00–£22.00; double room from £42.00–£44.00
Dinner, Bed & Breakfast per person, per night: £31.00–£32.00
Evening meal: 1900 (last orders 2000)

Bedrooms: 1 single, 2 double, 1 twin, 1 triple
Bathrooms: 4 en-suite, 1 private
Parking: 5 spaces

120 Coningsby ◆◆◆◆◆ Gold Award

6 Macclesfield Road, Buxton, Derbyshire SK17 9AH **Tel:** (01298) 26735 **Fax:** (01298) 26735
E-mail: coningsby@btinternet.com

We take great pleasure in welcoming guests to our Victorian home where we try to add those special touches that make all the difference when staying away from home. Our guests are assured superior accommodation, good food and impeccable cleanliness in a relaxed atmosphere where the hosts care and have time to talk. If you would like more details we would be pleased to send you our colour brochure upon request. Please, no smoking, children or pets.

Bed & Breakfast per night: double room from £55.00–£70.00
Evening meal: Monday–Thursday 1900 (last bookings 1600)

Bedrooms: 3 double
Bathrooms: 3 en-suite
Parking: 6 spaces
Open: February–October

121 Ditch House

Chelmorton, Buxton, Derbyshire SK17 9SG **Tel:** (01298) 85719 **Fax:** (01298) 85719

Comfortable and spacious rooms in newly restored cottage set on the edge of Peakland village with superb views. Good walking area, packed lunches available. Close to Buxton, Bakewell and Chatsworth. Christmas walking breaks available.

Bed & Breakfast per night: single occupancy from £23.00–£30.00; double room from £40.00–£54.00

Bedrooms: 1 double, 1 twin
Bathrooms: 2 en-suite
Parking: 4 spaces

Blue John

The Derbyshire town of Castleton lies in the White Peak, a rolling limestone plateau carved into steep gorges and valleys by the last ice age. As glaciers melted they forced tremendous volumes of water downwards through joints in the limestone to form turbulent underground rivers, gouging out the rock into an impressive network of caverns. Castleton boasts four separate cave systems in its immediate vicinity.

Two of these, Treak Cliff Cavern and Blue John Cavern, contain deposits of Britain's rarest mineral, a beautifully veined fluorspar known as blue john, found nowhere else in the world. The origin of its name is uncertain, but it may derive from the French bleu-jaune (blue-yellow), two of the mineral's predominant colours (much of the stone found its way to French workshops). Its use for ornamental purposes may date back to Roman times, but it was not until the 18th century that blue john was commercially mined and worked on a large scale. The architect Robert Adam used the mineral to decorate fireplaces in the music room at Kedleston Hall (tel: 01332 842191) in 1762, and also created the famous Chatsworth Tazza, the largest bowl ever constructed from a single piece of blue john (Chatsworth House, tel: 01246 582204).

The caverns provided useful access to many of the deposits of the valuable mineral. Extracting it, however, was no easy matter. Blue john occurs in two distinct formations, either as cylindrical nodules completely buried by clay, or as flat veins sandwiched between hard layers of limestone. In the past, the deposits were extensive; the mines yielded over 20 tons annually at their peak of production, and the size of individual formations was correspondingly impressive; some nodules measured more than a foot (30cm) in diameter. Today only about half a ton is produced and few large formations are ever found. Consequently most is used for small items of jewellery, cutlery handles and small bowls, on sale in Castleton's souvenir shops.

Guided tours of Blue John Cavern (tel: 01433 620638) and Treak Cliff Cavern (tel: 01433 620571) provide a fascinating insight into a unique Peak District industry, while the massive scale of the caves and the superb formations of stalactites cannot fail to impress by their sheer natural grandeur.

Entries are cross referenced by number to the maps on pages 68–69

122 Maynard Arms Hotel

★ ★ ★ Silver Award

Main Road, Grindleford, Derbyshire S32 2HE **Tel:** (01433) 630321 **Fax:** (01433) 630445

Established in 1898 in the heart of the Peak National Park, the Maynard Arms is an idyllic location for pleasure or business. Superior bedrooms have views over the Derwent Valley. The best local produce is served for both lunch (1200–1400) and dinner (1900–2130) accompanied by our extensive wine list, in the Padley Restaurant overlooking the hotel gardens. The Longshaw Bar satisfies the heartiest of appetites between 1200–1400 and 1900–2130, also serving traditional hand-pulled beers.

Bed & Breakfast per night: single occupancy from £67.00–£87.00; double room from £77.00–£97.00
Lunch available: 1200–1400
Evening meal: 1900 (last orders 2130)

Bedrooms: 8 double, 2 twin
Bathrooms: 10 en-suite
Parking: 80 spaces
Cards accepted: Mastercard, Visa, Switch/Delta, Amex, Eurocard

123 Woodlands

♦♦♦♦

Hathersage Road, Grindleford, Derbyshire S30 1JH **Tel:** (01433) 631593

A late Georgian farmhouse, ideally situated in Hope Valley in the Peak District. Sympathetically restored in 1983. Large twin-bedded room with en-suite luxury bathroom which has bath, shower, washbasin, bidet and wc. Full generous and varied English breakfast, plus continental or vegetarian. Set in over an acre of lawns, including a walled garden with furniture. Paddocks and ponies in eight acres. 15 minutes from Bakewell. Fabulous hotels and pubs nearby – the nearest just two minutes.

Bed & Breakfast per night: double room from £50.00–£60.00

Bedrooms: 1 twin
Bathrooms: 1 en-suite
Parking: 4 spaces

124 The Stud Farm Countryside Bed and Breakfast

♦♦♦♦ Silver Award

Hardstoft, Pilsley, Chesterfield, Derbyshire S45 8AE **Tel:** (01773) 875994

Charming 17th-century farmhouse set in picturesque farmland, home to the family sheep and competition horses. Overlooking Hardwick Hall and close to Chatsworth House and all the delights of the Derbyshire Peak District. High class en-suite accommodation. Large indoor heated swimming pool to relax in, or enjoy the peace and tranquillity of a large garden. Close to the M1. Ideal base for business visitors and tourists.

Bed & Breakfast per night: single occupancy max £26.00; double room max £40.00
Dinner, Bed & Breakfast per person, per night: max £40.00
Evening meal: 1900 (last orders 2000)

Bedrooms: 1 double, 2 twin
Bathrooms: 3 en-suite
Parking: 7 spaces

At-a-glance symbols are explained on the flap inside the back cover

125 Riber Hall

★★★ Silver Award

Matlock, Derbyshire DE4 5JU **Tel:** (01629) 582795 **Fax:** (01629) 580475
Web: http://www.riber-hall.co.uk **E-mail:** info@riber-hall.co.uk

Relax in this tranquil and historic Derbyshire country house and enjoy AA 2 Rosette cuisine. Stroll in the old walled gardens amidst glorious birdsong and enjoy afternoon tea by the log fire. Recommended by all major guides. Two day breaks available. 20 minutes from the M1 junction 28.

Bed & Breakfast per night: single occupancy from £92.50–£107.00; double room from £118.50–£162.00
Dinner, Bed & Breakfast per person, per night: £87.25–£109.00
Lunch available: 1200–1330 (last orders)

Evening meal: 1900 (last orders 2130)
Bedrooms: 12 double, 2 twin
Bathrooms: 14 en-suite
Parking: 50 spaces
Cards accepted: Mastercard, Visa, Switch/Delta, Amex, Diners, Eurocard, JCB

126 The Kings at Ivy House

◆◆◆◆

Biggin-by-Hartington, Buxton, Derbyshire SK17 0DT **Tel:** (01298) 84709 **Fax:** (01298) 84710
Web: http://www.smoothhound.co.uk/hotels/kingsivy.html **E-mail:** kings.ivyhouse@lineone.net

Set in the Peak Park, Ivy House is a beautifully restored Georgian coaching inn featuring log fires, flagstone floors and our listed barns, all within two acres of grounds which include our vegetable and herb gardens. All rooms are en-suite with baths and the views to the front are spectacular. However, the best features of all are the superb home-cooked evening meals and relaxed, friendly atmosphere. As our guests frequently say, "home from home!".

Bed & Breakfast per night: single occupancy from £29.00–£39.00; double room £58.00
Dinner, Bed & Breakfast per person, per night: £44.00–£54.00
Evening meal: 1930

Bedrooms: 2 double, 1 twin, 1 family
Bathrooms: 4 en-suite
Parking: 12 spaces

127 Cairn Grove

◆◆◆◆

Ashes Lane, Fenny Bentley, Ashbourne, Derbyshire DE6 1LD **Tel:** (01335) 350538 or 07973 859992
E-mail: keith.wheeldon@virgin.net

Spacious limestone house set in a one-acre grove. Cherry tree drive approach to pleasant aspect overlooking Fenny Bentley village in the Peak Park with views of typical Derbyshire Dales countryside. Tastefully decored en-suite rooms, all with tea/coffee making facilities and television. Central heating for year round accommodation. Convenient for Buxton, Chatsworth, Haddon, White Peak, Alton Towers and local to Ashbourne, Dovedale, Carsington Water and the Tissington Trail. Excellent evening meals locally, the nearest being five minutes' walk.

Bed & Breakfast per night: single occupancy from £22.00–£27.00; double room from £38.00–£50.00

Bedrooms: 2 double, 1 twin
Bathrooms: 2 en-suite, 1 private
Parking: 3 spaces

128 Omnia Somnia

◆◆◆◆◆ Gold Award

The Coach House, The Firs, Ashbourne, Derbyshire DE6 1HF **Tel:** (01335) 300145 or 07711 547799 **Fax:** (01335) 300958
E-mail: omnia.somnia@talk21.com

A private house, formerly a Victorian coach house, nestling amongst mature trees in a quiet location near Ashbourne town centre. Our rooms are very different, each one special in its own way: Oriens – a room with every facility and many, many pictures, and the superb bathroom has a bath big enough for two! Occidens – enter into your own sitting room, then climb the stairs to a romantic hideaway bedroom. Meridies – a sumptuous, panelled room with a hand-crafted, fully draped four-poster bed.

Bed & Breakfast per night: double room from £60.00–£70.00
Dinner, Bed & Breakfast per person, per night: £49.50–£54.50
Evening meal: 1900 (last orders 2030)

Bedrooms: 3 double
Bathrooms: 3 en-suite
Parking: 3 spaces
Cards accepted: Mastercard, Visa, Switch/Delta, JCB, Solo

129 Reevsmoor

◆◆◆◆

Hoargate Lane, Hollington, Ashbourne, Derbyshire DE6 3AG **Tel:** (01335) 330318

Reevsmoor is situated in the picturesque Derbyshire Dales countryside, six miles from Ashbourne and seven miles from Derby. Tom and Helen Livesey extend a very warm welcome for you to come and stay in our comfortable family home. Enjoy a traditional English breakfast in our elegant dining room. We are ideally situated for touring the Peak District and the Potteries. Both our rooms are ground floor, en-suite, non-smoking with colour television and coffee making facilities.

Bed & Breakfast per night: single occupancy from £18.00–£26.00; double room from £36.00–£44.00

Bedrooms: 1 double, 1 twin
Bathrooms: 2 en-suite
Parking: 10 spaces
Open: March–October

130 October House

◆◆◆◆

The Water Meadows, Swarkestone, Derby, Derbyshire DE73 1JA **Tel:** (01332) 705849

Situated in the ancient riverside village of Swarkestone, October House is a charming converted farm building in a peaceful, rural location. A delightful beamed sitting room opens onto the walled garden for the private enjoyment of visitors. There are just two well-appointed guest bedrooms with television, beverage tray, robes, hairdryer and private facilities. Canal and riverside footpaths. Three miles from Calke Abbey (National Trust) and with easy access to the M1 and East Midlands airport. Evening meals by arrangement.

Bed & Breakfast per night: single occupancy from £24.00; double room from £44.00
Dinner, Bed & Breakfast per person, per night: £34.00–£36.00
Evening meal: 1800 (last orders 2000)

Bedrooms: 1 double (2nd double by arrangement)
Bathrooms: 1 private
Parking: 4 spaces

At-a-glance symbols are explained on the flap inside the back cover

131 The Old School House

 Silver Award

Castle Hill Road, Alton, Stoke-on-Trent, Staffordshire ST10 4AJ **Tel:** (01538) 702151 **Fax:** (01538) 702151
Web: http://members.tripod.co.uk/old_school_house/ **E-mail:** old_school_house@talk21.com

The Grade II listed Old School House has been tastefully restored and contains many original features. Located in the peaceful conservation part of the village with pubs and restaurants within walking distance. The attractive village of Alton is situated in the picturesque Churnet Valley with many signed walks. Alton Towers is one mile away and the Peak District is nearby. Guests are assured of a warm and friendly welcome in our beautiful home.

Bed & Breakfast per night: double room from £50.00–£60.00

Bedrooms: 3 double
Bathrooms: 3 en-suite

132 Lee House Farm

♦♦♦♦

Leek Road, Waterhouses, Stoke-on-Trent, Staffordshire ST10 3HW **Tel:** (01538) 308439

A charming 18th-century house in the centre of a picturesque village in the Peak District National Park. Lee House is full of character: all bedrooms are non-smoking, centrally heated and en-suite, with colour television and tea/coffee making facilities. Ideally situated for walking and cycling in the Manifold Valley, visiting stately homes, touring the Staffordshire Moorlands, the Peak District and the famous Potteries. Waterhouses is midway between Leek and Ashbourne on the A523. 6 miles from Alton Towers.

Bed & Breakfast per night: single occupancy £30.00; double room from £40.00–£50.00

Bedrooms: 2 double, 1 twin
Bathrooms: 3 en-suite
Parking: 4 spaces

133 Bank House

♦♦♦♦♦ Gold Award

Farley Road, Oakamoor, Stoke-on-Trent, Staffordshire ST10 3BD **Tel:** (01538) 702810 **Fax:** (01538) 702810
Web: http://www.smoothhound.co.uk/hotels/bank.html **E-mail:** john.orme@dial.pipex.com

A luxurious, elegant and peaceful licensed country home offering the highest standards of food and comfort, a third of a mile south of the village. Each en-suite or private-bath bedroom has a beautiful view of the picturesque Churnet Valley, England's little Rhineland. Within the Staffordshire Moorlands, next to the National Park, one mile from Alton Towers, and amidst superb countryside for walking, it is also convenient for visiting the Potteries, Derbyshire Dales, numerous great houses, gardens and other attractions.

Bed & Breakfast per night: single occupancy from £44.00–£53.00; double room from £58.00–£76.00
Dinner, Bed & Breakfast per person, per night: £57.00–£60.00
Evening meal: by arrangement

Bedrooms: 1 double, 2 twin
Bathrooms: 2 en-suite, 1 private
Parking: 8 spaces
Cards accepted: Mastercard, Visa, Diners, Eurocard

Entries are cross referenced by number to the maps on pages 68–69

134 Ley Fields Farm

◆◆◆◆ Silver Award

Leek Road, Cheadle, Stoke-on-Trent, Staffordshire ST10 2EF **Tel:** (01538) 752875

This attractive, listed, Georgian farmhouse is set on a working dairy farm in beautiful countryside. Spacious, traditionally furnished accommodation includes elegant lounge and dining room where delicious breakfasts are served using local produce and home-made preserves. Luxury en-suite bedrooms, including family suite with two bedrooms and private lounge, have hot drink facilities and many extras provided for your comfort. We extend a warm welcome to our guests.

Bed & Breakfast per night: single occupancy from £20.00–£24.00; double room from £36.00–£40.00

Bedrooms: 1 double, 2 family
Bathrooms: 3 en-suite
Parking: 4 spaces

135 The Olde House on the Green

◆◆◆◆

Fulford, Stoke-on-Trent ST11 9QS **Tel:** (01782) 394555

In the country, close to the city, aptly describes the location of Olde House. This pretty 16th-century house is set in peaceful gardens and lies in the centre of a country village (no traffic noise or fumes), yet only ten minutes from many of the Potteries' factory shops, tours and museums. Enjoy delightful accommodation, tap into a wealth of local knowledge and relax with a welcome that is both warm and genuine.

Bed & Breakfast per night: single occupancy from £22.00–£45.00; double room from £36.00–£55.00

Bedrooms: 2 double, 1 twin
Bathrooms: 1 en-suite, 1 public
Parking: 5 spaces

136 Pen-y-Dyffryn Country Hotel

★★★ Silver Award

Rhyd-y-Croesau, Oswestry, Shropshire SY10 7DT **Tel:** (01691) 653700 **Fax:** (01691) 650066
Web: http://www.go2.co.uk/penydyffryn **E-mail:** penydyffryn@go2.co.uk

Once a Georgian rectory, now an 'away-from-it-all' country hotel in the most peaceful of situations in the lovely Shropshire Hills, midway between Shrewsbury and Chester. With an easy-going atmosphere and unpretentious comfort, the hotel has ten bedrooms (including one on the ground floor and two with private patios), all with lovely hill views. The restaurant, with its AA 2 Rosette food award, utilises much local and organic produce. Several National Trust castles nearby. Guests return again and again.

Bed & Breakfast per night: single room from £57.00–£60.00; double room from £78.00–£94.00
Dinner, Bed & Breakfast per person, per night: £56.00–£63.00 (min 2 nights)
Evening meal: 1900 (last orders 2030)

Bedrooms: 1 single, 4 double, 4 twin, 1 family
Bathrooms: 10 en-suite
Parking: 15 spaces
Open: All year except January
Cards accepted: Mastercard, Visa, Switch/Delta, Amex, Eurocard

At-a-glance symbols are explained on the flap inside the back cover

137 Lyth Hill House

◆◆◆◆

Old Coppice, Lyth Hill, Shrewsbury, Shropshire SY3 0BP **Tel:** (01743) 874660 **Fax:** (01743) 874660
Web: http://www.lythhillhouse.co.uk **E-mail:** B&B@lythhill.globalnet.co.uk

Lyth Hill House is situated in a quiet rural location with views over miles of open countryside. It is a non-smoking house, which is unsuitable for children. There are numerous countryside walks nearby. All rooms are on the ground floor. Television and tea/coffee making facilities are provided in the bedrooms. Separate guest lounge and dining room. Use of indoor swimming pool during the summer months. Ample car parking is available on site. For more information see www.lythhillhouse.co.uk

Bed & Breakfast per night: single occupancy from £27.00–£33.00; double room from £44.00–£56.00
Dinner, Bed & Breakfast per person, per night: £34.00–£43.00 (min 2 nights, 2 sharing)
Evening meal: 1800 (last orders 2100)

Bedrooms: 1 double, 1 twin
Bathrooms: 1 en-suite, 1 private
Parking: 4 spaces

The Shropshire Hills

The 'Shropshire Alps' and 'Little Switzerland' are not altogether fanciful names for that dramatically hilly part of the county sandwiched between the Welsh border and the River Severn. Here, ancient earth movements have tilted up great layers of different rock strata, each now forming its own ridge of hills stretching in a roughly south-westerly to north-easterly direction.

Most easterly of the ridges are the Clee Hills, formed of rich red sandstone, topped with basalt, and consisting of two separate ridges, Brown Clee Hill (1,792ft - 546m) and Titterstone Clee Hill (1,749ft - 533m). To their west the River Corve flows through a gentle wooded valley, before the land rises again to Wenlock Edge, a well-defined and steep-sided ridge of limestone flanked with trees. West of the Edge the hump of Caer Caradoc (1,506ft - 459m) dominates the Caradoc Hills around Church Stretton, and beyond rises the forbidding plateau of the Long Mynd (1,696ft - 517m). This 10-mile (16km) ridge of moorland, composed of heather-covered grit and shale, is a favourite launch point for gliders, and also provides some of the best walking country in Shropshire. An ancient path of unknown age, the Port Way, runs the entire length of the crest, commanding magnificent views of the Wrekin (1,335ft - 407m), which protrudes dramatically from the Shropshire Plain, its volcanic rocks the oldest in England. The eastern flank of the Long Mynd is eroded by streams into a series of deep ravines, of

which the popular Carding Mill Valley (shown above) is considered the most beautiful; two others are Callow Hollow and Ashes Hollow. Westward again are the Stiperstones, a sombre rocky outcrop where devils are believed to gather on Midwinter Night and, at 1,731ft (528m), a dramatic vantage point.

Aside from its superb scenery the area is rich in other attractions, with appealing towns, such as Shrewsbury, Bridgnorth, Bewdley and Ludlow all within easy reach. It boasts a string of impressive castles and fortified manors (Ludlow, Clun, Stokesay are three of many), some fine ecclesiastical ruins (Buildwas and Wenlock), and a fascinating industrial heritage (Ironbridge). At the heart of the hills is Church Stretton, an appealing little town which became something of a land-locked resort in the 19th century, a perfect base, then and now, from which to explore the slopes. Contact Church Stretton Tourist Information Centre (tel: 01694 723133) for details of sights and walks (guided hikes are available) throughout the region.

Entries are cross referenced by number to the maps on pages 68–69

138 Coalbrookdale Villa

◆◆◆◆ Gold Award

Paradise, Coalbrookdale, Ironbridge, Telford, Shropshire TF8 7NR **Tel:** (01952) 433450
E-mail: coalbrookdalevilla@bunmail

Coalbrookdale Villa is a large, Victorian ironmaster's house set in Paradise which is just off the main wharfage in Ironbridge. You can walk into town and be standing on the bridge in approximately ten minutes, or you can be at the Museum of Iron in the opposite direction in five minutes. Newly refurbished luxury en-suite bedrooms offer our guests a comfortable and tranquil stay. We have ample private parking spaces in the drive and the house is surrounded by a large garden. For the comfort and safety of our guests Coalbrookdale Villa is a non-smoking household. Contact June Ashdown on 01952 433450 for further information.

Bed & Breakfast per night: single occupancy from £30.00–£45.00; double room from £44.00–£55.00

Bedrooms: 3 double, 1 twin
Bathrooms: 3 en-suite, 1 private
Parking: 10 spaces

139 The Wenlock Edge Inn

◆◆◆◆ Silver Award

Hilltop, Wenlock Edge, Much Wenlock, Shropshire TF13 6DJ **Tel:** (01746) 785678 **Fax:** (01746) 785285
E-mail: jpwonwei@enta.net

Situated in a peaceful location on Wenlock Edge – an Area of Outstanding Natural Beauty. Run by two generations of the Waring family for the last 16 years, the atmosphere of the inn is informal and friendly. Guests can relax in the comfort and cosiness of Silver Award-winning rooms and enjoy wholesome country cooking with fresh local produce and organic bread for breakfast.

Bed & Breakfast per night: single occupancy from £41.50–£48.00; double room from £63.00–£75.00
Lunch available: 1200–1400 (not Mondays)
Evening meal: 1900 (last orders 2100)

Bedrooms: 2 double, 1 twin
Bathrooms: 3 en-suite
Parking: 40 spaces
Cards accepted: Mastercard, Visa, Switch/Delta, Amex, JCB, Visa Electron

140 The Albynes

◆◆◆◆◆ Silver Award

Nordley, Bridgnorth, Shropshire WV16 4SX **Tel:** (01746) 762261

The Albynes is a beautiful country house set in large informal gardens which are surrounded by parkland. The large lounge and superb Tudor-panelled dining room each have magnificent views. The spacious bedrooms are attractively furnished and have private facilities. We offer you a very warm welcome and invite you to enjoy the Shropshire countryside whilst visiting the many local attractions. Quietly situated (off the B4373) midway between Bridgnorth and Ironbridge.

Bed & Breakfast per night: single room from £25.00–£30.00; double room from £40.00–£44.00

Bedrooms: 1 single, 1 double, 1 twin
Bathrooms: 2 en-suite, 1 private
Parking: 8 spaces

141 Old Vicarage Hotel

★★★ Gold Award

Worfield, Bridgnorth, Shropshire WV15 5JZ **Tel:** (01746) 716497 **Fax:** (01746) 716552
Web: http://www.oldvicarageworfield.com **E-mail:** admin@the-old-vicarage.demon.co.uk

An Edwardian vicarage set in two acres of grounds on the edge of a conservation village in glorious Shropshire countryside, close to Ironbridge Gorge, Severn Valley Railway and Welsh border towns. With an award-winning (AA 3 Rosettes) dining room and cellar, the Old Vicarage is personally run by Peter and Christine Iles. Two-night leisure breaks available at any time of the year which include half-price golf at Hawkstone Park with half-price admission to the Follies.   **Category 2**

Bed & Breakfast per night: single occupancy from £70.00–£105.00; double room from £107.50–£170.00
Dinner, Bed & Breakfast per person, per night: £72.50–£105.00 (min 2 nights)
Lunch available: by prior arrangement

Evening meal: 1900 (last orders 2100)
Bedrooms: 8 double, 5 twin, 1 triple
Bathrooms: 14 en-suite
Parking: 30 spaces
Cards accepted: Mastercard, Visa, Amex

142 Middleton Lodge

◆◆◆◆

Middleton Priors, Bridgnorth, Shropshire WV16 6UR **Tel:** (01746) 712228 **Fax:** (01746) 712675

An imposing stone building in a one-acre garden with spacious bedrooms overlooking Brown Clee Hill, Middleton Lodge is within easy reach of many places of interest, including Severn Valley Railway, Ironbridge, and the historic towns of Ludlow, Shrewsbury, Much Wenlock, Bridgnorth and Church Stretton.

Bed & Breakfast per night: single occupancy from £30.00–£35.00; double room from £45.00–£50.00

Bedrooms: 2 double, 1 twin
Bathrooms: 2 en-suite, 1 private
Parking: 4 spaces

143 Sayang House

◆◆◆◆

Hope Bowdler, Church Stretton, Shropshire SY6 7DD **Tel:** (01694) 723981
E-mail: madegan@aol.com

Set in a superb location amongst the Shropshire Hills. Ideal for walking, cycling and golf. We can collect from the station 1.5 miles away. En-suite bedrooms, beautiful beamed lounge for visitors' use only, overlooking an acre of landscaped garden. Evening meals available on request, all home prepared using local produce.

Bed & Breakfast per night: single occupancy £28.00; double room £50.00
Dinner, Bed & Breakfast per person, per night: £40.50
Evening meal: 1900 (last orders 1930)

Bedrooms: 1 twin, 2 triple
Bathrooms: 3 en-suite
Parking: 6 spaces

144 Chadstone

◆◆◆◆◆ Silver Award

Aston Munslow, Craven Arms, Shropshire SY7 9ER **Tel:** (01584) 841675
E-mail: chadstone.lee@btinternet.com

Chadstone is a spacious, modern, centrally-heated dormer bungalow set in two acres of grounds in the renowned Corvedale, enjoying outstanding panoramic views of the Clee Hills. A friendly, personal service and luxurious en-suite accommodation, all enhanced by the peace and quiet of the south Shropshire countryside. To quote our guests: "Warmest possible welcome", "Home from home"; "Superb accommodation"; "Excellent food"; "Lovely views and very comfortable"; "Days to treasure and a splendid tonic".

Bed & Breakfast per night: single occupancy from £22.50–£25.00; double room from £45.00–£50.00
Dinner, Bed & Breakfast per person, per night: £37.50–£40.00
Evening meal: 1830 (last bookings 1200)

Bedrooms: 1 double, 2 twin
Bathrooms: 3 en-suite
Parking: 6 spaces

145 Knock Hundred Cottage

◆◆◆◆ Silver Award

Abcott, Clungunford, Craven Arms, Shropshire SY7 0PX **Tel:** (01588) 660594 **Fax:** (01588) 660594

Situated in the scenic Clun Valley, Knock Hundred Cottage is believed to originate from the 16th century and enjoys an open aspect with extensive views. Many places of interest are within easy reach, including National Trust and English Heritage properties and gardens, the Heart of Wales Railway and the Ironbridge museums. There are also historic towns to visit and an abundance of walks to enjoy. Guests are promised a warm and friendly welcome.

Bed & Breakfast per night: double room £45.00
Evening meal: by prior arrangement

Bedrooms: 1 double, 1 twin
Bathrooms: 1 en-suite, 1 private
Parking: 2 spaces

146 Lower House

◆◆◆◆

Adforton, Leintwardine, Craven Arms, Shropshire SY7 0NF **Tel:** (01568) 770223 **Fax:** (01568) 770592
Web: http://www.sy7.com/lowerhouse **E-mail:** cutler@sy7.com

Lower House originates from the early 17th century and is situated in North Herefordshire in the Welsh Marches. There is excellent walking in the surrounding hills and the area is quiet and unspoilt. There are many castles, gardens and National Trust properties within an easy drive. We offer first class, home-cooked food served in our elegant dining room. We are unlicensed, but guests are welcome to bring their own wine.

Bed & Breakfast per night: single occupancy from £26.00–£28.00; double room from £52.00–£56.00
Dinner, Bed & Breakfast per person, per night: £43.00–£46.00
Evening meal: 1900 (last orders 1930)

Bedrooms: 2 double, 2 twin
Bathrooms: 3 en-suite, 1 private
Parking: 10 spaces

At-a-glance symbols are explained on the flap inside the back cover

147 Bromfield Manor ◆◆◆◆

Bromfield, Ludlow, Shropshire SY8 2JU **Tel:** (01584) 856536 or 07850 713340 **Fax:** (01584) 856536
Web: http://www.go2.co.uk/bromfield **E-mail:** john.mason9@virgin.net

Relax in the informal, friendly atmosphere of a house with character while enjoying the personal attention of the owners. Bromfield Manor is a stone-built Grade II listed building situated in the village of Bromfield, two miles north of Ludlow. Gardens of one acre have views of the surrounding hills. Bedrooms and drawing room enjoy a south facing vista to the Whitcliffe beauty spot. Get a taste of country house living – you may like it.

Bed & Breakfast per night: single occupancy from £35.00–£50.00; double room £50.00

Bedrooms: 1 double, 1 twin
Bathrooms: 2 private
Parking: 10 spaces

148 Number Twenty Eight ◆◆◆◆◆ Silver Award

28 Lower Broad Street, Ludlow, Shropshire SY8 1PQ **Tel:** (01584) 876996 **Fax:** (01584) 876860
Web: http://www.go2.co.uk/no28 **E-mail:** ross.no28@btinternet.com

These listed town houses, all within yards of each other in this historic street, offer superior, en-suite bed and breakfast accommodation. All rooms are individually furnished to provide every comfort. Each house (just two rooms in each) has a sitting room and a garden for your enjoyment and relaxation. The houses are within the conservation area of this 'most lovely of English towns' and within walking distance of more Michelin-starred restaurants than anywhere else on earth!

Bed & Breakfast per night: single occupancy from £65.00–£75.00; double room from £65.00–£80.00

Bedrooms: 4 double, 2 twin
Bathrooms: 6 en-suite
Cards accepted: Mastercard, Visa, Amex

149 Brockencote Hall ★★★ Gold Award

Chaddesley Corbett, Kidderminster, Worcestershire DY10 4PY **Tel:** (01562) 777876 **Fax:** (01562) 777872

Nestling in the heart of the Worcestershire countryside, Brockencote Hall is set in seventy acres of private parkland with its own lake. It is the perfect place for relaxation. Proprietors Alison and Joseph Petitjean have created a charming Gallic oasis in the heart of England, combining traditional French comfort and friendliness with superb French cuisine. The hotel offers a choice of seventeen magnificent en-suite bedrooms, including one that has been especially designed to make stays comfortable for disabled guests.

Bed & Breakfast per night: single occupancy from £110.00–£130.00; double room from £135.00–£170.00
Dinner, Bed & Breakfast per person, per night: £82.50–£112.50 (2 sharing)
Lunch available: 1200–1330

Evening meal: 1900 (last orders 2130)
Bedrooms: 13 double, 3 twin, 1 triple
Bathrooms: 17 en-suite
Parking: 50 spaces
Cards accepted: Mastercard, Visa, Switch/Delta, Amex, Diners

Entries are cross referenced by number to the maps on pages 68–69

150 Home Farm

◆◆◆◆ Silver Award

Great Witley, Worcester, Worcestershire WR6 6JJ **Tel:** (01299) 896825 **Fax:** (01299) 896176

Home Farm offers a warm welcome to all its guests. It is a Grade II* listed moated farmhouse, surrounded by beautiful gardens, with breathtaking views of Worcestershire. Each bedroom has a character of its own, being spacious and individually decorated, with many 'personal' touches. Breakfast incorporates a large choice of local and seasonal produce to suit all tastes. Enjoy a relaxing, peaceful stay and visit the many nearby places of interest.

Bed & Breakfast per night: single room from £20.00–£22.50; double room from £40.00–£55.00

Bedrooms: 2 single, 2 twin
Bathrooms: 1 en-suite, 1 public
Parking: 12 spaces

---

151 Highfield

◆◆◆◆

Ivington Road, Leominster, Herefordshire HR6 8QD **Tel:** (01568) 613216

Highfield is a charming Edwardian house standing in a large garden with unspoilt views of open farmland and distant hills. It is the home of twins Catherine and Marguerite Fothergill whose aim is for everyone to be contented. There are three very pleasant comfortable bedrooms, two attractive sitting rooms and truly delicious home-prepared food to suit all tastes is served in the delightful dining room. A happy and relaxed stay is assured.

Bed & Breakfast per night: double room £44.00
Dinner, Bed & Breakfast per person, per night: £32.50–£34.50
Evening meal: 1900 (last bookings 1200)

Bedrooms: 1 double, 2 twin
Bathrooms: 1 en-suite, 2 private
Parking: 3 spaces
Open: All year except January and February

---

152 The Paddock

◆◆◆◆ Silver Award

Shobdon, Leominster, Herefordshire HR6 9NQ **Tel:** (01568) 708176 **Fax:** (01568) 708829

Situated in idyllic countryside bordering Wales, The Paddock offers a warm welcome, wonderful service and delightful en-suite accommodation. All the well-equipped rooms are on the ground floor and include a mechanical ventilation system and underfloor central heating. Guests have their own entrance, a comfortable lounge with satellite television, and a large garden and patio. We serve a substantial breakfast and offer a delicious three-course dinner. Visit The Paddock for a truly relaxing break.

Bed & Breakfast per night: single occupancy £30.00; double room from £40.00–£45.00
Dinner, Bed & Breakfast per person, per night: £35.00–£45.00
Evening meal: 1900

Bedrooms: 4 double, 1 twin
Bathrooms: 5 en-suite
Parking: 10 spaces

At-a-glance symbols are explained on the flap inside the back cover

153 Broxwood Court

Broxwood, Leominster, Herefordshire HR6 9JJ **Tel:** (01544) 340245 **Fax:** (01544) 340573

This beautiful home, with its sweeping lawns where peacocks roam, magnificent trees and lake, and uninterrupted views of the Black Mountains, offers an atmosphere of peace and tranquillity. Relax in the cosy library, enjoy the views from the drawing room, play tennis on the all-weather court, swim in the heated outdoor pool, or walk in the lovely thirty-acre garden. Mike and Anne are a relaxed and well-travelled couple who will give you a very warm welcome.

Bed & Breakfast per night: single occupancy £50.00; double room from £66.00–£76.00
Dinner, Bed & Breakfast per person, per night: £53.00–£70.00 (min 2 nights at weekends)
Evening meal: 1900 (last orders 2100)

Bedrooms: 1 double, 2 twin
Bathrooms: 2 en-suite, 1 private
Parking: 15 spaces
Open: All year except February
Cards accepted: Mastercard, Visa, Eurocard

Cruck-framed Houses

The Midlands are particularly rich in timber-framed or, to use the popular term, half-timbered buildings – 'half-timbered' being a reference to the early medieval period when the timbers were formed by cutting logs in half. These buildings are classified as either box-frame construction or cruck construction. By far the more common type was box-frame, where jointed horizontal and vertical timbers formed a wall and either the panels were infilled or the whole wall was covered with some sort of cladding. In the cruck construction, the structure was supported by pairs of inclined, slightly curved timbers that normally met at the ridge of the roof and were tied by a collar or tie-beam, making an A shape. These timbers, called crucks or blades, were spaced at regular intervals along the building to take the weight of the roof and often of the walls too. Wherever possible crucks were cut from the trunk of one tree split along its length to get a symmetrical arch. Alternatively, they were taken from trees with a natural curve in the trunk and blades matched as closely as possible.

There were various forms of cruck construction, the most important being full cruck, base or truncated cruck, raised cruck and jointed cruck. Full crucks extend from ground level to the apex. Base or truncated begin on the ground but stop below the apex and are joined by a tie-beam or collar that supports the roof. Raised crucks start a few feet off the ground in a solid wall, and in jointed cruck construction the curving blade is jointed to a vertical post that begins on the ground.

Many crucks have been incorporated into larger buildings, hidden behind a cladding of stone or brick or plastered over, but where they are visible as the gable end they are an attractive and striking feature. Cruck-framing is particularly prevalent in the Midlands, the North and West (and is more or less entirely absent in East Anglia and the South-East, where box-framing predominates), and it is in Hereford & Worcester that the greatest concentration of cruck buildings is to be found. There are some fine examples in Weobley, unsurpassed for its black-and-white buildings. Explore its streets and you cannot fail to admire the skills of the 15th-, 16th- and 17th-century craftsmen. Other towns in the county worth visiting for their half-timbering are Eardisley, Eardisland, Pembridge and Dilwyn. Some excellent examples of cruck-framed buildings have been reconstructed at the Avoncroft Museum of Historic Buildings in Bromsgrove (tel: 01527 831886).

154 The Old Vicarage

◆◆◆◆ Silver Award

Vowchurch, Herefordshire HR2 0QD **Tel:** (01981) 550357 **Fax:** (01981) 550357
Web: http://www.golden-valley.co.uk/vicarage

This Victorian vicarage, set in the heart of the beautiful Golden Valley, near the Black Mountains and Welsh border, was once the home of Lewis Carroll's brother. You are invited to our home – to share its interesting old family treasures and hospitality. Small 'special occasion' parties are most welcome. Much thought and care is given to the preparation and presentation of your breakfasts and imaginative dinners, using local and home grown produce for real taste. So much to see and do in this unspoilt, most rural of counties.

Bed & Breakfast per night: single room from £21.00–£26.00; double room from £42.00–£52.00
Dinner, Bed & Breakfast per person, per night: £34.00–£46.00
Evening meal: 1900

Bedrooms: 1 single, 1 double, 1 family
Bathrooms: 2 en-suite, 1 private

155 Mill Orchard

◆◆◆◆ Gold Award

Kingstone, Hereford HR2 9ES **Tel:** (01981) 250326 **Fax:** (01981) 250520
Web: http://www.travel-uk.net/millorchard **E-mail:** handjcleveland@compuserve.com

Situated between the Wye Valley and Golden Valley, Mill Orchard is a country house set in one acre of south-facing gardens overlooking lovely countryside. In this delightful home you are offered a warm welcome and high quality accommodation. Bedrooms are spacious and well-equipped. We serve delicious breakfasts using local or home-grown seasonal produce. Evening meals by arrangement. Good pubs and restaurants nearby. Ideal for exploring the beautiful border counties. Discounts available.

Bed & Breakfast per night: single occupancy from £28.00–£30.00; double room from £46.00–£50.00
Dinner, Bed & Breakfast per person, per night: £33.00–£40.00 (min 2 sharing)

Bedrooms: 2 double, 1 twin
Bathrooms: 2 en-suite, 1 private
Parking: 6 spaces
Open: All year except January and December

156 Felton House

◆◆◆◆

Felton, Hereford HR1 3PH **Tel:** (01432) 820366 **Fax:** (01432) 820366
Web: http://www.smoothhound.co.uk/hotels/felton.html

Felton House is truly somewhere very special where you can relax on arrival with refreshments in the library, drawing room, conservatory or in the tranquil four-acre gardens. Eat an excellent evening meal in a local inn, then sleep in a historic bed and awake refreshed to enjoy, in a superb Victorian dining room, the breakfast you have chosen from a wide selection of traditional and vegetarian dishes. The highest levels of quality, hospitality and service just 20 minutes by car from Hereford, Leominster, Bromyard and Ledbury.

Bed & Breakfast per night: single room £23.00; double room £46.00

Bedrooms: 1 single, 2 double, 1 twin
Bathrooms: 2 en-suite, 2 private
Parking: 6 spaces

157 The Steppes

★★ Silver Award

Ullingswick, Hereford HR1 3JG **Tel:** (01432) 820424 **Fax:** (01432) 820042

This award-winning country house hotel with an intimate atmosphere abounds in antique furniture, inglenook fireplaces, oak beams and flag-stoned floors. The old dairy now houses a magnificent cobbled bar with Dickensian atmosphere, and a restored timber-framed barn and converted stable accommodate six large luxury en-suite bedrooms. Outstanding cordon bleu cuisine (AA 2 Rosettes) is served by candle light, and highly praised breakfasts come with an imaginative selection.

Bed & Breakfast per night: single occupancy from £40.00–£55.00; double room from £80.00–£90.00
Dinner, Bed & Breakfast per person, per night: £66.00–£71.00
Evening meal: 1930 (last bookings 1830)

Bedrooms: 5 double, 1 twin
Bathrooms: 6 en-suite
Parking: 8 spaces
Open: All year except January and December
Cards accepted: Mastercard, Visa, Switch/Delta, Amex, Eurocard

158 The Old Cowshed

◆◆◆◆

Avenbury Court Farm, Bromyard, Herefordshire HR7 4LA **Tel:** (01885) 482384 **Fax:** (01885) 482367
Web: http://www.ruralb.b.clara.co.uk **E-mail:** ruralb.b@clara.co.uk

Come to 'badger and buzzard' country in a location so peaceful you can almost hear it. Richard and Helen Combe invite you to relax in their spacious home in attractively converted farm buildings. Comfortable, tastefully furnished private suites with their own bath/shower. Ground floor rooms. Inglenook fireplace in guest drawing room, galleried beamed kitchen/dining room, large walled garden, magnificent views, off-road parking. High level of personal service our speciality. Beautiful countryside location.

Bed & Breakfast per night: single occupancy from £22.50–£25.00; double room from £45.00–£50.00

Bedrooms: 1 twin, 2 triple
Bathrooms: 3 private
Parking: 6 spaces

159 Hidelow House

◆◆◆◆ Silver Award

Acton Green, Acton Beauchamp, Worcester, Worcestershire WR6 5AH **Tel:** (01886) 884547 **Fax:** (01886) 884060
Web: http://www.hidelow.co.uk **E-mail:** accommodation@hidelow.co.uk

Near Malvern. Lovely, small, stone country house and converted 17th-century tithe barn amongst peaceful pastureland, 250 metres off the road on the Herefordshire/Worcestershire borders. Tastefully refurbished en-suite rooms, magnificent residents' lounge, grand piano and log fires on cooler days, sun terrace overlooking extensive gardens with fish pool and waterfall, and stunning open views across unspoilt Herefordshire countryside. Suite with four-poster bed. Disabled persons' accommodation possible for B&B in adjoining adapted cottage. Home-cooked evening meals by arrangement. Personal transport service.

Bed & Breakfast per night: single occupancy from £24.50–£29.50; double room from £49.00–£59.00
Dinner, Bed & Breakfast per person, per night: £39.00–£44.00
Evening meal: 1900

Bedrooms: 2 double, 1 twin
Bathrooms: 3 en-suite
Parking: 10 spaces

Entries are cross referenced by number to the maps on pages 68–69

160 Wyche Keep Country House

♦♦♦♦ Silver Award

22 Wyche Road, Malvern, Worcestershire WR14 4EG **Tel:** (01684) 567018 **Fax:** (01684) 892304
Web: http://www.jks.org/wychekeep **E-mail:** wyche-keep-tours@england.com

Wyche Keep is a stunning arts and crafts style house, perched high on the Malvern Hills, built by the family of Sir Stanley Baldwin, Prime Minister, to enjoy the spectacular sixty-mile views, and having a long history of elegant entertaining. Three large luxury double suites, including a four-poster. Traditional English cooking is a speciality and guests can savour memorable four-course candlelit dinners. Fully licensed. Magical setting with private parking. A no smoking establishment.

Bed & Breakfast per night: single occupancy from £38.00–£40.00; double room from £56.00–£60.00
Dinner, Bed & Breakfast per person, per night: £47.00–£49.00
Evening meal: 1930 (last orders 2000)

Bedrooms: 1 double, 2 twin
Bathrooms: 3 en-suite
Parking: 6 spaces

---

161 The Cottage in the Wood Hotel

★★★ Silver Award

Holywell Road, Malvern Wells, Malvern, Worcestershire WR14 4LG **Tel:** (01684) 575859 **Fax:** (01684) 560662

Stunningly set high on the Malvern Hills, looking across thirty miles of the Severn Plain to the horizon formed by the Cotswold Hills. Owned and run by the Pattin family for twelve years, the aim is to provide a relaxing and peaceful base from which to tour this area of outstanding natural beauty. The restaurant provides exceptional food backed by an extensive wine list of over five hundred bins. The daily half board price is based on a minimum two-night stay, and the weekly price offers seven nights for the price of six. Special breaks all week, all year. AA 2 Rosettes.

Bed & Breakfast per night: single occupancy from £74.00–£84.00; double room from £89.50–£139.00
Dinner, Bed & Breakfast per person, per night: £55.00–£95.00
Lunch available: 1230–1400

Evening meal: 1900 (last orders 2100)
Bedrooms: 16 double, 4 twin
Bathrooms: 20 en-suite
Parking: 40 spaces
Cards accepted: Mastercard, Visa, Switch/ Delta, Amex, Eurocard, JCB, Visa Electron

---

162 Welland Court

♦♦♦♦

Upton-upon-Severn, Worcestershire WR8 0ST **Tel:** (01684) 594426 **Fax:** (01684) 594426
Web: http://www.upton.enta.net **E-mail:** archer@wellandcourt.demon.co.uk

Welland Court is a gem of a small manor house of great character and charm. Built in about 1250, it was enlarged in the 18th-century when the Georgian façade was added. This gorgeous house has been recently rescued from a dilapidated state and graciously modernised to today's high standard of comfort. Truly beautiful countryside surrounds Welland Court from all angles. There is a two-acre lake, heavily stocked with trout, which is available for use by guests at no extra charge.

Bed & Breakfast per night: single occupancy from £35.00–£45.00; double room from £55.00–£75.00

Bedrooms: 1 double, 2 twin
Bathrooms: 3 en-suite
Parking: 13 spaces

At-a-glance symbols are explained on the flap inside the back cover

163 Holdfast Cottage Hotel

★★ Silver Award

Marlbank Road, Little Malvern, Malvern, Worcestershire WR13 6NA **Tel:** (01684) 310288 **Fax:** (01684) 311117
Web: http://www.holdfast-cottage.co.uk **E-mail:** holdcothot@aol.com

Pretty wisteria-covered country house hotel, set in two acres of gardens and private woodland, tucked into the foot of the Malvern Hills. Highly recommended for its freshly-prepared menu which changes daily and uses the best local and seasonal produce. Delightful dining room and bar. Cosy lounge with log fire. Enchanting en-suite bedrooms are individually furnished. A personal welcome plus care and attention throughout your stay is assured by the resident proprietors, Stephen and Jane Knowles.

Bed & Breakfast per night: single room from £48.00; double room from £88.00–£90.00
Dinner, Bed & Breakfast per person, per night: £60.00–£64.00
Evening meal: 1900 (last orders 2100)

Bedrooms: 1 single, 5 double, 2 twin
Bathrooms: 8 en-suite
Parking: 20 spaces
Cards accepted: Mastercard, Visa, Switch/Delta, Eurocard

Elgar and the Three Choirs Festival

No one actually knows when the tradition of annual music-making involving the three cities of Hereford, Worcester and Gloucester, now known as the Three Choirs Festival, began. It is probable that it was well established by the end of the 17th century, making it the oldest musical festival of its type in Europe. From the start it revolved around the three great cathedrals (Gloucester Cathedral is shown here) and consisted of a couple of days' performances of religious music each year in a different city. Even at this early stage, much informal music-making probably went on 'out of hours' and, by the mid-18th century, secular concerts had become an established part of the event.

Over the years the meetings expanded, becoming by the 1830s the 'festival' in existence today, with large-scale choral works held in the cathedral and secular and orchestral performances in various venues around the city, spread over a period of a week in August. During the 20th century the festival has played an important rôle in fostering new British composers, seeing the world premieres of works now well established in the musical repertoire by composers such as Parry, Vaughan

Williams, Holst, Delius, Walton, Bliss and Britten. Of all those associated with the festival, the most famous is Edward Elgar, whose music is inextricably linked with the Three Choirs and its history.

Elgar was born at Broadheath, 3 miles (5km) west of Worcester, and his birthplace is now open as a museum (tel: 01905 333224). His early career was not promising, and when his overture *Froissart* was first accepted by the festival committee in 1890 he, at 32, had not yet made a name for himself. It was the start of a more productive period however, and by the time his great *Dream of Gerontius* was premiered at the festival in 1902 his reputation was firmly established. From the end of the First World War until his death in 1934, Elgar made frequent appearances at the festival, a grand old man, knighted, frequently wearing his court dress, and often conducting his own works. Though his fame inevitably took him to London, he never lost touch with his beloved Malverns, taking homes in the area, cycling around its lanes and drawing inspiration from its calm English beauty. A detailed Elgar route is available from tourist offices, taking in sites associated with the composer. Elgar's music continues to be heard at the Three Choirs Festival and also at Malvern's Elgar Festival held in late May and early June.

164 Feathers Hotel

★★★ Silver Award

High Street, Ledbury, Herefordshire HR8 1DS **Tel:** (01531) 635266 **Fax:** (01531) 638955
E-mail: feathers@ledbury.kc3ltd.co.uk

The Feathers Hotel is a part timber-framed Elizabethan coaching inn, retaining many original features, situated in the heart of picturesque Ledbury. Spend a weekend with us and relax in our individually furnished bedrooms, enjoy award-winning local food and while away an hour in our leisure spa with swimming pool, jacuzzi, steam room, solarium and gym. Ledbury has many corners to explore and the surrounding Herefordshire countryside is famed for its beauty.

Bed & Breakfast per night: single occupancy from £69.50–£77.50; double room from £89.50–£125.00
Dinner, Bed & Breakfast per person, per night: from £57.50 (min 2 nights, 2 sharing)
Lunch available: 1200–1400 weekdays,

1200–1430 weekends
Evening meal: 1830 (last orders 2130)
Bedrooms: 12 double, 4 twin, 3 triple
Bathrooms: 19 en-suite **Parking:** 30 spaces
Cards accepted: Mastercard, Visa, Switch/Delta, Amex, Diners, Eurocard

165 The Chase Hotel

★★★ Silver Award

Gloucester Road, Ross-on-Wye, Herefordshire HR9 5LH **Tel:** (01989) 763161 **Fax:** (01989) 768330

A country house hotel set in 11 acres of gardens and grounds within close proximity of the town centre. All rooms have en-suite facilities, hair dryers, colour satellite televisions, radios and hospitality trays. The AA 2 Rosette award-winning restaurant provides excellence in food, service and cuisine. All public rooms overlook the gardens and, with ample parking, this hotel offers an ideal situation to enjoy a relaxing time while touring the area. Leisure breaks from £45 per person per night.

Bed & Breakfast per night: single occupancy from £60.00–£85.00; double room from £75.00–£100.00
Dinner, Bed & Breakfast per person, per night: £45.00–£65.00 (min 2 nights, 2 sharing)
Lunch available: 1200–1400

Evening meal: 1900 (last orders 2145)
Bedrooms: 16 double, 21 twin, 1 triple
Bathrooms: 38 en-suite
Parking: 200 spaces
Cards accepted: Mastercard, Visa, Switch/Delta, Amex, Diners, Eurocard

166 Forest Edge

◆◆◆◆

4 Noden Drive, Lea, Ross-on-Wye, Herefordshire HR9 7NB **Tel:** (01989) 750682
Web: http://www.wood11.freeserve.co.uk **E-mail:** don@wood11.freeserve.co.uk

A warm welcome and friendly atmosphere awaits you at our modern luxury home. Situated in a quiet rural area just four miles from Ross-on-Wye, its location is very central for the exploration of the many attractions of this beautiful area. The house has a secluded, attractive, well-stocked garden with conservatory offering fine views towards the Royal Forest of Dean. En-suite bedrooms are furnished and equipped to a very high standard. Ample private parking.

Bed & Breakfast per night: double room from £40.00–£45.00

Bedrooms: 1 double, 1 twin
Bathrooms: 2 en-suite
Parking: 4 spaces

167 Royal Spring Farm

(A4136), Longhope, Gloucestershire GL17 0PY **Tel:** (01452) 830550

A 14-acre fruit farm ten miles west of Gloucester with a spacious, beamed farmhouse backing onto our orchards, grazing and woodland. Comfortably furnished with antique family furniture in public rooms, and log fires in winter. Our meals use home-grown or local produce and breakfast offers our fruit and home-made jams and marmalade. A convenient centre for beautiful Forest of Dean, Wye Valley, Cotswolds and historic Gloucester, Tewkesbury, Ross-on-Wye. Woodland walks from the door.

Bed & Breakfast per night: single room from £20.00–£22.00; double room from £40.00–£44.00
Evening meal: 1900 (last orders 2100)

Bedrooms: 1 single, 1 double/family, 1 twin/family
Bathrooms: 1 en-suite, 2 private
Parking: 20 spaces

168 The Old Rectory

Hope Mansell, Ross-on-Wye, Herefordshire HR9 5TL **Tel:** (01989) 750382 **Fax:** (01989) 750382

An attractive Georgian house in peaceful surroundings in hills bordering the River Wye and the Forest of Dean, designated as an Area of Outstanding Natural Beauty. The house is surrounded by mature gardens, a small orchard and has an all-weather tennis court. The comfortable rooms have period furniture. A wealth of local information is provided and the library includes a wide selection of reference and general reading books for all ages. Families are welcomed.

Bed & Breakfast per night: single occupancy from £20.00–£22.50; double room £40.00

Bedrooms: 2 double, 1 twin
Bathrooms: 1 private, 1 public
Parking: 4 spaces

169 Norton House

◆◆◆◆ Gold Award

Whitchurch, Ross-on-Wye, Herefordshire HR9 6DJ **Tel:** (01600) 890046 **Fax:** (01600) 890045
E-mail: jackson@osconwhi.source.co.uk

A 17th-century Grade II listed former farmhouse, which has been beautifully renovated with pine shutters and doors, oak beams, flagstone floors and inglenook fireplaces. It oozes old fashioned charm but offers all the modern comfort our guests could wish for. Delicious Aga-cooked meals served by candle light make for a romantic escape. Situated in the beautiful Wye Valley, a short walk from the River Wye and five minutes' drive from Yat Rock, making it an ideal touring centre.

Bed & Breakfast per night: single occupancy from £25.00–£30.00; double room from £40.00–£44.00
Dinner, Bed & Breakfast per person, per night: £29.50–£33.50
Evening meal: 1930

Bedrooms: 2 double, 1 twin
Bathrooms: 3 en-suite
Parking: 3 spaces

Entries are cross referenced by number to the maps on pages 68–69

170 Wyndham Arms

★★★ Silver Award

Clearwell, Coleford, Gloucestershire GL16 8JT **Tel:** (01594) 833666 **Fax:** (01594) 836450

A 14th-century village inn with 20th-century amenities. At the edge of the Royal Forest of Dean, just above the Wye Valley, the Wyndham Arms has been in the Stanford family's competent ownership since 1973. All bedrooms en-suite, award-winning restaurant, traditional beers, lots of different malt whiskies, and very pretty gardens. Just the place for a get-away weekend. Stay free on Sundays if you dine in the restaurant.

Bed & Breakfast per night: single room £50.50; double room from £80.00–£100.00
Dinner, Bed & Breakfast per person, per night: £50.00–£68.00
Lunch available: 1200–1400
Evening meal: 1845 (last orders 2130)

Bedrooms: 2 single, 4 double, 9 twin, 2 triple, 1 suite
Bathrooms: 18 en-suite
Parking: 52 spaces
Cards accepted: Mastercard, Visa, Switch/Delta, Amex, Diners, Eurocard, JCB

171 Stretton Lodge Hotel

◆◆◆◆

Western Road, Cheltenham, Gloucestershire GL50 3RN **Tel:** (01242) 570771 **Fax:** (01242) 528724
Web: http://www.strettonlodge.demon.co.uk **E-mail:** info@strettonlodge.demon.co.uk

The Victorian Stretton Lodge Townhouse is now a family-managed hotel nestling in the heart of Cheltenham, yet located in a quiet area with its own garden and parking. Each en-suite bedroom is individually decorated, whilst the elegant sitting and dining rooms reflect a past age of gracious living. Light meals and snacks are served throughout the day and home-cooked meals each evening. Please contact Carol and Christopher Tallis for further assistance and to make your reservation.

Bed & Breakfast per night: single room from £40.00–£55.00; double room from £58.00–£80.00
Dinner, Bed & Breakfast per person, per night: £46.00–£52.00 (min 2 nights)
Evening meal: 1700 (last orders 1930)

Bedrooms: 1 single, 2 double, 1 twin, 1 triple
Bathrooms: 5 en-suite
Parking: 6 spaces
Cards accepted: Mastercard, Visa, Switch/Delta, Amex, Eurocard, JCB

172 Hotel on the Park

★★★ Gold Award

Evesham Road, Cheltenham, Gloucestershire GL52 2AH **Tel:** (01242) 518898 **Fax:** (01242) 511526
Web: http://www.hotelonthepark.co.uk **E-mail:** stay@hotelonthepark.co.uk

This exclusive town house hotel is set within a classic example of a Regency villa and successfully combines the highest standards of traditional hotel-keeping with the charm and character of a period house. The twelve individually-designed bedrooms and suites and the elegant, candlelit public rooms complement a restaurant serving some of the best modern British cooking on offer today. Situated opposite Pittville Park and five minutes from the racecourse and the town centre. 2 AA Rosettes.

Bed & Breakfast per night: single occupancy from £86.50; double room from £108.50–£168.50
Dinner, Bed & Breakfast per person, per night: £70.50–£98.00 (min 2 nights)
Lunch available: 1200–1400

Evening meal: 1900 (last orders 2130)
Bedrooms: 8 double, 4 twin
Bathrooms: 12 en-suite
Parking: 10 spaces
Cards accepted: Mastercard, Visa, Switch/Delta, Amex, Diners, Eurocard

At-a-glance symbols are explained on the flap inside the back cover

173 Beechworth Lawn Hotel ♦♦♦♦

133 Hales Road, Cheltenham, Gloucestershire GL52 6ST **Tel:** (01242) 522583 **Fax:** (01242) 574800

Near to the town centre and conveniently located for shopping and leisure activities, Beechworth Lawn offers a period hotel carefully restored. Decorated and furnished with the highest quality beds, linen and soft-furnishings for your complete comfort and pleasure. There is high-quality accommodation and food with discreet friendly service. With our all-year low rates, twenty-four hour access and off-street parking, we will make your stay in Cheltenham a memorable and happy one. Your hosts: Peter and Claire Christensen.

Bed & Breakfast per night: single occupancy from £40.00–£48.00; double room from £55.00–£65.00
Evening meal: 1830 (last bookings 1200)

Bedrooms: 2 double, 2 twin, 2 triple
Bathrooms: 6 en-suite
Parking: 12 spaces
Cards accepted: Mastercard, Visa

174 Charlton Kings Hotel ★★★ Silver Award

London Road, Charlton Kings, Cheltenham, Gloucestershire GL52 6UU **Tel:** (01242) 231061 **Fax:** (01242) 241900

Situated in an area of outstanding natural beauty on the edge of Cheltenham Spa. An ideal touring centre for the walker (the famous Cotswold Way is only a half mile away) or motorist (ask for your free 'Romantic Road' when booking). Whatever you choose, come back and enjoy the creative skills of our talented chef. Although we have high standards, the hotel is informally run by the proprietor and his team of enthusiastic staff.

Bed & Breakfast per night: single room from £59.90–£79.90; double room from £90.00–£104.00
Dinner, Bed & Breakfast per person, per night: £60.00–£70.75
Lunch available: 1200–1400
Evening meal: 1900 (last orders 2045)

Bedrooms: 2 single, 8 double, 2 twin, 1 triple, 1 family
Bathrooms: 14 en-suite
Parking: 26 spaces
Cards accepted: Mastercard, Visa, Switch/Delta, Amex, Eurocard, JCB, Solo

175 The Firs Bed and Breakfast ♦♦♦♦♦

Selsley Road, North Woodchester, Stroud, Gloucestershire GL5 5NQ **Tel:** (01453) 873088 **Fax:** (01453) 873053
E-mail: cwalsh3088@aol.com

The Firs is located in a quiet Cotswold village where the famous Woodchester Pavement is buried. A fine Georgian house with many period features and panoramic views of the Cotswold escarpment. Within walking distance are several excellent pubs and restaurants. Ideally situated for Bath, the Cotswold Way, Woodchester Park and Mansion, Cheltenham, Westonbirt Arboretum, Gatcombe, Badminton, Cirencester, Gloucester Docks and Bristol. Both rooms are en-suite and individually decorated, with colour television and tea and coffee facilities. Laundry and cycle hire available.

Bed & Breakfast per night: single occupancy from £25.00–£30.00; double room from £44.00–£48.00

Bedrooms: 1 double, 1 triple
Bathrooms: 2 en-suite
Parking: 5 spaces

Entries are cross referenced by number to the maps on pages 68–69

176 Highlands ◆◆◆◆

Shortwood, Nailsworth, Stroud, Gloucestershire GL6 0SJ **Tel:** (01453) 832591 **Fax:** (01453) 833590

We welcome our guests all year to enjoy our comfortable, elegantly furnished home, situated on the edge of Nailsworth amidst open countryside, yet close to town centre. Guests can enjoy country walking and breathtaking views of Cotswold valleys. Sightsee around pretty Cotswold villages, enjoy a day out in Bath or Cheltenham (30 minutes' drive) and return, in the winter, to a large log fire in the lounge, or dine in one of the excellent local restaurants.

Bed & Breakfast per night: single occupancy from £18.50–£25.00; double room from £39.50–£45.00
Dinner, Bed & Breakfast per person, per night: £29.50–£32.50

Bedrooms: 2 double, 1 twin
Bathrooms: 2 en-suite, 1 private
Parking: 4 spaces

177 The Old Rectory ◆◆◆◆ Gold Award

Didmarton, Gloucestershire GL9 1DS **Tel:** (01454) 238233 **Fax:** (01454) 238909

Relax by the log fire or in the pretty, walled garden before walking to the village pub for dinner. Finally returning to a comfortable non-smoking bedroom in this Grade II listed former rectory. A good touring base, close to the M4/5 and halfway between Bath and Cirencester. Excellent walking country. We are five minutes from Westonbirt Arboretum and less than ten from Tetbury with its many antique shops. Parking is in the small courtyard at the rear.

Bed & Breakfast per night: single occupancy from £30.00–£35.00; double room from £40.00–£46.00

Bedrooms: 2 double, 1 twin
Bathrooms: 2 en-suite, 1 private
Parking: 4 spaces

178 Tavern House ◆◆◆◆◆ Gold Award

Willesley, Tetbury, Gloucestershire GL8 8QU **Tel:** (01666) 880444 **Fax:** (01666) 880254
Web: http://www.tavernhousehotel@ukbusiness.com

A delightfully situated 17th-century Grade II listed former staging-post, this elegant Cotswold-stone country house is only one mile from Westonbirt Arboretum which has one of Europe's largest collections of trees and shrubs. The four en-suite bedrooms have direct-dial telephone, television, hairdryer and much more. A charming secluded garden offers peace and tranquillity, far from the madding crowd. Convenient for Bath, Gloucester, Cheltenham and Stow. A country house atmosphere with attention to detail being our keynote. ETB 'England for Excellence' Silver Award, 1993.

Bed & Breakfast per night: single occupancy from £47.50–£57.50; double room from £63.00–£68.00

Bedrooms: 3 double, 1 twin
Bathrooms: 4 en-suite
Parking: 4 spaces
Cards accepted: Mastercard, Visa

At-a-glance symbols are explained on the flap inside the back cover

179 The Swan Hotel

★★★ Gold Award

Bibury, Cirencester, Gloucestershire GL7 5NW **Tel:** (01285) 740695 **Fax:** (01285) 740473
Web: http://www.swanhotel.co.uk **E-mail:** swanhot1@swanhotel-cotswolds.co.uk

A luxurious hotel with cosy parlours, elegant dining room, sumptuous bedrooms (a few with four-poster beds) and lavish bathrooms (some with large jacuzzi baths). Our head chef, Shaun Naen, presents a regularly changing menu in a modern European style which is occasionally influenced by oriental cuisine. An ideal base for touring the Cotswolds, visiting Shakespeare's Stratford, Roman Bath, antiques in Burford and the Oxford colleges. Take pleasure in our private garden on the banks of the River Coln – enjoy the ambience or fish for your own trout. Licensed for weddings. Ideal venue for special occasions.

Bed & Breakfast per night: single occupancy from £99.00–£125.00; double room from £165.00–£250.00
Dinner, Bed & Breakfast per person, per night: £97.50–£142.50 (min 2 nights)
Lunch available: 1200–1430

Evening meal: 1930 (last orders 2130)
Bedrooms: 13 double, 4 twin, 1 family
Bathrooms: 18 en-suite **Parking:** 20 spaces
Cards accepted: Mastercard, Visa, Switch/Delta, Amex, Diners, Eurocard, JCB, Visa Electron, Solo

Westonbirt Arboretum

When Captain Robert Holford planted his first tree on his father's land in 1829 he did so, in part, for posterity, knowing he could never live to see the mature fulfilment of his botanical vision. The eldest son of the owner of the wealthy Westonbirt estate on the edge of the Cotswolds, Holford was just 21 when he began the outstanding collection of tree specimens which now forms Westonbirt Arboretum. Today, almost 170 years later, visitors may view the spectacular culmination of his life's work.

Holford was primarily a plantsman. His aim was to collect as many species as possible, nurturing them in a climate and ecosystem which was, in many cases, very different from that of their country of origin. Today some 4,000 species flourish here, with exotic specimens at every turn: the Chilean fire-bush, the tulip tree, the corkscrew hazel, the handkerchief tree...

Holford aimed not only to grow a wide range of species, but also to create a landscape of great beauty, designed to provide colour and interest throughout the year. In what is now the main arboretum, he began planting a series of rides and glades laid out to create ever-changing vistas. Here, sheltered by especially planted belts of evergreens, azaleas, camellias and rhododendrons flourish, a mass of vivid colour in spring. Summer is the best time to appreciate the 'colour circle' designed by Holford as a congenial picnic spot, while autumn sets the trees on fire, especially acers and maples.

Later, with the help of his son, George, who inherited his father's passion, Holford cut further drives and avenues through nearby Silk Wood. Here he devoted space to collections of oak, beech, ash and lime, creating an opportunity to see familiar native species side by side with more exotic foreign cousins. The giant evergreen conifers – pines, spruces, sequoias, cedars and cypresses – are particularly impressive in winter, especially when covered in snow.

In total the arboretum covers 600 acres (242.5 hectares) of woodland with 17 miles (27.2km) of paths and 18,000 listed specimens of plants. To view it in its entirety is an impossible challenge, but by its nature it rewards many visits throughout the year (tel: 01666 880220).

Entries are cross referenced by number to the maps on pages 68–69

180 Lansdowne House ◆◆◆◆

Lansdowne, Bourton-on-the-Water, Cheltenham, Gloucestershire GL54 2AT **Tel:** (01451) 820812 **Fax:** (01451) 822484
Web: http://www.smoothhound.co.uk/hotels/lansdn1.html **E-mail:** lansdowne-house@ukf.net

A traditionally-built period Cotswold stone family house, a few minutes' walk from the centre of the village. The tastefully furnished en-suite rooms have colour television, tea/coffee tray and central heating. We offer comfort with a combination of old and antique furnishings. A delicious, freshly cooked, full English breakfast is served each morning, and our wide selection of tourist information and guide books are available for guests' use. Go on, spoil yourself!

Bed & Breakfast per night: single occupancy from £30.00–£35.00; double room from £35.00–£40.00

Bedrooms: 2 double, 1 triple
Bathrooms: 3 en-suite
Parking: 4 spaces

181 Coombe House ◆◆◆◆

Rissington Road, Bourton-on-the-Water, Gloucestershire GL54 2DT **Tel:** (01451) 821966 or (01451) 822367 **Fax:** (01451) 810477
Web: http://www.smoouthound.co.uk/hotels/coombeho.html

Quietly located just a riverside walk from the centre of this beautiful Cotswold village, Coombe House offers a haven of tranquillity, comfort and personal attention from your hosts, Chris and Stephie. The charming bedrooms, reception rooms and lovely gardens with unusual plants will delight you. A perfect central base from which to explore the Cotswolds' famous gardens, historic houses, castles and glorious villages. We are totally non-smoking. Private parking to the rear of the house.

Bed & Breakfast per night: single occupancy from £55.00–£65.00; double room from £65.00–£75.00

Bedrooms: 4 double, 2 twin
Bathrooms: 6 en-suite
Parking: 6 spaces
Open: April–October
Cards accepted: Mastercard, Visa, Switch/Delta, Diners, Eurocard

182 Farncombe ◆◆◆◆

Clapton, Bourton-on-the-Water, Cheltenham, Gloucestershire GL54 2LG **Tel:** (01451) 820120 or 07714 703142 **Fax:** (01451) 820120

Farncombe provides peace and tranquillity, with superb views of the Windrush Valley, in Clapton-on-the-Hill, 2.5 miles from Bourton-on-the-Water, in the centre of the Cotswolds. A comfortable, non-smoking, family Cotswold home set in large gardens. Two double rooms with showers and basins, and one en-suite twin room, each with hairdryer and radio. Large dining room with tea/coffee making facilities. Television lounge.

Bed & Breakfast per night: double room from £39.00–£43.00

Bedrooms: 2 double, 1 twin
Bathrooms: 1 en-suite, 2 rooms with private shower
Parking: 3 spaces

At-a-glance symbols are explained on the flap inside the back cover

183 Kings Head Inn and Restaurant ◆◆◆◆

The Green, Bledington, Oxford, Gloucestershire OX7 6XQ **Tel:** (01608) 658365 **Fax:** (01608) 658902
Web: http://www.btinternet.com/~kingshead **E-mail:** kingshead@btinternet.com

History comes hot buttered at this quintessential 15th-century Cotswold inn which nestles on the village green, complete with brook and attendant ducks. The inn has always served as a hostelry and indeed Prince Rupert of the Rhine supposedly lodged here prior to the battle of Stow in 1642. To this day much of the medieval character remains with exposed stone walls, an inglenook fireplace, settles and pews. Delightful bedrooms complement with full facilities and thoughtful extras. Our award-winning restaurant offers bar fayre, table d'hôte and à la carte. Excellent value and ideal for exploring many attractions – Blenheim, Warwick, Stratford, Oxford etc.

Bed & Breakfast per night: single occupancy £45.00; double room from £65.00–£90.00
Evening meal: 1900 (last orders 2200)

Bedrooms: 10 double, 2 twin
Bathrooms: 12 en-suite
Parking: 60 spaces
Cards accepted: Mastercard, Visa, Switch/Delta, Eurocard

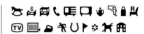

184 Number Nine ◆◆◆◆ Silver Award

9 Park Street, Stow-on-the-Wold, Cheltenham, Gloucestershire GL54 1AQ **Tel:** (01451) 870333 **Fax:** (01451) 870445

We will be delighted to welcome you to our elegant 17th-century Cotswold stone house situated in the centre of the charming town of Stow-on-the-Wold. The three spacious and luxurious en-suite bedrooms are tastefully furnished with every facility for your comfort and are non-smoking. Excellent breakfasts using fresh local produce with home-made preserves and speciality breads are served in our attractive dining room. The beamed guest lounge area has open log fires in winter.

Bed & Breakfast per night: single occupancy from £35.00–£40.00; double room from £50.00–£55.00

Bedrooms: 2 double, 1 twin
Bathrooms: 3 en-suite
Cards accepted: Mastercard, Visa, Switch/Delta, Amex, Eurocard

185 Aston House ◆◆◆◆

Broadwell, Moreton-in-Marsh, Gloucestershire GL56 0TJ **Tel:** (01451) 830475
Web: http://www.netcomuk.co.uk/~nmfa/aston_house.html **E-mail:** fja@netcomuk.co.uk

Guests, and children over ten years, are welcomed to our home in this quiet village, just 1.5 miles from Stow-on-the-Wold and central for touring the Cotswold villages and surrounding towns. All rooms (one on the ground floor) are comfortably furnished and have tea/coffee making facilities, radio, colour television, armchairs and electric blankets for those colder nights. Bedtime drinks and biscuits are provided. Good English breakfast. No smoking. Pub within walking distance.

Bed & Breakfast per night: double room from £43.00–£46.00

Bedrooms: 2 double, 1 twin
Bathrooms: 2 en-suite, 1 private
Parking: 3 spaces
Open: All year except January and December

Entries are cross referenced by number to the maps on pages 68–69

186 Grapevine Hotel

★★★ Silver Award

Sheep Street, Stow-on-the-Wold, Gloucestershire GL54 1AU **Tel:** (01451) 830344 **Fax:** (01451) 832278
Web: http://www.vines.co.uk **E-mail:** enquiries@vines.co.uk

An historic 17th-century award-winning hotel in the antiques centre of the Cotswolds. The Grapevine has a country house feel, with each bedroom individually designed and furnished with antiques; rich warm fabrics complement the mellowed Cotswold stone. The romantic conservatory is home to the historic Hamburg vine, which canopies the restaurant and gives the hotel its name. Consistent, fine cuisine and excellent service have earned the hotel its AA 2 Rosettes for the fourth consecutive year.

Bed & Breakfast per night: single occupancy from £82.00–£102.00; double room from £127.00–£147.00
Dinner, Bed & Breakfast per person, per night: £75.50–£95.50
Lunch available: 1200–1400

Evening meal: 1900 (last orders 2130)
Bedrooms: 1 single, 7 double, 12 twin, 2 triple
Bathrooms: 22 en-suite
Parking: 23 spaces
Cards accepted: Mastercard, Visa, Amex, Diners, JCB

187 Guiting Guesthouse

◆◆◆◆◆ Gold Award

Post Office Lane, Guiting Power, Cheltenham, Gloucestershire GL54 5TZ **Tel:** (01451) 850470 **Fax:** (01451) 850034
Web: http://www.freespace.virgin.net/guiting.guest_house/ **E-mail:** guiting.guest_house@virgin.net

The house is a delightful and carefully-restored 16th-century Cotswold stone farmhouse. Everywhere there are exposed beams, inglenook fireplaces, open fires and polished solid elm floors from the Wychwood forest. Three rooms have four-poster beds and are en-suite, whilst the other room has totally private facilities. Television and generously-filled hospitality tray in each room. Access to the guesthouse is available at all times. Delicious evening meals, served by candle light, are prepared and presented by the hosts (with the exception of Sunday and Monday).

Bed & Breakfast per night: single occupancy £35.00; double room from £56.00–£60.00
Dinner, Bed & Breakfast per person, per night: £45.00
Evening meal: 1845 (last orders 1845)

Bedrooms: 3 double, 1 twin
Bathrooms: 3 en-suite, 1 private
Parking: 4 spaces
Cards accepted: Mastercard, Visa, Switch/Delta, JCB

188 Isbourne Manor House

◆◆◆◆◆ Gold Award

Castle Street, Winchcombe, Cheltenham, Gloucestershire GL54 5JA **Tel:** (01242) 602281 **Fax:** (01242) 602281

This beautiful listed house is quietly situated within attractive gardens which are bordered by the River Isbourne. We are adjacent to the lovely grounds of Sudeley Castle and only two minutes' walk away from both stunning Cotswold countryside and the centre of historic Winchcombe. All rooms are decorated and furnished to the highest standard, combining modern comfort with family antiques and beautiful fabrics. Guests have the sole use of two elegant reception rooms, private parking and garden.

Bed & Breakfast per night: single occupancy from £40.00–£60.00; double room from £50.00–£70.00

Bedrooms: 2 double, 1 twin
Bathrooms: 2 en-suite, 1 private
Parking: 4 spaces

189 Sudeley Hill Farm

◆◆◆◆

Winchcombe, Cheltenham, Gloucestershire GL54 5JB **Tel:** (01242) 602344 **Fax:** (01242) 602344

A friendly welcome awaits you on our 800-acre sheep and arable farm. The 15th-century listed farmhouse is situated above Sudeley Castle, with a large garden and panoramic views across the valley. A comfortable lounge, log fires, separate dining room, no smoking en-suite bedrooms with television and facilities for hot drinks. Central for exploring the Cotswolds. Good pub food in Winchcombe, half a mile away.

Bed & Breakfast per night: single occupancy from £30.00–£34.00; double room from £48.00–£50.00

Bedrooms: 1 double, 2 triple
Bathrooms: 3 en-suite
Parking: 10 spaces

190 Wings Cottage

◆◆◆◆ Gold Award

Wing Lane, Kemerton, Tewkesbury, Gloucestershire GL20 7JG **Tel:** (01386) 725273 **Fax:** (01386) 725273
Web: http://www.wingscottage.demon.co.uk/index.html **E-mail:** jway@wingscottage.demon.co.uk

Wings Cottage offers the peace and tranquillity of a bygone age. Restoration work has revealed the beautiful beams and old Cotswold stonework which have been hidden for many years. Enjoy our garden, open under the National Garden Scheme in August. Explore the ancient market town of Tewkesbury or visit the Cotswold Hills and towns nearby. We offer old fashioned courtesy and modern comfort to our guests and many return time after time as welcome friends.

Bed & Breakfast per night: double room from £48.00–£52.00
Evening meal: 1900

Bedrooms: 1 double, 1 twin
Bathrooms: 1 en-suite, 1 private
Parking: 4 spaces
Open: All year except January and December

191 The Lygon Arms

★★★★ Gold Award

Broadway, Worcestershire WR12 7DU **Tel:** (01386) 852255 **Fax:** (01386) 854470
Web: http://www.savoy-group.co.uk **E-mail:** info@the-lygon-arms.co.uk

The 16th-century Lygon Arms is the centrepiece of Broadway, one of the Cotswolds' prettiest villages. Recently restored rooms and suites are furnished in country house style. The historic Great Hall combines the best traditional British foods with innovative modern cooking, whilst Oliver's Brasserie and the Patio Restaurant specialise in lighter fare. The adjoining Country Club boasts a magnificent galleried pool, and provides health and beauty treatments. The Inn provides the perfect base to explore the surrounding countryside.

Bed & Breakfast per night: single room from £135.13–£173.90; double room from £209.15–£264.38
Dinner, Bed & Breakfast per person, per night: £139.83
Lunch available: 1230–1400

Evening meal: 1930 (last orders 2115)
Bedrooms: 2 single, 48 double, 9 twin, 6 triple
Bathrooms: 65 en-suite
Parking: 153 spaces
Cards accepted: Mastercard, Visa, Switch/Delta, Amex, Diners, Eurocard, JCB

Entries are cross referenced by number to the maps on pages 68–69

192 Dormy House

★★★ Silver Award

Willersey Hill, Broadway, Worcestershire WR12 7LF **Tel:** (01386) 852711 **Fax:** (01386) 858636
E-mail: reservations@dormyhouse.co.uk

The 17th-century Dormy House is ideally located for visiting the picturesque villages of the Cotswolds as well as Shakespeare's Stratford-upon-Avon. Enjoy the beautifully appointed rooms, superb restaurant and high standard of cuisine and service. Our croquet lawn, putting green, sauna/steam room, gym, games room and nature trail offer the chance to combine leisure with pleasure. Pamper yourself with a Champagne Weekend or a carefree midweek break in the Heart of England.

Bed & Breakfast per night: single occupancy from £73.00–£97.00; double room from £146.00–£174.00
Dinner, Bed & Breakfast per person, per night: £100.00–£122.00
Lunch available: 1230–1400 (except Saturday)

Evening meal: 1900 (last orders 2130)
Bedrooms: 3 single, 18 double, 26 twin, 1 family
Bathrooms: 48 en-suite **Parking:** 90 spaces
Cards accepted: Mastercard, Visa, Switch/Delta, Amex, Diners, Eurocard

193 Whiteacres Guesthouse

◆◆◆◆

Station Road, Broadway, Worcestershire WR12 7DE **Tel:** (01386) 852320
E-mail: whiteacres@btinternet.com

Whiteacres is just a short walk from the centre of Broadway village. This beautiful Edwardian property offers five en-suite bedrooms, two with four-poster beds, all with colour television, tea/coffee making facilities, hair dryers and many thoughtful extras. There is a guests' lounge, an attractive dining room and ample car parking space. The house is decorated to a high standard and our aim is to provide a comfortable, happy base for a perfect holiday.

Bed & Breakfast per night: single occupancy from £40.00–£45.00; double room from £50.00–£54.00

Bedrooms: 4 double, 1 twin
Bathrooms: 5 en-suite
Parking: 6 spaces

194 The Mill at Harvington

★★★ Silver Award

Anchor Lane, Harvington, Evesham, Worcestershire WR11 5NR **Tel:** (01386) 870688 **Fax:** (01386) 870688

Friendly, owner-run hotel, sensitively converted from a beautiful Georgian house and former baking mill. Situated on the banks of the River Avon in acres of private parkland, our hotel offers peace, tranquillity and a view over the garden and river towards the morning sun from every bedroom. Find gentle elegance without formality, good food without fussiness (AA 2 Rosettes), and friendly staff who will help you relax immediately.

Bed & Breakfast per night: single occupancy from £63.00–£79.00; double room from £86.00–£119.00
Dinner, Bed & Breakfast per person, per night: £49.50–£60.50 (min 2 nights)
Lunch available: 1145–1345

Evening meal: 1900 (last orders 2045)
Bedrooms: 16 double, 5 twin
Bathrooms: 21 en-suite **Parking:** 45 spaces
Cards accepted: Mastercard, Visa, Switch/Delta, Amex, Diners, JCB, Maestro, Visa Electron, Solo

At-a-glance symbols are explained on the flap inside the back cover

195 Lowerfield Farm ◆◆◆◆

Willersey, Broadway, Worcestershire WR11 5HF **Tel:** (01386) 858273 or 07703 343996 **Fax:** (01386) 854608
Web: http://www.lowerfield-farm.co.uk **E-mail:** info@lowerfield-farm.co.uk

Genuine farmhouse comfort and hospitality on a mixed sheep and cereal farm where ewes and lambs, working sheep dogs, horses and ponies all form part of the scene. This late 17th-century Cotswold stone farmhouse has delightful accommodation, all en-suite with panoramic views over hills. A peaceful location providing an ideal base to explore the Cotswolds, Hidcote Gardens, Stratford-upon-Avon and beyond. A wealth of good eating houses nearby or evening meals by arrangement. Colour brochure available.

Bed & Breakfast per night: double room from £45.00–£55.00
Dinner, Bed & Breakfast per person, per night: £35.00–£40.00
Evening meal: 1900

Bedrooms: 2 double, 1 twin
Bathrooms: 3 en-suite
Parking: 6 spaces

196 M'Dina Courtyard ◆◆◆◆ Silver Award

Park Road, Chipping Campden, Gloucestershire GL55 6EA **Tel:** (01386) 841752 **Fax:** (01386) 840942
E-mail: chilver@globalnet.co.uk

Charming Cotswold stone house in an idyllic courtyard setting incorporating a 200-year-old cottage and apartment. Conveniently located at the quieter end of Chipping Campden's historic high street. All rooms are en-suite and thoughtfully equipped to a very high standard. An extensive breakfast menu, using local produce wherever possible, is served in the cosy dining room with its feature inglenook fireplace. Homely atmosphere for non-smokers. Reduction for stays over three nights.

Bed & Breakfast per night: double room from £48.00–£60.00

Bedrooms: 2 double, 1 triple
Bathrooms: 3 en-suite
Parking: 4 spaces

197 Sandalwood House ◆◆◆◆

Back-Ends, Chipping Campden, Gloucestershire GL55 6AU **Tel:** (01386) 840091 **Fax:** (01386) 840091

Peacefully located just five minutes' walk from the centre of the historic market town. Highly recommended quality accommodation for non-smokers. Large light and airy rooms containing everything for comfort and convenience with wash basins, shaving points, colour television, radios, hostess tray, private bathrooms. Cosy relaxing lounge. A perfect base for touring by car or foot, exploring the many interesting Cotswold villages. Convenient for Stratford-upon-Avon, the National Trust garden at Hidcote and Snowshill Manor.

Bed & Breakfast per night: single occupancy from £35.00–£38.00; double room from £46.00–£48.00

Bedrooms: 1 twin, 1 triple
Bathrooms: 2 private
Parking: 5 spaces

Entries are cross referenced by number to the maps on pages 68–69

198 Folly Farm Cottage

◆◆◆◆ Gold Award

Ilmington, Shipston-on-Stour, Warwickshire CV36 4LJ **Tel:** (01608) 682425 **Fax:** (01608) 682425
Web: http://www.follyfarm.co.uk **E-mail:** slowe@cwcom.net

A large country cottage in a delightful, undiscovered and quiet Cotswold village, with country pubs and pretty cottages. Within easy reach of Stratford-upon-Avon and Warwick. Offering outstanding B&B accommodation for that special occasion. Romantic en-suite double or four-poster rooms, with television, video, free video library and hospitality tray. As an added luxury, breakfast may be served in your room overlooking the pretty cottage gardens or in our new dining room. Luxury honeymoon apartment suite with double whirlpool bath also available.

Bed & Breakfast per night: double room
from £52.00–£78.00

Bedrooms: 3 double
Bathrooms: 3 en-suite
Parking: 8 spaces

---

199 The Grange

◆◆◆◆ Gold Award

Long Marston, Stratford-upon-Avon, Warwickshire CV37 8RH **Tel:** (01789) 721800 or 07785 577048 **Fax:** (01789) 721901
Web: http://www.stratford-upon-avon.co.uk/grange.htm **E-mail:** grangeline@bigfoot.com

The Grange is a beautiful, atmospheric home dating from 1590, in a peaceful rural location perfect for touring Shakespeare Country and the Cotswolds. Set in one acre of garden with large car parking area. We promise you a stay of total relaxation and pampering, with luxurious bedrooms and en-suite bathrooms, and every comfort from soft bathrobes to exquisite toiletries! The friendly service includes home-baked afternoon tea on arrival and a superb selection of cooked breakfasts.

Bed & Breakfast per night: single
occupancy from £35.00–£45.00; double room
from £44.00–£65.00

Bedrooms: 2 double, 1 twin
Bathrooms: 3 en-suite
Parking: 6 spaces
Cards accepted: Mastercard, Visa,
Switch/Delta

---

200 Loxley Farm

◆◆◆◆

Loxley, Warwick, Warwickshire CV35 9JN **Tel:** (01789) 840265 **Fax:** (01789) 840265

Picturesque thatched, half-timbered farmhouse and barn, surrounded by one and a half acres of garden and orchard, in a quiet village on the edge of the Cotswolds. Three and a half miles from Stratford-upon-Avon, seven miles from Warwick. Accommodation is in the recently restored single-storey barn, which has two private suites of rooms, one of which includes a small kitchen. Traditional English breakfasts are served in the farmhouse dining room. Mrs Horton is happy to book theatre tickets at no extra charge.

Bed & Breakfast per night: single
occupancy from £40.00–£45.00; double room
from £60.00–£65.00

Bedrooms: 2 double
Bathrooms: 2 en-suite
Parking: 10 spaces

At-a-glance symbols are explained on the flap inside the back cover

201 Glebe Farm

◆◆◆◆◆ Gold Award

Loxley, Warwick, Warwickshire CV35 9JW **Tel:** (01789) 842501 **Fax:** (01789) 842501
Web: http://www.glebefarmhouse.com **E-mail:** scorpiolimited@msn.com

Glebe Farm House is a fine country house set in 30 acres of Warwickshire countryside and yet only two miles from Stratford. Warwick Castle, England's finest, is only ten minutes away and the National Exhibition Centre 20 minutes. All rooms have four-poster beds and en-suite bathrooms and are richly decorated. Our menu fully reflects the quality of our home-produced organic ingredients. Mark and Kate look forward to welcoming you into this oasis of hospitality.

Bed & Breakfast per night: single occupancy from £69.50; double room from £85.00–£95.00
Dinner, Bed & Breakfast per person, per night: £67.50–£72.50
Evening meal: 1800 (last orders 2200)

Bedrooms: 3 double
Bathrooms: 3 en-suite
Parking: 12 spaces
Cards accepted: Mastercard, Visa, Switch/Delta, Amex

Packwood Yew Garden

There is something rather surreal about the famous Yew Garden at Packwood House. On the manicured green lawn, smooth and flat as a billiard table, immaculately clipped yew bushes stand to attention. Seen from a distance they are strangely people-like, resembling a gathering of hooded figures, poised waiting, listening, ready to hurry off about their business. It is no wonder that a human symbolism has been attributed to them; the arrangement of trees with its single large yew 'the Master' standing atop a mound, surrounded by a 'multitude' of others, is said to represent the 'Sermon on the Mount'. Further refinements to the scheme include four large trees near the 'Master' known as 'the Apostles', and a row of twelve on a raised terrace called 'the Evangelists'.

Whether the original designer of the garden intended such a scheme is unknown, for references to the 'Sermon on the Mount' idea do not appear in documents until the late 19th century, some 200 years after the first trees were planted. All that is known about the origins of the Yew Garden is that John Fetherston, who inherited Packwood in 1634, laid out at least part of it between 1650 and 1670, but it is possible that many of the trees were planted some time later.

It was probably John Fetherston's father, another John, who began the fine timber-framed mansion which still forms the core of the present house. Though less famous than the garden, this too is of considerable interest. During the course of the Fetherston family's ownership the original Tudor building underwent considerable alterations, in particular the addition of fine stables and outbuildings in the 1670s. Packwood left the Fetherston family in 1869 and was eventually bought by Alfred Ash, a wealthy industrialist, in 1905. Ash's son, Graham Baron Ash, lavished meticulous care on it, restoring it to match his vision of the perfect Tudor mansion. He was a punctiliously correct and obsessively tidy man who kept everything, including the gardens, in perfect order. The restoration of his house became his passion – until he tired of it and bought a moated castle in Sussex. Donating Packwood to the National Trust, he hoped it would be kept forever as he created it, and so it has been. It remains the kind of museum piece it always was in his lifetime, a perfect monument to the Tudor age. Packwood House (tel: 01564 783294) is 2 miles (3.2km) east of Hockley Heath on the A3400.

202 Sambourne Hall Farm ◆◆◆◆

Wike Lane, Sambourne, Redditch, Worcestershire B96 6NZ **Tel:** (01527) 852151

Beautiful 16th-century farmhouse set in 500 acres in picturesque village. Large comfortable bedrooms, own sitting room, walled garden. Coughton Court one mile, Ragley Hall five miles, Stratford-upon-Avon ten miles. Ideal for business or vacations. Easy access to NEC and Cotswolds. Good local pub in village.

Bed & Breakfast per night: single occupancy from £30.00–£35.00; double room from £45.00–£48.00

Bedrooms: 1 double, 1 family
Bathrooms: 1 en-suite, 1 private
Parking: 6 spaces

203 Payton Hotel ◆◆◆◆

6 John Street, Stratford-upon-Avon, Warwickshire CV37 6UB **Tel:** (01789) 266442 **Fax:** (01789) 294410
Web: http://www.payton.co.uk **E-mail:** info@payton.co.uk

Situated in the centre of Stratford-upon-Avon in a quiet exclusive location, yet only three minutes' walk to both the theatre and Shakespeare's birthplace. Experience the delights of a stay in this charming listed Georgian house where the caring proprietors – Peter and Brenda Wardle – will warmly welcome you. Tasteful, individually-furnished, cosy bedrooms include a king-size bed and a four-poster room. An excellent four-course breakfast is served until 1000 at weekends. Special dietary requirements are welcomed.

Bed & Breakfast per night: single occupancy from £32.00–£45.00; double room from £49.00–£68.00

Bedrooms: 3 double, 2 twin
Bathrooms: 4 en-suite, 1 room with private shower
Parking: 3 spaces
Cards accepted: Mastercard, Visa, Switch/Delta, Amex, Eurocard, JCB, Solo

204 Stratford Victoria ★★★★ Silver Award

Arden Street, Stratford-upon-Avon, Warwickshire CV37 6QQ **Tel:** (01789) 271000 **Fax:** (01789) 271001
E-mail: stratfordvictoria@compuserve.com

The Stratford Victoria provides all the facilities one would expect in a superior hotel. For special occasions the hotel has four-poster rooms and a luxurious suite. With ample free parking, the hotel is just a few minutes' walk to the town centre and its many attractions. All guests can enjoy free use of Stratford Leisure Centre during their stay or use our gymnasium and relax in our large whirlpool spa or our beauty salon.

Bed & Breakfast per night: single room from £87.50–£95.00; double room from £107.50–£127.50
Dinner, Bed & Breakfast per person, per night: £67.50 (min 2 nights)
Lunch available: 1200–1400

Evening meal: 1800 (last orders 2200)
Bedrooms: 10 single, 37 double, 2 twin, 9 triple, 42 family
Bathrooms: 100 en-suite **Parking:** 95 spaces
Cards accepted: Mastercard, Visa, Switch/Delta, Amex, Diners, Eurocard

At-a-glance symbols are explained on the flap inside the back cover

205 Northleigh House

♦♦♦♦ Silver Award

Five Ways Road, Hatton, Warwick, Warwickshire CV35 7HZ **Tel:** (01926) 484203 or 0374 101894 **Fax:** (01926) 484006
Web: http://www.northleigh.co.uk

A personal welcome, the individually-designed rooms with colour co-ordinated furnishings, en-suite bathrooms, television, fridge, kettle and many thoughtful extras make this the perfect hide-away in rural Warwickshire. A full English breakfast is freshly cooked to suit guests' individual tastes. Evening meals can be arranged, although there are excellent country pubs nearby, as well as the historic towns of Stratford-upon-Avon and Warwick, and the exhibition centres. Please call Sylvia Fenwick for brochures. No smoking.

Bed & Breakfast per night: single room from £35.00–£42.00; double room from £50.00–£60.00
Evening meal: by prior arrangement

Bedrooms: 1 single, 5 double, 1 twin
Bathrooms: 7 en-suite
Parking: 8 spaces
Open: All year except January and December
Cards accepted: Mastercard, Visa, Eurocard

206 High House

♦♦♦♦

Old Warwick Road, Rowington, Warwick, Warwickshire CV35 7AA **Tel:** (01926) 843270 **Fax:** (01926) 843689

Beautiful country house built in 1690, having antique four-poster beds, beamed rooms and open fireplaces. Home-produced bread, preserves, and eggs from genuine free-range hens – like everything else at High House, breakfasts are extra special. Perfectly positioned in a rural, secluded spot, ideal for visiting Warwick, Stratford, Birmingham's National Exhibition Centre, National Trust houses and NAC Royal Showground. Many country pubs serving excellent food, all within two miles.

Bed & Breakfast per night: single room £35.00; double room £60.00

Bedrooms: 1 single, 1 double, 1 twin
Bathrooms: 3 en-suite
Parking: 20 spaces

207 Nailcote Hall Hotel and Restaurant

★★★★ Silver Award

Nailcote Lane, Berkswell, West Midlands CV7 7DE **Tel:** (024) 7646 6174 **Fax:** (024) 7647 0720
Web: http://www.nailcotehall.co.uk **E-mail:** info@nailcotehall.co.uk

A charming Elizabethan country house hotel set in 15 acres of gardens and surrounded by countryside. Built in 1640, the house was used by Cromwell during the Civil War. Enjoy the relaxing atmosphere of the Piano Bar Lounge and the intimate Tudor Oak Room restaurant or the lively Mediterranean style of Rick's Garden Café and Bar with regular live entertainment. Leisure facilities include a championship 9-hole par 3s golf course which is host venue to the British Professional Short Course Championship each year, a superb indoor leisure complex with Roman-style swimming pool, gymnasium, steam room, solarium, and health and beauty salon.

Bed & Breakfast per night: single occupancy from £140.00; double room from £150.00
Lunch available: 1200–1400
Evening meal: 1900 (last orders 2130)

Bedrooms: 25 double, 13 twin
Bathrooms: 38 en-suite
Parking: 130 spaces
Cards accepted: Mastercard, Visa, Switch/Delta, Amex, Diners, JCB

208 Oak Tree Farm

◆◆◆◆◆ Gold Award

Hints Road, Hopwas, Tamworth, Staffordshire B78 3AA **Tel:** (01827) 56807 or 07836 387887 **Fax:** (01827) 56807

A country farmhouse with river frontage. Maintained to luxurious standards. Large, warm and welcoming bedrooms, all en-suite, with all comforts provided – sofas, courtesy tray, trouser press, hairdryer, iron, mineral water, etc. Set in the pretty village of Hopwas, between the River Tame and the Fazely Canal, Oak Tree Farm offers tranquil surroundings, but is very convenient for Tamworth, Lichfield, NEC and the airport.

Bed & Breakfast per night: single occupancy from £50.00; double room from £64.00

Bedrooms: 3 double, 1 twin, 2 triple
Bathrooms: 6 en-suite
Parking: 10 spaces
Cards accepted: Mastercard, Visa

209 The Golden Lion Inn of Easenhall

◆◆◆◆

Easenhall, Rugby, Warwickshire CV23 0JA **Tel:** (01788) 832265 **Fax:** (01788) 832878
Web: http://www.rugbytown.co.uk/goldlion.htm **E-mail:** james.austin@btinternet.com

Charm, character and friendly atmosphere combined with the luxury of modern-day comforts make this 16th-century inn an ideal venue for business or pleasure. A few minutes' drive from main motorway junctions, relax and enjoy the tranquillity of the countryside. Plenty of local interest and with easy access to many major towns and cities. Comfortable en-suite bedrooms, delicious fresh food, fine wine and ales served in the attractive oak-beamed restaurant and bar all ensure a practical and relaxing visit.

Bed & Breakfast per night: single room from £45.00; double room from £65.00
Evening meal: 1800 (last orders 2200)

Bedrooms: 2 single, 1 double, 1 twin
Bathrooms: 4 en-suite
Parking: 60 spaces
Cards accepted: Mastercard, Visa, Switch/Delta, Amex, Eurocard

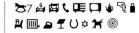

210 The Old Rectory

◆◆◆◆

Main Street, Harborough Magna, Rugby, Warwickshire CV23 0HS **Tel:** (01788) 833151 or 07803 054509 **Fax:** (01788) 833151
Web: http://www.rugbytown.co.uk/hotels/harborough/The_Old_Rectory.htm

Situated in a peaceful village in half an acre of walled garden, we offer a relaxed and friendly atmosphere with personal care and attention. There are spacious public areas and bright, tastefully furnished bedrooms with all modern amenities and views over the surrounding countryside. Good local pubs are close by, offering excellent food. We are conveniently placed for the M6, M1 and A14, the NEC at Birmingham, and we are an ideal centre for touring the Cotswolds and Shakespeare country.

Bed & Breakfast per night: single occupancy from £30.00–£35.00; double room from £50.00–£60.00

Bedrooms: 2 double, 1 twin
Bathrooms: 3 en-suite
Parking: 7 spaces

211 Chapter House ◆◆◆◆

High Street, Roade, Northampton, Northamptonshire NN7 2NW **Tel:** (01604) 862523 **Fax:** (01604) 864117

This magnificent 17th-century listed building is steeped in history and stands back from the High Street in its own grounds. Formerly a Baptist chapel where it is thought John Bunyan preached, now a beautiful property with one of the main features being the bedrooms which lead onto a galleried area overlooking the main hall. Within a few miles of Northampton, Silverstone, Stoke Bruerne (canal museum) and the M1. Walking distance from restaurant and two pubs.

Bed & Breakfast per night: single occupancy from £29.50–£45.00; double room £50.00

Bedrooms: 1 double, 2 twin
Bathrooms: 3 en-suite
Parking: 3 spaces
Cards accepted: Mastercard, Visa, Switch/Delta, Eurocard, JCB, Maestro

212 Lake Isle Hotel ★★ Silver Award

16 High Street East, Uppingham, Oakham, Leicestershire LE15 9PZ **Tel:** (01572) 822951 **Fax:** (01572) 822951

The personal touch we provide will make your stay extra special, starting with a decanter of sherry, home-made biscuits and fresh fruit in your room. Our AA 2 Rosette restaurant menus, changed weekly, offer fresh produce and a list of over 300 wines, with special 'Wine Dinners' held throughout the year. Whirlpool baths and cottage suites are available. The shops of this sleepy market town surround us, yet we are within a short drive of Rutland Water, Burghley House and many pretty villages.

Bed & Breakfast per night: single room from £45.00–£62.00; double room from £65.00–£85.00
Dinner, Bed & Breakfast per person, per night: £54.00–£60.00
Lunch available: 1230–1345

Evening meal: 1930 (last orders 2130)
Bedrooms: 1 single, 9 double, 2 twin
Bathrooms: 12 en-suite
Parking: 7 spaces
Cards accepted: Mastercard, Visa, Amex, Diners, Eurocard

213 Honeyholes ◆◆◆◆

South Farm, Hackthorn , Lincoln, Lincolnshire LN2 3PW **Tel:** (01673) 861868 or (01673) 861838 **Fax:** (01673) 861868

Step free from the stresses of life and enjoy the relaxing atmosphere of our Edwardian farmhouse. Stroll through the cottage-style gardens or unwind by a flickering open fire on cooler days. Rediscover the tastes of home cooking and baking, using local produce when possible. Centrally located for exploring Lincolnshire. Go racing at Market Rasen. Local golf, fishing and horse riding. Explore cathedral, castles and country houses, five minutes from county showground and Hemswell antique centre.

Bed & Breakfast per night: single occupancy from £20.00–£25.00; double room from £38.00–£44.00
Dinner, Bed & Breakfast per person, per night: £33.00–£39.00

Bedrooms: 2 double, 1 twin
Bathrooms: 1 en-suite, 1 public
Parking: 6 spaces

Entries are cross referenced by number to the maps on pages 68–69

214 Glebe Farm

♦♦♦♦

Benniworth, Market Rasen, Lincolnshire LN8 6JP **Tel:** (01507) 313231 **Fax:** (01507) 313231

Panoramic views of the unspoilt Lincolnshire Wolds, large en-suite rooms and superb home cooking are the hallmarks of 18th-century Glebe Farm at Benniworth, near Market Rasen. All rooms are furnished to the highest standards, including fresh fruit, biscuits and flowers. All you need bring with you is a good appetite. Sally and Ian Selby grow their own vegetables and make their own sausages. The eggs served at breakfast come from thier own free-range hens and the pork, beef, lamb and game they serve at dinner is all from neighbouring farms. Evening meal, by arrangement, from £12.50. The countryside really doesn't get any better than this!

Bed & Breakfast per night: single occupancy from £25.00–£30.00; double room from £46.00–£50.00
Evening meal: by prior arrangement

Bedrooms: 2 double, 1 twin
Bathrooms: 2 en-suite, 1 private
Parking: 8 spaces

215 D'isney Place Hotel

♦♦♦♦ Silver Award

Eastgate, Lincoln, Lincolnshire LN2 4AA **Tel:** (01522) 538881 **Fax:** (01522) 511321
Web: http://www.disney-place.freeserve.co.uk **E-mail:** info@disney-place.freeserve.co.uk

Conjure up a spacious and elegant townhouse a stone's throw from the cathedral, in the heart of historic Lincoln. Built in 1735 for John D'isney, the house was extended in the reign of Queen Victoria. Each bedroom is unique with every comfort including fresh milk on your tea tray. Waken to a freshly cooked breakfast served to your room on finest English bone china. D'isney Place rekindles the charm and elegance of a night away.

Bed & Breakfast per night: single room from £51.50–£61.50; double room from £63.00–£79.00

Bedrooms: 1 single, 11 double, 3 twin, 2 family
Bathrooms: 17 en-suite
Parking: 5 spaces
Cards accepted: Mastercard, Visa, Switch/Delta, Amex, Diners, Eurocard

216 Georgian House

♦♦♦♦

Station Road, Sutterton, Boston, Lincolnshire PE20 2JH **Tel:** (01205) 460048 **Fax:** (01205) 460048

Georgian House is a Grade II listed 17th-century house with a large Victorian-style conservatory overlooking a lovely landscaped garden. For cold winter evenings the lounge, with its inglenook fireplace, is available for guests. All rooms are en-suite and are furnished with antique furniture. We are situated next to the 12th-century village church and there are many things to see and do within a short drive of the village. Brochure on request.

Bed & Breakfast per night: single room from £23.00–£25.00; double room from £36.00–£40.00

Bedrooms: 1 single, 1 double, 1 triple
Bathrooms: 3 en-suite
Parking: 6 spaces

At-a-glance symbols are explained on the flap inside the back cover

217 Barnsdale Lodge Hotel

★★★ Silver Award

The Avenue, Exton, Oakham, Leicestershire LE15 8AH **Tel:** (01572) 724678 **Fax:** (01572) 724961

Set in the heart of Rutland's beautiful countryside overlooking Rutland Water, this 17th-century farmhouse welcomes you with luxury and warmth. Traditional English fayre, using fresh, locally-grown produce, is served in an Edwardian dining room. International wines complement the menus. Afternoon tea, elevenses and buttery lunches are available in the conservatory. Our 45 en-suite bedrooms are filled with antique furniture. The ideal retreat from everyday life. Come and discover the tranquillity of Rutland.

Bed & Breakfast per night: single room £65.00; double room from £89.00–£109.50
Dinner, Bed & Breakfast per person, per night: from £65.00 (min 2 nights to include Friday, Saturday or Sunday nights)
Lunch available: 1200–1415

Evening meal: 1900 (last orders 2145)
Bedrooms: 8 single, 27 double, 8 twin, 2 triple
Bathrooms: 45 en-suite
Parking: 220 spaces
Cards accepted: Mastercard, Visa, Switch/Delta, Amex, Diners, Eurocard

218 Abbey House and Coach House

◆◆◆◆

West End Road, Maxey, Peterborough PE6 9EJ **Tel:** (01778) 344642 or (01778) 347499 **Fax:** (01778) 342706
Web: http://www.abbeyhouse.co.uk **E-mail:** info@abbeyhouse.co.uk

Grade II listed building formerly owned by Peterborough Abbey in a quiet village close to historic Stamford and Rutland Water. There is an elegant dining room, a guest lounge with medieval features and, outside, spacious well-tended gardens. Accommodation is shared between the main house and coach house. Abbey House provides an ideal base from which to visit the stately homes, abbeys and cathedrals of the eastern shires and also for those interested in gardens, wildfowl, golf, aviation, history and Shakespeare. Telephone or fax for brochure.

Bed & Breakfast per night: single room from £30.00–£36.00; double room from £49.00–£59.00

Bedrooms: 1 single, 5 double, 3 twin, 1 family
Bathrooms: 10 en-suite
Parking: 12 spaces

219 Pipwell Manor

◆◆◆◆

Washway Road, Saracens Head, Holbeach, Spalding, Lincolnshire PE12 8AL **Tel:** (01406) 423119 **Fax:** (01406) 423119

This handsome listed Georgian manor house, circa 1730, has many original features and is situated in a small village in the Lincolnshire Fens, in the midst of the flower-growing area. Guests are welcomed with afternoon tea in the comfortable sitting room, which has a log fire in winter. Traditional English breakfast is served in the elegant dining room and includes home-made preserves and home-produced fruit and eggs. Pipwell Manor is a lovely place to stay.

Bed & Breakfast per night: single room from £30.00; double room from £44.00

Bedrooms: 1 single, 2 double, 1 twin
Bathrooms: 2 en-suite, 2 private
Parking: 4 spaces

Entries are cross referenced by number to the maps on pages 68–69

220 Corfield House

◆◆◆◆ Silver Award

Sporle, Swaffham, Norfolk PE32 2EA **Tel:** (01760) 723636
E-mail: corfield.house@virgin.net

Corfield House is an attractive brick-built house standing in half an acre of lawned gardens in the peaceful village of Sporle near Swaffham, an ideal base for touring Norfolk. Some of the comfortable en-suite bedrooms (one ground floor) have fine views across open fields and all have television, clock radio and a fact-file on places to visit. Full English or continental breakfast prepared to order. No smoking throughout.

Bed & Breakfast per night: double room from £39.00–£47.00

Bedrooms: 2 double, 2 twin
Bathrooms: 4 en-suite
Parking: 5 spaces
Open: April–December
Cards accepted: Mastercard, Visa, Eurocard

221 Felbrigg Lodge

◆◆◆◆◆ Silver Award

Aylmerton, Norfolk NR11 8RA **Tel:** (01263) 837588 **Fax:** (01263) 838012
Web: http://www.felbrigglodge.co.uk **E-mail:** info@felbrigglodge.co.uk

Set in beautiful countryside two miles from the coast, Felbrigg Lodge is hidden in eight acres of spectacular woodland gardens. Time has stood still since Edwardian ladies came here in their carriages to take tea and play croquet. Great care has been taken to preserve this atmosphere with large comfortable en-suite rooms all luxuriously decorated and with every facility. This is a true haven of peace and tranquillity. A nature lover's paradise. Delicious candlelit dinners and copious breakfast. Indoor heated pool and gym.

Bed & Breakfast per night: single occupancy from £45.00–£65.00; double room from £60.00–£110.00
Dinner, Bed & Breakfast per person, per night: £54.50–£79.50 (min 2 sharing)

Evening meal: 1945 (last orders 1945)
Bedrooms: 2 double, 1 twin
Bathrooms: 3 en-suite
Parking: 8 spaces
Cards accepted: Mastercard, Visa

222 Mill Common House

◆◆◆◆

Mill Common Road, Ridlington, North Walsham, Norfolk NR28 9TY **Tel:** (01692) 650792 **Fax:** (01692) 651480
Web: http://www.broadland.com/millcommon **E-mail:** johnpugh@millcommon.freeserve.co.uk

English 'country house' bed and breakfast at its best with complete peace and comfort for short or longer breaks. Superb breakfasts of local produce are served in the large, elegant conservatory. This delightfully-furnished Georgian farmhouse with open log fires is set in a beautiful garden with paddocks. It is ideally located for the sandy beaches, wonderful golf courses, the many National Trust properties, open gardens, historic churches and of course the wildlife of Norfolk's Broads and reserves.

Bed & Breakfast per night: double room from £45.00–£56.00
Dinner, Bed & Breakfast per person, per night: £37.50–£46.00
Evening meal: 1900 (last orders 2100)

Bedrooms: 1 double, 1 twin
Bathrooms: 1 en-suite, 1 private
Parking: 4 spaces

223 Regency Guesthouse

The Street, Neatishead, Norwich, Norfolk NR12 8AD **Tel:** (01692) 630233 **Fax:** (01692) 630233

17th-century guest house in the centre of a picturesque and quiet Norfolk Broads village. Five bedrooms tastefully Laura Ashley decorated. Oak-panelled breakfast room. Two beamed-ceiling sitting rooms. Enclosed garden. With accent on personal service, the owners have built up a reputation over 20 years for very generous English breakfasts and happily cater for vegetarians/special diets. Two good eating hostelries within walking distance. Ideal base for touring East Anglia, bird watching, wildlife, rambling, cycling, fishing, boating. Ten miles from the medieval city of Norwich, six miles to the coast.

Bed & Breakfast per night: double room from £42.00–£48.00

Bedrooms: 2 double, 2 twin
Bathrooms: 3 en-suite, 2 public
Parking: 8 spaces
Cards accepted: Diners

Norfolk Lavender

The Romans used lavender daily. They used it as a healing agent and as an insect repellent, in massage oils and to scent their bath water. Indeed, the name of the genus to which all species of lavender belong, Lavandula, derives from the Latin word meaning 'for washing'. Whether the Romans brought lavender to England or whether it was already growing here is uncertain, but Roman soldiers settling here would certainly have planted it as part of their herbal first-aid kit. Similarly, lavender was grown for medicinal uses in medieval monastic gardens. The dried flowers were used in Tudor times to scent chests and closets and to keep bedbugs at bay. Its cleansing properties were particularly valued during the plague of 1665, when the street cries of lavender sellers were part of everyday urban life. Victorian women used lavender perfume lavishly to scent themselves, their linen and their clothes.

In Victorian days there were a number of famous lavender fields in the south of England but in the early years of this century the bushes were attacked by a deadly disease, shab, and very little has been grown since. However, Norfolk Lavender at

Heacham in Norfolk (tel: 01485 570384), which was planted in 1932, still grows seven varieties of lavender – five for distilling and two for drying. The fields are harvested – mechanically – from about mid-July, about one third of the crop being used as flowers for potpourris and sachets, two-thirds for distilling. The flowers for drying are packed loosely into sacks through which warm air is blown for several days. The flower heads are then removed from the stalks and sifted. The distilling process is an ancient one. Lavender's fragrance is contained in the oil stored in glands at the base of each floret and this oil is extracted by steam distillation. About 500lb (227kg) of flowers, stalks and all, are loaded into each still while one of the workers stands in it treading them down. Steam is then passed through the still and the mixture of steam and oil vapour passes to the condenser. The pure essential oil then collects in the separator and is drawn off, at the rate of about half a litre per still-load. The oil is matured for a year before being blended with other oils and fixatives.

Entries are cross referenced by number to the maps on pages 68–69

224 The Old Pump House ◆◆◆◆

Holman Road, Aylsham, Norwich, Norfolk NR11 6BY **Tel:** (01263) 733789 **Fax:** (01263) 733789

A warm, welcoming Georgian house which is full of character, The Old Pump House is ideally situated close to Norwich, the Norfolk Broads, the coast, nature reserves and stately homes (we are one mile from Blickling Hall). The tastefully decorated rooms are mainly en-suite and breakfasts, which are freshly cooked to order, are served in the elegant Red Room which overlooks a peaceful garden. There is adequate off-road parking, with good pubs and restaurants nearby.

Bed & Breakfast per night: single room £18.00; double room £46.00
Evening meal: by arrangement

Bedrooms: 1 single, 3 double, 2 twin
Bathrooms: 4 en-suite, 1 public
Parking: 6 spaces
Cards accepted: Mastercard, Visa, Eurocard

225 Westwood Barn ◆◆◆◆

Crabgate Lane South, Wood Dalling, Norwich, Norfolk NR11 6SW **Tel:** (01263) 584108

Westwood Barn is an exclusive 15th-century building converted to provide two double and one twin en-suite ground-floor bedrooms, including a four-poster bedroom. Magnificent rooms with original beams and countryside views. Idyllic rural location for discovering the charms and tranquillity of North Norfolk: two miles from the picturesque village of Heydon, with National Trust properties, Norwich, the coast and Broads within a twelve mile radius, and Sandringham an easy drive. A warm welcome to all.

Bed & Breakfast per night: single occupancy from £32.00–£35.00; double room from £46.00–£52.00

Bedrooms: 2 double, 1 twin
Bathrooms: 3 en-suite
Parking: 10 spaces

226 Witch Hazel ◆◆◆◆

Church Lane, Wicklewood, Wymondham, Norfolk NR18 9QH **Tel:** (01953) 602247 **Fax:** (01953) 602247

Peter and Eileen welcome you to Witch Hazel – a spacious detached house in a peaceful rural environment with mature gardens in which to relax. We offer good home cooking using fresh produce from our garden or purchased locally. Evening meals are available on request. Wicklewood is close to the historic market town of Wymondham and is within easy reach of Norwich, the Norfold Broads, the coast and Norfolk's many attractions. All rooms en-suite. Non-smoking throughout.

Bed & Breakfast per night: single occupancy max £26.00; double room max £42.00
Dinner, Bed & Breakfast per person, per night: £31.00–£33.50 (min 2 sharing)
Evening meal: 1800–2000

Bedrooms: 3 double
Bathrooms: 3 en-suite
Parking: 3 spaces

At-a-glance symbols are explained on the flap inside the back cover

227 The Old Vicarage

48 The Street, Brooke, Norwich, Norfolk NR15 1JU **Tel:** (01508) 558329

Situated in the award-winning village of Brooke in a peaceful and secluded situation with extensive gardens. Within seven miles of the centre of Norwich, on the B1332 Norwich–Bungay road, and within easy reach of the Suffolk heritage coast and Norfolk Broads. One large four-poster room with adjoining private bathroom and one twin bedroom with en-suite shower room. Private sitting room with television available for guests' use. We are a no smoking house. No children under 15 years.

Bed & Breakfast per night: single occupancy £21.00; double room £42.00
Dinner, Bed & Breakfast per person, per night: £35.00

Bedrooms: 1 double, 1 twin
Bathrooms: 1 en-suite, 1 private
Parking: 3 spaces

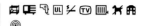

228 Holly Cottage

11 Mill Lane, Corton, Lowestoft, Suffolk NR32 5HZ **Tel:** (01502) 731224

Found down a quiet, quaint lane in Corton, a coastal village on the Norfolk/Suffolk border, Holly Cottage offers a lovely twin bedroom with dual aspects overlooking our delightful secluded garden. The spacious en-suite includes toilet, shower and twin washbasins. A delicious breakfast is served in a beamed dining room with french doors opening into the conservatory which guests are most welcome to use. The sea and two pubs are within short strolls. A warm, friendly welcome is assured.

Bed & Breakfast per night: single occupancy from £25.00; double room from £40.00

Bedrooms: 1 twin
Bathrooms: 1 en-suite

229 Earsham Park Farm

Harleston Road, Earsham, Bungay, Suffolk NR35 2AQ **Tel:** (01986) 892180 or 07798 728936 **Fax:** (01986) 892180

Park Farm has historic links with the 14th-century and the Duke of Norfolk. The beautiful Victorian farmhouse, set on a hill overlooking the Waveney Valley, is secluded with superb views. All the en-suite rooms are spacious, centrally heated, well-fitted and include television and beverage facilities. Enjoy the large gardens, farm walks and superb farmhouse breakfasts using our own and the best local produce. All your comforts will be cared for in this non-smoking home-from-home.

Bed & Breakfast per night: single occupancy from £30.00–£45.00; double room from £40.00–£65.00
Evening meal: 1800 (last orders 2000)

Bedrooms: 2 double, 1 twin
Bathrooms: 3 en-suite
Parking: 11 spaces
Cards accepted: Mastercard, Visa, Switch/Delta, Diners

Entries are cross referenced by number to the maps on pages 68–69

230 Poplar Hall

◆◆◆◆

Frostenden Corner, Frostenden, Wangford, Suffolk NR34 7JA **Tel:** (01502) 578549
Web: http://www.southwold.demon.co.uk/poplar-hall/index.html

An early 16th-century, thatched house set in lovely gardens and surrounded by gentle Suffolk countryside, yet only 3.5 miles from the delightful seaside town of Southwold. Poplar Hall offers luxury Bed & Breakfast in a beautifully furnished home with beams and inglenooks. Sumptuous breakfasts are served in a delightful dining room where guests enjoy fresh and local produce and home-made preserves, whilst watching the activity at the bird tables scattered around the garden. A haven of tranquillity.

Bed & Breakfast per night: single room from £20.00–£25.00; double room from £44.00–£52.00

Bedrooms: 1 single, 2 double
Bathrooms: 1 en-suite, 1 public
Parking: 8 spaces

231 Chippenhall Hall

◆◆◆◆◆ Silver Award

Fressingfield, Eye, Suffolk IP21 5TD **Tel:** (01379) 588180 or (01379) 586733 **Fax:** (01379) 586272
Web: http://www.chippenhall.co.uk **E-mail:** info@chippenhall.co.uk

A listed Tudor manor of Saxon origin, recorded in the Domesday Book, enjoying total rural seclusion in seven acres of gardens with ponds, and a heated outdoor pool set in a rose-covered courtyard. The manor is heavily beamed with inglenook log fireplaces. For that special anniversary with friends, arrange for pre-dinner drinks served in the bar and fine food and wines served by candle light. Located one mile south of Fressingfield, B1116.

Bed & Breakfast per night: single occupancy from £70.00–£76.00; double room from £72.00–£80.00
Dinner, Bed & Breakfast per person, per night: £63.00–£68.00
Lunch available: 1215–1400

Evening meal: 1930 (last bookings 1700)
Bedrooms: 4 double
Bathrooms: 4 en-suite
Parking: 12 spaces
Cards accepted: Mastercard, Visa, Eurocard

232 Rose Farm

◆◆◆◆

Middleton, Saxmundham, Suffolk IP17 3NG **Tel:** (01728) 648456 or 07885 194945

Situated 'just off the beaten track' on the edge of the pretty village of Middleton, halfway between Aldeburgh and Southwold, our two studios 'The Dairy' and 'The Stable' have been converted to offer spacious and superbly furnished en-suite bed and breakfast accommodation. Both are ground floor and each has its own private entrance off a garden courtyard. A hearty English breakfast is served in the charming farmhouse dining room and a very warm welcome is assured at Rose Farm. No smoking, pets or children.

Bed & Breakfast per night: single occupancy from £42.00–£55.00; double room from £52.00–£64.00

Bedrooms: 2 double/twin
Bathrooms: 2 en-suite
Parking: 6 spaces
Open: All year except November and December

At-a-glance symbols are explained on the flap inside the back cover

233 North Lodge

 Silver Award

6 North Entrance, Saxmundham, Suffolk IP17 1AY **Tel:** (01728) 603337

Explore Suffolk and its heritage coastline from the comfort of our beautifully renovated Grade II listed guest house. Providing six quality bedrooms (all en-suite), we can guarantee to make everyone feel special. Relax on the leather couches in our library. Unwind with a drink in our residents' lounge, with its grand piano and, in winter, open fire. Amble in our conservatory and walled garden. Enjoy the delights of good home cooking from our kitchen. Let us spoil you.

Bed & Breakfast per night: single occupancy from £32.50–£45.00; double room from £50.00–£70.00
Evening meal: 1900 (last orders 2000)

Bedrooms: 3 double, 2 twin, 1 family
Bathrooms: 6 en-suite
Parking: 6 spaces
Cards accepted: Mastercard, Visa, Switch/Delta, Eurocard

Brasses of East Anglia

East Anglia has a plethora of superb churches that house a wealth of medieval art. One branch of this is that of the monumental brass. Created to mark a grave and to glorify the dead person, brasses are now a lesson in medieval life. The inscriptions provide information on local families, the coats of arms give genealogical material, the depictions of the men, women and children are a source book for costume.

The earliest brasses date from the late 13th and early 14th centuries. In Isleham church in Cambridgeshire, for instance, Sir Geoffrey Bernard is dated to 1275 by the type of tailed surcoat he wears over his armour. Many soldiers are shown lying with a dog as a foot-rest – as at Trumpington, another Cambridgeshire church. This brass is in memory of Sir Roger Trumpington, who died in 1289, and here his dog bites the scabbard of his sword. Sir Roger was a Crusader – a fact indicated by his crossed legs. The most famous military brass in England, however, is that of Sir Robert de Bures in Acton, Suffolk, dated to 1302. He, too, was a Crusader and wears a splendid set of chainmail, with decorative knee-pieces of cuir-bouilli (boiled leather), pryck spurs and a surcoat whose folds are gathered with a waist-girdle.

Other brasses show husband and wife side by side, sometimes with rows of children too. John Daye, the printer, is commemorated in Little Bradley, Suffolk, with a wife, six sons and five daughters, plus two babies under the table. Weston Colville, Cambridgeshire has two good brasses: one to Sir Robert Leverer (1427), depicted in armour and surrounded by flowers, beside his wife in flowing head dress. In the same church, a brass in a much later style (1636) to Abraham Gates shows him with his wife at a prie-dieu and surrounded by cherubs, skulls and an angel with trumpet flying off to tell St Peter of his arrival. The earliest known brass of a priest in a cope is found in East Anglia, at Fulbourn, Cambridgeshire.

Since they are floor monuments, brasses have always been subjected to heavy wear and their conservation is now of great concern. The best places to take rubbings are brass-rubbing centres such as that in St Mary's Church, Bury St Edmunds (tel: 01284 706668), the Round Church, Cambridge (tel: 01223 871621), or Ely Cathedral (tel: 01353 667735), where replicas from all over Britain include the elegant Lady Margaret Peyton II of Isleham.

234 Mile Hill Barn

◆◆◆◆◆ Silver Award

Main Road, Kelsale, Saxmundham, Suffolk IP17 2RG **Tel:** (01728) 668519
Web: http://www.abreakwithtradition.co.uk **E-mail:** richard@milehillbarn.freeserve.co.uk

Welcome to our home in this superbly converted and characterful Suffolk oak barn. Three delightfully furnished ground floor en-suite rooms with colour television, beverage tray, own access and private parking. A choice of double, king-size and luxury super-king (or twin). Stroll in the grounds, relax in our enchanting walled garden or by the log fire in our beamed and vaulted lounge. Enjoy farmhouse-style Aga cooking using fresh local ingredients and home-made preserves for traditional breakfasts and candlelit dinners in our cosy dining room. Central for Minsmere, Snape, Aldeburgh and Southwold. A no smoking house.

Bed & Breakfast per night: double room from £55.00–£70.00
Dinner, Bed & Breakfast per person, per night: £43.50–£51.00
Evening meal: 1900 (last orders 1900)

Bedrooms: 3 double
Bathrooms: 3 en-suite
Parking: 12 spaces

---

235 Fieldway Bed & Breakfast

◆◆◆◆

Saxtead Road, Dennington, Framlingham, Woodbridge, Suffolk IP13 8AP **Tel:** (01728) 638456 **Fax:** (01728) 638456

Fieldway is located in the centre of the village overlooking the church and village green, just two miles from Framlingham Castle and close to the heritage coast. Stylish interiors, comfortable beds, lovely dining room with views over beautiful gardens. One double room with own conservatory, guests' sitting room.

Bed & Breakfast per night: single room £22.00; double room £40.00
Dinner, Bed & Breakfast per person, per night: £30.00
Evening meal: 1900 (last orders 2100)

Bedrooms: 1 single, 1 double, 1 twin
Bathrooms: 1 private, 1 public
Parking: 4 spaces

---

236 The Cretingham Bell

◆◆◆◆ Silver Award

The Street, Cretingham, Woodbridge, Suffolk IP13 7BJ **Tel:** (01728) 685419 **Fax:** (01728) 685419

The Cretingham Bell is an oak-beamed Tudor manor house situated in the quiet village of Cretingham. Ideal for the traveller who enjoys a stay in a tranquil setting. We offer mainly traditional home-cooked dishes which can be eaten in the non-smoking restaurant or bar areas. The Bell is ideally positioned for many of Suffolk's varied attractions. Virginia and Vic offer you a welcome as warm as our log fires.

Bed & Breakfast per night: single occupancy max £39.95; double room max £58.75
Lunch available: 1200–1400
Evening meal: 1900 (last orders 2100)

Bedrooms: 1 double, 1 twin
Bathrooms: 2 en-suite
Parking: 25 spaces
Cards accepted: Mastercard, Visa, Switch/Delta, Eurocard

237 The Old House ◆◆◆◆

Eyke, Woodbridge, Suffolk IP12 2QW **Tel:** (01394) 460213

Jan and Tony Warnock invite you to their lovely listed home, which dates from the 16th century. We have open fires, beams, a beautiful garden, and we overlook the Deben Valley on the edge of the heritage coast. Attractive forest and river walks are within easy reach. All rooms have central heating, en-suite facilities, sofas and easy chairs. We cater for all diets and offer a wide choice for breakfast. Evening meals by special arrangement.

Bed & Breakfast per night: single occupancy from £26.00–£30.00; double room from £42.00
Dinner, Bed & Breakfast per person, per night: £35.00–£44.00
Evening meal: 1800 (last bookings 1000)

Bedrooms: 2 double/twin, 1 twin
Bathrooms: 3 en-suite
Parking: 8 spaces

238 Seckford Hall Hotel ★★★ Silver Award

Woodbridge, Suffolk IP13 6NU **Tel:** (01394) 385678 **Fax:** (01394) 380610
Web: http://www.seckford.co.uk **E-mail:** reception@seckford.co.uk

A romantic Elizabethan mansion set in 32 acres of landscaped gardens and woodlands. Personally supervised by the owners, Seckford Hall is a haven of seclusion and tranquillity. Oak panelling, beamed ceilings, antique furniture, four-poster bedrooms, suites, leisure club with indoor pool, gym and spa bath and adjacent 18-hole golf course. Two restaurants featuring fresh lobster and game from local farms, extensive wine cellar. Picturesque Woodbridge with its tide mill, antique shops and yacht harbour is a short walk away. 'Constable Country' and Suffolk coast nearby.

Bed & Breakfast per night: single room from £79.00–£125.00; double room from £110.00–£165.00
Lunch available: 1200–1400
Evening meal: 1915 (last orders 2130)

Bedrooms: 3 single, 14 double, 10 twin, 1 triple, 4 family
Bathrooms: 32 en-suite
Parking: 102 spaces
Cards accepted: Mastercard, Visa, Switch/Delta, Amex, Diners, Eurocard, JCB

239 The Marlborough at Ipswich ★★★ Silver Award

Henley Road, Ipswich, Suffolk IP1 3SP **Tel:** (01473) 257677 **Fax:** (01473) 226927
E-mail: reception@themarlborough.co.uk

Privately owned by the Gough family for over 30 years, The Marlborough is a small hotel offering a friendly and relaxed atmosphere. Situated close to the beautiful Christchurch Park and just ten minutes' walk from the town centre. Our restaurant overlooks the floodlit garden and we are proud to boast AA 2 Rosettes for food. All bedrooms are en-suite and tastefully furnished. Ideal base for exploring Constable country and Suffolk's coastline.

Bed & Breakfast per night: single room from £59.00; double room from £84.00–£104.00
Dinner, Bed & Breakfast per person, per night: £59.50–£69.50
Lunch available: 1230–1400
Evening meal: 1930 (last orders 2130)

Bedrooms: 4 single, 13 double, 5 twin
Bathrooms: 22 en-suite
Parking: 60 spaces
Cards accepted: Mastercard, Visa, Switch/Delta, Amex, Diners

Entries are cross referenced by number to the maps on pages 68–69

240 Dairy House Farm

Bradfield Road, Wix, Manningtree, Essex CO11 2SR **Tel:** (01255) 870322 **Fax:** (01255) 870186

Set in the middle of our 700-acre arable and fruit farm, we are delighted to offer elegant, comfortable accommodation and friendly care to all our guests, with tea and home-made cakes in the sitting room upon arrival. A peaceful setting and relaxed atmosphere make Dairy House an ideal base for discovering Essex and the pretty villages of Suffolk – and we are only 15 minutes from Harwich, so a perfect stepping stone to the continent.

Bed & Breakfast per night: single occupancy from £25.00–£26.00; double room from £37.00–£40.00

Bedrooms: 1 double, 2 twin
Bathrooms: 2 en-suite, 1 private
Parking: 5 spaces

Audley End

At the Dissolution of the Monasteries in 1536 Henry VIII gave the Benedictine Abbey of Walden to Lord Audley, who built himself a distinguished house in the grounds. This passed to Lord Howard of Walden, who in 1603 was created 1st Earl of Suffolk. Rather than enlarge the existing building, the Earl (who later became Lord High Treasurer) decided to construct a house which befitted his elevated status. Indeed the plans were on such a vast scale that James I tellingly declared it 'too big for a king, but might do for the Lord Treasurer'. When completed, Audley End had two enormous courts, built around the ruins of the Benedictine Abbey, and was one of the largest houses in the land.

In the early 1720s, the 5th Earl, keen to leave his mark on the building, called in the services of the talented Sir John Vanbrugh, playwright, society figure and architect of both Castle Howard and Blenheim Palace. Vanbrugh recommended that the outer court should be demolished, and also substantially altered the rest of the house, although he ensured that the Jacobean flavour of the exterior, with its balustraded roof and many turrets, was retained.

After a short period of neglect, the strangely named Sir John Griffin Griffin was the next to shape the look of Audley End. Sir John commissioned Robert Adam who, like his predecessor, Sir John Vanbrugh, kept the 17th-century façade but added many 18th-century devices to the interior, where his additions include the magnificent state rooms. Outside,

Lancelot 'Capability' Brown set about turning the park into the 18th-century ideal of the picturesque, with a Palladian bridge-cum-summerhouse, Temple of Victory, and the Temple of Concord (1781), from where there is a particularly fine vista.

Other highlights include the Jacobean Hall (largely untouched by Vanbrugh and Adam), some superb plaster ceilings, a chapel in the 'Strawberry Hill gothick' (highly ornate) style and some contemporary furniture and paintings. Some idea of the size of the earlier buildings can be gauged from the fact that Audley End is roughly half the size of its early 17th-century incarnation. The house (tel: 01799 522399) and its estate village of Audley End are 1 mile (1.6km) west of Saffron Walden.

241 Weavers ◆◆◆◆

25 High Street, Hadleigh, Ipswich, Suffolk IP7 5AG **Tel:** (01473) 827247 or (01473) 823185 **Fax:** (01473) 822803
E-mail: cyndymiles@aol.com

Weavers restaurant offers the unbeatable combination of first-class à la carte dining, the mellow ambience of our 500-year-old building and top quality service. Winter log fires, antique furnishings and luxury guest rooms make Weavers the perfect place for a relaxing break. Situated in the centre of the unspoilt market town of Hadleigh, in the heart of Constable country, we pride ourselves on making Weavers a really special experience.

Bed & Breakfast per night: double room from £45.00–£65.00
Evening meal: 1900 (last orders 2230)

Bedrooms: 3 double
Bathrooms: 3 en-suite
Parking: 3 spaces
Cards accepted: Mastercard, Visa, Switch/Delta, Eurocard, Visa Electron, Solo

242 Edge Hall ◆◆◆◆

2 High Street, Hadleigh, Ipswich, Suffolk IP7 5AP **Tel:** (01473) 822458 **Fax:** (01473) 827751

Beautiful Georgian house offering luxurious accommodation. Spacious rooms stylishly furnished. Elegant 19th-century four-poster. Family-run home offering a very high standard with personal service. Excellent location to explore this unspoilt county. Well situated to visit Lavenham and Constable country or travel to the coastal towns of Aldeburgh and Southwold. Quiet river and hillside walks. Ample off-street parking. Budget accommodation available in 'The Lodge' adjacent to the formal walled garden. Pets welcome.

Bed & Breakfast per night: single room from £35.00–£45.00; double room from £50.00–£75.00
Dinner, Bed & Breakfast per person, per night: £46.00–£66.00
Evening meal: 1900 (last orders 2000)

Bedrooms: 1 single, 4 double, 1 twin, 2 triple
Bathrooms: 8 en-suite
Parking: 20 spaces

243 Red House Farm ◆◆◆◆

Station Road, Haughley, Stowmarket, Suffolk IP14 3QP **Tel:** (01449) 673323 **Fax:** (01449) 675413

A warm welcome and homely atmosphere await you at our attractive farmhouse which is situated just half a mile from the picturesque village of Haughly. The bedrooms are comfortably furnished and all have en-suite shower rooms. There is also a guest sitting room and separate dining room. Mid Suffolk is an ideal base for exploring East Anglia and there are excellent facilities in the area for horse riding, swimming, fishing, golfing, walking, cycling and bird watching.

Bed & Breakfast per night: single room £25.00; double room £40.00

Bedrooms: 2 single, 1 double, 1 twin
Bathrooms: 4 en-suite
Parking: 3 spaces
Open: All year except December

Entries are cross referenced by number to the maps on pages 68–69

244 Brook Farm

◆◆◆◆

Drinkstone Road, Beyton, Bury St Edmunds, Suffolk IP30 9AQ **Tel:** (01359) 270733

Relax in our 15th-century, Grade II listed farmhouse situated on the outskirts of the pretty village of Beyton, five miles from Bury St Edmunds. Ideally situated for exploring Suffolk and South Norfolk, with Cambridge only 30 miles away. Guests are welcome to use the hall sitting room with its oak beams and log burning stove and enjoy the attractive gardens which are surrounded by a moat, with fields beyond. Evening meals are by arrangement and we are happy to cater for vegetarians.

Bed & Breakfast per night: double room from £45.00–£55.00
Evening meal: by prior arrangement

Bedrooms: 1 double, 1 twin
Bathrooms: 1 en-suite, 1 private
Parking: 4 spaces

245 The Red House

◆◆◆◆

29 Bolton Street, Lavenham, Sudbury, Suffolk CO10 9RG **Tel:** (01787) 248074
Web: http://www.lavenham.co.uk/redhouse

The Red House is a Victorian double-fronted town house and a most comfortable and friendly home. Situated in the heart of Lavenham, just a stone's throw from the Guildhall and Market Square. The three en-suite double bedrooms are attractively furnished and have tea and coffee making facilities. There is a pretty guest sitting room and a sunny country garden to relax in. Candlelit dinners can be arranged by prior notice.

Bed & Breakfast per night: double room £45.00
Dinner, Bed & Breakfast per person, per night: £37.50–£40.00

Bedrooms: 2 double, 1 twin
Bathrooms: 3 en-suite
Parking: 6 spaces
Open: All year except January

246 Lavenham Priory

◆◆◆◆◆ Gold Award

Water Street, Lavenham, Sudbury, Suffolk CO10 9RW **Tel:** (01787) 247404 **Fax:** (01787) 248472
Web: http://www.btinternet.com/~lavpriory **E-mail:** tim.pitt@btinternet.com.

Winner of the East of England Tourist Board's Best B&B for 1999. Lavenham Priory, a Grade I listed house, provides guests with a truly unique and unforgettable experience. Bed chambers feature crown posts, Elizabethan wall paintings and oak floors, with four-poster, lit bateau and polonaise beds. Lavenham is often described as one of the finest medieval villages in England, with its historic buildings and streets. A relaxed family atmosphere, good humour and a memorable visit are Gilli and Tim's objectives.

Bed & Breakfast per night: single occupancy from £59.00–£69.00; double room from £78.00–£98.00

Bedrooms: 2 double, 1 twin
Bathrooms: 3 en-suite
Parking: 13 spaces
Cards accepted: Mastercard, Visa, Switch/Delta, JCB, Maestro, Visa Electron, Solo

At-a-glance symbols are explained on the flap inside the back cover

247 The Great House Restaurant and Hotel ◆◆◆◆

Market Place, Lavenham, Sudbury, Suffolk CO10 9QZ **Tel:** (01787) 247431 **Fax:** (01787) 248007
Web: http://www.greathouse.co.uk **E-mail:** greathouse@clara.co.uk

Ideally located on the Market Square of the beautiful medieval village of Lavenham, we are the perfect place for a relaxing get-away. Our spacious bedrooms offer the best comfort, with luxury bathrooms and sitting rooms or sitting areas. The creative French cuisine of our award-winning restaurant is complemented by excellent and friendly service from our professional staff. Choose from the daily menu or from the à la carte for that 'something special'. Special leisure breaks from Monday to Thursday.

Bed & Breakfast per night: single occupancy from £55.00–£65.00; double room from £70.00–£120.00
Dinner, Bed & Breakfast per person, per night: £49.95–£58.95 (min 3 nights)
Lunch available: 1200–1430

Evening meal: 1900 (last orders 2130)
Bedrooms: 3 double, 1 twin, 1 triple
Bathrooms: 5 en-suite
Parking: 10 spaces
Cards accepted: Mastercard, Visa, Switch/Delta, Amex, Eurocard, JCB

248 Island House ◆◆◆◆

Lower Road, Lavenham, Sudbury, Suffolk CO10 9QJ **Tel:** (01787) 248181
Web: http://www.dialspace.dial.pipex.com/town/way/xgk42 **E-mail:** islandhouse@dial.pipex.com

The Island House is situated in a superb position, close to the Market Place, yet nestling in beautiful open countryside. Guests have use of a private sitting room and a deck which overlooks the lovely gardens, through which Lavenham Brook flows. Breakfast is cooked carefully and healthily, giving an interesting choice of menu. We endeavour to create a warm and relaxing environment to ensure that our guests have a memorable stay with us.

Bed & Breakfast per night: double room from £50.00

Bedrooms: 1 double, 1 twin
Bathrooms: 1 private, 1 en-suite shower
Parking: 5 spaces

249 White Horse Inn ◆◆◆◆

Hollow Hill, Withersfield, Haverhill, Suffolk CB9 7SH **Tel:** (01440) 706081

Considered to be one of Suffolk's most beautiful country inns. The owners are proud of the high standards of hospitality and service which are complemented by a warm and friendly atmosphere. Comfortable en-suite accommodation is provided in a converted cart lodge. All rooms are traditionally furnished. Breakfast and dinner are served in the cosy dining room overlooking the garden. The well-stocked bar has oak beams and an open log fire. An ideal base for exploring Cambridge or Newmarket.

Bed & Breakfast per night: single room from £45.00; double room from £65.00–£75.00
Evening meal: 1900 (last orders 2100)

Bedrooms: 2 single, 1 double, 1 twin
Bathrooms: 4 en-suite
Parking: 44 spaces
Cards accepted: Mastercard, Visa, Switch/Delta, Amex, Diners, Eurocard, Visa Electron

Entries are cross referenced by number to the maps on pages 68–69

250 Yardley's ◆◆◆◆

Orchard Pightle, Hadstock, Cambridge CB1 6PQ **Tel:** (01223) 891822 **Fax:** (01223) 891822

Yardley's, with pretty garden and conservatory, offers a high standard of food and comfort. Situated in a quiet location in the picturesque village of Hadstock within easy reach of M11, Cambridge and Stansted. Well-equipped bedrooms benefit from en-suite facilities or exclusive use of shower/bathroom. Good local pubs and restaurants. Evening meals by arrangement. Gillian and John make that extra effort to ensure the success of your visit, whether for business or pleasure.

Bed & Breakfast per night: single occupancy from £25.00–£35.00; double room from £44.00–£48.00
Dinner, Bed & Breakfast per person, per night: £32.00–£36.00
Evening meal: 1830 (last orders 2000)

Bedrooms: 1 double, 2 twin
Bathrooms: 1 en-suite, 2 private
Parking: 6 spaces
Cards accepted: Mastercard, Visa

251 The Meadow House ◆◆◆◆

2A High Street, Burwell, Cambridge, Cambridgeshire CB5 0HB **Tel:** (01638) 741926 or (01638) 741354 **Fax:** (01638) 743424

The Meadow House, Burwell is an exceptional, modern property set in two acres of wooded grounds. King-size luxury beds, suite of rooms with balcony available. Large car park. No smoking. Close to Cambridge and Newmarket.

Bed & Breakfast per night: single occupancy from £25.00–£30.00; double room from £40.00–£45.00

Bedrooms: 3 double
Bathrooms: 2 en-suite, 1 private
Parking: 14 spaces

252 Cathedral House ◆◆◆◆ Silver Award

17 St Mary's Street, Ely, Cambridgeshire CB7 4ER **Tel:** (01353) 662124 **Fax:** (01353) 662124
Web: http://www.cathedralhouseco.uk **E-mail:** farndale@cathedralhouse.co.uk

A warm welcome awaits at Cathedral House, a characterful Grade II listed house in the centre of Ely, close to the magnificent cathedral and the city's main attractions. There are three suites for guests, each with its own luxury bathroom with a cast iron bath and heated towel rail. All the bedrooms are individually furnished and overlook the delightful walled garden, as does the dining room where guests take breakfast together around the family table.

Bed & Breakfast per night: single occupancy from £35.00–£45.00; double room from £50.00–£60.00

Bedrooms: 1 double, 1 twin, 1 family
Bathrooms: 3 en-suite
Parking: 4 spaces

253 Denmark House ◆◆◆◆

58 Denmark Road, Cottenham, Cambridge, Cambridgeshire CB4 8QS **Tel:** (01954) 251060 or (01954) 250448
E-mail: denmark.house@tesco.net

Denmark House is a detached 1920-style residence with many original features and tastefully decorated, set in peaceful, delightful gardens with seating. It is situated in a popular village six miles north of the university city of Cambridge, ten miles from Ely with its ancient cathedral, and Newmarket, the home of horseracing. Cottenham has excellent local amenities and easy access to major routes, making this an ideal location for touring the East of England.

Bed & Breakfast per night: single occupancy from £25.00–£30.00; double room from £38.00–£46.00

Bedrooms: 2 double, 1 twin
Bathrooms: 3 en-suite
Parking: 2 spaces

254 Wallis Farm ◆◆◆◆

98 Main Street, Hardwick, Cambridge, Cambridgeshire CB3 7QU **Tel:** (01954) 210347 **Fax:** (01954) 210988
E-mail: wallisfarm@mcmail.com

A warm welcome awaits you at our traditional Victorian farmhouse on our working farm in the picturesque village of Hardwick. We are seven miles from the university town of Cambridge and ideally situated for touring Cambridgeshire, Norfolk and Suffolk. All rooms are ground floor, en-suite, twin/double, with four in a recently-converted barn, furnished to a high standard. Large gardens and farmland which guests are welcome to use. All have colour television and tea/coffee making facilities.

Bed & Breakfast per night: single occupancy from £35.00–£40.00; double room from £45.00–£50.00

Bedrooms: 2 double, 2 twin, 1 triple
Bathrooms: 5 en-suite
Parking: 8 spaces

255 Prince of Wales ◆◆◆◆

Potton Road, Hilton, Huntingdon, Cambridgeshire PE18 9NG **Tel:** (01480) 830257 **Fax:** (01480) 830257

The Prince of Wales is a friendly traditional inn situated in the picturesque village of Hilton. Set in the heart of rural Cambridgeshire it is only a short drive from Cambridge, Peterborough and Huntingdon. Guests can relax in the comfortably-furnished lounge, the congenial atmosphere of which is enhanced by a blazing log fire on cold winter nights. In these pleasant surroundings you can also enjoy a freshly-prepared three course meal or a simple bar snack chosen from our comprehensive menu. We are particularly proud of our reputation for fine real ales – the inn has been listed in the CAMRA Good Beer Guide for many years.

Bed & Breakfast per night: single room from £40.00–£45.00; double room £60.00
Lunch available: 1200–1400 (not Monday)
Evening meal: 1900 (last orders 2115)

Bedrooms: 2 single, 1 double, 1 twin
Bathrooms: 4 en-suite
Parking: 9 spaces
Cards accepted: Mastercard, Visa, Switch/Delta, Amex, Eurocard, JCB, Maestro, Visa Electron, Solo

Entries are cross referenced by number to the maps on pages 68–69

256 North End Barns

 ◆◆◆◆ Silver Award

North End Farm, Risley Road, Bletsoe, Bedford, Bedfordshire MK44 1QT **Tel:** (01234) 781320 **Fax:** (01234) 781320

North End Barns is on a working arable and sheep farm. A superb barn conversion in quiet north Bedfordshire countryside providing en-suite rooms with television and tea and coffee making facilities. Breakfast is served in a 16th-century farmhouse. Tennis court available along with miles of country walks. We are just off the main A6, north of Bedford, near the village of Bletsoe. There are several excellent pubs and restaurants in the area and lots of places of interest.

Bed & Breakfast per night: single occupancy from £25.00–£30.00; double room from £45.00–£50.00

Bedrooms: 4 twin
Bathrooms: 4 en-suite
Parking: 8 spaces
Cards accepted: Mastercard, Visa, Switch/Delta, Amex, Diners, Eurocard, JCB, Maestro, Visa Elect

Hat Making in Luton

Luton Town Football Club has long been known as 'the Hatters', a name which reveals the town's importance as the centre of the English hat-making industry. The main reason for the Bedfordshire town's pre-eminent position is the quality of the surrounding soil, which allows wheat grown in nearby fields to reach a considerable height. The long stems (or straws), once plaited, were ideal for use in making straw hats. These, together with other straw goods such as corn dollies, were sold in the markets of 17th- and 18th-century Luton and Dunstable.

Special schools known as 'plait schools' appeared in the town as demand for the high-quality products increased. Plaited straws were also imported from the town of Livorno, on Italy's Tuscan coast. Indeed the Italian connection in the history of English hat-making is important, and the word 'millinery' comes from the placename Milan (even preserving the now lost pronunciation, 'Millen'). When the Napoleonic wars meant that Italian imports became scarce, the Luton hat-making industry took off.

Trade continued to grow throughout the 19th century, although cheaper plait

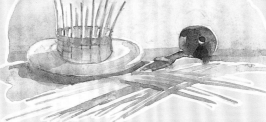

from the Far East was bought in from the 1870s onwards. The area of Luton known as Plaiters' Lea (now a conservation area) was where the hat factories, with their newly installed and adapted sewing machines, congregated. These were usually tall, narrow buildings, with each floor dedicated to a separate process, such as blocking (stretching the materials over metal moulds), machining, trimming, dyeing and so forth. Good examples of these factories can be seen in Bute and Guildford Streets.

The first half of this century saw continued prosperity in the hat trade, but in the 1960s the hat ceased to be an item of everyday wear and became instead an item of occasional wear. Nevertheless there are still almost 40 manufacturers in the town, and visitors can often view a working factory; check with the Tourist Information Centre (tel: 01582 401579) – itself housed in an old hat factory – for details. They also have leaflets about a millinery trail through Plaiters' Lea, while displays of past Luton-made hats (as well as occasional hat making demonstrations) can be seen at the Luton Museum and Art Gallery (tel: 01582 546722).

257 Highfield Farm

Great North Road, Sandy, Bedfordshire SG19 2AQ **Tel:** (01767) 682332 **Fax:** (01767) 692503

A tranquil and welcoming house with a warm and friendly atmosphere, set in its own grounds on an attractive arable farm, to which most guests return. Some rooms are on the ground floor and in delightfully converted stables. Highfield is set well back from the A1, giving quiet and peaceful seclusion, yet easily accessible and convenient for Cambridge, the RSPB, the Shuttleworth Aircraft Museum, London and much more. Ample safe parking. A no smoking house. Contact Mrs Margaret Codd.

Bed & Breakfast per night: single occupancy from £30.00–£45.00; double room from £50.00–£60.00

Bedrooms: 1 double, 3 twin, 1 triple, 1 family
Bathrooms: 4 en-suite, 1 private, 1 public
Parking: 14 spaces
Cards accepted: Mastercard, Visa, Switch/Delta, JCB, Solo

258 Tudor Cottage

Upwick Green, Albury, Ware, Hertfordshire SG11 2JX **Tel:** (01279) 771440 or 07770 898424

A delightfully spacious house of Tudor origin (Grade II listed) situated in a beautiful landscaped garden. Complete seclusion and stunning panoramic views. Ideally situated for London/Cambridge and Stansted Airport. Ten minutes from the airport and the M11, yet not under flight paths. Ample parking. All rooms are elegantly furnished to a high standard. Excellent breakfasts served in the dining room or on the terrace. Simply savour the peace, or use the house as a base for further exploration.

Bed & Breakfast per night: single room £33.00; double room £55.00

Bedrooms: 2 single, 1 double, 1 twin
Bathrooms: 1 en-suite, 3 private
Parking: 14 spaces

259 Marygreen Manor Hotel

★★★★ Silver Award

London Road, Brentwood, Essex CM14 4NR **Tel:** (01277) 225252 **Fax:** (01277) 262809
Web: http://www.marygreenmanor.co.uk **E-mail:** info@marygreenmanor.co.uk

16th-century timber-framed building, visited by King Henry VIII. Original Tudor bedrooms with four-poster beds (3). Garden rooms overlook olde-worlde garden. Restaurant with AA 2 Rosettes offers extensive à la carte or fixed price menus complemented by comprehensive award-winning wine list. Lunch served from 1230–1430, dinner served from 1915–2215. Two minutes from J28 on the M25. Motorway links to the Channel Tunnel, Stansted, Gatwick and Heathrow Airports.

Bed & Breakfast per night: single occupancy from £116.50–£139.00; double room from £137.50–£145.00
Lunch available: 1230–1430
Evening meal: 1915 (last orders 2215)

Bedrooms: 26 double, 17 twin
Bathrooms: 43 en-suite
Parking: 100 spaces
Cards accepted: Mastercard, Visa, Switch/Delta, Amex, Diners

Entries are cross referenced by number to the maps on pages 68–69

England's
West Country

HELEN·CLAIRE
BRIXHAM

► Hawker's Morwenstow

Morwenstow, near Bude, was the home of Robert Stephen Hawker, a remarkable 19th-century parson and poet who left his whimsical mark upon the village. The vicarage chimneys are built to resemble the various churches with which he had been connected, while a capital on the village church displays the message 'This is the house of God' carved upside-down – for a celestial readership! High on the cliffs near by is a tiny driftwood hut, now owned by the National Trust, where, often in a fug of opium, he composed much of his poetry.

► Lundy Island

Lundy is as remote an island as England has to offer and makes a magnificent day out from Ilfracombe and Bideford, both some 24 miles (38.5km) distant on the north Devon coast. The island, 3 miles (5km) long and never much more than half a mile (1km) wide, boasts some superb scenery, and there can be no better way of passing time here than strolling its gentle paths. The west coast is the highlight of the island: here Soay sheep and feral goats pick their way over stacks of granite tumbling hundreds of feet to the Atlantic while ravens wheel above.

An unrivalled coastline

The very pace of life seems to slow as you head west. The counties of Cornwall, Devon, Dorset, Somerset and Wiltshire somehow conduct their various businesses at a more civilised speed. Wiltshire alone is land-locked, so perhaps the sea's proximity has a relaxing effect. The magnificent coastline certainly draws people, but its huge length – the South-West Coastal Path, hugging the foreshore from Minehead to Poole, is 613 miles (986km) long – ensures that even on the sunniest of days, many beaches remain uncrowded. As always, those further from car parks are the quietest, but have fewest facilities. The well-known resorts, such as Torquay, Newquay and Ilfracombe, cater for all tastes and depths of pocket. Quieter havens to consider include Ladram Bay (near Sidmouth), Soar (a tiny bay south-west of Salcombe), Crinnis Beach (near St Austell), Pendower Beach (east of St Mawes), Portheras (west of St Ives), Lee Bay (near Ilfracombe) and St Audrie's Bay (just east of Watchet). Five minutes with a detailed map, especially of the superb southern coasts of Devon and Cornwall, will reveal countless other coves, bays and beaches, often with perfect sand.

Where the catch is landed

And if the weather is too cold for the beach, why not explore a Cornish or Devonian fishing village? These, as much a West Country speciality as Exmoor ponies or clotted cream, are one of the region's most engaging attractions. Some, such as Clovelly, on the northern coast of Devon, are justifiably famous. Tumbling in picturesque manner down the cliffs into the sea and with a main 'street' too steep and too narrow for cars, it nevertheless copes admirably with its visitors. Others – some popular, some little-known – to explore include Port Isaac (on the North Cornish coast and also without cars), Helford, Looe (both East and West), Gorran Haven, Gunwalloe, Porthcurno (all on the southern coast of Cornwall) and Beer (on Devon's southern shores).

Perfect bases for exploration

As the sumptuous fishing villages are mainly in the extreme south-west, so the historic towns and cities tend to be further east in Somerset, Dorset and Wiltshire. Here you can choose from the incomparable cities of Salisbury, Bath and Wells, each with a magnificent range of secular and ecclesiastical architecture. Sherborne, too, has a glorious abbey and many fine buildings dating from the 16th and 17th centuries, as well as two castles, one in ruins, the other home to a range of art treasures. Shaftesbury is the setting for one of England's best-loved views – the steep, cobbled Gold Hill was famously used for a bread commercial – but has other intriguing nooks and crannies. Marlborough's broad High Street is lined with substantial 18th-century houses, yet is only a mile from Savernake, England's largest privately owned forest, criss-crossed with footpaths. Ilchester dates from Roman times, but the town prospered in the medieval and Georgian periods; the houses round the green reveal the town's latter lineage. Looking further west, Salcombe, wonderfully situated on the Kingsbridge Estuary and enjoying the mildest of climates, became a resort in the 19th century. It has a gentle charm all its own, and is near Totnes, an appealing market town that has whole-heartedly embraced alternative culture. Just over the Tamar into Cornwall lies Launceston, a town of old-world character with two 16th-century bridges and a ruined medieval castle. Surrounded by unspoilt countryside, all make ideal bases for a long weekend's exploration.

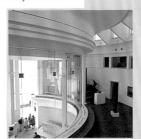

Pasties, scrumpy and Yarg

An important part of a weekend away is to indulge in local specialities. The West Country has its fair share, with few visitors able to resist the cream tea. Clotted cream, the essential ingredient, is widely available throughout the region. Cornwall has its pasty, now eaten the length and breadth of the land, but nowhere as good, so they say, as in its home. Somerset's many orchards have long produced cider and the earthier, more potent scrumpy. Many farms still produce – and a couple of museums at Dowlish Wake and Bradford-on-Tone celebrate – the heady brews. The name of Cheddar is synonymous with cheese, but there are many more beside, from Cornish Yarg to Somerset Brie. And throughout, sold in market, shop, pub and restaurant, are fresh fish of the finest quality. The West Country is a piscivore's paradise.

Getting away from it all

Few places in the West Country have an urban feel. Bristol and Plymouth are cities redolent of their maritime history yet remaining close to their rural hinterlands. Elsewhere, the predominant mood is of the country, and visitors are spoilt for choice when it comes to walking territory. The three moors – Bodmin, Exmoor and Dartmoor – are all wild enough to have challenging routes suitable for the experienced hiker only, but on their gentler fringes are endless, easier options that reveal some of England's most sublime countryside. The National Parks of Dartmoor and Exmoor have many suggestions for walks; outside these, areas particularly rewarding for exploration on foot include the Mendips in north Somerset, the Lizard in south-west Cornwall, the Marlborough Downs in north-east Wiltshire and the Quantock Hills just east of Exmoor. Thanks to the South-West Coastal Path, walking the coast is straightforward, though often strenuous. Other long-distance paths in the region include the Exe Valley Way (a 45-mile

▶ The Tate

At the end of the Second World War St Ives became home to an influential clan of artists. Following the death of the sculptress Barbara Hepworth in 1975, her studio was given to the Tate Gallery in London and is now open as a museum. The Tate slowly acquired other works by St Ives artists, but was unable to display them until the opening of the magnificent and airy former gasworks as a gallery in 1993. Overlooking Porthmeor beach, few arts venues can boast a closet specially designed for visitors to leave their surfboards...

▶ Wookey Hole

Since the 15th century visitors have come to peer into the dark caverns and subterranean passages of Wookey Hole, near Wells. Today, dramatic electric

lighting illuminates fantastic rock-formations and the glassy surface of an underground lake. There are a number of other attractions on offer too: paper-making demonstrations on the site of a 19th-century paper-mill; a collection of fairground art; a re-creation of Madame Tussaud's touring 'Cabinet of Curiosities'; and an exhibition of amusements from penny pier arcades. (Tel: 01749 672243.)

▶ Brunel's Bristol

The great engineer Isambard Kingdom Brunel was only 23 when he won a competition to design a bridge across the Avon Gorge at Bristol. This was the start of a long association with the city, one which produced its most famous landmarks. Brunel, chief engineer for the Great Western Railway, designed its splendid neo-Tudor station, Temple Meads, now a Grade I listed building. His great steam-ships SS *Great Western*, and SS *Great Britain* were built in Bristol: the latter, in the city docks, is now a museum (tel: 0117 926 0680).

▶ Chesil Beach

One of the stranger natural phenomena of the South Coast, Chesil Beach is a 16-mile (26km) strip of shingle running from the Dorset village of Abbotsbury to the Isle of Portland. Fashioned entirely by the sea to a height of some 30–40ft (9–12m), the bank forms a thin barrier between the Fleet, the largest lagoon in Britain, and the sea. Barely disturbed by mankind, the Fleet supports as many as 150 species of seaweed, as well as abundant fish and water-fowl. (Tel: 01305 760579.)

(72.5km) level route following the River Exe from Exmoor to its estuary), the West Devon Way, a shorter path that runs along Dartmoor's western edge from Plymouth to Okehampton, the Two Moors Way, a magnificent and demanding path extending over 100 miles (161km) and linking Dartmoor and Exmoor, the Liberty Trail, following the route taken by the Monmouth Rebellion through south Somerset and west Dorset, and The Saints Way, a 37-mile (59.5km) coast to coast route across Cornwall from Padstow to Fowey. Public transport links with many of these longer paths, allowing them to be walked in sections; most also have shorter, circular routes using part of their length. For the walker keen to get away from motor traffic, there is an alternative suggestion. The island of Lundy has a pub, church and shop but not a single road within 12 miles (19km). It also has spectacular cliff-top paths.

A celebration of words and music

Held annually in late May and early June, the Salisbury Festival presents both classical and jazz concerts, poetry and exhibitions, folk, circus and children's events. Further west, the Roman city of Bath hosts a festival of literature (February) and of music (May). The latter kicks off with opening-night celebrations featuring fireworks, and celebrates contemporary European jazz, early and classical music. On a smaller scale at roughly the same time of year, Chard, in southern Somerset, promotes music in a variety of styles composed by women. Held over six weeks or so in July and August, the Dartington Festival gives a series of concerts devoted to opera, dance and classical music in the medieval Dartington Hall and gardens. It is aimed as much at those who wish to partake as to listen. Also in July is the Exeter Festival, when the broad-ranging programme may include classical music in the Gothic cathedral, opera and fireworks, lectures, comedy, jazz, theatre and fringe events.

Houses of substance

The region's historic houses range from the large-scale – such as Longleat and Wilton House, both in Wiltshire – to the more compact Coleridge Cottage at Nether Stowey, where the eponymous poet found inspiration for *The Rime of the Ancient Mariner*. Little has changed in the two centuries since Coleridge moved in. Other remarkable – and visitable – residences of the region include Great Chalfield Manor (near Melksham), a 15th-century house of mellow stone with a fine great hall, and Forde Abbey, a former monastery near Chard now also known for its gardens. Not far away, in the sleepy countryside near Beaminster, is the Tudor mansion of Parnham, renowned for its furniture workshop. By contrast, Bristol and Bath each preserve a magnificent 18th-century townhouse: Bristol's is appropriately called The Georgian House, while Bath's proudly proclaims its address – No. 1 Royal Crescent. The latter was once the home of the Duke of York who famously marched his men up and down hills. Devon, meanwhile, invites you to a couple of castles a little out of the ordinary. Castle Drogo, perched above the River Teign near Drewsteignton is the work of Edwin Lutyens, and was not completed until the 1930s. Of more authentic age for a castle is Bickleigh, though it is in reality more fortified manor house than full-blooded medieval castle. One of its attractions is a display of gadgets used by Second World War spies. It is best to turn up at Pencarrow, a Georgian family home near Bodmin, in late spring or early summer when no fewer than 692 separate species of rhododendron welcome visitors, whether of a botanical bent or not. Trerice, a few miles south-east of Newquay, is a glorious Elizabethan house with unusual curved and scrolled gables. As well as an orchard of Cornish apple trees, there is a remarkable collection of lawn-mowers.

In search of St Hyacinth

Cornwall offers the church-hunter rich pickings. There are superb buildings – such as Launcells Church, inland from Bude, little altered since its completion in the 15th century. There are incomparable settings: the churches of St Anthony-in-Meneage on the Helford River and St Just-in-Roseland are two of the best. And there are the wondrous names. Churches in Cornwall are dedicated to St Petroc, St Hyacinth, St Nonna, St Germans and St Winnow. Other consecrated buildings to seek out in the West Country include St Brannock's in Braunton and St Andrew's in Cullompton (both Devon), St Andrew's in Banwell (Somerset) and St Mary's in Lydiard Tregoze (near Swindon).

Contact phone numbers
Perry's Cider Mills, Dowlish Wake, Ilminster (tel: 01460 52681)
Sheppy's Farmhouse Cider, Bradford-on-Tone, Taunton (tel: 01823 461233)
Dartmoor National Park (tel: 01822 890414)
Exmoor National Park (tel: 01398 323665)
Salisbury Festival (tel: 01722 323883)
Bath Literature Festival (tel: 01225 463362)
Bath International Music Festival (tel: 01225 463362)
Chard Festival of Women in Music (tel: 01460 66115)
Dartington International Summer School (tel: 01803 865988)
Exeter Festival (tel: 01392 265118)
Longleat, Warminster (tel: 01985 844400)
Wilton House, Wilton (tel: 01722 746720)
Coleridge Cottage, Nether Stowey (tel: 01278 732662)
Great Chalfield Manor, Melksham (tel: 01225 782239)
Forde Abbey, Chard (tel: 01460 220231)
Parnham, Beaminster (tel: 01308 862204)
The Georgian House, Bristol (tel: 0117 921 1362)
No. 1 Royal Crescent, Bath (tel: 01225 428126)
Castle Drogo, Drewsteignton (tel: 01647 433306)
Bickleigh Castle, Tiverton (tel: 01884 855363)
Pencarrow, Bodmin (tel: 01208 841369)
Trerice, Newquay (tel: 01637 875404)

► Swindon, the Railway Town
In the hundred years between 1830 and 1930, Swindon's population increased from 1,740 to 65,000. The reason was the arrival of the Great Western Railway (GWR) and the setting up of its manufacturing works in the town. The company built a 'railway village' to house its growing workforce: no. 34 Faringdon Road is now a museum (tel: 01793 466553) furnished as it might have been in the late 19th century. The company's hostel for male workers is now the GWR museum (tel: 01793 466555), displaying locomotives and railway memorabilia.

► Dartmoor Longhouses
A defining feature of the longhouse is that humans and livestock lived under a single roof. This arrangement, common on the continent, is very rare in England, and only occurs where it was vital to keep livestock warm and near at hand in harsh winter conditions. Around a hundred longhouses remain on Dartmoor: low, rectangular buildings, built between 1150 and 1700 from huge blocks of granite, often partly recessed into the hillside to maximise shelter.

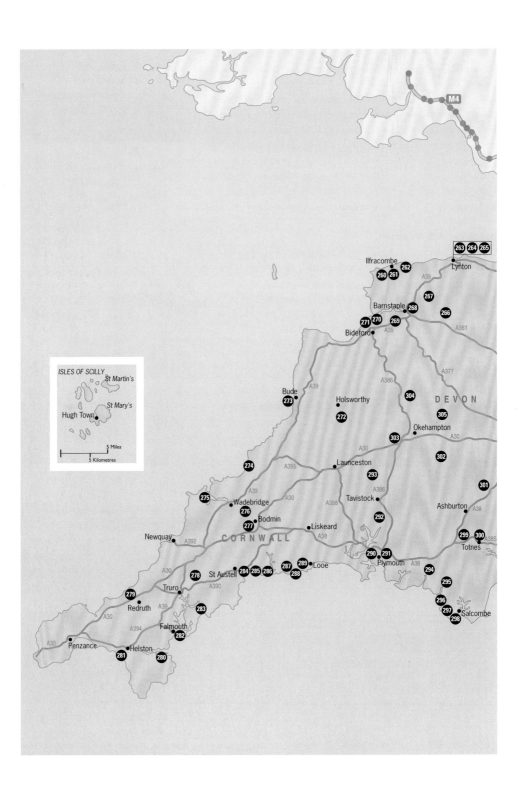

ISLES OF SCILLY
St Martin's
St Mary's
Hugh Town
5 Miles
5 Kilometres

Ilfracombe
260 261 262
Lynton
263 264 265
A39
267
266
Barnstaple 268
A361
271 270 269
Bideford
A39
DEVON
A386
A377
Bude
273
A39
Holsworthy
304
272
Okehampton
305
303
A30
302
Launceston
A395
293
301
A30
274
A388
Tavistock
Ashburton
A38
275
A39
A386
292
Wadebridge
A30
Newquay
276
Bodmin
299 300
277
Totnes
A392
CORNWALL
Liskeard
A385
290 291
Looe
Plymouth
294
A30
287 289
A38
278 St Austell
284 285 286 288
295
Truro
A390
296
279
283
297
Salcombe
Redruth
A39
298
A30
A394
Falmouth
Penzance
282
A30
Helston
281
320

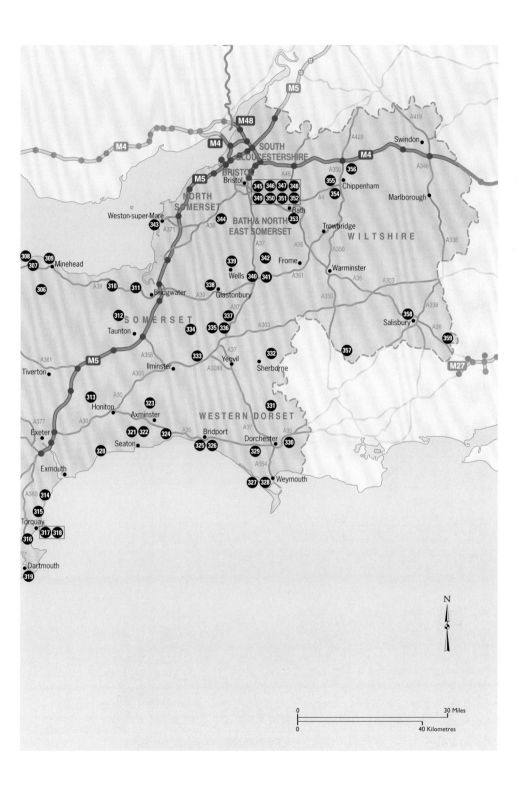

260 Watersmeet Hotel

★★★ Silver Award

Mortehoe, Woolacombe, Devon EX34 7EB **Tel:** (01271) 870333 **Fax:** (01271) 870890
Web: http://www.watersmeethotel.co.uk **E-mail:** watersmeethotel@compuserve.com

Set on the National Trust Atlantic coastline with panoramic views of Hartland Point and Lundy Island, the three acres of garden enclose a lawn tennis court, an open air swimming pool and steps to the beach below. A superb new indoor pool and spa is popular with everybody. The resident owners ensure the Watersmeet offers the comfort and peace of a country house, and all the main bedrooms, lounges and the octagonal restaurant overlook the sea. The Watersmeet offers a wine list to complement its national award-winning cuisine and service.

Bed & Breakfast per night: single room from £60.00–£122.00; double room from £90.00–£214.00
Dinner, Bed & Breakfast per person, per night: £68.00–£120.00
Lunch available: 1200–1400

Evening meal: 1900 (last orders 2030)
Bedrooms: 3 single, 9 double, 8 twin, 2 triple
Bathrooms: 22 en-suite **Parking:** 50 spaces
Open: All year except January and December
Cards accepted: Mastercard, Visa, Switch/Delta, Amex, Diners

The Tarka Trail

The writer Henry Williamson (1895–1977) was born and bred in London, but in 1921 he decided to leave the city, mounted his motorcycle and headed south-west. His eventual destination was the Devonshire village of Georgeham, near Barnstaple, where he rented a small cottage and stayed for many years. Here he was given an orphaned otter cub which he reared and cared for. It gave him the inspiration for his famous book, *Tarka the Otter*, in which he displayed not only his fascination for these shy and beautiful creatures, but also his deep knowledge and love of the wildlife and landscapes of this most beautiful part of Devon.

An area roughly corresponding to that featured in the book is now being promoted as Tarka Country, a region which extends along Devon's north coast from Bideford to Lynton and southwards to the northern fringes of Dartmoor. As part of a major eco-tourism initiative, the Tarka Country Tourism Association has set up a long-distance route – the Tarka Trail – designed to encourage the visitor to explore the countryside without the use of the car. Describing an irregular figure of eight, the trail loops between Exmoor and Dartmoor, with Barnstaple at its centre, covering 180 miles (290km) of varied and often stunning scenery.

It is of course possible to walk the entire length of the Tarka Trail (except the section between Eggesford and Barnstaple which is a train journey), but shorter walks and cycle routes with starting points on or near the trail have also been devised. Some are circular, some involve a return by bus. Full details of all the different options are available from the Tarka Country Tourism Association (tel: 01271 345008).

The Tarka Trail passes many places mentioned in Williamson's famous book. Tarka's fictional birthplace, for example, is on the Torridge, just upstream from Bideford, while remote Cranmere Pool on Dartmoor was visited by Tarka after the death of his mate, Greymuzzle. But don't expect to see any otters on your travels. Due to river pollution and loss of habitat, otters are one of Europe's most endangered mammals. The best place to see them is at the Tamar Otter Sanctuary, near Launceston, Cornwall (about 25 miles - 40km - from Barnstaple) where otters are bred and re-introduced to the wild in a bid to save them from extinction (tel: 01566 785646).

Entries are cross referenced by number to the maps on pages 130–131

261 Glen Tor Hotel ◆◆◆◆

Torrs Park, Ilfracombe, Devon EX34 8AZ **Tel:** (01271) 862403 **Fax:** (01271) 862403

Wendy, Tony and Joan would like to spoil you with personal attention you thought had gone for ever. Excellent en-suite accommodation and spacious rooms with many extras. Quiet situation yet close to all amenities and at the foot of the famous Torrs Walks. Enjoy a scrumptious breakfast and set off to explore this lovely area. Walking, cycling, fishing – or whatever takes your fancy. Come home and relax in our comfortable, friendly bar. Excellent evening meals are optional.

Bed & Breakfast per night: single room from £21.00–£23.00; double room from £42.00–£46.00
Dinner, Bed & Breakfast per person, per night: £31.00–£33.00 (min 2 nights)
Evening meal: 1830

Bedrooms: 1 single, 4 double, 1 twin, 1 family
Bathrooms: 6 en-suite, 1 private
Parking: 3 spaces

262 Bessemer Thatch Hotel and Restaurant ◆◆◆◆ Silver Award

Berrynarbor, Devon EX34 9SE **Tel:** (01271) 882296 **Fax:** (01271) 882296

Situated in one of Devon's prettiest villages and only two miles from the Exmoor border, Bessemer Thatch is the perfect retreat from life's stresses and strains. Four-poster bedrooms with charming decor and furnishings complement this lovely old 13th-century building that offers peace and quiet, with more than a little comfort. In the dining room with its cosy inglenook fireplace enjoy the very best of traditional English menus which are always carefully prepared and presented. Truly somewhere special.

Bed & Breakfast per night: single occupancy from £25.00–£38.00; double room from £50.00–£76.00
Dinner, Bed & Breakfast per person, per night: £40.00–£53.00
Evening meal: 1830 (last orders 2130)

Bedrooms: 5 double, 1 twin
Bathrooms: 6 en-suite
Open: All year except Christmas
Cards accepted: Mastercard, Visa, Switch/Delta, Eurocard

263 Seawood Hotel ★ Silver Award

North Walk Drive, Lynton, Devon EX35 6HJ **Tel:** (01598) 752272 **Fax:** (01598) 752272

Seawood is situated at one of the loveliest spots on the North Devon coast, right in the heart of Lorna Doone country. Nestling on wooded cliffs 400ft above the sea, the hotel has some magnificent views. It looks right out across Lynmouth Bay and the Grand Headland of Countisbury where Exmoor meets the sea. On a clear night you can easily see the twinkling lights of Wales.

Bed & Breakfast per night: single room from £27.00–£29.00; double room from £54.00–£58.00
Dinner, Bed & Breakfast per person, per night: £42.50–£44.50
Evening meal: 1900 (last orders 1930)

Bedrooms: 1 single, 9 double, 2 twin
Bathrooms: 12 en-suite
Parking: 10 spaces
Open: April–October

At-a-glance symbols are explained on the flap inside the back cover

264 Rockvale Hotel

Lee Road, Lynton, Devon EX35 6HW **Tel:** (01598) 752279 or (01598) 753343

Delightful Victorian property situated in its own grounds on the sunny south-facing slopes of Hollerday Hill. Central location with glorious, panoramic views across the town towards Countisbury and Watersmeet Valley. Award-winning home cooking and hospitality. Substantial vegetarian range and special diets catered for. Peaceful and relaxing. Cosy bedrooms with many thoughtful extras. Large level car park. The perfect location for walking, touring or just relaxing. Totally non-smoking. Enjoy being spoilt!

Bed & Breakfast per night: single room from £22.00–£24.00; double room from £48.00–£52.00
Dinner, Bed & Breakfast per person, per night: £38.00–£42.00
Evening meal: 1900 (last bookings 1600)

Bedrooms: 1 single, 5 double, 2 triple
Bathrooms: 6 en-suite, 2 private
Parking: 10 spaces
Open: March–October
Cards accepted: Mastercard, Visa, Switch/Delta, Eurocard, Maestro, Solo

265 Kingford House

Longmead, Lynton, Devon EX35 6DQ **Tel:** (01598) 752361

Nestling under Hollerday Hill, close to the 'Valley of Rocks'. All rooms are comfortably appointed to a high standard with colour television, clock radio, hairdryer and tea making facilities. Traditional home cooking, a choice of menu (changed daily) and selective wine list. Ideal situation for walkers, with the coastal path close by, or for touring Exmoor by car. Ample off-street parking available. Managed by resident, caring proprietors offering a warm welcome and relaxed, friendly atmosphere.

Bed & Breakfast per night: single room from £18.50–£21.00; double room from £37.00–£42.00
Dinner, Bed & Breakfast per person, per night: £30.00–£32.50
Evening meal: 1900 (last bookings 1700)

Bedrooms: 2 single, 3 double, 1 twin
Bathrooms: 4 en-suite, 2 private
Parking: 8 spaces
Open: All year except January

266 Rockley Farmhouse

◆◆◆◆ Silver Award

Brayford, Barnstaple, Devon EX32 7QR **Tel:** (01598) 710429 **Fax:** (01598) 710429
Web: http://www.hicon.co.uk/rockley **E-mail:** rockley@hicon.co.uk

Red deer can often be seen grazing around our delightful farmhouse which is situated in spectacular seclusion within Exmoor National Park. We are not a working farm, but we do have farmyard friends. Rockley is an ideal base for coastal and moorland walks, riding or enjoying the moor. There is a stream-bordered garden for you to relax in and we offer traditional bed and breakfast in high quality accommodation. Evening meal optional. North Devon Marketing Bureau Super Service Award 1999 - Highly Commended.

Bed & Breakfast per night: single occupancy from £20.00–£23.00; double room from £40.00–£46.00
Evening meal: 1800

Bedrooms: 2 double, 1 twin
Bathrooms: 1 en-suite, 1 public
Parking: 5 spaces
Open: All year except Christmas

Entries are cross referenced by number to the maps on pages 130–131

267 Bracken House Country Hotel

 ◆◆◆◆◆ Gold Award

Bratton Fleming, Barnstaple, Devon EX31 4TG **Tel:** (01598) 710320

On the western edge of Exmoor. An attractive former Victorian rectory set in eight peaceful acres of garden, pasture, pond and woodland. Extensive views. A haven of rural tranquillity. Eight en-suite bedrooms, including two on the ground floor. Interesting Devon food cooked with care in the Aga. Friendly and efficient service. Dogs welcome to bring well-trained owners. Convenient for Arlington, Rosemoor, Marwood and the spectacular Exmoor coastline. **Category 3**

Bed & Breakfast per night: double room from £56.00–£80.00
Dinner, Bed & Breakfast per person, per night: £45.00–£57.00
Evening meal: 1900 (last bookings 1800)

Bedrooms: 4 double, 4 twin
Bathrooms: 8 en-suite
Parking: 12 spaces
Open: April–October
Cards accepted: Mastercard, Visa, Eurocard

268 Bradiford Cottage

 ◆◆◆◆

Bradiford, Barnstaple, Devon EX31 4DP **Tel:** (01271) 345039 **Fax:** (01271) 345039

The cottage is a creaky, lived-in, 17th-century converted farm building with good country taste. Along the flagstone passage there is a large, homely drawing room leading out to a secluded patio, the flower garden and the lawn which stretches up the hill. There is a bathroom with a huge bath under a sloping ceiling and a delightful main bedroom with wiggly walls. The village pub, swimming pools, sandy beaches and Exmoor are nearby.

Bed & Breakfast per night: single room from £16.00–£17.00; double room from £32.00–£34.00

Bedrooms: 1 single, 2 double, 1 twin
Bathrooms: 2 public
Parking: 4 spaces

269 The Red House

 ◆◆◆◆

Brynsworthy, Roundswell, Barnstaple, Devon EX31 3NP **Tel:** (01271) 345966 **Fax:** (01271) 379966

A period country house situated in an elevated position with panoramic views. Although being within two miles of the historic market town of Barnstaple, the house is set in the countryside with its own half acre garden. All rooms have colour television, shower, hairdryer, tea/coffee making facilities and central heating. Visitors will find that they are well situated for visiting the historic towns, sandy beaches and natural beauty of the Moors, and can enjoy a good and varied selection of pub food, all within a short driving distance.

Bed & Breakfast per night: single room from £20.00–£24.00; double room from £36.00–£42.00

Bedrooms: 1 single, 1 double, 1 twin
Bathrooms: 2 rooms with private shower, 1 public bathroom
Parking: 6 spaces
Open: All year except January and December

At-a-glance symbols are explained on the flap inside the back cover

270 Yeoldon Country House Hotel and Restaurant ★★★ Silver Award

Durrant Lane, Northam, Bideford, Devon EX39 2RL **Tel:** (01237) 474400 **Fax:** (01237) 476618

Set in two acres of gardens overlooking the River Torridge, Yeoldon House offers real hospitality and a refreshingly casual atmosphere in this uniquely unspoilt part of Devon. Individually decorated rooms with an air of elegance and charm – all en-suite with tea/coffee making facilities. Imaginative à la carte cuisine using fresh local produce and an extensive wine list. Restaurant awarded an AA Rosette in 1997 and 1998.

Bed & Breakfast per night: single occupancy from £45.00–£55.00; double room from £65.00–£95.00
Dinner, Bed & Breakfast per person, per night: £63.50–£73.50
Evening meal: 1900 (last orders 2100)

Bedrooms: 7 double, 3 twin
Bathrooms: 10 en-suite
Parking: 22 spaces
Cards accepted: Mastercard, Visa, Switch/Delta, Amex, Diners, Eurocard

271 Eversley ◆◆◆◆

1 Youngaton Road, Westward Ho!, Bideford, Devon EX39 1HU **Tel:** (01237) 471603

Two minutes' walk from the sea shore and the south west coast path, Eversley has been described as a country hotel in a seaside village, but without the grounds! The Victorian house, with its galleried landing, has three guest rooms so you are assured of our personal attention. The house is tastefully furnished and each bedroom is individually styled with the usual amenities. North Devon is easily accessed from Eversley, with Clovelly, North Cornwall, Barnstaple and beyond within easy driving distance.

Bed & Breakfast per night: single occupancy from £24.00–£27.00; double room from £36.00–£42.00

Bedrooms: 1 double, 1 twin, 1 family
Bathrooms: 1 en-suite, 1 public

272 Court Barn Country House Hotel ★★ Silver Award

Clawton, Holsworthy, Devon EX22 6PS **Tel:** (01409) 271219 **Fax:** (01409) 271309
Web: http://www.holsworthy.co.uk

Pure Devon air, magical skies and countryside, combined with crackling log fires, antiques and fresh flowers, create a warm and relaxing atmosphere for a romantic break. Set in park-like grounds, Court Barn is one of the South West's great small touring hotels. Close to the Atlantic heritage coast, Blue Flag beaches, nature walks, cycle trails, National Trust houses and gardens, and midway between the Moors. Our award-winning restaurant, which features an extensive wine list, teas and hospitality make Court Barn a place to remember. Romantic breaks. Reduced golf fees.

Bed & Breakfast per night: single room from £35.00–£40.00; double room from £70.00–£90.00
Dinner, Bed & Breakfast per person, per night: £52.00–£58.00 (min 2 nights, 2 sharing)
Lunch available: 1200–1400

Evening meal: 1900 (last orders 2130)
Bedrooms: 1 single, 3 double, 2 twin, 2 triple
Bathrooms: 8 en-suite
Parking: 17 spaces
Cards accepted: Mastercard, Visa, Switch/Delta, Amex, Diners, Eurocard

Entries are cross referenced by number to the maps on pages 130–131

273 The Falcon Hotel

★★★ Silver Award

Breakwater Road, Bude, Cornwall EX23 8SD **Tel:** (01288) 352005 **Fax:** (01288) 356359

Overlooking the famous Bude Canal, with beautiful walled gardens and yet only a short stroll from the beaches and shops, the Falcon has one of the finest settings in North Cornwall. Established in 1798, it still retains an old-world charm and atmosphere. The bedrooms are furnished to a very high standard, and have televisions with Teletext and Sky. Excellent local reputation for the quality of the food, both in the bar and candlelit restaurant.

Bed & Breakfast per night: single room from £38.00–£40.00; double room from £76.00–£80.00
Dinner, Bed & Breakfast per person, per night: £52.00–£54.00
Lunch available: 1200–1400
Evening meal: 1900 (last orders 2100)

Bedrooms: 6 single, 15 double, 5 twin
Bathrooms: 26 en-suite
Parking: 40 spaces
Cards accepted: Mastercard, Visa, Switch/Delta, Amex, Diners, Eurocard, Visa Electron, Solo

The South-West Coast Path

'Poole 500 miles' reads the signpost pointing west along the Somerset coast at Minehead. In this daunting manner begins the South-West Coast Path, a walk around England's 'toe' taking in some of the most magnificent coastal scenery in the land. The walk starts dramatically as it enters the Exmoor National Park, hugging steep, wooded slopes that drop precipitously down to the sea, with stupendous views of the Welsh coast. Further on, the section of Devon coastline from Westward Ho! (the only British placename to include an exclamation mark) to the Cornish border is equally lovely as it passes the huddled village of Clovelly and the heights of Hartland Point with fine views of Lundy Island.

The Cornish Coast, both north and south, displays a stunning array of rocky promontories and soaring cliffs, interspersed with superb sandy beaches and fishing villages nestling in tiny coves. In general, the south coast, here and further on, is harder to negotiate than the north because of the many estuaries cutting into the lower-lying terrain, often requiring long detours inland.

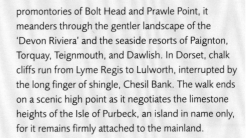

The path re-enters Devon and, almost immediately, Plymouth, the largest city on its route. After rounding the wild promontories of Bolt Head and Prawle Point, it meanders through the gentler landscape of the 'Devon Riviera' and the seaside resorts of Paignton, Torquay, Teignmouth, and Dawlish. In Dorset, chalk cliffs run from Lyme Regis to Lulworth, interrupted by the long finger of shingle, Chesil Bank. The walk ends on a scenic high point as it negotiates the limestone heights of the Isle of Purbeck, an island in name only, for it remains firmly attached to the mainland.

As well as offering stunning scenery, the walk is rich in historical interest, from prehistoric hillforts in Dorset to Palmerston forts in Plymouth, or the abandoned village of Tyneham (Dorset) taken over by the army in 1943. In Cornwall, defunct engine houses and empty pilchard 'palaces' are relics of a rich industrial past.

The naturalist, as well as the historian, will find much of interest. The protruding coastline provides a landfall for migrating birds, while sub-tropical species of plants flourish in the mild climes of the South-West. The Lizard, in particular, supports a unique flora, while army ranges at Lulworth, untouched by modern farming practices, have preserved a rare botanical habitat.

There are several guides to the South-West Coast Path available, some suggesting shorter, circular walks and offering advice on accommodation, local attractions and other practical information.

274 Port William Inn

◆◆◆◆

Trebarwith Strand, Tintagel, Cornwall PL34 0HB **Tel:** (01840) 770230 **Fax:** (01840) 770936
E-mail: william@eurobell.co.uk

Probably the best located inn in Cornwall, romantically situated 50 yards from the sea, overlooking sea, beach and cliffs on the unspoilt north coast at Trebarwith Strand. All rooms are en-suite and overlook the sea. We are renowned for the quality of our home-cooked traditional fayre and local sea food, which also includes vegetarian alternatives. We have a good selection of real ales, including local brews.

Bed & Breakfast per night: single occupancy from £50.00–£67.00; double room from £65.00–£79.00
Lunch available: 1200–1430
Evening meal: 1800 (last orders 2130)

Bedrooms: 2 double, 1 twin, 1 triple, 2 family
Bathrooms: 6 en-suite
Parking: 50 spaces
Cards accepted: Mastercard, Visa, Switch/Delta, Amex, Eurocard

275 The Dower House

◆◆◆◆◆ Gold Award

Fentonluna Lane, Padstow, Cornwall PL28 8BA **Tel:** (01841) 532317 **Fax:** (01841) 532667
E-mail: dower@btinternet.com

As you step on to our terrace and smile at this beautiful old house, you'll glance to your right over the rooftops of old Padstow, and marvel at the magnificent view of the Camel Estuary and distant hills of Bodmin Moor. Paul and Patricia will greet and introduce you to their house. You will be delighted with the individually-decorated rooms and the care with which your breakfast is freshly prepared and presented in their elegant dining room.

Bed & Breakfast per night: single room from £43.50–£50.00; double room from £58.00–£84.00
Lunch available: 1130–1430
Evening meal: 1900

Bedrooms: 1 single, 3 double, 2 twin
Bathrooms: 6 en-suite
Parking: 8 spaces
Open: All year except January and December
Cards accepted: Mastercard, Visa, Switch/Delta, Eurocard

276 Trehellas House

★★ Silver Award

Washaway, Bodmin, Cornwall PL30 3AD **Tel:** (01208) 72700 **Fax:** (01208) 73336
Web: http://www.crescom.co.uk/trehellas

Delightful, early 18th-century former posting inn with exposed beams and slate floors, together with its attractive converted barn. Our Courtroom Suite is complete with beautiful French antique furniture. Rooms have wrought-iron bedsteads, patchwork quilts, telephone, colour television and en-suite bathroom. Attractive garden with heated swimming pool. Great Cornish breakfasts. Dinner is available in the Memories of Malaya restaurant which serves superb food from the Pacific Rim using aromatic herbs and spices.

Bed & Breakfast per night: single room £30.00; double room from £60.00– £100.00
Dinner, Bed & Breakfast per person, per night: £50.00–£70.00
Evening meal: 1900 (last orders 2100)
Bedrooms: 1 single, 11 double

Bathrooms: 12 en-suite
Parking: 30 spaces
Open: All year except January
Cards accepted: Mastercard, Visa, Switch/Delta, Amex, Eurocard, JCB

Entries are cross referenced by number to the maps on pages 130–131

277 Bokiddick Farm

◆◆◆◆◆ Gold Award

Lanivet, Bodmin, Cornwall PL30 5HP **Tel:** (01208) 831481 **Fax:** (01208) 831481

Character, Georgian farmhouse with oak beams and wood panelling, on 180-acre, family-run dairy farm. Magnificent views and peaceful location. Our superb situation in the centre of Cornwall makes us an ideal base for exploring all of Cornwall, close to National Trust Lanhydrock House and on the Saints Way Walk. Lovely en-suite bedrooms. Delicious farmhouse breakfasts cooked on the Aga. Enjoy a holiday or short break here at any time of year. The warmest of welcomes awaits you.

Bed & Breakfast per night: single occupancy from £25.00–£30.00; double room from £40.00–£44.00

Bedrooms: 2 double, 1 triple
Bathrooms: 3 en-suite
Parking: 4 spaces

---

278 Bissick Old Mill

◆◆◆◆

Ladock, Truro, Cornwall TR2 4PG **Tel:** (01726) 882557 **Fax:** (01726) 884057

Bissick Old Mill is known to be 300 years old and continued as a flour mill until the mid-1960s. Its conversion has been sympathetically conceived to provide modern conveniences whilst maintaining its former character, including slate floors, natural stone walls and beamed ceilings. Our aim is to provide you with the perfect environment in which to relax and enjoy the beauty of Cornwall, all areas of which are readily accessible from our central location.

Bed & Breakfast per night: single room £39.95; double room from £54.40–£69.00
Evening meal: 1900 (last bookings 1700)

Bedrooms: 1 single, 2 double, 1 twin
Bathrooms: 4 en-suite
Parking: 9 spaces
Cards accepted: Mastercard, Visa, Switch/Delta, Eurocard, JCB, Visa Electron

---

279 Aviary Court Hotel

★★ Silver Award

Marys Well, Illogan, Redruth, Cornwall TR16 4QZ **Tel:** (01209) 842256 **Fax:** (01209) 843744
E-mail: aviarycourt@connexions.co.uk

A charming 300-year-old Cornish country house set in its own grounds on the edge of Illogan Woods, ideal for touring the South West peninsula and its many local attractions. Six well-equipped individual bedrooms with tea/coffee making facilities, biscuits, mineral water, fresh fruit, direct dial telephone, remote control television and a view of the gardens. The resident family proprietors ensure personal service, offering well-cooked varied food that uses as much Cornish produce as possible.

Bed & Breakfast per night: single occupancy from £40.00–£42.50; double room from £60.00–£62.50
Dinner, Bed & Breakfast per person, per night: £43.00–£45.00 (min 2 sharing)
Lunch available: 1230–1330 (Sunday only)

Evening meal: 1900 (last orders 2030)
Bedrooms: 4 double, 1 twin, 1 triple
Bathrooms: 6 en-suite
Parking: 25 spaces
Cards accepted: Mastercard, Visa, Switch/Delta, Solo

At-a-glance symbols are explained on the flap inside the back cover

280 Tregildry Hotel

★★ Silver Award

Gillan, Manaccan, Helston, Cornwall TR12 6HG **Tel:** (01326) 231378 **Fax:** (01326) 231561
Web: http://www.cornwall-online.co.uk/tregildry **E-mail:** trgildry@globalnet.co.uk

An elegant small hotel with stunning sea views. Tucked away in an undiscovered corner of the Lizard Peninsula, this is for those seeking relaxed and stylish comfort in 'away from it all' surroundings. Large, light lounges with panoramic sea views have comfy sofas, fresh flowers and the latest books and magazines. The stylish restaurant has won awards for cuisine and the pretty sea-view bedrooms are attractively decorated with colourful fabrics. Near coastal path walks and an ideal peaceful base for exploring Cornwall.

Dinner, Bed & Breakfast per person, per night: £65.00–£75.00
Evening meal: 1900 (last orders 2030)

Bedrooms: 1 single, 6 double, 3 twin
Bathrooms: 10 en-suite
Parking: 15 spaces
Open: March–October
Cards accepted: Mastercard, Visa, Switch/Delta, Eurocard, JCB

The Lizard

If it's Britain's most southerly point you're after, then come to the Lizard (Land's End is the westernmost point). This small Cornish peninsula has much to interest the visitor besides its location, being especially rich both geologically and botanically. Like almost every part of the county, the Lizard also has many historical connections and a glorious coastline.

Opinions vary as to how it got its name: some claim it means high palace, others that it derives from a Celtic word for outcast. Both explanations are plausible, for the Lizard is a level moorland plateau about 200ft (61m) above sea level, almost cut off from the rest of the county. Much of the peninsula is formed of serpentine stone, a soft, easily-worked material used in local churches (and on sale in the shops of Lizard village). A farmer reputedly chanced upon its ornamental qualities when he erected some large rocks in his field as rubbing posts for his cows. He soon noticed that the 'polished' areas showed patterns resembling snakeskin, and colours ranging from grey-green to pink. Once Queen Victoria had chosen it for Osborne House its popularity was assured. In the church of St Winwalloe at Landewednack it can be seen alternated with granite. This, the most southerly church in Britain, is where the last sermon was preached in Cornish (1678).

Kynance Cove, owned by the National Trust, is typical of the majestic coastline of the Lizard. Its rocky outcrops enjoy some unlikely names, including Man-o'-War Rock, the Devil's Postbox, the Devil's

Bellows and Asparagus Island (where the plant grows wild). There are some intriguing caves (the Parlour and the Drawing Room), but take care not to be stranded by the incoming tide.

The flora of the Lizard is a botanist's delight. Here can be found plants too tender to grow outdoors elsewhere in the country (such as tamarisks and the Hottentot fig) and others which are unique to this corner of England, such as Cornish Heath. These plants have to be able to withstand the frequent onslaught of sea gales, something which countless local vessels have not managed. More shipwrecks have occurred here than almost anywhere else in the country. Off the eastern coast of the peninsula are the Manacles, a group of ferocious rocks extending over a couple of square miles. In 1770 parishioners of the nearby church of St Arkerveranus (in the village of St Deverne) redesigned the steeple as a landmark to warn passing ships. They may have been successful, but there are still over 400 victims of shipwrecks buried in the churchyard.

281 Tye Rock Country House Hotel

◆◆◆◆◆ Silver Award

Loe Bar Road, Porthleven, Helston, Cornwall TR13 9EW **Tel:** (01326) 572695 **Fax:** (01326) 572695
Web: http://ourworld.compuserve.com/homepages/tyerockhotel

Tye Rock is situated in the most superb location, overlooking the sea from Lands End to Lizard, and suits the discerning guest seeking elegance, peace and tranquillity with personal service. Our 3.5 acres of clifftop grounds back onto National Trust coastal paths yet are only a short walk from the pretty harbour. The hotel has been completely refurbished and each of our seven bedrooms has a separate theme, and all are en-suite with sea views.

Bed & Breakfast per night: single occupancy from £65.00–£75.00; double room from £81.00–£99.00
Dinner, Bed & Breakfast per person, per night: £58.00–£68.00
Evening meal: 1930 (last orders 2030)

Bedrooms: 7 double
Bathrooms: 7 en-suite
Parking: 20 spaces
Cards accepted: Mastercard, Visa, Switch/Delta, Eurocard

282 Green Lawns Hotel

★★★ Silver Award

Western Terrace, Falmouth, Cornwall TR11 4QJ **Tel:** (01326) 312734 or (01326) 312700 **Fax:** (01326) 211427
Web: http://www.green-lawns-hotel.co.uk **E-mail:** info@green-lawns-hotel.co.uk

Where can you relax in an elegant, centrally positioned, chateau-style hotel with views across a beautiful bay? The Green Lawns Hotel and the famous Garras restaurant! If you are looking for a holiday where high standards and personal attention are paramount, you will enjoy an excellent choice of imaginative cuisine from a table d' hôte or à la carte menu. All our guests enjoy free membership of the Garras Leisure Club with its magnificent indoor swimming pool. 'Britain in Bloom' winners for six years running.

Bed & Breakfast per night: single room from £50.00–£90.00; double room from £90.00–£140.00
Dinner, Bed & Breakfast per person, per night: £63.00–£110.00
Lunch available: 1200–1345
Evening meal: 1845 (last orders 2145)

Bedrooms: 6 single, 16 double, 9 twin, 2 triple, 6 family
Bathrooms: 39 en-suite
Parking: 60 spaces
Cards accepted: Mastercard, Visa, Switch/Delta, Amex, Diners, Eurocard

283 The Hundred House Hotel

★★ Silver Award

Ruan Highlanes, near Truro, Cornwall TR2 5JR **Tel:** (01872) 501336 **Fax:** (01872) 501151

Delightful 19th-century Cornish country house set in three acres. Near St Mawes on the Fal estuary and surrounded by superb countryside and unspoilt sandy coves. It is now a charming small hotel, beautifully decorated and furnished like an elegant English home. Delicious candlelit dinners, Cornish cream teas, log fires and croquet on the lawn make a relaxing short break or a longer stay a memorable delight. Ideal for exploring Cornwall, its sub-tropical gardens or walking the coastal path. AA Rosette for food.

Bed & Breakfast per night: single room max £45.00; double room max £90.00
Dinner, Bed & Breakfast per person, per night: £55.00–£70.00
Evening meal: 1930 (last orders 2000)

Bedrooms: 2 single, 4 double, 4 twin
Bathrooms: 10 en-suite
Parking: 15 spaces
Open: March–October
Cards accepted: Mastercard, Visa, Switch/Delta, Amex, Eurocard

At-a-glance symbols are explained on the flap inside the back cover

284 Horizon House

Sea Road, Carlyon Bay, St Austell, Cornwall PL25 3SG **Tel:** (01726) 817221 **Fax:** (01726) 817221

Horizon House overlooks National Trust coastline in a quiet and tranquil position, yet close to renowned gardens, restaurants, pubs and sandy beaches. Golf and Charlestown Harbour are ten minutes away by the coastal path. Our guest accommodation comprises spacious rooms (one double and one twin), both en-suite with sea views, own entrance, colour television, radio/alarm, hairdryer and tea/coffee facilities. Ample parking space.

Bed & Breakfast per night: double room from £60.00–£70.00

Bedrooms: 1 double, 1 twin
Bathrooms: 2 en-suite
Parking: 2 spaces
Open: March–October

285 Cliff Head Hotel Limited

★★★ Silver Award

Sea Road, Carlyon Bay, St Austell, Cornwall PL24 3RB **Tel:** (01726) 812345 **Fax:** (01726) 815511
Web: http://www. cornishriviera.co.uk/cliffhead **E-mail:** cliffheadhotel@btconnect.com

Prestigious, privately owned hotel standing in grounds of delightful multi-coloured hydrangeas – this is the ideal base for touring Cornwall. From the moment you enter this charming hotel you are aware of the friendly atmosphere which is enhanced by high standards of service, tasteful decor and comfortable furnishings. Expressions Restaurant offers international and British fayre combined with a superb wine list and good service. We also have a heated pool, sauna and sunbed. Golfing breaks available.

Bed & Breakfast per night: single room from £45.00–£55.00; double room from £75.00–£85.00
Dinner, Bed & Breakfast per person, per night: £45.00–£58.00 (min 2 nights, must include Friday or Saturday)
Lunch available: 1200–1345

Evening meal: 1900 (last orders 2130)
Bedrooms: 19 single, 17 double, 15 twin, 8 triple
Bathrooms: 59 en-suite
Parking: 80 spaces
Cards accepted: Mastercard, Visa, Switch/Delta, Amex, Diners

286 Marina Hotel

★★ Silver Award

Esplanade, Fowey, Cornwall PL23 1HY **Tel:** (01726) 833315 **Fax:** (01726) 832779
Web: http://www.cornwall-online.co.uk/marina_hotel/ **E-mail:** marina.hotel@dial.pipex.com

This Georgian hotel, originally built as the summer residence of the Bishop of Truro, is situated on the waterside with its own moorings. The hotel faces south and most rooms (four have balconies) overlook the estuary. The walled garden provides an ideal spot for observing the waterside traffic. The award-winning restaurant overlooking the water provides a feast of local fish, shellfish and meat. Early and late season offers of two nights for the price of one.

Bed & Breakfast per night: single occupancy from £48.00–£60.00; double room from £66.00–£104.00
Dinner, Bed & Breakfast per person, per night: £51.00–£70.00
Lunch available: 1200–1700

Evening meal: 1900 (last orders 2030)
Bedrooms: 7 double, 4 twin
Bathrooms: 11 en-suite
Open: All year except January and February
Cards accepted: Mastercard, Visa, Switch/Delta, Amex, Eurocard

Entries are cross referenced by number to the maps on pages 130–131

287 Trenderway Farm

◆◆◆◆◆

Pelynt, Polperro, Cornwall PL13 2LY **Tel:** (01503) 272214 **Fax:** (01503) 272991
E-mail: trenderwayfarm@hotmail.com

Built in the late 16th century, this mixed working farm is set in peaceful, beautiful countryside at the head of the Polperro Valley. Bedrooms here are truly superb – with bathrooms as big as some hotel bedrooms – and are decorated with the flair of a professional interior designer. A hearty farmhouse breakfast is served in the sunny conservatory, using local produce. Although an evening meal is not provided, an excellent range of restaurants can be recommended. Totally no smoking.

Bed & Breakfast per night: double room from £60.00–£70.00

Bedrooms: 3 double, 1 twin
Bathrooms: 4 en-suite
Parking: 4 spaces
Open: All year except December

288 Talland Bay Hotel

 ★★★ Silver Award

Talland Bay, Looe, Cornwall PL13 2JB **Tel:** (01503) 272667 **Fax:** (01503) 272940

A delightful old Cornish manor house set in two acres of gardens overlooking the sea. All bedrooms are furnished to a high standard and many have sea views. Dinners feature fresh regional produce – local seafood, Cornish lamb, West Country cheeses. AA Rosette. Talland Bay is a magically peaceful spot from which to explore this part of Cornwall. Breathtaking cliff paths lead to Looe and Polperro, and there are fascinating sub-tropical gardens and National Trust properties within easy reach.

Bed & Breakfast per night: single room from £49.00–£79.00; double room from £98.00–£158.00
Dinner, Bed & Breakfast per person, per night: £67.00–£96.00
Lunch available: 1230–1400 (1230–1330 on Sunday)

Evening meal: 1930 (last orders 2100)
Bedrooms: 3 single, 5 double, 9 twin, 2 family
Bathrooms: 19 en-suite **Parking:** 20 spaces
Open: All year except January and part February
Cards accepted: Mastercard, Visa, Switch/Delta, Amex, Diners, Eurocard

289 Fieldhead Hotel

 ★★ Silver Award

Portuan Road, Hannafore, West Looe, Looe, Cornwall PL13 2DR **Tel:** (01503) 262689 **Fax:** (01503) 264114
Web: http://www.chycor.co.uk/fieldhead **E-mail:** field.head@virgin.net

Built in 1896, the hotel occupies a commanding site on West Looe, providing remarkable views across Looe Bay to Rame Head, Eddystone Lighthouse and the intriguing Looe Island. Set in one acre of landscaped tropical gardens with heated outdoor pool, the Fieldhead has 14 individually styled en-suite bedrooms, most with sea views, including four superior and two with balconies. Mainly fresh produce and locally caught seafood are served in the stylish restaurant. On-site private car park.

Bed & Breakfast per night: single occupancy from £31.00–£58.00; double room from £52.00–£94.00
Dinner, Bed & Breakfast per person, per night: £42.00–£63.00 (min 2 sharing)
Evening meal: 1830 (last orders 2045)

Bedrooms: 10 double, 2 twin, 1 triple, 1 family
Bathrooms: 14 en-suite
Parking: 15 spaces
Cards accepted: Mastercard, Visa, Switch/Delta, Amex, Solo

290 Berkeleys of St James ◆◆◆◆

4 St James Place East, The Hoe, Plymouth, Devon PL1 3AS **Tel:** (01752) 221654 **Fax:** (01752) 221654
Web: http://www.smoothhound.co.uk/hotels/berkely2.html

Elegant, non-smoking, Victorian guesthouse in a quiet square on Plymouth Hoe. An ideal location for visiting the historic Barbican or touring Devon and Cornwall. Luxury en-suite rooms. Excellent English breakfast menu. A comfortable and quiet stay assured.

Bed & Breakfast per night: single room from £28.00–£30.00; double room from £40.00–£60.00

Bedrooms: 1 single, 3 double, 1 triple
Bathrooms: 4 en-suite, 1 private
Parking: 3 spaces
Cards accepted: Mastercard, Visa, Switch/Delta, Eurocard, JCB, Maestro, Visa Electron, Solo

West Country Cheeses

The West Country is ideal cattle-rearing country: its climate is mild and damp, its grass lush, and much of its landscape too hilly and higgledy-piggledy to make good arable farmland. At one time almost every small region had its own variety of cheese, and though many have disappeared, the region has preserved some of its most popular old varieties and has developed many new ones, too.

Somerset is the home of the acknowledged 'king of cheeses', the great and versatile Cheddar. Sixty percent of all cheese produced in creameries throughout England and Wales is Cheddar. First recorded in the early 16th century, it got its name because visitors to the famous Cheddar Gorge bought the flavoursome hard cheese there. Today visitors to the Cheddar Rural Village (tel: 01934 742810) may watch cheesemaking displays, while not far away, Chewton Cheese Dairy, near Wells (open to the public, tel: 01761 241666) continues to make Cheddar to traditional methods.

Cheddar's nearest rival, also a full-flavoured hard cheese, is Double Gloucester, originally made from the rich milk of the Gloucester black cattle. A 'single' variety, known as the 'haymaking cheese' was made from early-season milk, and was matured quickly, resulting in a light colour. The larger 'double' Gloucesters were allowed to mature longer and were consequently darker. Both are made at Old Ley Court near Birdwood, Gloucestershire (tel: 01452 750225), where cheese-making demonstrations can be seen on certain days.

At one time, Dorset Blue Vinney, a hard blue-veined cheese, was made on numerous farms throughout Dorset. Though it went out of production in the 1980s, it is again produced near Sherborne (not open to the public, but the cheese is readily available in local shops). Cornish Yarg, by contrast, is a recent innovation, a crumbly white cheese with a black covering of nettle leaves, first produced in the 1980s by the Gray family – Yarg is Gray backwards – at Lynher Dairies near Liskeard (open in summer: tel: 01579 362244).

Another new development is the creation in the West Country of French-type soft cheeses, with Somerset Brie and Somerset Camembert now widely available. The range of West Country cheeses is wide, and although little can beat a slice of tasty traditional farmhouse Cheddar, look out for some more unusual varieties: Brendon Blue, Vulscombe, Cloisters, Tala, Wedmore, Little Rydings, Hazlewood, Devon Oke, Blackdown, Capricorn and the irresistible Stinking Bishop.

Entries are cross referenced by number to the maps on pages 130–131

291 Bowling Green Hotel ◆◆◆◆◆

9-10 Osborne Place, Lockyer Street, Plymouth, Devon PL1 2PU **Tel:** (01752) 209090 **Fax:** (01752) 209092
Web: http://www.smoothhound.co.uk/hotels/bowling.html

Situated in the historic naval city of Plymouth opposite the world famous 'Drake's Bowling Green', this elegant Georgian hotel has superbly appointed bedrooms offering all the modern facilities the traveller requires. With a full breakfast menu and friendly and efficient family staff, you can be sure of a memorable visit to Plymouth. The Bowling Green Hotel is centrally situated for the Barbican, Theatre Royal, leisure/conference centre and ferry port, with Dartmoor only a few miles away.

Bed & Breakfast per night: single room from £38.00; double room from £48.00–£54.00

Bedrooms: 1 single, 8 double, 2 triple, 1 family
Bathrooms: 12 en-suite
Parking: 4 spaces
Cards accepted: Mastercard, Visa, Switch/Delta, Amex, Diners, Eurocard, Visa Electron, Solo

292 Uppaton Country Guest House ◆◆◆◆

Buckland Monachorum, Yelverton, Devon PL20 7LL **Tel:** (01822) 855511

Uppaton House is one of those very special places that one constantly seeks but rarely finds. Surrounded by three acres of gardens and orchards, the house nestles directly within the Dartmoor National Park. Our public and guest bedrooms enjoy superb views over the gardens and the River Tamar. The heart of Uppaton is the kitchen where Alison and James create fine cuisine with local quality produce, coupled with a tempting wine list. Tranquillity and relaxation in a perfect setting.

Bed & Breakfast per night: single room from £25.00–£32.50; double room from £40.00–£50.00
Dinner, Bed & Breakfast per person, per night: £35.00–£40.00
Evening meal: 1800 (last orders 2000)

Bedrooms: 1 single, 2 double, 1 twin
Bathrooms: 3 en-suite, 1 private
Parking: 10 spaces

293 Tor Cottage ◆◆◆◆◆ Gold Award

Chillaton, Lifton, Devon PL16 0JE **Tel:** (01822) 860248 **Fax:** (01822) 860126
Web: http://www.torcottage.demon.co.uk **E-mail:** info@torcottage.demon.co.uk

Enjoy the ambience of this special place. A national winner of the English Tourist Board's 'England for Excellence' Award and holder of a 1999 Gold Award. Tor Cottage has a warm and relaxed atmosphere and nestles in its own private valley. Streamside setting, lovely gardens and 18 acres of wildlife hillsides. Peace, tranquillity and complete privacy in beautiful en-suite bedsitting rooms, each with a log fire and private garden/terrace. Superb traditional and vegetarian breakfasts. Heated pool (summer). Early booking advisable.

Bed & Breakfast per night: single occupancy from £76.00–£79.00; double room from £90.00–£98.00

Bedrooms: 2 double, 1 twin
Bathrooms: 3 en-suite
Parking: 8 spaces
Open: All year except January and December
Cards accepted: Mastercard, Visa, Switch/Delta

294 Ermewood House Hotel

★★ Silver Award

Totnes Road, Ermington, Ivybridge, Devon PL21 9NS **Tel:** (01548) 830741 **Fax:** (01548) 830982
Web: http://www.ermewood-house.co.uk **E-mail:** info@ermewood-house.co.uk

Ermewood House, a Grade II listed former rectory, is located in a warm, sheltered vale between Dartmoor and the unspoilt coastline of South Devon. All ten bedrooms are en-suite, have views over open countryside and are centrally heated. Our licensed restaurant provides a high standard of traditional, freshly prepared cuisine using mainly local produce. In colder months log fires create a warm and welcoming atmosphere. Summer or winter, Ermewood is the ideal place to stay.

Bed & Breakfast per night: single room from £40.00–£45.00; double room from £65.00–£78.00
Dinner, Bed & Breakfast per person, per night: £45.00–£51.00 (min 3 nights, 2 sharing)
Evening meal: 1830 (last orders 2030)

Bedrooms: 2 single, 6 double, 2 twin
Bathrooms: 10 en-suite
Parking: 20 spaces
Cards accepted: Mastercard, Visa, Switch/Delta, Eurocard, Maestro, Solo

295 Helliers Farm

♦♦♦♦

Ashford, Aveton Gifford, Kingsbridge, Devon TQ7 4ND **Tel:** (01548) 550689 **Fax:** (01548) 550689

Helliers Farm is a small sheep farm set on a hill overlooking a lovely valley in the South Hams. An ideal centre for touring the coasts, moors, golf courses (Bigbury, Thurlestone and Dartmouth), National Trust houses and walks, and the city of Plymouth. Tastefully appointed en-suite bedrooms and a comfortable lounge and dining room where excellent farmhouse breakfasts are served. No smoking.

Bed & Breakfast per night: single room from £22.00; double room from £44.00–£50.00

Bedrooms: 1 single, 2 double, 1 twin, 1 family
Bathrooms: 3 en-suite, 1 public
Parking: 6 spaces

296 Thurlestone Hotel

★★★★ Gold Award

Thurlestone, Kingsbridge, Devon TQ7 3NN **Tel:** (01548) 560382 **Fax:** (01548) 561069
Web: http://www.thurlestone.co.uk **E-mail:** enquiries@thurlestone.co.uk

An intimate atmosphere, characteristic of grand establishments, distinguishes us from others due to our location on the Devon coast, in an area of outstanding natural beauty. Sixty four en-suite bedrooms (includes four suites), well furnished with every facility, including video in some rooms. A restaurant with a reputation for fine rosette food, superb wine and long-serving staff. Leisure activities include indoor swimming pool, spa bath, sauna, solarium, 9-hole championship golf course and tennis, squash and badminton courts as well as opportunities for walks and fishing. Please telephone for brochure.

Bed & Breakfast per night: single room from £42.00–£90.00; double room from £84.00–£180.00
Dinner, Bed & Breakfast per person, per night: £53.00–£97.00 (min 2 nights)
Lunch available: 1200–1400

Evening meal: 1930 (last orders 2100)
Bedrooms: 5 single, 18 double, 24 twin, 13 triple, 4 family
Bathrooms: 64 en-suite **Parking:** 119 spaces
Cards accepted: Mastercard, Visa, Switch/Delta, Amex, Eurocard, JCB, Visa Electron

Entries are cross referenced by number to the maps on pages 130–131

297 Heron House Hotel

★★★ Silver Award

Thurlestone Sands, Salcombe, Devon TQ7 3JY **Tel:** (01548) 561308 or (01548) 561600 **Fax:** (01548) 560180

The hotel commands one of the most outstanding locations on the south coast. At the sea's edge, 50 yards from the large sandy beach and bird reserve in a National Trust protected area, surrounded by unspoilt countryside. All rooms enjoy superb views of sea or country and the bar lounge is elegant and spacious. For quieter moments another small lounge overlooks the outdoor pool. The modern, well-equipped kitchen produces high quality meals and has been awarded an AA Rosette for its food.

Bed & Breakfast per night: single occupancy from £40.00–£65.00; double room from £80.00–£150.00
Dinner, Bed & Breakfast per person, per night: £50.00–£85.00
Evening meal: 1900 (last orders 2050)

Bedrooms: 8 double, 6 twin, 3 family
Bathrooms: 17 en-suite
Parking: 50 spaces
Cards accepted: Mastercard, Visa, Switch/Delta, Eurocard

298 Tides Reach Hotel

★★★ Silver Award

South Sands, Salcombe, Devon TQ8 8LJ **Tel:** (01548) 843466 **Fax:** (01548) 843954
Web: http://www.tidesreach.com **E-mail:** book@tidesreach.com

Located in a tree-fringed sandy cove where country meets the sea, with a glorious view across the Salcombe Estuary, you can relax in style in this beautifully furnished and decorated hotel. Pamper yourself in the superb leisure complex, extensively equipped and with a sunny tropical atmosphere. Award-winning creative cuisine (AA 2 Rosettes) served with courtesy and care in our garden-room restaurant.

Bed & Breakfast per night: single occupancy from £50.00–£86.00; double room from £90.00–£192.00
Dinner, Bed & Breakfast per person, per night: £50.00–£120.00
Evening meal: 1900 (last orders 2100)

Bedrooms: 18 double, 17 twin, 3 family
Bathrooms: 38 en-suite
Parking: 100 spaces
Open: All year except January and December
Cards accepted: Mastercard, Visa, Switch/Delta, Amex, Diners, Eurocard, JCB

299 Knowle Farm

◆◆◆◆

Rattery, Nr Totnes, Devon TQ10 9JY **Tel:** (01364) 73914 **Fax:** (01364) 73914

Four-poster, pretty linen, beams, wood-panelled dining room and Aga-cooked breakfasts in our 17th-century Devon longhouse. Set in 44 acres of beautiful farmland, Knowle Farm is close to Totnes and Dartmoor, and within easy reach of the wonderful coastline and sandy beaches. Pet farm animals abound. There is a heated pool from May to September, tennis, an indoor purpose-built toddlers' soft play area and table tennis. We have a king-size four-poster room and a twin room, both en-suite, as well as a children's twin room adjacent (adaptable for adults) which shares the en-suite facilities.

Bed & Breakfast per night: single occupancy from £35.00–£40.00; double room from £48.00–£55.00

Bedrooms: 1 double, 2 twin
Bathrooms: 2 en-suite
Parking: 9 spaces

300 The Old Forge at Totnes ◆◆◆◆

Seymour Place, Totnes, Devon TQ9 5AY **Tel:** (01803) 862174 **Fax:** (01803) 865385

This beautiful 600-year-old building is a haven of comfort and relaxation, not far from the town centre. Rooms are delightfully co-ordinated, offering hairdryer, radio alarm, telephone, central heating, colour television, beverage tray, continental bedding and direct dial telephone. We also have ground floor rooms and a family cottage suite. Leisure lounge with whirlpool spa. Enjoy breakfast in the Tudor-style dining room which offers a wide choice of menu with vegetarian options. Specialities: golf breaks (near 15 courses) and 'hands on' blacksmithing. No smoking indoors. Extensive afternoon tea menu served in the walled tea garden or conservatory.

Bed & Breakfast per night: single room from £42.00–£50.00; double room from £52.00–£72.00

Bedrooms: 1 single, 5 double, 2 twin, 2 family
Bathrooms: 9 en-suite, 1 private
Parking: 10 spaces
Cards accepted: Mastercard, Visa, Switch/Delta, Eurocard

301 Edgemoor Hotel ★★★ Silver Award

Haytor Road, Bovey Tracey, Devon TQ13 9LE **Tel:** (01626) 832466 **Fax:** (01626) 834760
Web: http://www.edgemoor.co.uk **E-mail:** edgemoor@btinternet.com

'Loaded with charm', this wisteria-clad country house hotel is personally run by resident proprietors Rod and Pat Day. With its beautiful gardens and lovely en-suite bedrooms (including some four-posters) the Edgemoor provides the ideal setting in which to unwind from the cares of modern life. Good food (AA 2 Rosettes), fine wines and beautiful countryside combine to help make your stay memorable and enjoyable.

Bed & Breakfast per night: single room from £50.00–£57.50; double room from £80.00–£100.00
Dinner, Bed & Breakfast per person, per night: £55.00–£65.00 (min 2 nights)
Lunch available: 1200–1345
Evening meal: 1900 (last orders 2100)

Bedrooms: 3 single, 9 double, 3 twin, 1 triple, 1 family
Bathrooms: 17 en-suite
Parking: 50 spaces
Cards accepted: Mastercard, Visa, Switch/Delta, Amex, Eurocard, JCB, Visa Electron

302 Mill End Hotel ★★★ Silver Award

Sandypark, Chagford, Devon TQ13 8JN **Tel:** (01647) 432282 **Fax:** (01647) 433106
E-mail: millendhotel@talk21.com

Converted from a working mill, Mill End has retained all its rural charm. The mill wheel still turns in the courtyard and the Teign, which runs by the door, is one of the ten best sea-trout rivers in the country, with fishing available to guests. The gardens and walks are delightful and the hotel is ideal as a touring centre for the West. Then again, you could just sleep! Award-winning (AA 2 Rosettes) cuisine.

Bed & Breakfast per night: single room from £51.00–£79.00; double room from £72.00–£100.00
Dinner, Bed & Breakfast per person, per night: £55.00–£160.00
Lunch available: 1230–1345
Evening meal: 1930 (last orders 2100)

Bedrooms: 2 single, 5 double, 8 twin, 2 triple
Bathrooms: 15 en-suite, 2 private
Parking: 21 spaces
Cards accepted: Mastercard, Visa, Switch/Delta, Eurocard

Entries are cross referenced by number to the maps on pages 130–131

303 Staddlestones

Thorndon, Thorndon Cross, Okehampton, Devon EX20 4NG **Tel:** (01837) 861389

Attractive converted barn and round house near Dartmoor in the heart of rural West Devon. Guest accommodation consists of a ground floor twin-bedded room, private sitting room and private bathroom. Guests have full use of the secluded garden. Ideal for all Devon and Cornwall, National Trust properties, golf, riding, boating, fishing, bird watching and good walks. This is a no smoking establishment. We give our guests a warm welcome.

Bed & Breakfast per night: single occupancy £22.00; double room £44.00

Bedrooms: 1 twin
Bathrooms: 1 private
Parking: 4 spaces

Clapperbridges

Near Ashway in Exmoor, the River Barle flows wide and shallow over its brown stony bed. On either side, the road ends abruptly in a somewhat intimidating ford, but walkers may remain dry-shod, crossing the Barle via a magnificent walkway of vast stone slabs, known as Tarr Steps.

Tarr Steps is a type of ancient bridge known as a clapperbridge, and at 177ft (54m) in length is the largest and most elaborate of its type in England. The term 'clapperbridge' is used for any bridge constructed from large, flat slabs of stone forming a level pathway over a river or stream; the word probably developed from the Anglo Saxon cleaca meaning 'stepping stones'. Indeed a number of clapperbridges may well have begun as simple stepping-stones, which later formed the piers upon which linking slabs of stone were balanced. While some clapperbridges consist simply of a single slab thrown across the stream, multi-span bridges have typically between two and five spans (Tarr Steps with its magnificent 17 spans, is actually something of an anomaly).

No-one knows exactly when Tarr Steps was built, and, although for many years considered a pre-historic monument, it is now thought to be of much more recent construction. Most clapperbridges were built in the 14th century on packhorse routes, but a few appeared as late as the 18th and 19th centuries. They were simple and functional, and when routes changed or more superior structures superseded

them, they were very often allowed to disappear. Today, only about 40 remain in England.

Clapperbridges are found in parts of the country where the local rock yields large slabs of strong stone. There are consequently two main concentrations: one in North and West Yorkshire, the other in Devon and Cornwall. The greatest number are in Dartmoor, which boasts a wide range of variations. Postbridge, a lonely village in the heart of the Moor, has one of the finest of its type (shown above). It consists of three vast slabs of granite, some 17ft (5m) by 7ft (2m) in size, supported by four piers of granite blocks. Also on Dartmoor are Teignhead's bridge, built in 1790, and one over the Cowsic River at Two Bridges, built in 1837. At Wallabrook is a single-span clapperbridge, while the bridge at Yar Tor Down, Hexworthy, has three spans. Runnage bridge, near Postbridge, is a late example fitted with parapets.

304 Parsonage Farm

◆◆◆◆

Iddesleigh, Winkleigh, Devon EX19 8SN **Tel:** (01837) 810318

A warm welcome awaits you in our period farmhouse, home of the famous parson Jack Russell, situated approximately one mile from the picturesque village of Iddesleigh and within 3.5 miles of the market town of Hatherleigh. An ideal base to explore Dartmoor, Exmoor and both coastlines. This is an area of outstanding natural beauty and very peaceful. Woodland and river walks around our farm allow you to see a great variety of wildlife.

Bed & Breakfast per night: single occupancy from £18.00; double room from £36.00

Bedrooms: 1 double, 1 family
Bathrooms: 2 en-suite
Parking: 2 spaces
Open: April–October

305 Lower Nichols Nymet Farm

◆◆◆◆ Silver Award

Lower Nichols Nymet, North Tawton, Devon EX20 2BW **Tel:** (01363) 82510 **Fax:** (01363) 82510
E-mail: pylefamlnn@aol.com

We offer a haven of comfort and rest on our farm that is set in rolling countryside in the centre of Devon. On holiday, food becomes important – we serve hearty and healthy breakfasts and candlelit dinners using local produce. Our elegantly furnished en-suite bedrooms have glorious views. There are many National Trust properties and other attractions to visit. This is a perfect base for exploring the beauties of the West Country. A no smoking establishment. Brochure available.

Bed & Breakfast per night: single occupancy £25.00; double room from £40.00– £45.00
Dinner, Bed & Breakfast per person, per night: £30.00–£32.50
Evening meal: 1830

Bedrooms: 1 double, 1 family
Bathrooms: 2 en-suite
Parking: 4 spaces
Open: March–October

306 Little Brendon Hill Farm

◆◆◆◆◆ Gold Award

Wheddon Cross, Exmoor, Somerset TA24 7BG **Tel:** (01643) 841556 **Fax:** (01643) 841556
E-mail: Larry.Maxwell@btinternet.com

Our aim is to give our guests the very best of everything – excellent food prepared with fresh wholesome ingredients presented on fine china, cut glass and silver in the loveliest surroundings. Your comfort is paramount. Log fires. Central heating. Non-smoking. All rooms en-suite. Relaxed short stays or long lazy weeks. Please ask for our brochure.

Bed & Breakfast per night: single occupancy £30.00; double room from £40.00– £44.00
Dinner, Bed & Breakfast per person, per night: £33.00–£37.00
Evening meal: 1900 (last orders 1200)

Bedrooms: 1 double, 2 twin
Bathrooms: 3 en-suite
Parking: 10 spaces

Entries are cross referenced by number to the maps on pages 130–131

307 Porlock Vale House

★★ Silver Award

Porlock Weir, Somerset TA24 8NY **Tel:** (01643) 862338 **Fax:** (01643) 863338
Web: http://www.porlockvale.co.uk **E-mail:** info@porlockvale.co.uk

Formerly a hunting lodge, now a magnificent Edwardian country house hotel in a wonderful situation. Set in twenty five acres of grounds which sweep down to the sea, Porlock Vale House nestles at the foot of the ancient wooded fringe where Exmoor meets the coast. A friendly, unpretentious hotel where you can enjoy good food and fine wines served in a relaxed, informal atmosphere, with beautiful, uninterrupted views across Porlock Bay. Whether you enjoy the great outdoors or sitting by a log fire, Porlock Vale is the perfect place for a short break at any time of the year.

Bed & Breakfast per night: single occupancy from £39.00–£59.00; double room from £60.00–£95.00
Dinner, Bed & Breakfast per person, per night: £45.00–£68.00
Lunch available: 1200–1400

Bedrooms: 10 double, 5 twin
Bathrooms: 15 en-suite
Parking: 20 spaces
Cards accepted: Mastercard, Visa, Switch/Delta, Amex

308 Fern Cottage

◆◆◆◆

Allerford, Nr Porlock, Exmoor National Park, Somerset TA24 8HN **Tel:** (01643) 862215 **Fax:** (01643) 862215

A large traditional Exmoor cottage dating back to the early 16th century in a tiny National Trust village in a wood-fringed vale within Exmoor National Park. Walks in spectacular scenery start on the doorstep! Much acclaimed for our traditional and bistro style food. Dinner is served around our large table in an informal 'dinner party' style or, depending on guest numbers, a more intimate setting. A comprehensive wine cellar with over 85 different wines, including some vintages at surprisingly pleasant prices.

Bed & Breakfast per night: single occupancy £36.50; double room £53.00
Dinner, Bed & Breakfast per person, per night: £39.00
Evening meal: 1900 (last bookings 1800)

Bedrooms: 3 triple
Bathrooms: 3 en-suite
Parking: 8 spaces
Cards accepted: Mastercard, Visa, Switch/Delta, Eurocard, JCB, Maestro, Visa Electron, Solo

309 Channel House Hotel

★★ Silver Award

Church Path, Off Northfield Road, Minehead, Somerset TA24 5QG **Tel:** (01643) 703229 **Fax:** (01643) 708925
Web: http://www.channelhouse.co.uk **E-mail:** channel.house@virgin.net

An elegant Edwardian country house perfectly located for exploring the beauty of Exmoor and situated on the lower slopes of Minehead's picturesque North Hill where it nestles in two acres of award-winning gardens. The high standards of cuisine and accommodation will best suit those seeking superior quality and comfort. If you would like to experience smiling service in the tranquil elegance of this lovely hotel, we will be delighted to send you our brochure and sample menu.

Bed & Breakfast per night: single occupancy £70.00; double room £110.00
Dinner, Bed & Breakfast per person, per night: £51.00–£65.00
Evening meal: 1900 (last orders 2030)

Bedrooms: 2 double, 5 twin, 1 triple
Bathrooms: 8 en-suite
Parking: 10 spaces **Open:** March–November
Cards accepted: Mastercard, Visa, Switch/Delta, Amex, Diners, Eurocard, JCB, Maestro, Visa Elect

At-a-glance symbols are explained on the flap inside the back cover

310 Combe House Hotel

★★ Silver Award

Holford, Bridgwater, Somerset TA5 1RZ **Tel:** (01278) 741382 **Fax:** (01278) 741322
E-mail: enquiries@combehouse.co.uk

In the heart of the Quantock Hills (renowned as an area of outstanding natural beauty) lies this 17th-century house of great character. Once a tannery, this cottage-style hotel offers absolute peace and quiet in beautiful surroundings. Inside the beamed building, with its charming collection of pictures, pottery and period furniture, the visitor will find the relaxed atmosphere and friendly service ideal to enjoy Combe House, its AA Rosette restaurant, the Quantocks and the many attractions in the area.

Bed & Breakfast per night: single room from £28.00–£38.00; double room from £56.00–£87.00
Dinner, Bed & Breakfast per person, per night: £46.75–£55.25 (min 2 nights)
Evening meal: 1930 (last orders 2030)

Bedrooms: 4 single, 5 double, 7 twin
Bathrooms: 16 en-suite
Parking: 20 spaces
Cards accepted: Mastercard, Visa, Switch/Delta, Amex, Eurocard

311 Blackmore Farm

◆◆◆◆◆

Cannington, Bridgwater, Somerset TA5 2NE **Tel:** (01278) 653442 **Fax:** (01278) 653427
E-mail: Dyerfarm@aol.com

A rare Grade I listed 14th-century manor house retaining many period features including oak beams, stone archways, log fires and its own private chapel. A traditional farmhouse breakfast is served in the Great Hall. All the bedrooms are en-suite, one with a four-poster bed. You can be assured of a warm welcome to this family home situated in a quiet, rural location, with views of the Quantock Hills. An ideal base for touring Bath, Somerset and Exmoor. Facilities for disabled guests. ♿ **Category 2**

Bed & Breakfast per night: single occupancy from £30.00–£40.00; double room from £42.00–£52.00

Bedrooms: 3 double, 1 triple
Bathrooms: 4 en-suite
Parking: 6 spaces
Cards accepted: Mastercard, Visa, Switch/Delta

312 Redlands

◆◆◆◆

Trebles Holford, Combe Florey, Taunton, Somerset TA4 3HA **Tel:** (01823) 433159
E-mail: redlandshouse@hotmail.com

A warm welcome awaits our guests at Redlands, a peacefully located barn conversion set beside a stream adjacent to the Quantock Hills. There is excellent walking, riding and cycling locally, or just enjoy the steam era on the restored West Somerset railway. Within easy reach are gardens, National Trust properties and the coast. A ground floor room is suitable for disabled guests, but whatever your needs we try to ensure an enjoyable stay. 🚶 **Category 3**

Bed & Breakfast per night: single occupancy £25.00; double room £50.00

Bedrooms: 1 double, 1 twin
Bathrooms: 2 en-suite
Parking: 4 spaces

Entries are cross referenced by number to the maps on pages 130–131

313 Stafford Barton

◆◆◆◆◆ Gold Award

Broadhembury, Honiton, Devon EX14 3LU **Tel:** (01404) 841403 **Fax:** (01404) 841403
E-mail: anne@devonfarms.co.uk

Come and share our lovely home for a holiday treat. Just a short walk through leafy lanes from picturesque thatched village. Glorious views of rolling hills and our beautiful gardens from the lounge with picture windows. Day trips may take you to Honiton, Sidmouth, National Trust properties or Exeter. The dining room has a table licence and offers the very best of farmhouse cooking in a relaxed and informal atmosphere. Log fire for your warmth on those dark and cool evenings. Arrive as a guest, leave as a friend.

Bed & Breakfast per night: single occupancy from £25.00–£30.00; double room from £45.00–£50.00
Dinner, Bed & Breakfast per person, per night: £35.00–£37.50
Evening meal: 1800 (last orders 1930)

Bedrooms: 2 double, 1 twin
Bathrooms: 3 en-suite
Parking: 3 spaces

314 Thomas Luny House

◆◆◆◆◆ Silver Award

Teign Street, Teignmouth, Devon TQ14 8EG **Tel:** (01626) 772976

Thomas Luny House – built by the marine artist Thomas Luny around 1800 – is tucked away in a conservation area. It is now the home of Alison and John Allan and their young family. The house, which is surrounded by a secluded garden, is furnished tastefully with antiques and has four themed en-suite rooms, two with views to the river. Drive under an archway (beware: the entrance is narrow) and enjoy a warm welcome.

Bed & Breakfast per night: single occupancy from £30.00–£35.00; double room from £50.00–£70.00

Bedrooms: 2 double, 2 twin
Bathrooms: 4 en-suite
Parking: 6 spaces
Cards accepted: Mastercard, Visa

315 Suite Dreams Hotel

◆◆◆◆

Steep Hill, Maidencombe, Torquay TQ1 4TS **Tel:** (01803) 313900 **Fax:** (01803) 313841
Web: http://www.suitedreams.co.uk **E-mail:** suitedreams@suitedreams.co.uk

Set in the tranquil heart of the West Country with spectacular, panoramic valley and sea views, we are able to guarantee our guests a relaxing stay in peaceful surroundings. The hotel itself is spaciously fitted to the highest standard, whilst all the rooms offer a wide range of facilities including colour television, hospitality tray, fridge and en-suite bathroom. This special combination of style and comfort allows us to ensure that we offer an excellent service.

Bed & Breakfast per night: single occupancy from £20.50–£44.00; double room from £41.00–£68.00

Bedrooms: 9 double, 3 twin
Bathrooms: 12 en-suite
Parking: 12 spaces
Cards accepted: Mastercard, Visa, Switch/Delta, Eurocard, JCB, Solo

At-a-glance symbols are explained on the flap inside the back cover

316 Wynncroft Hotel ◆◆◆◆

2 Elmsleigh Park, Paignton, Devon TQ4 5AT **Tel:** (01803) 525728 **Fax:** (01803) 526335
Web: http://www.wynncroft.co.uk **E-mail:** wynncroft@FSBDial.co.uk

Enjoy a relaxing, friendly stay at the Wynncroft. Comfort, service and a warm, friendly welcome await you in our family-run Victorian hotel, only a short level walk from the beach or town. Free transport from the coach and railway station, or park in our large private car park. A la carte menu using fresh local produce, catering for a range of special diets, including gluten free. Well-appointed en-suite rooms with television, clock radio, hairdryer, etc.

Bed & Breakfast per night: single occupancy from £20.00–£32.00; double room from £40.00–£64.00
Dinner, Bed & Breakfast per person, per night: £29.00–£41.00
Evening meal: 1800 (last orders 1900)

Bedrooms: 6 double, 2 twin, 2 triple
Bathrooms: 9 en-suite, 1 public
Parking: 8 spaces
Open: All year except November and December
Cards accepted: Mastercard, Visa, Switch/Delta, Eurocard, Maestro

317 Blue Haze Hotel ◆◆◆◆

Seaway Lane, Torquay, Devon TQ2 6PS **Tel:** (01803) 607186 or (01803) 606205 **Fax:** (01803) 607186
Web: bluehazehotel.co.uk **E-mail:** mail@bluehazehotel.co.uk

'That something special!' - attractive, peaceful and surrounded by lovely grounds, in a quiet country lane leading down to the sea. Cheerful service with free smiles for everyone. On arrival – Devonshire cream tea with home-made scones. Superior quality bedrooms, sparkling clean, well appointed and all non-smoking. Splendid breakfasts to start your day – freshly cooked to order or chosen from the tempting buffet. Easy parking in our large, pleasant, private car park well away from the road.

Bed & Breakfast per night: double room from £62.00–£66.00

Bedrooms: 4 double, 2 twin, 2 triple, 1 family
Bathrooms: 9 en-suite
Parking: 15 spaces
Open: April–October
Cards accepted: Mastercard, Visa, Switch, Amex, Eurocard, JCB

318 Osborne Hotel & Langtry's Restaurant ★★★ Silver Award

Hesketh Crescent, Meadfoot Beach, Torquay, Devon TQ1 2LL **Tel:** (01803) 213311 **Fax:** (01803) 296788

This 29-bedroomed hotel, centrepiece of an elegant Regency crescent, overlooks the seclusion of Meadfoot Beach. The hotel offers the friendly ambience of a country home complemented by superior standards of comfort, five acres of gardens, indoor/outdoor pools, tennis court, gym, sauna, solarium, snooker room and putting green. Langtry's guide-acclaimed restaurant offers superlative food every evening and is one of the foremost restaurants on the English Riviera. The all-day Brasserie serves an international selection of food and drinks.

Bed & Breakfast per night: single room from £52.00–£70.00; double room from £104.00–£170.00
Dinner, Bed & Breakfast per person, per night: £68.00–£100.00
Evening meal: 1900 (last orders 2145)

Bedrooms: 1 single, 26 double, 2 family
Bathrooms: 29 en-suite
Parking: 100 spaces
Cards accepted: Mastercard, Visa, Switch/Delta, Amex

319 Royal Castle Hotel ★★★ Silver Award

11 The Quay, Dartmouth, Devon TQ6 9PS **Tel:** (01803) 833033 **Fax:** (01803) 835445
Web: http://www.r-castle-hotel.co.uk **E-mail:** enquiry@r-castle-hotel.co.uk

A 17th-century coaching hostelry in the heart of the historic port of Dartmouth – an unrivalled location ideal for short breaks at any time of year. 25 luxuriously appointed en-suite bedrooms, all individually decorated and furnished, some with four-poster or brass beds and jacuzzi. The elegant restaurant on the first floor overlooks the estuary and specialises in select regional produce and locally-caught seafood. Two bars serve delicious food, traditional ales and a good choice of wines. We look forward to welcoming you.

Bed & Breakfast per night: single room from £41.95–£58.55; double room from £84.00–£130.00
Dinner, Bed & Breakfast per person, per night: £53.00–£76.00
Lunch available: 1200–1400

Evening meal: 1845 (last orders 2200)
Bedrooms: 4 single, 10 double, 8 twin, 3 triple
Bathrooms: 25 en-suite
Parking: 17 spaces
Cards accepted: Mastercard, Visa, Switch/Delta, Amex, Eurocard, Solo

320 Royal York and Faulkner Hotel ★★ Silver Award

Esplanade, Sidmouth, Devon EX10 8AZ **Tel:** 0800 220714 **Fax:** (01395) 577472
Web: http://www.royal-york-hotel.co.uk **E-mail:** yorkhotel@eclipse.co.uk

Charming Regency hotel in the centre of Sidmouth's delightful Esplanade and adjacent to the picturesque town centre. Long established family-run hotel offering all amenities and excellent facilities, coupled with personal, efficient service. 68 well appointed bedrooms, mainly en-suite, many enjoying sea views. Ample tastefully furnished lounge and bar areas. Sea facing dining room offering excellent cuisine with a varied choice of menu. Attractive leisure complex comprising jacuzzi, sauna, solarium and exercise equipment. Indoor short-mat bowls, rink and full-size snooker table.

Bed & Breakfast per night: single room from £28.50–£48.50; double room from £57.00–£97.00
Dinner, Bed & Breakfast per person, per night: £36.50–£56.50
Lunch available: 1200–1400
Evening meal: 1915 (last orders 2030)

Bedrooms: 22 single, 9 double, 29 twin, 8 triple
Bathrooms: 66 en-suite, 2 private
Parking: 20 spaces
Open: All year except January
Cards accepted: Mastercard, Visa, Switch/Delta, Eurocard, JCB, Visa Electron

321 St Edmund's ♦♦♦♦ Silver Award

Swan Hill Road, Colyford, Colyton, Devon EX24 6QQ **Tel:** (01297) 552626 **Fax:** (01297) 553829

Offering individually furnished en-suite bed and breakfast facilities for all the family (including a large four-poster bedroom), St Edmund's is ideally located in East Devon's beautiful Axe Valley. The pretty village of Colyford, between Lyme Regis in Dorset and Sidmouth in Devon, also has two excellent pubs and a restaurant with extensive menus. Miles of unspoilt coastal and countryside walks can be found in this lovely area where a warm welcome awaits you.

Bed & Breakfast per night: single room from £25.00–£30.00; double room from £44.00–£56.00

Bedrooms: 1 single, 3 double, 1 twin, 1 triple, 1 family
Bathrooms: 7 en-suite **Parking:** 8 spaces
Open: All year except January and December
Cards accepted: Mastercard, Visa, Switch/Delta, Visa Electron

At-a-glance symbols are explained on the flap inside the back cover

322 Swallows Eaves Hotel

 ★★ Silver Award

Colyford, Colyton, Devon EX24 6QJ **Tel:** (01297) 553184 **Fax:** (01297) 553574

Enjoy the beauty and treasures of Devon and Dorset from this attractive wisteria-clad small hotel. Pretty village setting in the Sidmouth-Lyme Regis area, two miles from the sea, with glorious views towards the heritage coast. Only eight delightful en-suite rooms. For breakfast taste real pork sausages, freshly made by the village butcher, and smother thick slices of toast with locally made chunky marmalade before walking the coastal footpath, visiting glorious gardens and viewing the abundance of National Trust properties. Red Rosette dinners. Ground floor room and easy parking. We regret no children, no dogs and no smoking. Complimentary use of indoor heated pool.

Bed & Breakfast per night: single room from £37.00–£52.00; double room from £54.00–£84.00

Dinner, Bed & Breakfast per person, per night: £47.00–£64.00

Evening meal: 1900 (last orders 2000)

Bedrooms: 1 single, 3 double, 4 twin
Bathrooms: 8 en-suite
Parking: 10 spaces
Cards accepted: Mastercard, Visa, Switch/Delta

À la Ronde

This extraordinary building, on the outskirts of Exmouth in Devon, was the brainchild of a pair of energetic and creative cousins, Jane and Mary Parminter. Built on an octagonal plan, it has windows on each of its eight corners. Its steep conical roof was originally thatched and had a little cupola on the top surrounded by four chimneys and topped by a weather vane. In the 1880s one stunned visitor wrote of it that it 'would not be out of place in one of the South Sea islands', and indeed with its thatched roof and limewashed walls the building did have something of the air of a tropical mud hut, though on

a grander scale. Its model was, in fact, the octagonal basilica of San Vitale in Ravenna. The intrepid cousins had visited Ravenna on a ten year grand tour which they completed in 1795, and on their return determined to build themselves a house which would remind them of their travels and provide a home for their souvenirs.

More intriguing even than the building itself is the interior of À la Ronde (tel. 01395 265514). In the 18th century it was fashionable for ladies of leisure to craft elaborate decorations for their homes; at À la Ronde a vast range of these skills has been employed to prodigious – almost ludicrous – effect. The rooms, in particular the gallery and drawing room, are adorned with pictures and patterns created with feathers, shells, dried flowers, marbled paint, cut paper, sand, and even seaweed and straw.

When Mary Parminter died in 1849 she left clear instructions that À la Ronde and its contents should be preserved and that only unmarried kinswomen should inherit the property. These conditions were observed for several generations, until changes in conveyancing law allowed a male relative finally to take over the house. Under the ownership of Rev Oswald Reichel in the 1890s major changes were made, including the replacement of the thatch with tiles, the addition of dormer windows, the demolition of an internal wall and the insertion of a gargantuan central heating system. Nevertheless, most of the cousins' extraordinary legacy has been preserved.

323 Lea Hill Hotel

★★ Silver Award

Membury, Axminster, Devon EX13 7AQ **Tel:** (01404) 881881 or (01404) 881388 **Fax:** (01404) 881890
Web: http://www.leahillhotel.co.uk

Award-winning, 14th-century hotel set in eight acres of grounds overlooking a secluded valley in peaceful Devon countryside, only eight miles from the coast. Mellow stone, oak beams and inglenook fireplaces enhance the relaxed, tranquil and friendly atmosphere. The beamed restaurant offers Rosette cuisine taking advantage of fresh local produce. Lea Hill is ideally situated for touring the West Country, walking, bird-watching, visiting National Trust properties or simply relaxing away from it all on our terraces or in our gardens.

Bed & Breakfast per night: single occupancy from £59.00–£63.00; double room from £98.00–£116.00
Dinner, Bed & Breakfast per person, per night: £82.00–£86.00
Lunch available: 1200–1400

Evening meal: 1900 (last orders 2100)
Bedrooms: 7 double, 4 twin
Bathrooms: 11 en-suite **Parking:** 50 spaces
Open: All year except January and February
Cards accepted: Mastercard, Visa, Switch/Delta, Amex, Eurocard

324 Thatch Lodge Hotel

◆◆◆◆◆ Gold Award

The Street, Charmouth, near Lyme Regis, Dorset DT6 6PQ **Tel:** (01297) 560407 **Fax:** (01297) 560407

'Picture postcard' 14th-century thatched hotel, originally a monks' retreat for nearby Forde Abbey. Four-poster, half-tester bedrooms and a Garden-View Suite, all with many thoughtful extras. Antiques, grapes cascading from a 200-year-old vine, and beautiful walled gardens make this an ideal retreat. Situated in an area of outstanding natural beauty, just three minutes' walk from the world-famous fossil beach. Discover the coastal location chosen for 'Emma', 'Restoration' and BBC's 'Harbour Lights'. We offer tranquillity, discerning quality and superb chef-inspired, AA 2 Rosette cuisine. Non-smoking throughout.

Bed & Breakfast per night: double room from £78.00–£120.00
Dinner, Bed & Breakfast per person, per night: £66.50–£87.50
Evening meal: 1930 (last orders 1930)

Bedrooms: 5 double, 1 twin
Bathrooms: 6 en-suite **Parking:** 10 spaces
Open: All year except January and February
Cards accepted: Mastercard, Visa, Switch/Delta, Eurocard, JCB, Visa Electron, Solo

325 Roundham House Hotel

★★ Silver Award

Roundham Gardens, West Bay Road, Bridport, Dorset DT6 4BD **Tel:** (01308) 422753 **Fax:** (01308) 421500

Owned and personally managed by Daphne and Jeremy Thomas, Roundham House is situated in an enviable position within an acre of feature gardens, with westerly views over the Dorset countryside and Lyme Bay. Built of local stone in 1903, the hotel offers every modern amenity for the discerning guest and is renowned for its excellent food, wine and hospitality. The table d'hôte and à la carte menus offer a wide choice, including vegetarian options, and feature local produce and fresh vegetables from the kitchen garden. The hotel is an ideal base for walking, touring or just relaxing in an area of outstanding beauty.

Bed & Breakfast per night: single room from £35.00–£40.00; double room from £60.00–£80.00
Dinner, Bed & Breakfast per person, per night: £50.00–£55.00

Evening meal: 1900 (last orders 2030)
Bedrooms: 1 single, 3 double, 2 twin, 2 family
Bathrooms: 7 en-suite, 1 private
Parking: 12 spaces
Open: All year except January and February
Cards accepted: Mastercard, Visa, JCB

At-a-glance symbols are explained on the flap inside the back cover

326 Britmead House

◆◆◆◆

West Bay Road, Bridport, Dorset DT6 4EG **Tel:** (01308) 422941 **Fax:** (01308) 422941

An elegant and spacious, recently refurbished detached house. Situated between Bridport and West Bay harbour with its beaches, Chesil Beach and the Dorset Coastal Path. An ideal base from which to discover Dorset. The spacious south-west facing dining room and lounge overlook an attractive garden and open countryside beyond. Well-appointed en-suite bedrooms, all with many thoughtful extras. Optional dinners. Quite simply everything, where possible, is tailored to suit your needs.

Bed & Breakfast per night: single occupancy from £26.00–£38.00; double room from £52.00–£60.00
Dinner, Bed & Breakfast per person, per night: £41.00–£54.00
Evening meal: 1900

Bedrooms: 4 double, 3 twin
Bathrooms: 6 en-suite, 1 private
Parking: 8 spaces
Cards accepted: Mastercard, Visa, Switch/Delta, Eurocard

327 Kenora Private Hotel

◆◆◆◆

5 Stavordale Road, Weymouth, Dorset DT4 OAB **Tel:** (01305) 771215
E-mail: kenora.hotel@wdi.co.uk

Conveniently situated, in a quiet cul-de-sac, 500 metres from the sandy beach and less to the town and harbour. The Kenora is perfectly placed to discover the delights of Weymouth, or as a base to explore the beauty of Hardy's Wessex. The hotel is run by Jean and Chris Lamb and has been for the last 22 years. They aim to provide good food, using local fresh produce whenever possible, and well-maintained comfortable accommodation.

Bed & Breakfast per night: single room from £28.00–£37.00; double room from £55.00–£63.00
Dinner, Bed & Breakfast per person, per night: £39.00–£42.00 (min 2 nights)

Bedrooms: 3 single, 7 double, 2 twin, 2 triple, 1 family
Bathrooms: 13 en-suite, 1 public
Parking: 15 spaces **Open:** April–September
Cards accepted: Mastercard, Visa, Delta

328 Bay Lodge

◆◆◆◆◆ Silver Award

27 Greenhill, Weymouth, Dorset DT4 7SW **Tel:** (01305) 782419 **Fax:** (01305) 782828
Web: http://www.baylodge.co.uk **E-mail:** barbara@baylodge.co.uk

Bay Lodge is set in a tranquil position in its own grounds at the centre of Weymouth Bay and enjoys panoramic sea views towards the harbour and surrounding cliffs. The luxurious bedrooms, some of which are on the ground floor, are furnished to accentuate their own unique features with king-size beds, jacuzzi bathrooms and open log fires. We have an elegant dining room where our chef prides himself on serving fresh local produce. The lounges have deep, comfortable armchairs and, together with the dining room, have open log/coal fires. Private car park. Two-day bargain breaks from £85 per person.

Bed & Breakfast per night: single room from £39.50; double room from £60.00
Dinner, Bed & Breakfast per person, per night: £42.50–£47.50 (min 2 nights, 2 sharing)
Evening meal: 1830 (last orders 1900)

Bedrooms: 1 single, 6 double, 4 twin, 1 triple
Bathrooms: 12 en-suite
Parking: 18 spaces
Cards accepted: Mastercard, Visa, Switch/Delta, Amex, Diners, Eurocard, JCB, Solo

Entries are cross referenced by number to the maps on pages 130–131

329 The Old Rectory ◆◆◆◆

Winterbourne Steepleton, Dorchester, Dorset DT2 9LG **Tel:** (01305) 889468 **Fax:** (01305) 889737
Web: http://www.trees.eurobell.co.uk **E-mail:** trees@eurobell.co.uk

Genuine 1850 Victorian rectory situated in a quiet hamlet, surrounded by breathtaking countryside. Close to historic Dorchester and Weymouth's sandy beaches. We specialise in providing a quiet comfortable night's sleep followed by a copious English, vegetarian or continental breakfast, with fresh organic home produce. The Crystal Dining Room is available for celebration dinners and cordon bleu cuisine (minimum 6 people). Enjoy our superbly appointed lounge, croquet lawn and putting green. Local pub within walking distance.

Bed & Breakfast per night: double room from £45.00–£100.00

Bedrooms: 3 double
Bathrooms: 3 en-suite
Parking: 8 spaces

330 Yalbury Cottage Hotel and Restaurant ◆◆◆◆◆

Lower Bockhampton, Dorchester, Dorset DT2 8PZ **Tel:** (01305) 262382 **Fax:** (01305) 266412
Web: http://www.smoothhound.co.uk/hotels/yalbury.html **E-mail:** yalbury.cottage@virgin.net

Nestling amidst woodlands and green fields and just 200 metres from the River Frome, Yalbury Cottage is the perfect place to 'relax and unwind'. This friendly 17th-century thatched hotel resides in a quiet hamlet at the heart of Thomas Hardy country and just a mile from his birthplace. The award-winning (AA 2 Rosette) food of head chef Russell Brown is complemented by oak beams and inglenook fireplaces in our pretty no smoking restaurant. Our meals are prepared from top quality Dorset produce and are accompanied by an extensive international wine list.

Bed & Breakfast per night: single occupancy £51.00; double room £78.00
Dinner, Bed & Breakfast per person, per night: £52.00–£71.00 (min 2 nights)
Evening meal: 1900 (last orders 2100)

Bedrooms: 6 double, 1 twin, 1 triple
Bathrooms: 8 en-suite
Parking: 19 spaces
Open: All year except January
Cards accepted: Mastercard, Visa, Switch/Delta, Eurocard, JCB, Solo

331 Holyleas House ◆◆◆◆ Silver Award

Buckland Newton, Dorchester, Dorset DT2 7DP **Tel:** (01300) 345214 **Fax:** (01305) 264488

The family Labrador, Holly, will welcome you to this warm, friendly country house with lovely walled gardens in a peaceful village between Dorchester and Sherborne, surrounded by rolling hills yet only 30 minutes from the coast. Rooms are beautifully decorated with antique furniture and enjoy fine views. Guests' sitting room and dining room have log fires in winter. Delicious breakfast includes our own free-range eggs, home-made marmalade, etc. Vegetarians catered for. Good pubs nearby for evening meals.

Bed & Breakfast per night: single room £25.00; double room from £45.00–£50.00

Bedrooms: 1 single, 1 double, 1 twin
Bathrooms: 1 en-suite, 2 private
Parking: 12 spaces

At-a-glance symbols are explained on the flap inside the back cover

332 The Old Vicarage ◆◆◆◆

Sherborne Road, Milborne Port, Sherborne, Dorset DT9 5AT **Tel:** (01963) 251117 **Fax:** (01963) 251515
Web: http://www.milborneport.freeserve.co.uk

A Victorian Gothic listed building set in three acres of beautiful grounds affording glorious views of open country. The property is privately owned and run by two ex-London restaurateurs. Every room has a different character and the spacious lounge is furnished with antiques. Dinner of the highest standard is served on Friday and Saturday. On other nights pubs within five minutes' walk serve good food. Situated on the edge of a charming village and two miles from the historic town of Sherborne with its magnificent Abbey and two castles. Within easy reach are stately homes and gardens. The most attractive Dorset coast is only 30 miles away.

Bed & Breakfast per night: single room from £27.00–£30.00; double room from £53.00–£90.00
Dinner, Bed & Breakfast per person, per night: £43.00–£63.00
Evening meal: 1930 (last orders 2100)

Bedrooms: 1 single, 3 double, 2 twin, 1 triple
Bathrooms: 7 en-suite
Parking: 15 spaces
Open: All year except January
Cards accepted: Mastercard, Visa, Switch/Delta, Amex, Eurocard

333 Penryn ◆◆◆◆

Southay, East Lambrook, South Petherton, Somerset TA13 5HQ **Tel:** (01460) 241358
E-mail: pjandea@tesco.net

Come and relax in a peaceful, rural setting. Our bungalow is set in an acre of garden surrounded by cider orchards. Enjoy freshly cooked, appetising meals using our own and local produce. The twin bedroom looks onto the garden. The en-suite has bath and separate shower. The lounge/dining room opening onto the patio and garden is for your exclusive use. Discover Somerset – gardens, historic buildings, 'Hamstone' villages, 'The Levels' and interesting towns. Two miles off the A303.

Bed & Breakfast per night: double room from £40.00–£42.00
Dinner, Bed & Breakfast per person, per night: £27.50–£28.50
Evening meal: 1800 (last orders 2000)

Bedrooms: 1 twin
Bathrooms: 1 en-suite
Parking: 4 spaces
Open: April–October

334 Muchelney Ham Farm ◆◆◆◆◆ Gold Award

Muchelney, Langport, Somerset TA10 0DJ **Tel:** (01458) 250737

Beautiful luxury farmhouse, mainly 17th century, tastefully furnished to a very high standard with period and antique furniture, beams and inglenook. Centrally heated throughout. Country house atmosphere, lovely views over unspoilt countryside on the Somerset Levels. Peaceful relaxing garden. Ideal for touring or business. All rooms have their own facilities.

Bed & Breakfast per night: single occupancy from £30.00–£35.00; double room from £50.00–£65.00
Dinner, Bed & Breakfast per person, per night: £45.00–£48.00

Bedrooms: 2 double, 1 twin
Bathrooms: 3 en-suite
Parking: 12 spaces

Entries are cross referenced by number to the maps on pages 130–131

335 Lower Farm ◆◆◆◆

Kingweston, Somerton, Somerset TA11 6BA **Tel:** (01458) 223237 or 07860 350426 **Fax:** (01458) 223276
E-mail: lowerfarm@kingweston.demon.co.uk

A warm welcome is guaranteed at this award-winning bed and breakfast. The attractive comfortable rooms are well-equipped and an excellent breakfast is served in the farmhouse dining room. This unusual Grade II listed building was formerly a coaching inn and guests have been welcomed here over the centuries. It is now our family home and the heart of our farming enterprise. Kingweston is conveniently placed to visit much of Somerset, including Glastonbury, Wells and Bath.

Bed & Breakfast per night: single room
£22.00; double room £44.00

Bedrooms: 1 single, 1 double, 1 twin
Bathrooms: 3 en-suite
Parking: 7 spaces
Cards accepted: Mastercard, Visa, Switch/Delta, JCB, Visa Electron, Solo

336 Still Cottage ◆◆◆◆

North Street, Somerton, Somerset TA11 7NY **Tel:** (01458) 272323

A warm welcome awaits guests in this lovingly restored, listed Georgian townhouse situated on the outskirts of Somerton, the ancient capital of Wessex. The rooms are imaginatively furnished with antiques and old pine and the lovely walled garden offers a peaceful haven after a day of sightseeing. Locally produced food is served in the breakfast room, where the Aga in the adjoining kitchen adds to the warmth and ambience of this attractive home.

Bed & Breakfast per night: single room from
£28.00–£30.00; double room from
£45.00–£48.00
Evening meal: 1930

Bedrooms: 1 single, 1 double, 1 twin
Bathrooms: 1 public

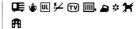

337 Stangray House ◆◆◆◆

Church Street, Keinton Mandeville, Somerton, Somerset TA11 6ER **Tel:** (01458) 223984 **Fax:** (01458) 223992
E-mail: dpm@euphony.com

A friendly, family-run country house in the pleasant, rural surroundings of South Somerset. This quiet location is ideally suited as a base to explore the numerous delights of the area. All bedrooms and the guest lounge have colour television, with a log fire in the lounge in winter. Parking for six to eight cars in the large drive with access to the rear garden which is available for guest use. A no smoking establishment.

Bed & Breakfast per night: single
occupancy from £20.00–£25.00; double room
from £40.00–£45.00
**Dinner, Bed & Breakfast per person, per
night:** £28.00–£30.50
Evening meal: 1900 (by arrangement)

Bedrooms: 1 double, 1 twin, 1 triple
Bathrooms: 1 en-suite, 1 public
Parking: 6 spaces

338 Avalon Barn

◆◆◆◆

Lower Godney, Glastonbury, Somerset BA5 1RZ **Tel:** (01458) 835005 **Fax:** (01458) 835005
E-mail: william.n@virgin.net

Avalon Barn is a comfortable, quiet and attractively converted barn with views stretching across the Somerset Levels to the Mendip Hills. Your car is parked near the front door where a warm and friendly welcome awaits you. Evening meals are available at local pubs, one just around the corner! Easy access to Glastonbury, Wells and places of historic interest. Cycle on the Somerset Levels. Coarse fishing in ponds and rivers. Bird watching reserves. Walk the Mendip Hills.

Bed & Breakfast per night: double room from £35.00–£45.00

Bedrooms: 2 double, 1 twin
Bathrooms: 1 en-suite, 1 public
Parking: 3 spaces
Cards accepted: Mastercard, Visa

Arthurian Legends of the South West

No one knows if Arthur actually existed. What is certain is that when the Romans left Britain in the early 5th century AD, recorded history went with them, at least for several hundred years. So the shadowy figures from these 'Dark Ages' are inevitably reconstructions by later clerics or deductions by latter-day archaeologists.

In fact, historians think Arthur did exist, probably a 5th- or 6th-century British chieftain who fought the invading Anglo-Saxons. His base – Camelot? – may have been at South Cadbury, near Sherborne, since excavations have revealed that this Iron Age hillfort on the troubled frontline between Saxon and Briton, was reoccupied and refortified in the late 5th or early 6th century.

The complex web of Arthurian myth, however, claims earlier beginnings. One story has Joseph of Arimathea sailing to Cornwall, perhaps to trade in tin. With him on one trip to the West Country is the young Christ who walks on the Mendips at Priddy. Another version has Joseph hiding the Holy Grail, the cup Christ used at the Last Supper, on Glastonbury Tor, his staff, stuck firmly into the ground miraculously growing shoots and known as the Glastonbury Thorn. The quest for the Holy Grail – a metaphor for the search for spiritual perfection – preoccupies many of Arthur's knights in several myths.

The British king is said to have visited Glastonbury at least twice, once to rescue his wife Guinevere from the clutches of Melwas, and again when he went to Avalon (often equated with Glastonbury) to die. Glastonbury Tor indeed resembles the description of the Isle of Avalon, looming dramatically above the Somerset wetlands, which in Arthur's day were regularly inundated by the sea. In 1191 the monks of Glastonbury Abbey (shown here) found a tomb, apparently inscribed with the words 'Here lies the famous King Arthur in the Isle of Avalon'. Only the cynical would see this as a clever (and successful) ploy to attract pilgrims to an abbey recently devastated by fire.

Other West Country Arthurian sites can be found at Amesbury (where Guinevere became abbess after Arthur's death), Dozmary Pool on Bodmin Moor (where Excalibur was caught by a mysterious hand), Tintagel (Arthur's birthplace) and Badbury Rings in Dorset (one of a number of possible locations for the site of the Battle of Mount Badon, at which Arthur was mortally wounded).

Entries are cross referenced by number to the maps on pages 130–131

339 Beryl ◆◆◆◆

Beryl, Wells, Somerset BA5 3JP **Tel:** (01749) 678738 **Fax:** (01749) 670508

'Beryl' – a precious gem in a perfect setting. Small 19th-century Gothic mansion, set in peaceful gardens, one mile from the centre of Wells. Well placed for touring the area. Offers comfortable, well-equipped bedrooms and relaxed use of the beautifully furnished reception rooms. Dinner is served with elegant style using fresh produce from the vegetable garden and local supplies. Children and pets are welcome. Outdoor heated pool, June-September. Open all year, except Christmas.

Bed & Breakfast per night: single occupancy from £50.00–£65.00; double room from £65.00–£95.00
Dinner, Bed & Breakfast per person, per night: £52.50–£67.50 (min 2 sharing)
Evening meal: 2000

Bedrooms: 3 double, 4 twin
Bathrooms: 7 en-suite
Parking: 14 spaces
Open: All year except Christmas
Cards accepted: Mastercard, Visa, Switch/Delta

340 Bowlish House  ◆◆◆◆ Silver Award

Coombe Lane, Shepton Mallet, Somerset BA4 5JD **Tel:** (01749) 342022 **Fax:** (01749) 342022

An elegant Georgian restaurant with rooms, wonderfully counterbalanced by the relaxed atmosphere. The award-winning restaurant and wine list are famous for their range and eclectic mix of modern classics and local produce. Shepton Mallet is a market town on the south-west slopes of the Mendip Hills, just ten minutes from the cathedral city of Wells. It is an ideal centre for exploring nearby Bath, Stourhead, Longleat, Glastonbury and Cheddar.

Bed & Breakfast per night: single occupancy from £48.00; double room from £58.00
Dinner, Bed & Breakfast per person, per night: £51.50 (min 2 sharing)
Lunch available: first Sunday of each month, or by prior arrangement

Evening meal: 1900 (last orders 2130)
Bedrooms: 2 double, 1 twin
Bathrooms: 3 en-suite
Parking: 10 spaces
Cards accepted: Mastercard, Visa, Switch/Delta

341 Burnt House Farm ◆◆◆◆ Silver Award

Waterlip, West Cranmore, Shepton Mallet, Somerset BA4 4RN **Tel:** (01749) 880280 **Fax:** (01749) 880004

Our charming refurbished period farmhouse offers character features, low beamed ceilings, pitch pine floors, and an inglenook fireplace (fires lit in the winter). Heated bedrooms have private showers or bathrooms, lace-canopied beds, colour televisions, complimentary refreshments/toiletries, clock radios, trouser presses and flowers. Morning newspapers can be ordered to accompany your plentiful, choice breakfast. Quality meals in nearby pub. Spacious parking or garage space available. Full sized snooker table. Hot hydro garden spa. No smoking. A warm welcome and attentive service. Mendip Hill location.

Bed & Breakfast per night: single occupancy £30.00; double room from £44.00–£48.00

Bedrooms: 2 double, 1 twin
Bathrooms: 1 en-suite, 2 private
Parking: 14 spaces

342 Ring O' Roses

♦♦♦♦ Silver Award

Stratton Road, Holcombe, Bath, Somerset BA3 5EB **Tel:** (01761) 232478 **Fax:** (01761) 233737
Web: http://www.ringoroses.co.uk **E-mail:** ringorosesholcombe@tesco.net

We have restored this 17th-century inn which takes its name from the old nursery rhyme when the plague devastated the ancient village of Holcombe. Nestling in the Mendip Hills away from busy roads and enjoying superb views across the fields towards Downside Abbey. The bedrooms are spacious and tastefully furnished with private bathrooms. Interesting and creative cooking, real ale and fine wines. Packed with antiques and atmosphere, it is an unexpected hidden treasure not to be missed!

Bed & Breakfast per night: single occupancy from £52.00–£55.00; double room from £65.00–£75.00
Dinner, Bed & Breakfast per person, per night: £45.00–£55.00 (min 2 nights)
Evening meal: 1900 (last orders 2100)

Bedrooms: 8 double
Bathrooms: 8 en-suite
Parking: 30 spaces
Cards accepted: Mastercard, Visa, Switch/Delta

343 Braeside Hotel

♦♦♦♦

2 Victoria Park, Weston-super-Mare BS23 2HZ **Tel:** (01934) 626642 **Fax:** (01934) 626642
Web: http://www.smoothhound.co.uk/hotels/braeside.html **E-mail:** braeside@tesco.net

Delightful, family-run hotel close to the sea front and sandy beach; in a quiet location with sea views and unrestricted on-street parking. Why not borrow one of our Ordnance Survey maps and explore the surrounding countryside; then finish your day by visiting one of Weston's excellent restaurants, all within easy walking distance. Directions: with the sea on your left, take the first right after the Winter Gardens, then first left into Lower Church Road. Victoria Park is the cul-de-sac on the right after the left-hand bend.

Bed & Breakfast per night: single room £25.00; double room £50.00

Bedrooms: 2 single, 5 double, 1 twin, 1 triple
Bathrooms: 9 en-suite

344 Butcombe Farm

♦♦♦♦

Aldwick Lane, Butcombe, Bristol BS40 7UW **Tel:** (01761) 462380 **Fax:** (01761) 462300
Web: http://www.butcombe-farm.demon.co.uk **E-mail:** info@butcombe-farm.demon.co.uk

Dating back to the late 14th century, Butcombe Farm is a beautiful manor house with individually decorated, en-suite bed and breakfast rooms. Set in several acres of field and woodland, amid the tranquil Somerset countryside, the fantastic views combine perfectly with our excellent facilities. Winter weekend offers available. Activities include fishing, horse riding, cycle hire, wine tasting, aromatherapy massage and art & craft workshops. For more information please contact Barry and Josephine Harvey.

Bed & Breakfast per night: single occupancy from £25.00–£39.00; double room from £35.00–£49.00

Bedrooms: 3 double, 2 triple
Bathrooms: 5 en-suite
Parking: 20 spaces
Cards accepted: Mastercard, Visa, Switch/Delta, Eurocard

Entries are cross referenced by number to the maps on pages 130–131

345 Villa Magdala Hotel

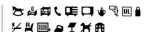 ◆◆◆◆ Gold Award

Henrietta Road, Bath BA2 6LX **Tel:** (01225) 466329 **Fax:** (01225) 483207
Web: http://www.villamagdala.co.uk **E-mail:** office@villamagdala.co.uk

Ideally situated, this charming Victorian town house hotel enjoys a peaceful location overlooking Henrietta Park, only five minutes' level walk to the city centre and the Roman Baths. The spacious rooms all have private bathrooms, televisions, direct dial telephones and refreshment trays. Private parking for guests is available in the hotel grounds. Special mid-week short breaks are available from November to March.

Bed & Breakfast per night: single room from £65.00–£85.00; double room from £80.00–£120.00

Bedrooms: 2 single, 9 double, 6 twin, 1 triple
Bathrooms: 18 en-suite
Parking: 18 spaces
Cards accepted: Mastercard, Visa, Switch/Delta, Amex, Eurocard, Visa Electron, Solo

346 Siena Hotel

◆◆◆◆

24/25 Pulteney Road, Bath BA2 4EZ **Tel:** (01225) 425495 **Fax:** (01225) 469029
E-mail: siena.hotel@dial.pipex.com

The Siena is one of the most attractive small hotels in Bath, situated within a few minutes' level walk from the centre. It is a fine example of early Victorian architecture, and is built within a walled garden, affording exceptional views of the city and the medieval Abbey. The interior combines elegant decoration with superb classical furnishings, creating an atmosphere of warmth and tranquillity. We pride ourselves on our quality accommodation, friendly approach and flexibility of service.

Bed & Breakfast per night: single room from £47.50–£70.00; double room from £72.50–£105.00

Bedrooms: 1 single, 9 double, 2 twin, 3 triple, 2 family
Bathrooms: 17 en-suite **Parking:** 16 spaces
Cards accepted: Mastercard, Visa, Switch/Delta, Amex, Diners, Eurocard, JCB, Maestro, Visa Elect

347 Gainsborough Hotel

◆◆◆◆

Weston Lane, Bath BA1 4AB **Tel:** (01225) 311380 **Fax:** (01225) 447411
Web: http://www.gainsboroughhotel.co.uk **E-mail:** gainsborough_hotel@compuserve.com

Spacious and comfortable country house style (B&B) hotel situated in our own grounds with nice views, near botanical gardens and city. The Abbey, Roman Baths and shops are a pleasant walk via the park. The hotel provides a warm and relaxing atmosphere for our guests' stay. All 17 tastefully furnished bedrooms are en-suite with some satellite televisions, beveridge facilities, telephones and hairdryers etc. Also a friendly bar, two sun terraces and private car park. A delicious five-course English breakfast is served daily.

Bed & Breakfast per night: single room from £37.00–£48.00; double room from £50.00–£85.00

Bedrooms: 1 single, 6 double, 6 twin, 3 triple, 1 family
Bathrooms: 17 en-suite
Parking: 18 spaces
Cards accepted: Mastercard, Visa, Switch/Delta, Amex, Eurocard

At-a-glance symbols are explained on the flap inside the back cover

348 County Hotel ◆◆◆◆

18-19 Pulteney Road, Bath BA2 4EZ **Tel:** (01225) 425003 **Fax:** (01225) 466493
E-mail: admin@county-hotel.co.uk

The County was completely refurbished in 1999 and is an ideal place for a short holiday or overnight stay. Situated within a five minute walk of the city centre, the elegant rooms have beautiful views across the cricket and rugby grounds to the Abbey. A friendly, family-run hotel offering exceptionally good breakfasts. Rarely for Bath, the hotel has ample car parking.

Bed & Breakfast per night: single room max £60.00; double room from £95.00–£185.00 **Lunch available:** 1200–1400 (bar snacks)	**Bedrooms:** 2 single, 18 double, 2 twin **Bathrooms:** 22 en-suite **Parking:** 50 spaces **Cards accepted:** Mastercard, Visa, Switch/Delta, Amex, Diners, Eurocard	

Claverton American Museum

The city of Bath, so quintessentially English, attracts American tourists like a magnet, so it is perhaps appropriate that just outside the city is a museum which offers a good measure of cultural exchange. Claverton Manor, a large 19th-century neo-classical mansion set in beautiful grounds overlooking the peaceful Avon valley, is now the American Museum in Britain (tel: 01225 460503) and is devoted entirely to the cultural history of the United States.

The museum has been based at Claverton since 1961 and was the brainchild of two Americans, Dallas Pratt and John Judkyn, whose desire it was to encourage greater mutual understanding between Britain and America. The bulk of the museum's collection takes the form of furnished rooms brought, often in their entirety, from houses in the United States, and representing different aspects of American society. Other galleries are devoted to specific crafts (pewter, silver, glass, textiles) or themes (North American Indians, maritime history, westward expansion).

The museum is something of a revelation in the sheer range and variety of cultural influences on display; it vividly demonstrates the enormous mixture of ethnic and social influences which were combined in the melting pot of American society, and the contrasts are immense. One room, for example, contains the austere furniture of the Shakers, a puritanical religious sect which settled in New England in the late 18th century. Utility and simplicity were the hallmarks of their plain, but beautiful, hand-made wooden furniture. Roughly contemporary, but a world apart, is the New Orleans bedroom. Its factory-made, dark mahogany furniture is heavily adorned with curly, baroque flourishes while curtains and carpets riot with elaborate patterns.

Displays on American Indians and Spanish colonists compete for space with less well-known ethnic groups. The Pennsylvania Dutch, for example (actually 17th-century refugees from Germany and Switzerland) brought a colourful decorative tradition manifested in vividly painted furniture and kitchenware.

The large number of different styles and traditions demanding representation has meant that the exhibits have spilled out into the manor's immediate surroundings. While one part of the grounds is planted as a colonial herb garden, another is a replica of George Washington's garden at Mount Vernon. An 18th-century Dutch summerhouse is furnished as a 19th-century American milliner's shop, and a stable block is devoted to American naive folk art.

Entries are cross referenced by number to the maps on pages 130–131

349 Holly Lodge

◆◆◆◆◆ Silver Award

8 Upper Oldfield Park, Bath BA2 3JZ **Tel:** (01225) 424042 or (01225) 339187 **Fax:** (01225) 481138
Web: http://www.hollylodge.co.uk **E-mail:** stay@hollylodge.co.uk

This charming Victorian town house commands panoramic views of the city and is delightfully furnished with individually-designed bedrooms, some with four-posters, and superb bathrooms. Elegant and stylish, it is owned and operated with meticulous attention to detail by George Hall. Superb breakfasts are enjoyed in the appealing breakfast room with yellow and green decor. Furnished with antiques, this immaculate establishment makes a pleasant base for touring Bath and the Cotswolds.

Bed & Breakfast per night: single room from £48.00–£55.00; double room from £79.00–£97.00

Bedrooms: 1 single, 4 double, 2 twin
Bathrooms: 7 en-suite
Parking: 8 spaces
Cards accepted: Mastercard, Visa, Switch/Delta, Amex, Diners, Eurocard, JCB, Maestro, Visa Elect

350 Bloomfield House

◆◆◆◆◆ Silver Award

146 Bloomfield Road, Bath BA2 2AS **Tel:** (01225) 420105 **Fax:** (01225) 481958
E-mail: bloomfieldhouse@compuserve.com

An elegant Georgian country house in a tranquil setting with glorious views over the city and with ample parking. French crystal chandeliers feature strongly and breakfast is served against a candlelit and open fire background. Half-tester and four-poster rooms, including the lavish principal bedroom of the Mayor and Mayoress of Bath (1902/03), are romantically presented. An easy ten minute walk to the city, and ideally situated for Somerset, Wessex and the South.

Bed & Breakfast per night: single room from £45.00–£55.00; double room from £70.00–£95.00

Bedrooms: 1 single, 6 double, 1 twin
Bathrooms: 5 en-suite, 3 private
Parking: 10 spaces
Cards accepted: Mastercard, Visa, Switch/Delta, Eurocard

351 The Lansdown Grove

★★★ Silver Award

Lansdown Road, Bath BA1 5EH **Tel:** (01225) 483888 **Fax:** (01225) 483838

Grade II listed building enjoying breathtaking views over the Georgian part of the city and wooded hills beyond. 48 comfortable bedrooms with private bathroom, remote-controlled colour television with satellite channels, trouser press, hair dryer and hospitality tray. For those special occasions there are superior rooms and a four-poster suite. Excellent restaurant offering a varied menu, complemented by friendly and professional staff. Free car parking. Ten minute stroll from the city centre.

Bed & Breakfast per night: single room from £79.00–£110.00; double room from £99.00–£161.00
Dinner, Bed & Breakfast per person, per night: from £65.00 (min 2 nights, 2 sharing)
Evening meal: 1900 (last orders 2130)

Bedrooms: 8 single, 29 double, 7 twin, 4 triple
Bathrooms: 48 en-suite
Parking: 35 spaces
Cards accepted: Mastercard, Visa, Switch/Delta, Amex, Diners, Eurocard

352 Meadowland

◆◆◆◆◆ Gold Award

36 Bloomfield Park, Bath BA2 2BX **Tel:** (01225) 311079 **Fax:** (01225) 311079
Web: http://www.bath.org/hotel/meadowland.html **E-mail:** meadowland@bath92.freeserve.co.uk

Set in its own quiet grounds offering the highest standards of en-suite accommodation, Meadowland has been elegantly furnished and decorated, the colour co-ordinated bedrooms have remote control television, hairdryers, trouser presses and a welcome tray. There is a comfortable lounge with a wide selection of books and magazines. A la carte breakfast is served in our charming dining room where guests can choose from an imaginative menu. Lovely gardens and private parking surround our house. A peaceful retreat for the discerning traveller. No smoking.

Bed & Breakfast per night: single occupancy from £50.00–£55.00; double room from £70.00–£75.00

Bedrooms: 2 double, 1 twin
Bathrooms: 3 en-suite
Parking: 6 spaces
Cards accepted: Mastercard, Visa, Eurocard

353 Monkshill

◆◆◆◆◆ Gold Award

Shaft Road, Monkton Combe, Bath BA2 7HL **Tel:** (01225) 833028 **Fax:** (01225) 833028

Five minutes from the centre of Bath lies this secluded and very comfortable country residence, surrounded by its own peaceful gardens and enjoying far-reaching views over one of the most spectacularly beautiful parts of the Avon Valley. You can be assured of a warm welcome at Monkshill, where the emphasis is on luxurious comfort and complete relaxation. The drawing room, with its fine antiques and open log fire, is for the exclusive use of the guests and the spacious bedrooms enjoy fine views over the gardens and valley below. Monkshill is situated within a designated Area of Outstanding Natural Beauty.

Bed & Breakfast per night: single occupancy from £45.00–£60.00; double room from £60.00–£75.00

Bedrooms: 2 double, 1 twin
Bathrooms: 2 en-suite, 1 private
Parking: 6 spaces
Cards accepted: Mastercard, Visa, Switch/Delta, Eurocard, JCB, Maestro, Visa Electron, Solo

354 Heatherly Cottage

◆◆◆◆

Ladbrook Lane, Gastard, Corsham, Wiltshire SN13 9PE **Tel:** (01249) 701402 **Fax:** (01249) 701412
Web: http://www.smoothhound.co.uk/hotels/heather3.html **E-mail:** ladbrook1@aol.com

A 17th-century cottage set in a quiet country lane with approximately two acres and views across open countryside. There is ample parking for up to eight cars. Guests have a separate wing of the house with their own entrance and staircase. All our rooms are en-suite with colour television, clock/radio, tea/coffee tray and hairdryer. Close to Bath, Lacock, Castle Combe, Avebury, Stonehenge and many National Trust properties. Pubs and restaurants nearby for good food.

Bed & Breakfast per night: single occupancy from £27.00–£30.00; double room from £43.00–£48.00

Bedrooms: 2 double, 1 twin
Bathrooms: 3 en-suite
Parking: 8 spaces

Entries are cross referenced by number to the maps on pages 130–131

355 Home Farm

Harts Lane, Biddestone, Chippenham, Wiltshire SN14 7DQ **Tel:** (01249) 714475 or 07966 549759 **Fax:** (01249) 701488
E-mail: smith@homefarmb-b.freeserve.co.uk

At Home Farm we welcome long and short stay visitors and business guests. A 17th-century farmhouse on a working farm, we are set in the picturesque village of Biddestone with its village greens and duck pond and two pubs just a stroll away. Breakfast is served in the oak-beamed dining room. Guests may use the garden or drawing room with log fire. Ample safe parking. We are well situated for easy M4 access and for visiting Bath, Castle Combe, Cotswolds, Cheddar etc.

Bed & Breakfast per night: single occupancy from £25.00–£30.00; double room from £40.00–£50.00

Bedrooms: 1 double, 1 triple, 1 family
Bathrooms: 2 en-suite, 1 private
Parking: 4 spaces

356 Gate Cottage

Sutton Benger, Chippenham, Wiltshire SN15 4RE **Tel:** (01249) 720121 or 07710 990201

Enjoy a relaxing stay in our delightful 250-year-old farm cottage. Situated on the edge of the village of Sutton Benger in the North Wiltshire countryside and within walking distance of two pubs and one restaurant. We are easily accessible for Bath, Malmesbury, Chippenham, Tetbury, Cirencester, Swindon and the Cotswolds and only two miles from Junction 17 of the M4. We are non-smoking and aim to make your stay with us as informal and enjoyable as possible.

Bed & Breakfast per night: single occupancy from £25.00–£30.00; double room from £40.00–£44.00

Bedrooms: 2 double, 1 twin
Bathrooms: 3 en-suite
Parking: 5 spaces

357 Glebe Cottage Farm

Ashmore, Salisbury, Dorset DP5 5AE **Tel:** (01747) 811974 **Fax:** (01747) 811104
E-mail: all@glebe.force9.co.uk

The warmest of welcomes awaits you in the tiny hilltop village of Ashmore, Dorset's highest village. Set in an area of outstanding natural beauty, high on the Wessex Downs, we are a farmhouse bed and breakfast situated in our own courtyard. Our rooms are spacious and full of character, with exposed beams and high quality furnishings. We provide sumptuous English breakfasts and can also offer a light supper in your room should you wish!

Bed & Breakfast per night: double room from £40.00–£50.00

Bedrooms: 1 double, 1 twin
Bathrooms: 2 en-suite
Parking: 2 spaces

358 Number Eighty Eight

◆◆◆◆

88 Exeter Street, Salisbury, Wiltshire SP1 2SE **Tel:** (01722) 330139

A delightful Victorian house in the heart of the city, enjoying magnificent views of Salisbury Cathedral. Five minutes' walk from the Market Square, shops and restaurants. A half hour's drive from Stonehenge, Stourhead, Wilton House and the New Forest. Number Eighty Eight is elegantly furnished and has been tastefully restored to include en-suite facilities. A traditional English breakfast is served, with variations if desired. Vegetarians and guests preferring a lighter diet are welcome. Number Eighty Eight is a non-smoking establishment. Special breaks available.

Bed & Breakfast per night: double room from £40.00–£55.00

Bedrooms: 1 double, 1 triple
Bathrooms: 1 en-suite, 1 private

359 Newton Farm House

◆◆◆◆ Silver Award

Southampton Road, Whiteparish, Salisbury, Wiltshire SP5 2QL **Tel:** (01794) 884416 **Fax:** (01794) 884416
Web: http://www.lineone.net/~newton.farmhouse.b-b/ **E-mail:** newton.farmhouse.b-b@lineone.net

Historic, listed 16th-century farmhouse, originally part of the Trafalgar Estate. Near the New Forest and convenient for Salisbury, Stonehenge, Romsey, Winchester, Portsmouth and Bath. Delightful en-suite bedrooms (five with genuine four-poster beds). Beamed dining room with flagstones, inglenook and bread oven plus Nelson memorabilia. Superb breakfasts include home-made breads and preserves, fresh fruits and free-range eggs. Extensive grounds with swimming pool. Dinner by arrangement using garden produce.

Bed & Breakfast per night: single occupancy from £25.00–£30.00; double room from £38.00–£50.00
Dinner, Bed & Breakfast per person, per night: £41.00–£46.00
Evening meal: 1900

Bedrooms: 3 double, 2 twin, 2 triple, 1 family
Bathrooms: 8 en-suite
Parking: 10 spaces

Key to Symbols

For ease of use, the key to symbols appears on the back of the cover flap and can be folded out while consulting individual entries. The symbols are designed to enable you to see at a glance what's on offer, and whether any particular requirements you have can be met. Most of the symbols are clear, simple icons and few require any further explanation, but the following points may be useful:

Alcoholic drinks: Alcoholic drinks are available at all types of accommodation listed in the guide unless the symbol UL (unlicensed) appears. However, even in licensed premises there may be some restrictions on the serving of drinks, such as being available to diners only.

Smoking: Some establishments prefer not to accommodate smokers, and if this is the case it will be indicated by the symbol ⅍. Other establishments may offer facilities for non-smokers such as no smoking bedrooms and parts of communal rooms set aside for non-smokers. Please check at the time of booking if the non-smoking symbol does not appear.

Pets: The symbol 🐕 is used to show that dogs are not accepted in any circumstances. Some establishments will accept pets, but we advise you to check this at the time of booking and to enquire as to whether any additional charge will be made to accommodate them.

South and South East England

▶ The Bloomsbury Group in Sussex

Inside the 12th-century church at Berwick, near Eastbourne, a surprise awaits. Its walls are covered with astonishing modern murals, created in the 1940s by Duncan Grant, Vanessa Bell and her son, Quentin Bell. The three, who lived at nearby Charleston Farmhouse, were members of an eccentric affiliation of writers and artists, the Bloomsbury Group. Charleston became a gathering place for the group and was vividly decorated in accordance with their artistic ideals. Virginia Woolf lived not far away, at Monk's House (NT), Rodmell. (Tel: 01323 411400.)

▶ The Tolpuddle Martyrs

In the Dorset of 1833 agricultural wages had fallen below the bread-line. When further reduction looked likely, six farmworkers joined – and swore loyalty to – a trade union. Landowners, desperate to prevent any return to the unrest of past years, secured conviction of the six under an obscure clause in the 1797 Mutiny Act in which administering false oaths was deemed a crime. Outcry greeted the sentence of seven years' transportation and after two years the six were fully pardoned. The Tolpuddle Martyrs Museum (tel: 01305 848237) tells their remarkable story.

Ancient and modern

History pervades every pore of south-eastern England. Despite the prosperity and modernity of these bustling counties, there lies a Roman villa, Saxon church, Tudor cottage, Georgian townhouse or Victorian railway station around almost every corner. Sometimes, the juxtaposition of old and modern is striking; at Folkestone, for example, visitors can choose to marvel at the engineering triumph of the Channel Tunnel or descend the steep cliffs to the Maritime Gardens in a lift built in 1885 and powered by water pressure. On other occasions, you will be hard-pushed to realise that you are now in the 21st century. Stroll through Chiddingstone, near Tonbridge (and not that far from the M25) and you leave the modern world behind. The houses are half-timbered, many dating from the Elizabethan and Jacobean periods, but the feel is of an idyllic, timeless age. Or hire a rowing boat at Odiham and explore the Basingstoke Canal. Trees shade the calm, quiet backwaters, the only sounds the gentle splash of oar and rustle of leaves.

An Englishman's home...

The region specialises in gorgeous villages. Some, such as Chiddingstone, are celebrated, others less so. Into this latter category fall the following. Wherwell (near Andover) is a shrine to the thatcher's art that also enjoys a magnificent setting on the banks of the Test. Across the Solent on the Isle of Wight lies sleepy Shorwell, sheltering in a wooded valley beneath the closely grazed downs. In West Sussex, just three miles from Petworth – itself a delightful small town dominated by the majestic Petworth House – is Fittleworth, a straggling settlement that offers another group of picturesque stone or brick cottages at each twist of the woodland la   prevailing material at Piddinghoe, just inland from Newhaven, where St John's Church has one of only three Norman round towers in Sussex. East Clandon, about four miles east of Guildford, is a compact community of brick-and-tile houses surrounding two of the staples of village life – the church and the inn. Milton Abbas is all tranquillity now, but two centuries ago Lord Dorchester provoked outrage from its residents when he razed it to the ground – in order to improve his view – and rebuilt it in a wooded valley a mile away. The replacement, six miles (10km) from Blandford Forum, is made up of regularly spaced, thatched cob cottages, so later generations have benefited from the landlord's ruthlessness. Pusey, down a 'no through road' east of Faringdon, is another appealing estate village, this one guarded by venerable beech and horse-chestnut trees. Swanbourne, in the Vale of Aylesbury, has been attractively rebuilt since an 18th-century fire. Smithfield Close, however, survived the conflagration, and is a handsome group of whitewashed, 16th-century thatched cottages.

Choose a clear day...

All of these villages make excellent centres to walk from, and most offer a pub for well-earned refreshment. If you believe all good walks should include some fine vistas, then try one of these four: Ditchling Beacon, a couple of miles north of Brighton, is arguably the best viewpoint in the South Downs. The stretch of the South Downs Way, leading west to the pair of windmills familiarly known as Jack and Jill, makes a rousing afternoon's hike. At the western end of the Way, and competing for the accolade of best viewpoint, is Butser Hill, highest point in the South Downs. The fort at Ditchling dates from the Iron Age; here Stone Age men and women flourished. The Queen Elizabeth Country Park – of which the hill is a part – provides leaflets for waymarked trails. Towards the northern end of the Chilterns – and at the end of the Ridgeway, a track used before the Romans arrived – is Ivinghoe Beacon; views extend to London, out over the Bedfordshire plain and south-west to the Chilterns, home to glorious, underrated countryside. The final vantage point is beside the Cerne Abbas giant, that uncompromising symbol of male fertility etched on the Dorset Downs. And Dorset comprises the entire view: untaxing, unspoilt and ineffably beautiful.

Walk this way

Many of the long-distance paths in south-eastern England follow the ridges of chalk downland, leading you past countless such viewpoints. With other rights-of-way criss-crossing these paths at regular intervals, it is a simple matter to devise shorter, circular walks. The 100-mile (161km) South Downs Way follows ancient tracks and old droveways in East and West Sussex and Hampshire. The North Downs Way, running 153 miles (246km) from Farnham to Canterbury, explores scenery of such splendour – sometimes wooded, sometimes grassland – it is hard to believe that for much of its length London is less than 30 miles (48km) away. The Ridgeway keeps to the tops of the Chilterns for its eastern stretch, descending to cross the Thames at Goring Gap, where it meets the Thames Path. A recent creation, this trail follows England's most famous river from source in Gloucestershire to the Thames Barrier at Woolwich, availing itself of 126 footbridges en route. The region has other longer paths that seek out the remoter corners of the countryside. Hampshire has the Hangers Way (17 miles (27km) through beechwoods between Alton and Petersfield) and The Solent Way (60 miles (96.5km) from Milford-on-Sea to Emsworth), and others besides. The Isle of Wight Coast Path circles the island in 69 glorious miles (111km).

How the other half lived

Those who enjoy that most intriguing of pastimes – having a good look round somebody else's house – can indulge themselves to their heart's content and without conscience. The choice is so wide that it can be a matter of choosing your scale, which starts at the very, very grand, such as Windsor Castle,

► **Sandham Memorial Chapel**

This chapel, at Burghclere in Berkshire, was built to house an extraordinary series of wall-paintings by the artist Stanley Spencer. He served in the army medical corps during World War I, and the murals record the everyday humdrum soldiers' duties: floor-cleaning, bed-making, laundry-sorting and a whole variety of other chores, but painted with exaggerated proportions and stylised perspective so that the scenes take on an aura of significance and horror. The chapel is dominated by a great Resurrection on the wall behind the altar (tel: 01635 278394).

Sir Stanley Spencer CBE RA

► **Selborne's Natural History**

Selborne, in a Hampshire backwater south of Alton, is largely synonymous with the work of late 18th-century clergyman-turned-naturalist, Gilbert White. Through a deep love of nature – and profound coach-sickness – White spent much of his time in the village of his birth. He eventually recorded his minute observation of natural phenomena in his masterpiece, The Natural History of Selborne, which has never been out of print since publication in 1789. His attractive home, The Wakes, is now a museum dedicated to his memory (tel: 01420 511275).

Nineteenth-century patron of the arts, bon viveur and local squire, 'Mad' Jack Fuller lives on thanks to his abiding passion for follies. His grave in the churchyard at Brightling, East Sussex, is a 25ft (7.5m)-high stone pyramid. Despite his wish to be interred at table, dressed for dinner and resplendent in top hat, he rests – in conventional repose – in the ground below. Nearby edifices include the 'Tower', a gothic-looking building with a battlemented top, and the Sugar Loaf, reputedly built in a night to enable Fuller to 'win' a bet that the spire of Dallington church was visible from his windows.

► **Folly Hill**
When Gerald Tyrwhitt-Wilson, 14th Baron Berners, opened his 140ft (43m) folly to his friends in 1935 he displayed the following notice above the entrance: 'Members of the public committing suicide from this tower do so at their own risk'. Berners was an aristocratic eccentric, an accomplished painter, writer and composer, who entertained lavishly. Those who climb his folly (just outside Faringdon) are rewarded by a panoramic view of several counties stretching to the Berkshire Downs and the White Horse of Uffington (tel: 01367 242191).

Blenheim Palace, Osborne House, Waddesdon Manor and Goodwood House, and includes some comparatively modest houses. Closer to this end of the spectrum is the 14th-century Alfriston Clergy House, the first property purchased by the National Trust for just £10 in 1896. Lamb House, in the near-perfect town of Rye, was the home of the novelist Henry James; the 18th-century building is surrounded by an attractive garden. Other, less celebrated historic homes include: Rousham House, a 17th-century Oxfordshire mansion now full of portraits but once used as a Royalist garrison in the Civil War; Haseley Manor, a rambling house of several periods happily rescued from dereliction in the 1970s; Dorney Court, Windsor, a 15th-century brick-and-timber house in the same ownership for almost 500 years; Chettle House, near Blandford Forum, an appealingly idiosyncratic, small Baroque country-house that feels – and is – very much a family home.

The coast is clear

England's southern coast has long been a playground for London, ensuring that most resorts offer a bewildering array of amenities. Margate, Eastbourne, Brighton, Bournemouth and Shanklin, amongst others, have long welcomed huge numbers of visitors. Escaping the hurly-burly can be more of a challenge on this stretch of coastline, but try Minnis Bay, on Kent's north-facing shore, west of Margate; Pevensey Bay, between Bexhill and Eastbourne; the sand dunes west of Littlehampton; Bracklesham Bay, near Selsey Bill; Lepe, a small stretch of sand and shingle facing the Isle of Wight; Luccombe Bay, ten minutes' walk from Shanklin; and Shipstal Point, giving on to a quiet stretch of Poole Harbour.

The artistic year

The cultural capital for livelier, broad-minded souls is Brighton, with its avant-garde galleries, arthouse cinemas and never-ending supply of clubs. The Brighton Festival – held each May, and one of England's largest celebrations of the arts – includes events such as conducted walks through Victorian cemeteries, dance, theatre, jazz and classical music. Not far away, Arundel puts out the bunting in August and invites you to open-air theatre in the castle grounds, jazz, fireworks and classical concerts. The centrepiece of the Canterbury Festival is the cathedral – used for operatic performances – while other venues host drama, dance and much more, each October. Similarly, Chichester Festival's focal point is its Norman cathedral, though the refurbished ballroom of Goodwood House has also been called into service in the past; the July festivities add exhibitions of contemporary sculpture and lectures to the round of concerts and plays. Guildford holds two festivals each year: music in March and books in October. Henley makes the most of its superb Thames-side setting when theatre takes to the streets and bridges of the town each July. At the end of September and in early October, it is the turn of Windsor to stage musical and literary events, some held in the Castle itself.

And for four weeks in February and March, the dance world turns its attention to north-western Surrey, the home of the Woking Dance Umbrella.

A break with history

Most of the festival towns and cities are ideal for short breaks. There are a hundred other attractive bases suitable for a weekend away, of which these form an eclectic sample. Winchester, the nation's capital until the reign of Canute, claims the longest cathedral in Europe and an impressive collection of Georgian townhouses, too. Midhurst, a busy market town beneath the South Downs, seems only to have glorious 16th-, 17th- and 18th-century buildings, some of the best in the appealingly named Knockhundred Row. Tunbridge Wells's prosperity arrived with the discovery of its chalybeate springs in 1606, and it has barely looked back since. Modern-day visitors can approach the springs along The Pantiles, a shopping area of sublime beauty. Arrive in early June and a cricket festival at one of the country's most picturesque grounds is in full swing. Hungerford, on the banks of the Kennet and close to more superb walking country, is a paradise for antique hunters. Thame, on the river of the same name, is equally popular with those not averse to spending an evening in a fine old coaching inn; the town boasts four that date from the 15th century.

Contact numbers

Basingstoke Canal (tel: 01252 370073)
The South Downs Way (tel: 02392 597618)
The North Downs Way (tel: 01622 221526)
The Ridgeway National Trail (tel: 01865 810224)
The Thames Path National Trail (tel: 01865 810224)
Hangers Way (tel: 01962 870500)
Solent Way (tel: 01962 870500)
Isle of Wight Coast Path (tel: 01983 813800)
Windsor Castle (tel: 01753 831118)
Blenheim Palace, Woodstock (tel: 01993 811325)
Osborne House, Isle of Wight (tel: 01983 200022)
Waddesdon Manor, Aylesbury (tel: 01296 653211)
Goodwood House, Chichester (tel: 01243 755000)
Alfriston Clergy House (tel: 01323 870001)
Lamb House, Rye (tel: 01892 890651)
Rousham House, Bicester (tel: 01869 347110)
Haseley Manor, Arreton, Isle of Wight (tel: 01983 865420)
Dorney Court, Windsor (tel: 01628 604638)
Brighton Festival (tel: 01273 700747)
Arundel Festival (tel: 01903 883690)
Canterbury Festival (tel: 01227 452853)
Chichester Festivities (tel: 01243 785718)
Guildford International Music Festival (tel: 01483 259167)
Guildford Book Festival (tel: 01483 444334)
Henley Festival (tel: 01491 843400)
Windsor Festival (tel: 01753 623400)
Woking Dance Umbrella (tel: 0208 741 8354)

► Pallant House

Built in 1712, Chichester's Pallant House (tel: 01243 774557) is an interesting setting for a modern-art collection. Each room, lovingly restored, reflects a period in the house's history and contains furniture, porcelain, textiles, even pictures from the period. But amongst all this grace and refinement, the raw colour and abstract form of the modern paintings on its walls strike an exciting note of contrast. Picasso, Sutherland, Nash, Piper, Moore and others are represented, most donated by Walter Hussey, Dean of Chichester Cathedral from 1955 to 1977.

► The Gardens of Stowe

Perhaps the finest statement of the art of the 18th-century garden lives on at Stowe, near Buckingham. John Vanbrugh, William Kent, James Gibbs and 'Capability' Brown – the most talented gardeners and architects of their day – went to great lengths to create a landscape remodelled and replanted to look as natural as possible, in order to match the aesthetic blueprint of ancient Rome. To this end, grottoes were built, lakes dug, columns erected and monuments – thirty, all told – sited with consummate care. The National Trust is now restoring these majestic gardens.

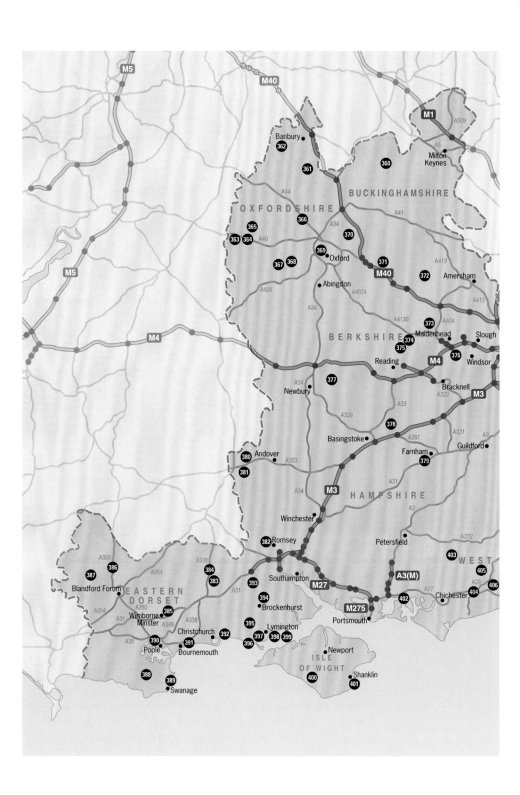

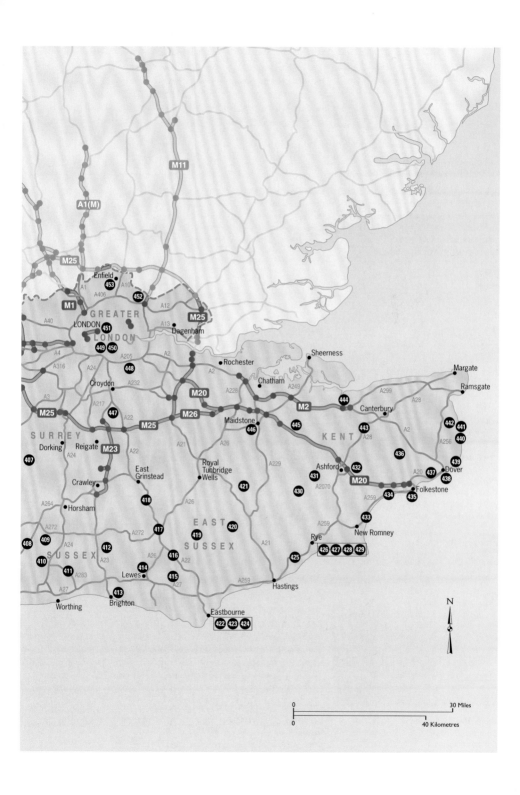

M11

A1(M)

M25

Enfield
453 454
452

M1
M25

GREATER
LONDON
A1
A406
A12
A13
A2
Dagenham
451
LONDON
449 450
A4
A205
A316
A24
448
A2
Rochester
Sheerness
Margate
A232
Croydon
A228
Chatham
A249
A299
Ramsgate
A3
A217
A22
M25
M20
M26
A2
Canterbury
A28
442 441
447
M25
Maidstone
445
444
440
A256
SURREY
A21
446
A28
443
KENT
436
439
Dorking Reigate
M23
A22
A26
A229
Ashford
432
A2
A20
437
Dover
407
A24
431
433
438
East
Grinstead
Royal
Tunbridge
Wells
421
430
A2070
M20
434
435
Folkestone
Crawley
418
A259
Horsham
A264
A26
417
EAST
420
A259
New Romney
A272
408 409
A24
412
419
SUSSEX
A21
Rye
426 427 428 429
410
A23
416
A22
425
411
A283
414
Lewes
415
A259
Hastings
413
A27
Worthing Brighton
Eastbourne
422 423 424

N

0   30 Miles
0   40 Kilometres

360 Villiers Hotel

★★★ Silver Award

3 Castle Street, Buckingham, Buckinghamshire MK18 1BS **Tel:** (01280) 822444 **Fax:** (01280) 822113
E-mail: villiers@villiers-hotels.demon.co.uk

When we created Villiers Hotel from the old Swan and Castle Inn, we set out to build a very special and individual hotel. Drawing upon the character of the 400-year-old hostelry we included the highest quality facilities and services, with comfort a priority for you, our guest – a home away from home. Henry's, our elegant air-conditioned restaurant, has been awarded AA 2 Rosettes for exceptional cuisine.

Bed & Breakfast per night: single room from £75–£95; double room from £100.00–£150.00
Dinner, Bed & Breakfast per person, per night: £120.00–£155.00
Lunch available: 1230–1400
Evening meal: 1900 (last orders 2230)

Bedrooms: 3 single, 19 double, 16 twin
Bathrooms: 38 en-suite
Parking: 36 spaces
Cards accepted: Mastercard, Visa, Switch/Delta, Amex, Diners, Eurocard

361 Holcombe Hotel & Restaurant

★★★ Silver Award

High Street, Deddington, Banbury, Oxfordshire OX15 0SL **Tel:** (01869) 338274 **Fax:** (01869) 337167

Delightful 17th-century, family-run hotel offering personal attention and traditional hospitality in a relaxed atmosphere. 16 en-suite bedrooms, each with its own character and every amenity including direct phone, PC socket and satellite television. The restaurant, known locally for its fine cuisine, offers modern and traditional English menus that can best be described as 'honest' food and holds an AA Rosette for the sixth consecutive year. Golfing can be arranged locally at a superb 18-hole course. Meeting room for up to 20 delegates. Free car park for 40 cars. Convenient to the M40 (junctions 10 or 11) on the A4260.

Bed & Breakfast per night: single room from £62.00–£75.00; double room from £85.00–£95.00
Dinner, Bed & Breakfast per person, per night: £60.00–£65.00 (min 2 nights, 2 sharing)
Lunch available: 1200–1400

Evening meal: 1900 (last orders 2200)
Bedrooms: 2 single, 8 double, 6 twin, 1 triple
Bathrooms: 17 en-suite
Parking: 40 spaces
Cards accepted: Mastercard, Visa, Switch/Delta, Amex, Eurocard

362 Partway House

♦♦♦♦♦

Swalcliffe, Banbury, Oxfordshire OX15 5HA **Tel:** (01295) 780246 **Fax:** (01295) 780988

A delightful Hornton stone house, offering an exceptionally high standard of accommodation, set in beautiful 2.5 acre gardens. All bedrooms and the guests' drawing room have lovely views of the garden, with rural vistas beyond. Our very warm welcome, personal attention and excellent breakfast menus ensure a most pleasurable stay. Complimentary afternoon tea on arrival. Eight miles west of the M40 junction 11. Within easy reach of Oxford, Stratford-upon-Avon and the Cotswolds. Approximately one hour from London and Birmingham.

Bed & Breakfast per night: single occupancy from £37.00–£39.50; double room from £54.00–£59.00

Bedrooms: 1 double, 1 twin
Bathrooms: 1 en-suite, 1 private
Open: All year except January and December

Entries are cross referenced by number to the maps on pages 176–177

363 The Old Bell Foundry ◆◆◆◆

45 Witney Street, Burford, Oxford, Oxfordshire OX18 4RX **Tel:** (01993) 822234 **Fax:** (01993) 822234

A charming, well-furnished, 16th-century stone cottage in a peaceful setting two minutes' walk from Burford's famous high street. The property benefits from ample private parking and extensive mature gardens leading down to the River Windrush. The en-suite accommodation is pleasingly situated at the rear of the property overlooking the gardens and church. The establishment is renowned for its hearty, traditional breakfasts which include home-made bread and conserves. An excellent base for touring the Cotswolds.

Bed & Breakfast per night: double room from £46.00–£50.00

Bedrooms: 1 triple
Bathrooms: 1 en-suite
Parking: 2 spaces

364 Burford House Hotel ◆◆◆◆◆ Silver Award

99 High Street, Burford, Oxford, Oxfordshire OX18 4QA **Tel:** (01993) 823151 **Fax:** (01993) 823240
Web: http://www.burford-house.co.uk

Situated in one of the Cotswold's most historic towns, Burford House is perfectly placed for exploring this lovely area. Run with care by owners Jane and Simon Henty, importance is placed on comfort, a relaxed atmosphere and attention to detail, and the house is cosy and intimate with a wealth of personal touches. Wonderful breakfasts are served and guests can return to traditional afternoon tea in the sitting rooms or delightful courtyard garden. A warm welcome awaits.

Bed & Breakfast per night: single occupancy from £75.00–£100.00; double room from £80.00–£120.00
Lunch available: 1200–1415

Bedrooms: 6 double, 1 twin
Bathrooms: 7 en-suite
Cards accepted: Mastercard, Visa, Switch/Delta, Amex

365 Courtlands ◆◆◆◆

6 Courtlands Road, Shipton-under-Wychwood, Oxford, Oxfordshire OX7 6DF **Tel:** (01993) 830551
Web: http://www.homepages.which.net/~j-jfletcher/j-jfletcher/index.html **E-mail:** j-jfletcher@which.net

A relaxed, friendly, modern house situated in a beautiful, quiet village in the picturesque Cotswolds. Courtlands offers rural peace and tranquillity together with being ideally situated for sightseeing. Oxford, Blenheim Palace, Shakespeare country, Cheltenham, walking the Oxfordshire Way or cycling. Here you will get personalised care and service (with home-made shortbreads and preserves). There is off-road parking and, as keen gardeners and National Trust members, we can direct you to all the best attractions.

Bed & Breakfast per night: single occupancy from £25.00–£30.00; double room from £45.00

Bedrooms: 2 double, 1 twin
Bathrooms: 2 en-suite, 1 private
Parking: 4 spaces

At-a-glance symbols are explained on the flap inside the back cover

366 Shipton Glebe

◆◆◆◆ Gold Award

Woodstock, Oxford, Oxfordshire OX20 1QQ **Tel:** (01993) 812688 **Fax:** (01993) 813142
E-mail: stay@shipton-glebe.com

This lovely country house, set in nine acres of garden/parkland, is situated on the edge of historic Woodstock, close to Blenheim Palace. All the rooms are luxuriously furnished, and incorporate sitting room facilities. Breakfasts are served in the conservatory overlooking the gardens, and evening meals – available by prior arrangement – can be served in the elegant dining room. You will find that Shipton Glebe is the perfect setting for that special and relaxing few days away. Winner of the Best Bed & Breakfast in the Southern region.

Bed & Breakfast per night: single occupancy from £55.00–£65.00; double room from £75.00–£90.00
Dinner, Bed & Breakfast per person, per night: £60.00–£62.50
Evening meal: 1930 (last orders 2030)

Bedrooms: 1 double, 2 twin, 1 family
Bathrooms: 3 en-suite, 1 private
Cards accepted: Mastercard, Visa, Switch/Delta

367 Chimney Farmhouse

◆◆◆◆

Chimney-on-Thames, Aston, Bampton, Oxfordshire OX18 2EH **Tel:** (01367) 870279 **Fax:** (01367) 870279

Come and enjoy the peace and quiet of Chimney Farm on the Thames Trail. Our recently refurbished late-Victorian farmhouse offers spacious, comfortable, en-suite accommodation. Guests' own lounge and dining room, colour television, tea and coffee facilities in bedrooms and central heating throughout. Enjoy walking, open golf courses nearby or a stroll round our mature garden. In easy reach of Oxford, Blenheim Palace and the Cotswolds. Variety of excellent pubs and restaurants in nearby villages. A warm welcome awaits you.

Bed & Breakfast per night: single room from £25.00–£30.00; double room from £42.00–£50.00

Bedrooms: 1 single, 1 double, 1 twin
Bathrooms: 3 en-suite
Parking: 3 spaces
Open: All year except January and December

368 Pinkhill Cottage

◆◆◆◆

45 Rack End, Standlake, Witney, Oxfordshire OX8 7SA **Tel:** (01865) 300544

A charming 17th-century thatched cottage in half-acre gardens fronting the River Windrush in a quiet Oxfordshire village, offering exclusive, private bed & breakfast accommodation for two. The old stable has been transformed into a sitting room from which leads a staircase to the hayloft – now an airy double bedroom with en-suite shower room. Many of the original beams are a feature of our cottage. Standlake is ideal for touring Oxford and the Cotswolds.

Bed & Breakfast per night: single occupancy from £30.00–£32.00; double room from £42.00–£46.00

Bedrooms: 1 double
Bathrooms: 1 en-suite
Parking: 1 space

Entries are cross referenced by number to the maps on pages 176–177

369 Pembroke House

379 Woodstock Road, Oxford, Oxfordshire OX2 8AA **Tel:** (01865) 310782 **Fax:** (01865) 310649

Situated on one of the most beautiful approach roads into Oxford, only ten minutes from the city centre. There is a frequent bus service stopping just outside the door, and buses also stop here for Blenheim Palace and Stratford-upon-Avon. All rooms have central heating, tea and coffee making facilities and television with video. The spacious bedrooms offer the perfect place to relax at the end of the day. Off-street parking is available.

Bed & Breakfast per night: single occupancy from £50.00–£70.00; double room from £70.00–£80.00

Bedrooms: 3 double
Bathrooms: 2 en-suite, 1 private

The Landmarks of White Horse Hill

The Lambourn Downs of South Oxfordshire, rising up bare and smooth from the Vale of the White Horse, are steeped in ancient history. Around 5000 years ago our ancestors settled here, built their forts, buried their dead and walked their pathways; today the Downs are liberally sprinkled with the relics of their existence. Some sites have been excavated, but alongside the scant archaeological evidence, a vein of myth and legend has come down over the centuries to provide explanations for the mysterious landmarks.

Dominating the valley which is named after it, the strange elongated shape of a galloping horse is cut into the chalk near Uffington. The Iron Age tribes who lived in the nearby hillfort are believed to have carved it in about 50BC as a representation of the horse goddess, Epona. Possibly the oldest chalk carving in the country, it is, intriguingly, the only one which faces right. In more recent centuries the white horse became the focus of a seven-yearly tradition: people would climb the hill to 'scour' the accumulated weeds and debris from the horse to the accompaniment of fairground revels.

Just below the horse is a mound known as Dragon's Hill. Whether natural or man-made is unknown, but local legend asserts that this is where St George killed the dragon. The patches of bare chalk on its top and sides, the story goes, were formed by hot streams of dragon's blood, over which the grass can never grow.

Running along the ridge of the Downs, just south of the White Horse, is the Ridgeway. This track – used by people of the New Stone Age, the builders of Stonehenge – is one of the oldest roads in Britain. It leads south-west past Wayland's Smithy, a neolithic burial chamber dating from around 2800BC. This remote spot is one of many places throughout Europe (usually either caves or burial mounds) imagined as the home of Wayland, the fearsome Saxon blacksmith-god.

The figure of the smith is also associated, somewhat menacingly, with another curiosity: a strangely-shaped stone beside the road leading south from Kingston Lisle, just east of the White Horse. The 'Blowing Stone', as it is called, was supposedly brought here by a blacksmith living in the nearby cottage who could blow into its many holes to create a gruesome, moaning roar. Another legend grew up that King Alfred summoned his troops to battle by blowing through the stone.

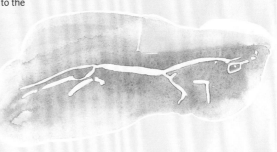

370 Studley Priory Hotel

★★★ Silver Award

Horton cum Studley, Oxford, Oxfordshire OX33 1AZ **Tel:** (01865) 351203 or (01865) 351254 **Fax:** (01865) 351613
Web: http://www.studley-priory.co.uk **E-mail:** res@studley-priory.co.uk

Timeless seclusion characterises the wooded setting of Studley Priory, whose exterior has scarcely altered since Elizabethan times. Enjoy fine views of the Chilterns and surrounding countryside. Our AA 2 Rosette restaurant offers modern English cooking complemented by our outstanding wine list. A short drive away are the dreaming spires of Oxford and magnificent Blenheim Palace at Woodstock. Public rooms and master bedrooms contain antique furniture. Log fires in public rooms in the winter months.

Bed & Breakfast per night: single room from £105.00–£130.00; double room from £140.00–£225.00
Dinner, Bed & Breakfast per person, per night: £90.00–£120.00 (min 2 nights)
Lunch available: 1200–1345

Evening meal: 1930 (last orders 2130)
Bedrooms: 3 single, 10 double, 5 twin
Bathrooms: 18 en-suite
Parking: 101 spaces
Cards accepted: Mastercard, Visa, Switch/Delta, Amex, Diners, Eurocard

371 The Dairy

♦♦♦♦♦ Gold Award

Moreton, Thame, Oxfordshire OX9 2HX **Tel:** (01844) 214075 **Fax:** (01844) 214075

This former milking parlour, set in over four acres, provides a beautiful, peaceful and comfortable stay. All bedrooms are bright and airy and include hairdryers, writing tables, fresh flowers, biscuits and comfortable sofas and chairs. There is a large open plan lounge with views of the Chilterns. The property is very convenient for London, either by train (50 minutes from local station), coach or car. Oxford is 20 minutes by car.

Bed & Breakfast per night: single occupancy from £56.00; double room from £79.00

Bedrooms: 2 double
Bathrooms: 2 en-suite
Parking: 6 spaces
Cards accepted: Mastercard, Visa, Amex, Eurocard

372 Cross Lanes Guest House

♦♦♦♦

Cross Lanes Cottage, Bledlow, Princes Risborough, Buckinghamshire HP27 9PF **Tel:** (01844) 345339 **Fax:** (01844) 274165

A warm welcome awaits you in this listed 16th-century cottage. All en-suite rooms have every attention to detail, even the little things you might forget. Characterful lounge and dining room add to the charm of this delightful home where hospitality and comfort are assured. An ideal location for enjoying Oxford, Waddesdon and the lovely Chiltern countryside, yet just a few miles from the M40. Secure parking. No pets, no children and no smoking.

Bed & Breakfast per night: single occupancy from £40.00–£45.00; double room from £55.00–£60.00

Bedrooms: 2 double, 1 twin
Bathrooms: 3 en-suite

Entries are cross referenced by number to the maps on pages 176–177

373 Danesfield House

★★★★ Silver Award

Medmenham, Marlow-on-Thames, Buckinghamshire SL7 2EY **Tel:** (01628) 891010 **Fax:** (01628) 890408

Danesfield House offers one of England's finest award-winning country house hotels, ideally set within the Chiltern Hills in an area of outstanding natural beauty, and yet within only one hour of London. Panoramic views of the River Thames from luxurious bedrooms, a beautiful terrace brasserie and the AA 2 Rosette Oak Room restaurant have helped establish Danesfield as a very popular destination. Luxury spa, including treatments, to open in summer 2000.

Bed & Breakfast per night: single room from £145.00–£165.00; double room from £185.00–£300.00
Lunch available: 1200–1500
Evening meal: 1830 (last orders 2200)

Bedrooms: 9 single, 59 double, 16 twin, 3 family
Bathrooms: 87 en-suite
Parking: 130 spaces
Cards accepted: Mastercard, Visa, Switch/Delta, Amex, Diners, Eurocard

374 The Knoll

◆◆◆◆

Crowsley Road, Shiplake, Henley-on-Thames, Oxfordshire RG9 3JT **Tel:** (01189) 402705 or 07885 755437 **Fax:** (01189) 402705
Web: http://www.saqnet.co.uk/users/the-knoll **E-mail:** milpops2@aol.com

The Knoll provides the perfect accommodation for an idyllic holiday or short stay. Beautifully restored by local craftsmen and fitted out with every modern convenience, you will be able to relax after a day's sightseeing or riverside walk in this private home with extensive landscaped gardens. The Knoll is situated in the quiet village of Shiplake, just two miles from Henley-on-Thames. Only 28 miles from London, you are also within easy driving distance of Windsor and Oxford.

Bed & Breakfast per night: single occupancy £48.00; double room from £50.00–£55.00

Bedrooms: 1 double, 1 twin/family
Bathrooms: 2 en-suite
Parking: 4 spaces

375 Holmwood

◆◆◆◆

Shiplake Row, Binfield Heath, Henley-on-Thames, Oxfordshire RG9 4DP **Tel:** (0118) 947 8747 **Fax:** (0118) 947 8637

Holmwood is an elegant Georgian country house with a galleried hall, mahogany doors and marble fireplaces. The house is set in three acres of beautiful gardens with extensive views over the Thames Valley. The large bedrooms are furnished with antique and period furniture – all have bathrooms en-suite, colour television and tea/coffee making facilities. Holmwood is convenient for Windsor, Oxford, London and Heathrow. Nearby are several pubs offering excellent evening meals. **Category 3**

Bed & Breakfast per night: single room £40.00; double room £60.00

Bedrooms: 1 single, 2 double, 2 twin
Bathrooms: 5 en-suite
Parking: 8 spaces
Cards accepted: Mastercard, Visa, Switch/Delta

At-a-glance symbols are explained on the flap inside the back cover

376 Moor Farm ◆◆◆◆

Ascot Road, Holyport, Maidenhead, Berkshire SL6 2HY **Tel:** (01628) 633761 **Fax:** (01628) 636167
E-mail: moorfm@aol.com

Guests can stay in the 700-year-old manor for bed and breakfast, or in the one and two-bedroom self-catering courtyard cottages. House guests have exclusive use of a wing with a sitting room, dining room and bedrooms with private bathrooms furnished with antiques. The cottages were converted from barns and stables and are furnished in antique pine. Good pubs are within walking distance. Close to Junctions 8 and 9 of the M4. Maidenhead's main line station is 1.5 miles and Windsor is 4 miles. Easy access to London and Heathrow.

Bed & Breakfast per night: single occupancy from £40.00–£45.00; double room from £50.00–£55.00

Bedrooms: 2 twin
Bathrooms: 1 en-suite, 1 private
Parking: 4 spaces

377 Regency Park Hotel ★★★★ Silver Award

Bowling Green Road, Thatcham, Newbury, Berkshire RG18 3RP **Tel:** (01635) 871555 **Fax:** (01635) 871571

In the heart of the Berkshire countryside but only minutes from the M4, the Regency Park is the perfect base from which to explore the Thames Valley and beyond. A warm welcome awaits you from staff commended for their courtesy and care. Executive standard bedrooms offer excellent facilities and the recently opened Watermark Restaurant has a contemporary setting where you can enjoy award-winning cuisine. June 2000 sees the opening of extensive indoor leisure facilities.

Bed & Breakfast per night: single room from £65.00–£130.00; double room from £90.00–£160.00
Dinner, Bed & Breakfast per person, per night: £62.50–£100.00
Lunch available: 1200–1400

Evening meal: 1900 (last orders 2200)
Bedrooms: 3 single, 29 double, 12 twin, 2 triple
Bathrooms: 46 en-suite
Parking: 125 spaces
Cards accepted: Mastercard, Visa, Switch/Delta, Amex, Diners

378 Tylney Hall Hotel ★★★★ Gold Award

Rotherwick, Basingstoke, Hampshire RG27 9AZ **Tel:** (01256) 764881 **Fax:** (01256) 768141
E-mail: sales@tylneyhall.com

Amidst sixty six acres of Hampshire countryside lies Tylney Hall, a privately-owned, Grade II listed country house hotel. The one hundred and ten bedrooms are beautifully decorated and fitted with all modern amenities. The award-winning Oak Room restaurant offers innovative menus for those dining for business or pleasure, complemented by an extensive wine cellar and attentive, yet discreet, service. Twelve individually designed function suites cater for up to one hundred people, whilst extensive and exclusive leisure facilities allow guests to relax in the luxurious surroundings.

Bed & Breakfast per night: single occupancy from £120.00–£299.00; double room from £152.00–£330.00
Dinner, Bed & Breakfast per person, per night: £97.50–£190.00 (min 2 nights, 2 sharing)
Lunch available: 1230–1400 (last orders 1330)

Evening meal: 1930 (last orders 2130)
Bedrooms: 95 double, 15 twin
Bathrooms: 110 en-suite
Parking: 120 spaces
Cards accepted: Mastercard, Visa, Switch/Delta, Amex, Diners

Entries are cross referenced by number to the maps on pages 176–177

379 | The Bishop's Table Hotel & Restaurant

★★★ Silver Award

27 West Street, Farnham, Surrey GU9 7DR **Tel:** (01252) 710222 **Fax:** (01252) 733494
E-mail: bishops.table@btinternet.com

An elegant, award-winning hotel where hospitality is at its best. All bedrooms are individually decorated. The walled garden is a walk into another world. The restaurant is well known and offers an excellent cuisine, including a full vegetarian menu.

Bed & Breakfast per night: single room from £90.00–£100.00; double room from £110.00–£145.00
Dinner, Bed & Breakfast per person, per night: £112.00–£122.00
Lunch available: 1230–1345

Evening meal: 1900 (last orders 2145)
Bedrooms: 6 single, 9 double, 2 twin
Bathrooms: 17 en-suite
Cards accepted: Mastercard, Visa, Amex, Diners, Eurocard

380 | May Cottage

♦♦♦♦ Silver Award

Thruxton, Andover, Hampshire SP11 8LZ **Tel:** (01264) 771241 or 07768 242166 **Fax:** (01264) 771770

May Cottage dates back to 1740 and is situated in the heart of this picturesque tranquil village with a Post Office and old inn. A most comfortable home with en-suite rooms, all having colour television, radio and tea tray. Guests' own sitting/dining room. Just off the A303, an ideal base for visiting ancient cities, stately homes and gardens, yet within easy reach of ports and airports. A non-smoking establishment.

Bed & Breakfast per night: single occupancy from £30.00–£35.00; double room from £50.00–£60.00

Bedrooms: 1 double, 2 twin
Bathrooms: 2 en-suite, 1 private
Parking: 4 spaces

381 | Lains Cottage

♦♦♦♦

Quarley, Andover, Hampshire SP11 8PX **Tel:** (01264) 889697 **Fax:** (01264) 889227
Web: http://dspace.dial.pipex.com/lains-cott-hols/ **E-mail:** lains-cott-hols@dial.pipex.com

Lains Cottage is a charming thatched house combining modern comforts with traditional cottage style. An ideal base from which to explore Stonehenge, Salisbury, the New Forest, Winchester and the South coast. The house is set in a quiet situation, yet only half a mile from the A303, giving access to London and the West Country.

Bed & Breakfast per night: single occupancy from £35.00–£50.00; double room from £50.00–£55.00

Bedrooms: 1 double, 2 twin
Bathrooms: 3 en-suite
Parking: 6 spaces

At-a-glance symbols are explained on the flap inside the back cover

382 The Mill Arms

◆◆◆◆

Barley Hill, Dunbridge, Romsey, Hampshire SO51 0LF **Tel:** (01794) 340401 **Fax:** (01794) 340401
Web: http://www.river-dun.demon.co.uk/ **E-mail:** the-mill-arms@river-dun.demon.co.uk

A former coaching inn which is centrally placed for touring the Test Valley and the New Forest. With award-winning gardens for al fresco dining in the summer and roaring log fires in the winter, each season has a different ambience. The excellent à la carte menu and robust home-made bar food is accompanied with a comprehensive wine list and ever-changing real ales. The rooms are decorated in warm tones and have an abundance of natural pine. All rooms are en-suite.

Bed & Breakfast per night: single occupancy from £35.00; double room from £55.00–£65.00
Dinner, Bed & Breakfast per person, per night: £32.50–£50.00 (min 2 sharing)
Lunch available: 1200–1430

Evening meal: 1900 (last orders 2130)
Bedrooms: 1 double, 4 twin, 1 family
Bathrooms: 6 en-suite
Parking: 42 spaces
Cards accepted: Mastercard, Visa, Switch/Delta, Eurocard

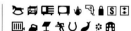

Romsey Abbey

If ever a building deserved to be better known, it is Romsey's parish church. It was built as part of a Benedictine nunnery, survived Henry VIII's dissolution of the monasteries because the people of Romsey bought it for £100, and is today one of the most flawless pieces of Norman architecture in Europe. It sits close to the River Test, its squat grey tower visible behind Romsey's market square. Inside is an untampered, uncluttered beauty that stops you in your tracks as you enter: tall round columns, perfectly proportioned rounded arches, superb arcading, zig-zagging, exuberantly carved capitals.

Stand at the west end and notice how, as your eye moves up the Nave toward the main altar, each bay is earlier in style than the last, for building work began at the east end, on the site of an earlier church, in about 1120 and progressed westwards, being completed about 1250. It makes a perfect textbook on Norman architecture. Then walk up the South Aisle to the South Transept to find the simple memorial to Earl Mountbatten, assassinated in 1979. The Mountbatten estate, Broadlands (tel: 01794 505010), is in Romsey.

Further up the South Aisle, and in the Retrochoir, are some particularly delightful carved capitals: several scalloped with birds and beasts. The one on the last pillar on the left of the South Aisle, together with its corresponding one in the North Aisle, tells a busy story. At the end of the South Aisle is one of the abbey's most precious treasures: a little low-relief

Saxon white stone crucifix set in the rounded wall behind the altar. There is another, larger, similarly dated to about 1000, outside, on the west wall of the South Transept. Pass the 12th-century wall painting in the Retrochoir, and from the North Aisle look across the Chancel to the three storeys of Norman arches. The arcading above the main arches is unique to Romsey: within each bay (the zig-zagging on the arches is wonderful here) is a pair of smaller arches with a small column in the space above. From the Chancel there is a clear view down the Nave. In the North Transept look for the 16th-century, Italian-style wooden painted reredos. Finally, turn left out of the South Door to see the carving above the Abbess's Doorway and the second Saxon crucifix. And all around the building look up at the corbels, a delightfully lively gallery of faces and creatures.

Entries are cross referenced by number to the maps on pages 176–177

383 Hucklesbrook Farm ◆◆◆◆

South Gorley, Fordingbridge, Hampshire SP6 2PN **Tel:** (01425) 653180
E-mail: j.sampson@virgin.net

Hucklesbrook Farm is a beautiful 17th-century farmhouse set in a peaceful position by the Huckles Brook. Ideally situated for exploring the New Forest, with riding stables, cycle hire, fishing, excellent pubs and restaurants all close by. Salisbury, Winchester and the Dorset coast are within easy reach. With their own entrance, the two charming bedrooms offer all private facilities plus colour television, wonderful views over open farmland and the New Forest beyond. A warm welcome awaits.

Bed & Breakfast per night: single occupancy £27.50; double room from £44.00–£48.00

Bedrooms: 1 double, 1 twin
Bathrooms: 1 en-suite, 1 private
Parking: 4 spaces

384 The Three Lions ◆◆◆◆◆ Gold Award

Stuckton, Fordingbridge, Hampshire SP6 2HF **Tel:** (01425) 652489 **Fax:** (01425) 656144

Built in 1863, The Three Lions nestles on the edge of the New Forest and is personally owned and run by Mike and Jayne Womersley. The rooms are all en-suite, airy and very peaceful, overlooking well-manicured gardens and the forest behind. There is also an open-air whirlpool therapy spa for residents' use. The restaurant is highly rated in all major UK food guides with AA 3 Rosettes and a 150-bin wine list.

Bed & Breakfast per night: single occupancy max £75.00; double room max £85.00
Lunch available: 1200–1400
Evening meal: 1900 (last orders 2100)

Bedrooms: 2 double, 1 twin
Bathrooms: 3 en-suite
Parking: 40 spaces
Cards accepted: Mastercard, Visa, Switch/Delta, Eurocard

385 Beechleas Hotel and Restaurant ★★ Silver Award

17 Poole Road, Wimborne Minster, Dorset BH21 1QA **Tel:** (01202) 841684

A delightful Georgian Grade II listed town-house hotel. Beautifully restored with nine tastefully furnished en-suite bedrooms of quality and an RAC Blue Ribbon and AA 2 Rosette award-winning restaurant. Many National Trust properties are within easy reach including Kingston Lacey, Corfe Castle and Badbury Rings. Walking, fishing, sailing, shopping, sandy beaches, the New Forest, Purbeck Hills, Poole and Bournemouth are all within a 20 minute drive.

Bed & Breakfast per night: single occupancy from £69.00–£89.00; double room from £89.00–£99.00
Evening meal: 1900 (last orders 2100)

Bedrooms: 7 double, 2 twin
Bathrooms: 9 private
Parking: 9 spaces
Open: mid January – Christmas Eve
Cards accepted: Mastercard, Visa, Amex

At-a-glance symbols are explained on the flap inside the back cover

386 Cleff House

◆◆◆◆◆ Gold Award

Brookmans Valley, Iwerne Minster, Blandford Forum, Dorset DT11 8NG **Tel:** (01747) 811129 or (01747) 811112 **Fax:** (01747) 811112

Big skies, rolling hills, sun setting beyond the church spire, peace and tranquillity – this is our valley. Set in nine acres in an area of outstanding natural beauty, Cleff House is a wonderful modern country house offering style, comfort and good cuisine using the pick of local produce. You are assured a warm welcome from your hosts who enjoy sharing their beautiful home with you.

Bed & Breakfast per night: single occupancy from £35.00–£40.00; double room from £55.00–£60.00

Bedrooms: 2 double, 1 twin
Bathrooms: 3 en-suite
Parking: 10 spaces
Open: All year except January and December

387 Swan Inn

◆◆◆◆

Market Place, Sturminster Newton, Dorset DT10 1AR **Tel:** (01258) 472208 **Fax:** (01258) 473767

In the heart of Thomas Hardy's Wessex, the 18th-century Swan Inn holds a long tradition of superb cuisine and quality accommodation. The attractive lounge bar is traditionally themed, serving home-cooked bar meals and daily specials, whilst the recently refurbished restaurant boasts an excellent à la carte menu. Acoommodation comprises five individually styled bedrooms with full en-suite facilities. Please discuss your requirements with the managers, Andy and Sandy Currie, who look forward to your visit.

Bed & Breakfast per night: single room from £40.00; double room from £49.50
Lunch available: 1200–1430
Evening meal: 1900 (last orders 2130)

Bedrooms: 1 single, 3 double, 1 twin
Bathrooms: 5 en-suite
Parking: 20 spaces
Cards accepted: Mastercard, Visa, Switch/Delta, Amex, Eurocard, Visa Electron

388 Mortons House Hotel

★★★ Silver Award

East Street, Corfe Castle, Wareham, Dorset BH20 5EE **Tel:** (01929) 480988 **Fax:** (01929) 480820

Mortons House is a 400-year-old Elizabethan manor in this fairytale village, built in the shape of an E to honour Queen Elizabeth I. The hotel offers both the history and charm of a private country house beautifully situated in the heart of the Purbeck Hills with the heritage coast close by. Seventeen character en-suite bedrooms, acclaimed cuisine (AA Rosette), log fire, pretty walled gardens and car parking. Open throughout the year. Special Christmas three-day holiday.

Bed & Breakfast per night: double room from £101.00–£111.00
Dinner, Bed & Breakfast per person, per night: £55.50–£74.50
Lunch available: 1200–1400
Evening meal: 1900 (last orders 2030)

Bedrooms: 13 double, 3 twin, 1 family
Bathrooms: 17 en-suite
Parking: 35 spaces
Cards accepted: Mastercard, Visa, Switch/Delta, Amex, Diners

Entries are cross referenced by number to the maps on pages 176–177

389 White Lodge Hotel

◆◆◆◆

Grosvenor Road, Swanage, Dorset BH19 2DD **Tel:** (01929) 422696 **Fax:** (01929) 425510
E-mail: whitelodge.hotel@virgin.net

Country-style hotel set within its own pretty gardens, including a car parking area. Situated on the south side of Swanage in a quiet location close to the coastal path and Durlston Country Park. Several of the bedrooms have superior sea views. All 13 bedrooms are fully en-suite. Extensive breakfast and dinner menus with food freshly prepared from local produce. Our public rooms consist of a 30-cover dining room, two lounges – one with a good supply of reading material – and a large lounge conservatory.

Bed & Breakfast per night: single room from £25.00–£29.00; double room from £50.00–£58.00
Dinner, Bed & Breakfast per person, per night: £39.50–£43.50
Evening meal: 1830 (last orders 1900)

Bedrooms: 1 single, 6 double, 4 twin, 2 triple
Bathrooms: 13 en-suite
Parking: 14 spaces
Cards accepted: Mastercard, Visa, Switch/Delta, Visa Electron

Brownsea Island

A short trip from Poole Quay across the sheltered waters of Poole Harbour leads to Brownsea Island. At just over 500 acres (202 hectares) this is the largest of the five islands in the harbour. Brownsea's recorded history begins before the Norman Conquest when Bruno, Lord of Studland, owned the island; his name lives on, in corrupt form, in the word Brownsea.

In 1722 William Benson bought Brownsea for £300. Dubbed 'Mad' Benson by locals, he was briefly certified insane amidst accusations of satanic worship and child sacrifice. Whatever the truth, Benson introduced many rare plants and trees and was instrumental in making the island the wildlife haven it is today. By 1852, when Colonel William Petrie Waugh purchased Brownsea, the price was £13,000. He and his wife were convinced that the island had all the raw materials necessary for a china clay business. A persuasive pair, the Waughs talked a London bank into investing £237,000 in Brownsea. When the clay proved good enough only for items such as drain pipes (remnants can be seen on much of the southern shore) the enterprise failed. As the Waughs fled to Spain so the island's economy – and the bank – collapsed.

Successive private owners stamped their mark on Brownsea: one briefly resurrected the pottery business; another turned the castle – originally one of Henry VIII's South Coast fortifications – into a luxurious dwelling; a third cut the island off from all outside influence between 1925 and 1961, so

allowing a range of rare fauna and flora to flourish away from the destructive habits of mankind. The National Trust, who inherited something of a jungle in 1961, has restored parts of the island to order, while leaving much to nature.

Today's visitors landing at Town Quay have plenty to discover. The northern shores and small lagoon now form a nature reserve populated by countless species of waders, gulls and waterfowl. There is a viewing hide not far from the quay and guided tours are available by arrangement. Look up into the pine trees and you may see red squirrels, for this is one of their last retreats in England; look down and you may glimpse the secretive sika deer. Come in late May or early June and two natural displays you cannot miss are the peacocks and the rhododendrons, the former flamboyantly and noisily strutting their stuff in front of the drab peahens, the latter creating huge splashes of purple in the sun. There are miles of glorious paths to explore, long sandy (if also a little muddy) beaches and an attractive little church. The castle is not open to the public. Further details from The National Trust on 01202 707744.

390 Tatnam Farm ◆◆◆◆

82 Tatnam Road, Poole, Dorset BH15 2DS **Tel:** (01202) 672969 **Fax:** (01202) 682732
E-mail: helenbishop@jrb.netkonect.co.uk

Tatnam Farm is a 300-year-old, Grade II listed farmhouse set in a half-acre walled garden. It offers a quiet and relaxed atmosphere whilst being only 15 minutes' walk from the centre of Poole. The accommodation is furnished in traditional country house style and has pretty bedrooms and an elegant bathroom. Guests may use the garden, which has a terrace with interesting pots and a pond set in the lawn, and is surrounded by mature trees and shrubs.

Bed & Breakfast per night: single room from £25.00–£27.00; double room from £50.00–£54.00

Bedrooms: 1 twin (plus additional single room by arrangement)
Bathrooms: 1 private
Parking: 2 spaces

391 Winter Dene Hotel ◆◆◆◆

11 Durley Road South, West Cliff, Bournemouth, Dorset BH2 5JH **Tel:** (01202) 554150 **Fax:** (01202) 555426
Web: http://www.bournemouth-hotels.co.uk/winterdene **E-mail:** wintdene@bournemouth-hotels.co.uk

The Winter Dene is an elegant Victorian villa which has been lovingly refurbished to offer comfortable surroundings for your holiday. Standing in spacious lawned gardens in a quiet area of the West Cliff just five minutes' walk from the sea and a short stroll to the town centre, pier and theatres. Spacious bedrooms are attractively furnished with antiques and pine. Licensed dining room offers excellent home cooking. High standards of service with the friendly atmosphere of a family-run hotel.

Bed & Breakfast per night: single room from £25.00–£30.00; double room from £50.00–£60.00
Dinner, Bed & Breakfast per person, per night: £32.00–£40.00
Evening meal: 1800 (last orders 1830)

Bedrooms: 2 single, 2 double, 2 twin, 3 triple, 4 family
Bathrooms: 13 en-suite
Parking: 12 spaces
Cards accepted: Mastercard, Visa, Eurocard

392 The White House ◆◆◆◆

428 Lymington Road, Highcliffe, Christchurch, Dorset BH23 5HF **Tel:** (01425) 271279 **Fax:** (01425) 276900
E-mail: thewhitehouse@themail.co.uk

The proprietors, Eileen and Fred, welcome you to their beautiful Victorian house which is decorated and furnished to a very high standard. Just a short walk from Highcliffe beach with its wonderful views of The Needles, or scenic cliff-top walks. Restaurants, shops and pubs are also within walking distance. Being close to the New Forest and golf courses makes this an ideal location. Colour television and tea/coffee facilities in all rooms. Generous breakfasts served in the delightfully decorated dining room. Private car park front and rear (free).

Bed & Breakfast per night: single occupancy from £22.00–£25.00; double room from £46.00–£50.00

Bedrooms: 4 double, 2 twin
Bathrooms: 5 en-suite, 1 public
Parking: 6 spaces

Entries are cross referenced by number to the maps on pages 176–177

393 Rufus House Hotel

♦♦♦♦ Silver Award

Southampton Road, Lyndhurst, Hampshire SO43 7BQ **Tel:** (023) 8028 2200 **Fax:** (023) 8028 2930

Welcome to Rufus House, a Victorian family-run hotel in the heart of the largest area of medieval forest left in Western Europe. Enjoy a relaxing break in beautiful surroundings. The guest lounge and many of our bedrooms have views across to the open forest opposite. All 11 bedrooms are well-appointed and have many extras. Our special turret rooms even have their own lounge areas. Our turreted home offers you yesterday's comforts with today's conveniences.

Bed & Breakfast per night: single room from £30.00–£40.00; double room from £55.00–£75.00

Bedrooms: 1 single, 8 double, 2 twin
Bathrooms: 11 en-suite

394 Whitley Ridge Country House Hotel

★★★ Silver Award

Beaulieu Road, Brockenhurst, Hampshire SO42 7QL **Tel:** (01590) 622354 **Fax:** (01590) 622856
Web: http://www.newforest-hotels.co.uk **E-mail:** whitleyridge@brockenhurst.co.uk

A charming Georgian country house hotel, formerly a royal hunting lodge, in five acres of New Forest parkland, Whitley Ridge has a very good reputation for its cuisine and friendly service. All en-suite bedrooms have recently been refurbished to a high standard and overlook extensive grounds which include a tennis court. In winter, log fires burn on cooler evenings, and the candlelit dining room (AA 2 Rosettes) creates a special atmosphere. Special midweek inclusive rates available.

Bed & Breakfast per night: single room from £60.00–£80.00; double room from £98.00–£120.00
Dinner, Bed & Breakfast per person, per night: £54.00–£65.00 (min 2 nights, 2 sharing)
Lunch available: 1200–1400 (Sunday only)

Evening meal: 1900 (last orders 2030)
Bedrooms: 2 single, 9 double, 3 twin
Bathrooms: 14 en-suite
Parking: 28 spaces
Cards accepted: Mastercard, Visa, Switch/Delta, Amex, Diners, Eurocard

395 The Nurse's Cottage

♦♦♦♦♦ Gold Award

Station Road, Sway, Lymington, Hampshire SO41 6BA **Tel:** (01590) 683402 **Fax:** (01590) 683402
E-mail: nurses.cottage@lineone.net

Nothing equals a visit to this cosy New Forest cottage, for over 70 years home to Sway's successive District Nurses. Lovingly refurbished in recent years, the award-winning guest accommodation offers every possible creature comfort, while chef/proprietor Tony Barnfield's enterprising dinner menu and extensive wine list make this the perfect escape for that very special occasion. Invariably fully booked months ahead, advance reservations are essential. The Garden Room Restaurant is open to non-residents for dinner, afternoon tea and Sunday luncheon. ⋔ **Category 3**

Bed & Breakfast per night: single room from £52.50–£62.50; double room £90.00
Dinner, Bed & Breakfast per person, per night: £47.50–£72.50 (min 2 nights)
Lunch available: by arrangement
Evening meal: 1830 (last orders 2030)

Bedrooms: 1 single, 1 double, 1 twin
Bathrooms: 3 en-suite
Parking: 4 spaces
Cards accepted: Mastercard, Visa, Switch/Delta, Amex, Eurocard, JCB, Maestro, Visa Electron, Solo

At-a-glance symbols are explained on the flap inside the back cover

396 Ha'penny House

16 Whitby Road, Milford-on-Sea, Lymington, Hampshire SO41 0ND **Tel:** (01590) 641210 **Fax:** (01590) 641219
E-mail: hapenny.house@talk21.co.uk

Set in a quiet area of the village of Milford-on-Sea, Ha'penny House is ideally situated for touring the New Forest, Bournemouth, Salisbury and the Isle of Wight. A traditional house with spacious rooms, it has a cosy lounge with an open fire and ample parking on site. A four-course breakfast is offered including vegetarian and 'healthy' options. Owners Carolyn and Roy endeavour to ensure their guests' comfort and enjoyment in a relaxed atmosphere.

Bed & Breakfast per night: single occupancy from £21.00–£25.00; double room from £42.00–£50.00

Bedrooms: 2 double
Bathrooms: 2 en-suite

397 Efford Cottage ◆◆◆◆◆ Gold Award

Everton, Lymington, Hampshire SO41 0JD **Tel:** (01590) 642315 **Fax:** (01590) 641030 or (01590) 642315
E-mail: effcottage@aol.com

A spacious Georgian cottage, offering high class, luxury en-suite accommodation for the discerning guest. Large well-equipped bedrooms contain many extra luxuries. A four-course breakfast from a wide and varied menu with home-grown produce, home-made bread and preserves, is prepared by Patricia, a qualified chef. Guests may relax in the large drawing room or in the one acre garden. Be assured of a warm and friendly stay – 'your comfort is our concern'.

Bed & Breakfast per night: double room from £46.00–£50.00

Bedrooms: 2 double, 1 double/twin
Bathrooms: 3 en-suite
Parking: 4 spaces

398 Rosefield House ◆◆◆◆◆ Gold Award

Sway Road, Lymington, Hampshire SO41 8LR **Tel:** (01590) 671526 **Fax:** (01590) 689007

Rosefield House offers a most enjoyable way to explore the Forest and nearby coastal resorts or 'just a night or two away from home'. Luxury accommodation in a beautiful country house surrounded by gardens. Large indoor heated swimming pool. Luxurious en-suite bedrooms all with zip-linked super king-size beds, television, video, video library, telephone and many other pampering ingredients. Superb lounge with wood-burning fire. Delicious breakfasts with our own free range eggs.

Bed & Breakfast per night: double room from £70.00–£80.00
Dinner, Bed & Breakfast per person, per night: £55.00–£65.00

Bedrooms: 2 double, 1 twin
Bathrooms: 3 en-suite

Entries are cross referenced by number to the maps on pages 176–177

399 The Hillsman House

 Silver Award

Milford Road, Lymington, Hampshire SO41 8DP **Tel:** (01590) 674737
E-mail: reservations@hillsman-house.co.uk

The Hillsman House has a unique style and is full of character and charm. A beautiful setting in 1.5 acres. Elegantly decorated and furnished with antiques. Luxurious en-suite guest rooms with views over the surrounding countryside. On arrival indulge in home-made chocolate cake and sit on the verandah overlooking palm trees and pampas grass, creating the relaxed atmosphere of the Carolinas. A perfect location for beaches, New Forest, Isle of Wight and the Georgian town of Lymington. Set yourself up for the day with a scrumptious English breakfast.

Bed & Breakfast per night: single room from £25.00–£27.00; double room from £50.00–£55.00

Bedrooms: 1 single, 2 double, 1 twin
Bathrooms: 4 en-suite

400 Northcourt

◆◆◆◆

Main Road, Shorwell, Newport, Isle of Wight PO30 3JG **Tel:** (01983) 740415 **Fax:** (01983) 740409

Large 17th-century manor house set in magnificent gardens of 15 acres, surrounded by hills, in a peaceful village. All rooms are large and en-suite, furnished in traditional style. Good base for walking, garden visiting or enjoying peaceful surroundings. Walk through the garden to the Crown Inn for meals. The sea, Osborne House, National Trust properties and Ventnor Botanic Gardens are all within 20 minutes' drive. Gardens of historic and botanical interest of exceptional variety and beauty. Ferries 10 miles away.

Bed & Breakfast per night: single occupancy from £25.00–£32.00; double room from £42.00–£55.00

Bedrooms: 2 double, 1 twin
Bathrooms: 3 en-suite
Parking: 10 spaces

401 Hope Lodge Hotel

◆◆◆◆

21 Hope Road, Shanklin, Isle of Wight PO37 6EA **Tel:** (01983) 863140 **Fax:** (01983) 863140
Web: http://www.placestostay.com **E-mail:** janetwf@aol.com

Situated above Shanklin Esplanade in an ideal position within easy reach of all amenities. We invite you to experience all-round luxury and a warm welcome. Great care and personal attention has been given to designing, decorating and furnishing the public rooms with your relaxation in mind. The dining room offers English and continental cuisine of the highest standard, and for those romantics among you we offer four-poster bedrooms.

Bed & Breakfast per night: single room from £19.50–£30.00; double room from £39.00–£60.00
Dinner, Bed & Breakfast per person, per night: £32.00–£42.00
Evening meal: 1815

Bedrooms: 2 single, 4 double, 1 twin, 1 triple
Bathrooms: 6 en-suite, 2 private
Parking: 10 spaces
Open: All year except January and February
Cards accepted: Mastercard, Visa, Switch, Diners, JCB, Eurocard

At-a-glance symbols are explained on the flap inside the back cover

402 Millstream Hotel and Restaurant

★★★ Silver Award

Bosham Lane, Bosham, Chichester, West Sussex PO18 8HL **Tel:** (01243) 573234 **Fax:** (01243) 573459
Web: http://www.millstream-hotel.co.uk **E-mail:** info@millstream-hotel.co.uk

A beautifully appointed country manor house dating from 1701, set in a picturesque quayside village, only four miles west of Chichester. The friendly staff will make you feel very welcome. Bedrooms are all individually furnished, with every modern facility. The Millstream Restaurant is renowned for its superb food and extensive wine list and has been awarded an AA Rosette for food excellence. Enjoy walking on the beautiful shoreline or the rolling South Downs. Fishbourne Roman Villa, Goodwood House and Chichester Festival Theatre are all within easy reach.

Bed & Breakfast per night: single room from £69.00–£72.00; double room from £112.00–£115.00
Dinner, Bed & Breakfast per person, per night: £60.00–£75.00
Lunch available: 1230–1400

Evening meal: 1900 (last orders 2130)
Bedrooms: 5 single, 16 double, 10 twin, 2 family
Bathrooms: 33 en-suite
Parking: 44 spaces
Cards accepted: Mastercard, Visa, Switch/Delta, Amex, Diners, Eurocard

403 Amberfold

◆◆◆◆

Heyshott, Midhurst, West Sussex GU29 0DA **Tel:** (01730) 812385

Miles of unspoilt woodland walks start on your doorstep. An ideal hideaway for nature lovers, yet only five minutes' drive from historic Midhurst and the local attractions of Goodwood, Chichester and the coast. Accommodation comprises two self-contained units with access all day. Double bedroom with shower room, toilet, central heating, television, electric kettle, cafetiere and toaster. A fridge, which is lavishly replenished daily with a selection of food, is provided for a self-service continental breakfast.

Bed & Breakfast per night: single occupancy from £35.00–£45.00; double room from £50.00–£60.00

Bedrooms: 2 double
Bathrooms: 2 en-suite
Parking: 6 spaces

404 Woodacre

◆◆◆◆

Arundel Road, Fontwell, Arundel, West Sussex BN18 0SD **Tel:** (01243) 814301 **Fax:** (01243) 814344
E-mail: wacrebb@aol.com

Conveniently located for Arundel, Chichester, Goodwood or the seaside, Woodacre offers bed and breakfast in a traditional family house, with annexed accommodation for up to ten guests. The house is set in an acre of garden surrounded by woodland. Our rooms are clean and spacious and comprise one en-suite double room and a family room on the ground floor and two twin rooms on the first floor. A full English breakfast is served in the conservatory or dining room overlooking the garden. Everyone is most welcome.

Bed & Breakfast per night: double room from £40.00–£45.00

Bedrooms: 1 double, 2 twin, 1 family
Bathrooms: 1 en-suite, 2 public
Parking: 20 spaces
Cards accepted: Mastercard, Visa, Switch/Delta, Eurocard

Entries are cross referenced by number to the maps on pages 176–177

405 White Horse Inn

◆◆◆◆

The Street, Sutton, Pulborough, West Sussex RH20 1PS **Tel:** (01798) 869221 **Fax:** (01798) 869291

Sutton is a picture-postcard village tucked away at the foot of the South Downs. Great sensitivity has been used to bring our charming Georgian inn up to the standards expected by the discerning traveller, whilst retaining its essential character. The bedrooms are elegantly furnished, each with its own spacious bathroom. The food has a strong emphasis on traditional country cooking, enhanced by a selection of other well-chosen dishes. Log fires in the winter and the garden in the summer! A no smoking policy applies to bedrooms.

Bed & Breakfast per night: single occupancy £48.00; double room from £58.00–£68.00
Lunch available: 1200–1400
Evening meal: 1900 (last orders 2145)

Bedrooms: 4 double, 2 twin
Bathrooms: 5 en-suite, 1 room with private shower
Parking: 10 spaces
Cards accepted: Mastercard, Visa, Switch/Delta, Amex

Arundel

Viewed from the south-west the attractive West Sussex town of Arundel has something of a French air. The warm red of clay rooftiles spills down a steep slope crowned by the Gothic-style Catholic cathedral and the huge fortifications of Arundel Castle. Both these buildings – and most of the town, for that matter – have strong connections with the Dukes of Norfolk, the family that has, in one sense or another, looked down upon the townsfolk for seven centuries. The castle, commanding a strategically important gap on the edge of the South Downs, was built in the 11th century. During the Civil War it suffered such damage at the hands of the Parliamentarians that little of the Norman original survives. Dating in large part from the 19th century, the battlements were designed as romantic rather than practical features. In the film version of *The Madness of King George* Arundel took on the starring role of Windsor Castle. It is open to the public (tel: 01903 883136).

The cathedral is dedicated to St Philip Howard, 13th Earl of Arundel, who was martyred in 1595 for his Catholic faith. Not to everyone's taste, it was designed in 1870 by one JA Hansom, inventor of the eponymous cab. Of greater architectural significance is the late 14th-century church of St Nicholas. One half, full of monuments to past Dukes of Norfolk, forms the Fitzalan Chapel where Catholic services are held; Anglican services are held in the other.

Over the past 20 years Arundel has also become a picturesque venue for international cricket with the touring team traditionally playing their opening game here against Lavinia, Duchess of Norfolk's XI. The town can also boast an intriguing museum dedicated to toys and militaria (tel: 01903 882908), though one of the most pleasant ways to pass time is to wander along streets full of Georgian and Victorian frontages (often concealing Tudor interiors). High Street, Maltravers Street and Tarrant Street are three of the best.

One theory about how Arundel came by its name claims it is a corruption of hirondelle, French for swallow. Whatever the truth, the town enjoys at least two avian connections; swallows appear on Arundel's coat of arms while near by is one of the South's best reserves for swans, geese, ducks and waders. Keen-eyed visitors to the Wildfowl and Wetlands Trust (tel: 01903 883355) may even be lucky enough to glimpse (or more probably hear the grunting of) the elusive water rail.

406 Burpham Country House Hotel

★★★ Silver Award

Burpham, Arundel, West Sussex BN18 9RJ **Tel:** (01903) 882160 **Fax:** (01903) 884627

Nestling in a fold of the famous Sussex South Downs, the hotel offers the most perfect location for a 'Stress Remedy Break'! The hamlet of Burpham is totally peaceful and unspoilt and the walks are truly spectacular. The dining room offers a regularly changing menu using only the best ingredients. Swiss-born Marianne Walker and husband George – the resident owners – are justly proud of their AA Rosette award-winning cuisine offered in the Rösti Room Restaurant and brand new conservatory. The comfort offered here is truly memorable. Please mention this guide when booking. Special breaks available.

Bed & Breakfast per night: single room from £42.50–£62.50; double room from £87.00–£105.00
Dinner, Bed & Breakfast per person, per night: £66.00–£76.00
Evening meal: 1915 (last orders 2045)

Bedrooms: 1 single, 6 double, 3 twin
Bathrooms: 10 en-suite
Parking: 12 spaces
Cards accepted: Mastercard, Visa, Amex, Eurocard

407 The Hurtwood Inn Hotel

★★★ Silver Award

Peaslake, Guildford, Surrey GU5 9RR **Tel:** (01306) 730851 **Fax:** (01306) 731390
E-mail: sales@hurtwoodinnhotel.freeserve.co.uk

A weekend stay at the Hurtwood Inn Hotel offers the perfect way to see the outstandingly beautiful villages and countryside of the Surrey Hills. Privately owned, the Hurtwood blends the character and uniqueness of a country inn with the professionalism of a metropolitan hotel. The emphasis is firmly on quality, comfort and hospitality in our 17 rooms, the renowned AA Rosette, fine dining restaurant 'Oscars' and the real country bar. We promise your stay will be something really special.

Bed & Breakfast per night: single room £57.50; double room from £65.00–£75.00
Lunch available: 1200–1400
Evening meal: 1900 (last orders 2130)

Bedrooms: 3 single, 11 double, 3 twin
Bathrooms: 17 en-suite
Parking: 25 spaces
Cards accepted: Mastercard, Visa, Switch/Delta, Amex, Diners, Eurocard

408 Chequers Hotel

★★ Silver Award

Old Rectory Lane, Pulborough, West Sussex RH20 1AD **Tel:** (01798) 872486 **Fax:** (01798) 872715
Web: http://www.chequershotel.com **E-mail:** admin@minotel.com

Situated in the heart of the local conservation area and facing out over the Arun Valley towards the South Downs, we pride ourselves upon being the quintessential small English country hotel. Built in 1548 and carefully extended and refurbished, we offer luxury en-suite bedrooms, fine food in our award-winning restaurant, a conservatory coffee shop, and ample parking. Right outside is our nine-acre meadow for walks for you and your dog.

Bed & Breakfast per night: single occupancy from £49.50–£59.50; double room from £85.00–£99.00
Dinner, Bed & Breakfast per person, per night: from £72.45
Lunch available: 1200–1400

Evening meal: 1900 (last orders 2045)
Bedrooms: 6 double, 2 twin, 3 triple
Bathrooms: 10 en-suite, 1 private
Parking: 16 spaces
Cards accepted: Mastercard, Visa, Switch/Delta, Eurocard

Entries are cross referenced by number to the maps on pages 176–177

409 New Barn Cottage

♦♦♦♦

New Barn Lane, off Harborough Hill, West Chiltington, Pulborough, West Sussex RH20 2PP **Tel:** (01798) 813231 **Fax:** (01798) 813231

A friendly welcome awaits you at our former herdsman's cottage which is approximately 400 years old. We are situated at the end of a private lane overlooking open countryside. The guest bedrooms have en-suite facilities with excellent views and a full English breakfast is included at a time to suit you. Centrally situated for exploring Sussex, with golf, horse racing, showjumping, the RSPB reserve, stately homes and local walks. Inns and restaurants with good food nearby.

Bed & Breakfast per night: single room £30.00; double room from £45.00–£55.00

Bedrooms: 1 single, 1 double
Bathrooms: 2 en-suite
Parking: 10 spaces

410 Hampers End

♦♦♦♦ Silver Award

Rock Road, Storrington, Pulborough, West Sussex RH20 3AF **Tel:** (01903) 742777 **Fax:** (01903) 742776
Web: http://www.hampersend.co.uk **E-mail:** info@hampersend.co.uk

Mike and Lorna Cheeseman welcome you to Hampers End – a lovely mellowed country house overlooking secluded gardens in a quiet location at the edge of the South Downs village of Storrington. Well-equipped en-suite bedrooms with colour television and beverage tray. Full English breakfast. Ample off-road parking. An ideal base for visiting historic stately homes, Roman villas, Arundel Castle, famous gardens, RSPB reserves and antique centres. Colour brochure, tariff and West Sussex information on request.

Bed & Breakfast per night: single occupancy from £32.50–£39.50; double room from £45.00–£59.00

Bedrooms: 3 double
Bathrooms: 3 en-suite
Parking: 6 spaces

411 The Old Tollgate Restaurant & Hotel

★★★ Silver Award

The Street, Bramber, Steyning, West Sussex BN44 3WE **Tel:** (01903) 879494 **Fax:** (01903) 813399
Web: http://www.home.fastnet.co.uk/otr **E-mail:** otr@fastnet.co.uk

In a lovely old Sussex village nestling at the foot of the South Downs, standing on the original Tollhouse site, a perfect blending of the old with the new. Award-winning, carvery-style restaurant – a well-known and popular eating spot – offers a magnificent hors d'oeuvres display followed by a vast selection of roasts, pies and casseroles, with delicious sweets and cheeses to add the final touch. Luxuriously-appointed bedrooms, including two four-posters with jacuzzi baths, and two suites.

Bed & Breakfast per night: single occupancy from £75.95–£101.95; double room from £82.90–£108.90
Dinner, Bed & Breakfast per person, per night: £61.95–£74.95 (min 2 nights, 2 sharing)
Lunch available: 1200–1400

Evening meal: 1900 (last orders 2130)
Bedrooms: 21 double, 10 twin
Bathrooms: 31 en-suite **Parking:** 60 spaces
Cards accepted: Mastercard, Visa, Switch/Delta, Amex, Diners, Eurocard, JCB, Visa Electron

At-a-glance symbols are explained on the flap inside the back cover

412 The Homestead

Homestead Lane, Valebridge Road, Burgess Hill, West Sussex RH15 0RT **Tel:** (01444) 246899 **Fax:** (01444) 246899
Web: http://www.burgess-hill.co.uk **E-mail:** homestead@burgess-hill.co.uk

Quiet, comfortable and friendly home in a peaceful setting of 7.5 acres at the end of a private lane. All rooms are en-suite with refreshment facilities and television. Two ground-floor bedrooms have wheelchair access. Glyndebourne, the South Downs Way, National Trust locations, numerous gardens and the Bluebell Steam Railway are all nearby. Close to mainline railway station – Brighton/Gatwick 15 minutes, London 50 minutes. Children over 12 welcome. Strictly no smoking.

Bed & Breakfast per night: single room from £19.00–£25.00; double room from £38.00–£50.00

Bedrooms: 1 single, 3 double/twin
Bathrooms: 4 en-suite
Parking: 6 spaces
Cards accepted: Mastercard, Visa, Delta

413 Adelaide Hotel

Silver Award

51 Regency Square, Brighton, East Sussex BN1 2FF **Tel:** (01273) 205286 **Fax:** (01273) 220904
E-mail: adelaide@pavilion.co.uk

This elegant Regency townhouse hotel centrally situated in Brighton's premier seafront square offers, among its hallmarks, a warm welcome, friendly service and delicious breakfasts, with vegetarian options always available. All the bedrooms include the extras that guarantee a relaxing and comfortable stay. Brighton's extensive and diverse shopping, many restaurants, theatre, etc., are all within easy walking distance, and parking is available in the square. An ideal centre from which to explore the Sussex hinterland. Discounted leisure breaks available.

Bed & Breakfast per night: single room from £41.00–£45.00; double room from £68.00–£82.00

Bedrooms: 3 single, 7 double, 1 twin, 1 triple
Bathrooms: 12 en-suite
Cards accepted: Mastercard, Visa, Switch/Delta, Amex, Diners, Eurocard, Visa Electron, Solo

414 Shelleys Hotel

★★★ Silver Award

High Street, Lewes, East Sussex BN7 1XS **Tel:** (01273) 472361 **Fax:** (01273) 483152

The town of Lewes, which is well known to opera lovers who attend the celebrated annual Glyndebourne Opera Festival, is nestled among the picturesque South Downs. Shelleys offers the highest standard of comfort. A short break can offer you the chance to explore some beautiful scenery, shop for antiques and visit the attractions of Brighton – about twenty minutes away – before returning to a peaceful country house hotel, renowned for its service and cuisine.

Bed & Breakfast per night: single room from £120.00–£135.00; double room from £165.00–£248.00
Dinner, Bed & Breakfast per person, per night: £70.00–£85.00
Lunch available: 1215–1415

Evening meal: 1900 (last orders 2115)
Bedrooms: 1 single, 9 double, 9 twin
Bathrooms: 19 en-suite **Parking:** 25 spaces
Cards accepted: Mastercard, Visa, Switch/Delta, Amex, Diners, Eurocard, JCB, Maestro, Visa Elect

Entries are cross referenced by number to the maps on pages 176–177

415 Eckington House　　　　◆◆◆◆

Ripe, Lewes, East Sussex BN8 6AV **Tel:** (01323) 811274 **Fax:** (01323) 811140
Web: http://www3.mistral.co.uk/suetj **E-mail:** suetj@mistral.co.uk

Beautiful 16th-century house with peaceful, mature garden in a rural village close to the South Downs and South coast. Facilities include oak-panelled guest sitting room with inglenook fireplace, croquet lawn and four-poster suite. Breakfast is served on the terrace during warm weather, with vegetarians catered for. Historic Lewes, famous Glyndebourne Opera House, and the coastal towns of Brighton and Eastbourne are nearby. London is one hour by rail from Lewes. Excellent for cycling, walking and sightseeing. Pub/restaurant within walking distance.

Bed & Breakfast per night: single occupancy from £25.00–£30.00; double room from £40.00–£55.00

Bedrooms: 3 double
Bathrooms: 3 en-suite
Open: March–October

416 Shortgate Manor Farm　　◆◆◆◆ Silver Award

Halland, Lewes, East Sussex BN8 6PJ **Tel:** (01825) 840320 **Fax:** (01825) 840320
Web: http://www.shortgate.co.uk **E-mail:** ewalt@shortgate.co.uk

A warm welcome awaits you at this 18th-century farmhouse set in eight acres. Superb gardens with a large variety of climbing and shrub roses, together with pergolas festooned with clematis and honeysuckle. This peaceful setting offers a warm and friendly atmosphere with wonderful views and is an ideal base for touring the county. There are many wonderful gardens, National Trust properties and historic houses within a short drive, and Glyndebourne is nearby. All rooms are en-suite. Wedding package from £140.

Bed & Breakfast per night: single occupancy from £35.00; double room from £50.00–£60.00

Bedrooms: 2 double, 1 twin
Bathrooms: 3 en-suite
Parking: 6 spaces

417 South Paddock　　　　◆◆◆◆◆ Silver Award

Maresfield Park, Uckfield, East Sussex TN22 2HA **Tel:** (01825) 762335

South East England Tourist Board 'Best Bed & Breakfast' runner up award. A comfortable country house, beautifully furnished with an atmosphere of warmth and elegance. All rooms face south, overlooking three and a half acres of mature gardens, landscaped for attractive colouring throughout the year. A peaceful setting for relaxing on the terrace, beside the fishpond and fountain or in spacious drawing rooms with log fires. Centrally located, 41 miles from London and within easy reach of Gatwick, the Channel ports, Glyndebourne, Nymans, Sissinghurst and Chartwell. Good restaurants locally.

Bed & Breakfast per night: single occupancy from £36.00–£40.00; double room from £54.00–£58.00

Bedrooms: 1 double, 2 twin
Bathrooms: 1 private, 1 public
Parking: 6 spaces

418 Ashdown Park Hotel

★★★★ Gold Award

Wych Cross, Forest Row, East Sussex RH18 5JR **Tel:** (01342) 824988 **Fax:** (01342) 826206
Web: http://www.ashdownpark.co.uk **E-mail:** sales@ashdownpark.co.uk

Ashdown Park Hotel is an impressive Victorian mansion set in the heart of Ashdown Forest - home to 'Pooh Bear' yet within easy reach of London, Gatwick Airport and the South coast. Each of the bedrooms and suites is beautifully decorated, many with breathtaking views of the surrounding gardens and parklands. The award-winning Anderida Restaurant offers an unforgettable dining experience which can be enjoyed following an energetic or relaxing visit to our extensive country club.

Bed & Breakfast per night: single room from £120.00–£299.00; double room from £152.00–£330.00
Lunch available: 1230–1400
Evening meal: 1930 (last orders 2130)

Bedrooms: 6 single, 42 double, 47 twin
Bathrooms: 95 en-suite
Parking: 120 spaces
Cards accepted: Mastercard, Visa, Switch/Delta, Amex, Diners, Eurocard

419 Iwood B&B

♦♦♦♦

Mutton Hall Lane, Heathfield, East Sussex TN21 8NR **Tel:** (01435) 863918 or 07768 917816

Quiet and secluded chalet bungalow set in a large, well-tended garden with distant views of the South Downs and the sea. Within walking distance of local shops, pubs and restaurants. Centrally located for visits to many East Sussex attractions. Excellent facilities include colour television in each room, off-road parking, use of garden and babysitting. You are assured of a warm welcome at this first class non-smoking establishment. Superb breakfasts from an extensive menu.

Bed & Breakfast per night: single room from £19.00; double room from £38.00–£40.00

Bedrooms: 1 single, 2 double
Bathrooms: 1 en-suite, 2 private
Parking: 3 spaces

420 Glydwish Place

♦♦♦♦♦ Silver Award

Fontridge Lane, Burwash, East Sussex TN19 7DG **Tel:** (01435) 882869 or 07860 624197 **Fax:** (01435) 882749
E-mail: dolores@barclays.net

Glydwish Place has been designed and built by the Collins family to share with their guests the ultimate experience in relaxation from the minute they arrive, with an in-house leisure centre for your enjoyment. It is a sanctuary, away from the noise of village and road, embedded in the richly wooded landscape of the Sussex Weald, yet only five minutes' drive from the village of Burwash. Within a radius of 20 miles there is a multitude of National Trust houses and gardens. The Channel ports are 50 minutes' drive away.

Bed & Breakfast per night: single room from £40.00–£45.00; double room from £60.00–£70.00

Bedrooms: 1 single, 3 double
Bathrooms: 2 en-suite, 2 private
Parking: 14 spaces

Entries are cross referenced by number to the maps on pages 176–177

421 Mount House

◆◆◆◆

Ranters Lane, Goudhurst, Cranbrook, Kent TN17 1HN **Tel:** (01580) 211230
E-mail: DavidMargaretSargent@compuserve.com

An 18th-century Grade II listed country house set in mature gardens of approximately two acres. Originally forming part of the Scotney Estate, the house has been fully restored and decorated in keeping with its period character. Set in rural countryside within the designated High Weald conservation area. We are ideally placed for visiting the many well known gardens in the area, including Sissinghurst, Scotney Castle, Great Dixter and Pashley Manor.

Bed & Breakfast per night: double room £45.00

Bedrooms: 1 double, 1 twin
Bathrooms: 1 en-suite, 1 private
Open: April–September

422 Lansdowne Hotel

★★★ Silver Award

King Edward's Parade, Eastbourne, East Sussex BN21 4EE **Tel:** (01323) 725174 **Fax:** (01323) 739721
Web: http://www.lansdowne-hotel.co.uk **E-mail:** the.lansdowne@btinternet.com

Traditional, privately-owned seafront hotel close to theatres and shops. The dining room offers the best of English cooking supported by a comprehensive wine list from around the world. Two lifts, two snooker rooms and games room. Sky Sports television in public room. Elegant lounges and foyer facing the sea. 22 lock-up garages and unrestricted street parking nearby. At lunchtime, enjoy our bar/lounge menu or traditional lunch on Sunday. Social/duplicate bridge weekends. Golfing breaks. Attractive Regency bar.

Bed & Breakfast per night: single room from £53.50–£61.00; double room from £87.00–£105.00
Dinner, Bed & Breakfast per person, per night: £41.00–£73.00 (min 2 nights)
Lunch available: 1200–1400

Evening meal: 1830 (last orders 2030)
Bedrooms: 38 single, 23 double, 51 twin, 4 triple
Bathrooms: 116 en-suite **Parking:** 22 spaces
Cards accepted: Mastercard, Visa, Switch/Delta, Amex, Diners, Eurocard, JCB

423 The Grand Hotel

★★★★★ Gold Award

King Edwards Parade, Eastbourne, East Sussex BN21 4EQ **Tel:** (01323) 412345 **Fax:** (01323) 412233

Benefiting from a complete restoration and spectacular improvement, the Grand takes pride of place as one of England's premier resort hotels. The atmosphere is restfully opulent but certainly not stuffy, with a wonderful location overlooking the sea in the elegant coastal town of Eastbourne. Boasting fine bedrooms and suites, two award-winning restaurants and comprehensive health and beauty facilities, including two pools, the Grand offers genuine service to match its elegant surroundings. ⬆ **Category 3**

Bed & Breakfast per night: single occupancy from £120.00–£360.00; double room from £152.00–£400.00
Dinner, Bed & Breakfast per person, per night: £95.50–£225.00 (min 2 nights, 2 sharing)
Evening meal: 1900 (last orders 2130)

Bedrooms: 28 double, 76 twin, 48 suites
Bathrooms: 152 en-suite
Parking: 60 spaces
Cards accepted: Mastercard, Visa, Amex, Diners, Eurocard

At-a-glance symbols are explained on the flap inside the back cover

424 Trevinhurst Lodge

 **Silver Award**

10 Baslow Road, Meads, Eastbourne, East Sussex BN20 7UJ **Tel:** (01323) 410023 **Fax:** (01323) 643238

Overlooking the sea on the edge of the South Downs we are perfectly located for those seeking a short break in a non-smoking environment. A warm welcome awaits the discerning and with just three bedrooms we can guarantee the individual attention you would expect. Fine food offered in our elegant dining room completes the picture and we can cater for any dietary needs. Speciality watercolour courses are also available (brochure on request).

Bed & Breakfast per night: single occupancy £30.00; double room from £52.00–£60.00
Dinner, Bed & Breakfast per person, per night: £44.00–£48.00 (min 2 nights)

Bedrooms: 2 double, 1 twin
Bathrooms: 2 en-suite, 1 private

The Royal Military Canal

Walk along the banks of the Royal Military Canal today in the company of none other than swans and the occasional angler, and it is hard to believe that such a peaceful haven of wildlife was created with the purpose of keeping Napoleon's marauding armies at bay. It was thought the French would try to land on the beaches between Hastings and Folkestone, and the suggestion was that a canal be built along the top of the Romney Marshes as a defensive barrier. There would be a road running parallel behind it to enable troops to move in safety and the canal would have regular dog-legs so that cannons, placed at each kink, could fire along the entire length.

With the enthusiastic backing of Pitt the Younger, who was just beginning his second term as Prime Minister in 1804, this amazing feat of engineering was soon under way. There were problems and delays in its construction, however, and by the time it was completed the French had been defeated at Trafalgar and the threat of invasion was over. The whole thing was just one costly military folly. The canal saw some commercial use until the railway opened in 1851 but it was never busy. From the start it was used to control the drainage of the Romney Marshes and this is still a vital role.

The Royal Military Canal Path is waymarked along its 27-mile (43.5km) length. At its eastern end it starts in Hythe, where rowing boats may be hired in summer, then it runs out into agricultural land, yellow waterlilies spreading across its surface. The whole canal is exceptionally rich in wildlife. The section between Hamstreet and Appledore is in the hands of the National Trust. You may see swans anywhere along the canal, but always at Appledore. The section between Appledore and Rye is perhaps the most interesting as the military road is still in use, and the path on top of the bank, where sheep rest beneath the trees, gives a good view of the whole thing. On the one side is the canal, the towpath and the front drain and, on the other, the military road and the back drain. At Iden Lock the canal runs into the River Rother as far as Rye, and from there the path runs across marshland past Henry VIII's Camber Castle to Winchelsea, and on across Pett Level to end in Cliff End. Rye Tourist Information Centre (tel: 01797 226696) has more details.

425 Manor Farm Oast

◆◆◆◆◆ Gold Award

Windmill Orchard, Workhouse Lane, Icklesham, Winchelsea, East Sussex TN36 4AJ **Tel:** (01424) 813787 **Fax:** (01424) 813787

A three roundel oasthouse built in the 19th century and nestling in acres of apple and cherry orchards. A truly peaceful haven of luxury, ideally situated for country walks or coastal visits. Set in 1066 Country, within easy reach of Rye, Winchelsea, Battle and Hastings. Christmas house parties catered for. Credit cards accepted. Licensed. Five-course dinner by arrangement.

Bed & Breakfast per night: single occupancy from £32.00–£40.00; double room from £55.00–£65.00
Dinner, Bed & Breakfast per person, per night: £47.50–£52.50
Evening meal: 1900 (last orders 2000)

Bedrooms: 2 double, 1 twin
Bathrooms: 2 en-suite, 1 private
Parking: 10 spaces
Cards accepted: Mastercard, Visa, Switch/Delta, Eurocard, JCB, Visa Electron, Solo

426 Playden Cottage Guesthouse

◆◆◆◆◆ Silver Award

Military Road, Rye, East Sussex TN31 7NY **Tel:** (01797) 222234
Web: http://www.smoothhound.co.uk/hotels/playden.html

On the old Saxon shore, less than a mile from Rye town and on what was once a busy fishing harbour, there is now only a pretty cottage with lovely gardens, a pond and an ancient right of way. The sea has long receded and, sheltered by its own informal gardens, Playden Cottage looks over the River Rother and across the sheep-studded Romney Marsh. It offers comfort, peace, a care for detail – and a very warm welcome.

Bed & Breakfast per night: double room from £56.00–£64.00
Dinner, Bed & Breakfast per person, per night: £40.00–£54.00 (min 2 nights at weekends)

Bedrooms: 1 double, 2 twin
Bathrooms: 3 en-suite
Parking: 7 spaces
Cards accepted: Mastercard, Visa, JCB

427 Jeake's House

◆◆◆◆◆ Silver Award

Mermaid Street, Rye, East Sussex TN31 7ET **Tel:** (01797) 222828 **Fax:** (01797) 222623
Web: http://www.s-h-systems.co.uk/hotels/jeakes.html **E-mail:** jeakeshouse@btinternet.com

Jeake's House stands on the most famous cobbled street in medieval Rye. Bedrooms have been individually restored to create a very special atmosphere, combining traditional elegance and luxury with modern amenities. Oak-beamed and panelled bedrooms with brass, mahogany or four-poster beds overlook the marsh and rooftops to the sea. Vegetarian or traditional breakfast is served in the galleried former chapel where soft chamber music and a roaring fire will make your stay a truly memorable experience. Private car park nearby.

Bed & Breakfast per night: single room £26.50; double room from £51.00–£91.00

Bedrooms: 1 single, 7 double, 1 twin, 2 triple, 1 family
Bathrooms: 9 en-suite, 1 private, 2 public
Cards accepted: Mastercard, Visa, Eurocard

At-a-glance symbols are explained on the flap inside the back cover

428 Rye Lodge Hotel

★★★ Silver Award

Hilders Cliff, Rye, East Sussex TN31 7LD **Tel:** (01797) 223838 or (01797) 226688 **Fax:** (01797) 223585
Web: http://www.ryelodge.co.uk **E-mail:** info@ryelodge.co.uk

Premier position on East Cliff, close to the historic 14th-century Landgate, High Street teashops, antique and art galleries, in this charming medieval Cinque port with its cobbled streets and picturesque period buildings. Rye Lodge offers elegance and charm in a relaxed atmosphere. The luxurious de luxe bedrooms are all en-suite. Room service – breakfast in bed as late as you like! Candlelit dinners in the elegant Terrace Room, delicious food and fine wines, attentive caring service, and an indoor swimming pool!

Bed & Breakfast per night: single room from £49.50–£85.00; double room from £80.00–£140.00
Dinner, Bed & Breakfast per person, per night: £55.00–£85.00 (min 2 nights)
Evening meal: 1900 (last orders 2100)

Bedrooms: 2 single, 11 double, 7 twin
Bathrooms: 20 en-suite
Parking: 20 spaces
Cards accepted: Mastercard, Visa, Switch/Delta, Amex, Diners, Eurocard, JCB

Martello Towers

One of the eccentricities inherited from the Georgian era is the chain of strange-looking gun towers constructed early in the 1800s along England's south-east coast. At war with France and faced with the greatest threat of invasion since 1066, the British government decided to fend off Napoleon's massing armies by strengthening coastal defences. Several military engineers had been impressed, ironically, by a French-built fortified tower at Mortella Point on Corsica, which with just three guns had repelled two heavily armed British warships in 1794. A proposal was put forward that a chain of similar forts be built between Suffolk and Sussex. Prime Minister William Pitt backed the plan with characteristic vigour and work started in 1804 on what became known as the Martello Towers.

By 1808, 73 towers, numbered from east to west, had been built between Dover in Kent and Eastbourne in Sussex. Work then started on another 29 towers along the coasts of Suffolk and Essex, plus one more at Seaford in Sussex, bringing the total to 103 by 1812. Resembling upturned flower pots in shape, the towers were built on three levels. A ladder, retractable in case of siege, gave entrance to the first floor, which was divided into three areas – living quarters for the officer and his 24 men, and a storeroom. Ammunition and provisions were kept on the ground floor, approached through a trap-door. The top floor was a gun platform, where a 2½-ton cannon was mounted on a revolving pivot. From here a 24lb (11kg) shot could be fired a

mile out to sea, and even the French acknowledged that, especially where the towers were just 600ft (182m) apart and their ships would be within range of 15 towers, the damage inflicted would be devastating.

However, the invasion never happened, Napoleon was defeated at Waterloo in 1815 and the most extensive defence system in the country's history stood like a string of follies. The towers were subsequently put to use by the Coastguard in its battle against the smuggling trade and a century later, in 1940, when Hitler threatened invasion, the War Department again prepared the towers for action – but once more the invasion never materialised. Now the number of towers has fallen to 43, many having sunk beneath the sea. Some are abandoned and in disrepair, some privately owned and converted to dwellings, others restored and open to the public. The following have a visitor centre or museum: No. 3 at East Cliff, Folkestone; No. 73, the Wish Tower, on Eastbourne seafront; No. 74, Seaford. Phone the Tourist Information Centre at Folkestone (tel: 01303 258594) for further details on No.3, at Eastbourne (tel: 01323 411400) for Nos. 73 and 74.

Entries are cross referenced by number to the maps on pages 176–177

429 Little Orchard House

◆◆◆◆◆ Silver Award

West Street, Rye, East Sussex TN31 7ES **Tel:** (01797) 223831 **Fax:** (01797) 223831

Elegant Georgian townhouse in a quiet cobbled street at the heart of ancient Rye. Perfectly situated for many excellent restaurants, shops, art/antique galleries as well as country/seaside walks, bird watching or touring nearby National Trust properties like Sissinghurst. Antique furniture throughout, open fires, fine art, books and bears create a relaxed house-party atmosphere. Large, secluded walled garden for guests' use. Generous country breakfasts feature local organic and free range products. Parking available.

Bed & Breakfast per night: single occupancy from £45.00–£65.00; double room from £64.00–£84.00

Bedrooms: 2 double, 1 twin
Bathrooms: 3 en-suite
Cards accepted: Mastercard, Visa, Eurocard

430 Little Silver Country Hotel

★★★ Silver Award

Ashford Road, St Michaels, Tenterden, Kent TN30 6SP **Tel:** (01233) 850321 **Fax:** (01233) 850647
Web: http://www.little-silver.co.uk **E-mail:** enquiries@little-silver.co.uk

Little Silver Country Hotel is set in its own landscaped gardens. The restaurant provides an intimate, tranquil atmosphere where local produce is enjoyed, pre-dinner drinks and after dinner coffee are offered in the beamed sitting room with its log fire. Breakfast is served in a Victorian conservatory overlooking the waterfall rockery. Luxury bedrooms, tastefully and individually designed, some with four-posters and jacuzzi baths, others with brass beds. Facilities for disabled. Personal attention, care for detail, warmth and friendliness create a truly memorable experience. RAC Restaurant Award. ↟ **Category 3**

Bed & Breakfast per night: single occupancy from £60.00–£85.00; double room from £85.00–£110.00
Dinner, Bed & Breakfast per person, per night: £60.00–£90.00 (min 2 nights)
Lunch available: 1200–1400 (pre–booked only)

Evening meal: 1830 (last orders 2200)
Bedrooms: 5 double, 3 twin, 1 triple, 1 family
Bathrooms: 10 en-suite
Parking: 50 spaces
Cards accepted: Mastercard, Visa, Switch/Delta, Amex, Eurocard, Visa Electron

431 Bethersden Old Barn

◆◆◆◆ Silver Award

The Old Barn, Bridge Farm, Bethersden, Ashford, Kent TN26 3LE **Tel:** 0870 7401180 **Fax:** (01233) 820547
Web: http://www.ukpages.net/annex.htm **E-mail:** info@ukpages.net

A warm welcome awaits you at The Old Barn, an 18th-century Kentish barn with many exposed beams, a pleasant ambience and pretty gardens. All rooms have en-suite or private bathrooms. Excellent breakfasts. Also available is our delightful four-room annexe, suitable for one or two people, with exposed beams and all facilities. Good base for visiting the gardens of Kent, Sissinghurst, Tenterden, Rye, Canterbury, Leeds Castle and the Channel Tunnel. Credit cards welcome.

Bed & Breakfast per night: single occupancy from £25.00–£35.00; double room from £48.00–£65.00

Bedrooms: 2 double, 1 twin
Bathrooms: 2 en-suite, 1 private
Parking: 6 spaces
Cards accepted: Mastercard, Visa, Switch/Delta

At-a-glance symbols are explained on the flap inside the back cover

432 Eastwell Manor Hotel

★★★★ Gold Award

Eastwell Park, Boughton Lees, Ashford, Kent TN25 4HR **Tel:** (01233) 213000 **Fax:** (01233) 635530
E-mail: eastwell@btinternet.com

'Breathtakingly beautiful: Eastwell Manor in the Garden of England.' Situated within a parkland of 3,000 acres and amidst 62 acres of its own well-tended gardens and natural woodland, enjoying seclusion and tranquillity, lies Eastwell Manor. The 23 elegant bedrooms in the Manor House are named after past owners – Lords, Ladies and Gentlemen – bearing witness to the hotel's rich history. Eastwell Mews, which are converted 18th-century stables, are situated within the grounds and comprise 19 courtyard apartments, all with en-suite facilities. AA 3 Rosettes for food. Situated off junction 9 of the M20 at Ashford. Eastwell Pavilion & Spa opens early 2000.

Bed & Breakfast per night: single occupancy from £160.00–£320.00; double room from £190.00–£350.00
Lunch available: 1200–1430
Evening meal: 1930 (last orders 2130)

Bedrooms: 14 double, 13 twin, 35 family
Bathrooms: 62 en-suite
Parking: 112 spaces
Cards accepted: Mastercard, Visa, Amex, Diners

433 Waterside Guest House

◆◆◆◆

15 Hythe Road, Dymchurch, Romney Marsh, Kent TN29 0LN **Tel:** (01303) 872253 **Fax:** (01303) 872253
Web: http://www.smoothhound.co.uk/hotels/watersid.html **E-mail:** water.side@cwcom.net

Feeling tired? Need a break? Look no further. At Waterside you will find comfortable accommodation, a relaxed atmosphere and good food with fresh vegetables, many home grown. Meals chosen from our varied à la carte menus, catering for all tastes, are served in the beamed dining room overlooking the attractive gardens and Romney Marsh. Locally there are pursuits and places of interest to suit all ages, and with ferry ports, the shuttle and Lydd airport close by, continental trips could not be easier.

Bed & Breakfast per night: single room from £18.00–£22.00; double room from £32.00–£40.00
Dinner, Bed & Breakfast per person, per night: £23.00–£29.00 (min 2 nights June–September)
Evening meal: 1730 (last orders 2000)

Bedrooms: 1 single, 2 double, 2 twin, 1 family
Bathrooms: 3 en-suite, 2 public
Parking: 7 spaces

434 The Hythe Imperial

★★★★ Silver Award

Prince's Parade, Hythe, Kent CT21 6AE **Tel:** (01303) 267441 **Fax:** (01303) 264610
Web: http://www.marstonhotels.co.uk **E-mail:** hytheimperial@marstonhotels.co.uk

An impressive sea-front resort hotel set within fifty acres in the historic Cinque port of Hythe. All the rooms enjoy sea or garden views with executive, four-poster, half-tester or jacuzzi rooms and suites available. Conference facilities available for up to two hundred and fifty, as well as superb leisure facilities, including 9-hole golf course, indoor swimming pool, luxurious spa bath, steam room, sauna, gym, sunbed, tennis, croquet, beauty salon and hairdressing. AA Rosette.

Bed & Breakfast per night: single room from £95.00; double room from £137.00
Dinner, Bed & Breakfast per person, per night: £77.50–£97.50 (min 2 nights, 2 sharing)
Lunch available: 1230–1400
Evening meal: 1900 (last orders 2100)

Bedrooms: 17 single, 45 double, 38 twin
Bathrooms: 100 en-suite
Parking: 202 spaces
Cards accepted: Mastercard, Visa, Switch/Delta, Amex, Diners

435 Harbourside Bed and Breakfast Hotel ◆◆◆◆◆ Gold Award

13/14 Wear Bay Road, Folkestone, Kent CT19 6AT **Tel:** (01303) 256528 or 07768 123884 **Fax:** (01303) 241299
Web: http://www.s-h-systems.co.uk/hotels/harbour.html **E-mail:** r.j.pye@dial.pipex.com

Two beautifully restored Victorian houses on the East Cliff, overlooking sea and harbour, provide luxury en-suite accommodation. The quality, hospitality, service, and value for money are truly special. We can be your perfect base from which to tour South East England, the best stop-over when crossing the Channel, or the centre point for a relaxing holiday. Phone, fax or e-mail us to reserve your room, ask for a colour brochure or just for more details.

Bed & Breakfast per night: single occupancy from £35.00–£40.00; double room from £60.00–£90.00
Lunch available: bar lunches to order
Evening meal: 1930 (last orders 2100)

Bedrooms: 4 double, 2 twin
Bathrooms: 5 en-suite, 1 private
Parking: 1 space
Cards accepted: Mastercard, Visa, Switch/Delta, Amex, Diners, Eurocard, Maestro, Visa Electron

436 Molehills ◆◆◆◆

Bladbean, Canterbury, Kent CT4 6LU **Tel:** (01303) 840051 or 780 8639942

The house, with one acre of gardens, is situated in a peaceful hamlet, off the beaten track, within the beautiful Elham Valley. We are within easy reach of the historic city of Canterbury and the Channel terminals. We produce good organic food and excellent home cooking. Our comfortable accommodation includes a sitting room with wood-burning stove, a conservatory and verandah for the use of our guests.

Bed & Breakfast per night: single occupancy from £25.00–£28.00; double room from £40.00–£45.00
Dinner, Bed & Breakfast per person, per night: £33.00–£36.00

Bedrooms: 1 double, 1 twin
Bathrooms: 2 en-suite
Parking: 3 spaces
Open: All year except Christmas

437 The Old Vicarage ◆◆◆◆◆ Gold Award

Chilverton Elms, Hougham, Dover, Kent CT15 7AS **Tel:** (01304) 210668 **Fax:** (01304) 225118
E-mail: vicarage@csi.com

Guests are welcomed in a warm and relaxed style by Judy and Bryan, the owners of this award-winning country house. In an outstanding position, set in wooded country gardens with open views over the Elms Vale, it is hard to believe that The Old Vicarage is only two miles from the bustle of the port of Dover. Many visitors come back time and again for a short break holiday, to share the elegance, peace and quiet, and enjoy the pubs, restaurants and attractions of East Kent.

Bed & Breakfast per night: double room from £60.00–£70.00
Evening meal: by arrangement

Bedrooms: 3 double
Bathrooms: 2 en-suite, 1 private
Parking: 6 spaces
Cards accepted: Mastercard, Visa, Eurocard

438 The Churchill

★★★ Silver Award

Dover Waterfront, Dover, Kent CT17 9BP **Tel:** (01304) 203633 **Fax:** (01304) 216320
Web: http://www.churchill-hotel.com **E-mail:** enquiries@churchill-hotel.com

The Churchill, Dover's only waterfront hotel, is situated in a beautiful Regency crescent, nestling under the famous White Cliffs, with views over the English Channel. A total of sixty eight bedrooms, all with en-suite facilities, satellite television, direct dial telephone, trouser press, and tea and coffee making facilities. Our spacious executive rooms also feature mini bars and bathrobes. Within the hotel is Winston's Restaurant, which offers a wide variety of classic English cuisine, with panoramic views over the English Channel. An alternative is a bar snack or light meal in the bar. The hotel also boasts a health club. Special offers and weekend breaks available on request.

Bed & Breakfast per night: single room
£68.00; double room £97.00
Lunch available: 1230–1415
Evening meal: 1930 (last orders 2115)

Bedrooms: 6 single, 37 double, 20 twin, 5 family
Bathrooms: 68 en-suite
Cards accepted: Mastercard, Visa,
Switch/Delta, Amex, Diners, Visa Electron

439 Wallett's Court Country House Hotel & Restaurant

★★★ Silver Award

Westcliffe, St-Margarets-at-Cliffe, Dover, Kent CT15 6EW **Tel:** (01304) 852424 **Fax:** (01304) 853430
Web: http://www.wallettscourt.com **E-mail:** wc@wallettscourt.com

Wallett's Court Country House is a 17th-century manor with 16 luxurious rooms, some with four-posters, others with sea views. Noted in major guides, the restaurant serves the finest local and organic produce, including some of the finest fish and seafood on the South Coast. In the grounds is a health spa with indoor pools, saunas and sun terrace set in seven acres of beautiful gardens in a tranquil, rural area of outstanding natural beauty on the White Cliffs of Dover.

Bed & Breakfast per night: single
occupancy from £70.00–£110.00; double room
from £80.00–£130.00
**Dinner, Bed & Breakfast per person, per
night:** £67.50–£92.50
Lunch available: 1200–1400

Evening meal: 1900 (last orders 2100)
Bedrooms: 11 double, 2 twin, 3 triple
Bathrooms: 16 en-suite
Parking: 20 spaces
Cards accepted: Mastercard, Visa,
Switch/Delta, Amex, Diners, Eurocard

440 Hardicot Guest House

♦♦♦♦

Kingsdown Road, Walmer, Deal, Kent CT14 8AW **Tel:** (01304) 373867 **Fax:** (01304) 373867

This spacious, detached Victorian house stands 100 yards from the Channel in three quarters of an acre of sheltered gardens with a garage and parking. Sea views, comfortable bedrooms with private facilities, substantial breakfasts with home-made preserves and a very warm welcome in elegant surroundings, guarantee a memorable visit. The area is steeped in history with Dover, Deal and Walmer Castles nearby and Canterbury a short drive away. Ideally situated for cliff walks, golf and cross-channel trips.

Bed & Breakfast per night: single
occupancy from £20.00–£22.00; double room
from £40.00–£44.00

Bedrooms: 1 double, 2 twin
Bathrooms: 1 en-suite, 2 private
Parking: 4 spaces

Entries are cross referenced by number to the maps on pages 176–177

441 The Sportsman

♦♦♦♦ Gold Award

23 The Street, Sholden, Deal, Kent CT14 0AL **Tel:** (01304) 374973 **Fax:** (01304) 374973

Three purpose-built, beautifully appointed en-suite rooms set in the tranquil gardens of this award-winning, 17th-century inn. Traditional beamed bar and restaurant offering good quality home cooked food and a fine range of wines and beers. Peaceful location, yet ideally placed for Deal and Sandwich with their championship golf courses and the port of Dover. A warm welcome, friendly atmosphere and personal service.

Bed & Breakfast per night: single occupancy from £45.00; double room from £55.00–£65.00
Lunch available: 1200–1400
Evening meal: 1900 (last orders 2100)

Bedrooms: 3 twin
Bathrooms: 3 en-suite
Parking: 20 spaces
Cards accepted: Mastercard, Visa, Switch/Delta, JCB, Solo

Flemings and Huguenots

The distinctive Flemish flavour of the streets of Sandwich, one of Southern England's most pleasant small towns, is difficult to miss. The clearest sign is the prevalence of Dutch gables – there are some on the corner of the church of St Peter (now the Tourist Information Centre during summer months) and others on Manwood Court, built in 1564 as a grammar school. Another indication is part of the local vocabulary; 'polder' – taken straight from the Dutch – is the word used by the townsfolk to describe the low-lying marshes between Sandwich and Canterbury.

In fact, the Flemings (as the immigrants from the Low Countries were known) were first invited by Edward III in the 14th century, since they were especially skilled in the art of weaving. The economy of this part of Kent had for some time been dependent upon trade through the port of Sandwich and upon cloth-making. The silting up of the harbour over many years (Sandwich is now some two miles from the sea) and the inefficiency of the old cloth-manufacturing techniques meant that the new arrivals were particularly welcome. Business boomed, and Sandwich's density of substantial timbered houses (Strand Street boasts some of the finest) bears witness to the fact that the town prospered greatly. The immigrants also brought other trades to this fertile corner of the land, such as hop-growing for the production of beer, and commercial market gardening; trades which have since become synonymous with Kent.

By the 16th century, many were fleeing the Low Countries to escape persecution for their Calvinist beliefs. Some French Protestants, too, had left their native land, but the Edict of Nantes in 1598 afforded them a measure of religious freedom. When in 1685 this was revoked, nearly half a million Protestants abandoned their homeland, many to cross the Channel to the South Coast. These new exiles, known as Huguenots, tended to stay on the eastern side of England, a significant number never leaving Kent. Echoing the achievements of their earlier Flemish counterparts, the Huguenots established in England the silk-weaving industry. At the peak of the trade, as many as 2,000 people were employed in the silk business in Canterbury alone. Indeed the contribution of the Huguenot community to the city was such that they were granted their own chapel within the cathedral.

442 Ilex Cottage ◆◆◆◆

Temple Way, Worth, Deal, Kent CT14 0DA **Tel:** (01304) 617026 **Fax:** (01304) 620890
Web: http://www.ilexcottage.co.uk **E-mail:** info@ilexcottage.co.uk

This carefully modernised home dating from 1736 retains many character features. Our well-appointed, spacious en-suite guest rooms have co-ordinated furnishings and rural views. The Georgian conservatory provides a delightful reception area for relaxing and enjoying refreshments. Non-smoking throughout. Children and pets welcomed. Secluded, peaceful location, yet conveniently near picturesque conservation village centre. Sandwich and Deal are five minutes away, and Canterbury, Dover and Ramsgate are 20 minutes away. Numerous local tourist attractions and leisure facilities. An idyllic holiday base.

Bed & Breakfast per night: single occupancy from £25.00–£35.00; double room from £40.00–£50.00

Bedrooms: 1 double, 2 twin
Bathrooms: 3 en-suite
Parking: 6 spaces

443 Stour Valley House ◆◆◆◆

Pilgrims Lane, Chilham, Canterbury, Kent CT4 8AA **Tel:** (01227) 738991 or 07768 074177 **Fax:** (01227) 738991
E-mail: fionaely@stourvalleyhouse.freeserve.co.uk

Stour Valley House is a beautifully decorated non-smoking establishment with magnificent views overlooking the Stour Valley and North Downs Way. Offering luxury accommodation, hearty breakfasts and weekday evening meals. All bedrooms have television, radio alarm, tea/coffee facilities, easy chairs and soft furnishings to match. Two minutes from the picturesque village of Chilham, six minutes from Canterbury and 25 minutes from Dover. Within easy walking distance of pub, bus and train. Come and relax, enjoy a peaceful setting with beautiful views and friendly hospitality.

Bed & Breakfast per night: single occupancy from £42.00–£55.00; double room from £50.00–£60.00
Dinner, Bed & Breakfast per person, per night: £37.00–£45.00

Bedrooms: 2 double, 1 twin
Bathrooms: 2 en-suite, 1 private
Parking: 3 spaces
Cards accepted: Mastercard, Visa, Amex

444 Preston Lea ◆◆◆◆ Silver Award

Canterbury Road, Faversham, Kent ME13 8XA **Tel:** (01795) 535266 **Fax:** (01795) 533388
Web: http://homepages.which.net/~alan.turner10 **E-mail:** preston.lea@which.net

This beautiful spacious house, built a century ago, was designed by a French architect and has many unique and interesting features, including two turrets, an oak-panelled hall, staircase, dining room and guest drawing room. Situated in lovely secluded gardens but by the A2, it is convenient for Canterbury, all the Channel ports, the M2 to London and beautiful countryside. Each bedroom is individually designed and all are large and sunny. A warm welcome is assured by caring hosts.

Bed & Breakfast per night: single occupancy £35.00; double room from £48.00–£55.00

Bedrooms: 2 double, 1 twin
Bathrooms: 2 en-suite, 1 private
Parking: 11 spaces
Cards accepted: Mastercard, Visa, Switch/Delta, Eurocard, JCB, Maestro, Visa Electron, Solo

Entries are cross referenced by number to the maps on pages 176–177

445 The Ringlestone Inn & Farmhouse Hotel ♦♦♦♦♦ Gold Award

Ringlestone Hamlet, Harrietsham, Maidstone, Kent ME17 1NX **Tel:** (01622) 859900 or 07973 612261 **Fax:** (01622) 859966
Web: http://www.ringlestone.com **E-mail:** bookings@ringlestone.com

Situated on the North Downs in the heart of Kent, just ten minutes from Leeds Castle, this character Kentish farmhouse is surrounded by eight acres of tranquil gardens and farmland. Luxuriously furnished in rustic oak throughout, with a canopied four-poster bed in the Elderflower Room. Opposite, the famous 16th-century Ringlestone Inn is recommended in major guides for help-yourself buffet lunch and interesting evening Kentish fare incorporating English fruit wines in the traditional recipes.

Bed & Breakfast per night: single occupancy from £86.00–£96.00; double room from £107.00–£142.00
Lunch available: 1200–1400
Evening meal: 1900 (last orders 2130)

Bedrooms: 2 double, 1 family
Bathrooms: 3 en-suite
Parking: 74 spaces
Cards accepted: Mastercard, Visa, Switch/Delta, Amex, Diners, Eurocard

446 Grove House ♦♦♦♦

Grove Green Road, Weavering Street, Maidstone, Kent ME14 5JT **Tel:** (01622) 738441

Attractive, detached comfortable home in quiet surroundings, with parking for six. Comfortable, double en-suite room and double and twin rooms with attractive guest bathroom. All rooms have their own colour television and tea/coffee making facilities. Easy access to motorways for London or the Channel Tunnel. Leeds Castle, Kent County Show Ground, restaurants and golf courses all nearby. Non-smoking.

Bed & Breakfast per night: single occupancy from £25.00–£35.00; double room from £40.00–£45.00

Bedrooms: 2 double, 1 twin
Bathrooms: 1 en-suite, 1 public
Parking: 6 spaces
Cards accepted: Mastercard, Visa, Switch/Delta

447 Coulsdon Manor Hotel ★★★★ Silver Award

Coulsdon Court Road, Coulsdon, Croydon, Surrey CR5 2LL **Tel:** (020) 8668 0414 **Fax:** (020) 8668 3118
Web: http://www.marstonhotels.co.uk **E-mail:** coulsdonmanor@marstonhotels.co.uk

Set in 140 acres of parkland, a large part of which is laid down as a challenging 18-hole golf course. Fifteen miles from central London and Gatwick, and easily accessible from all parts of the South East via the M25, M23, A23 or A22. A restored manor house with thirty five delightful bedrooms – many with enchanting views over the golf course – an award-winning restaurant and Reflections Leisure Club offering squash, sunbed, gymnasium, racketball, aerobics, sauna and steam.

Bed & Breakfast per night: single occupancy from £108.00; double room from £137.00
Dinner, Bed & Breakfast per person, per night: £77.50–£87.50 (min 2 nights, 2 sharing)
Evening meal: 1900 (last orders 2130)

Bedrooms: 16 double, 19 twin
Bathrooms: 35 en-suite
Parking: 200 spaces
Cards accepted: Mastercard, Visa, Switch/Delta, Amex, Diners

At-a-glance symbols are explained on the flap inside the back cover

448 Highfield Guest House

♦♦♦♦ Silver Award

12 Dowanhill Road, London SE6 1HJ **Tel:** (020) 8698 8038 **Fax:** (020) 8698 8039
Web: http://www.highfieldbb.co.uk **E-mail:** michel@highfieldbb.co.uk

Winner of the 1998 London Tourist Board 'Bed & Breakfast of the Year' Award. Highfield is a beautiful Victorian house situated in Hither Green, a quiet residential area in South-East London. It is convenient for Greenwich, Blackheath, central London, the Millennium Dome, the Kent countryside and cross-channel routes. A strong sense of style, bold colours and delicate details make this an ideal home for the discriminating traveller wishing to experience good taste with quality service. Easy parking. Entirely no smoking.

Bed & Breakfast per night: single occupancy from £35.00–£48.00; double room from £45.00–£65.00

Bedrooms: 2 double, 1 twin
Bathrooms: 1 en-suite, 1 public
Parking: 1 space + off-street parking
Cards accepted: Mastercard, Visa, Switch/Delta, Amex, Eurocard, JCB, Visa Electron

Epsom Derby

The Derby, the most famous horserace in the world, was first run in 1780, and has attracted huge audiences of ordinary people ever since. 'On Derby Day,' wrote Charles Dickens, 'a population rills and surges and scrambles through the place, that may be counted in millions.' Dickens was surely exaggerating, but so great was the race's popularity in the second half of the 19th century that Parliament was suspended for the day. Currently crowds of some 100,000 or so attend the race, held on the first Saturday in June.

The Derby is named after the 12th Earl of Derby, Edward Smith Stanley, who, together with his colourful uncle, General John Burgoyne, organised the first contest for three-year old fillies in 1779. The race over Epsom Downs was named 'The Oaks' after Burgoyne's rambling house, once a pub, near Epsom, and was won by Derby's filly, Bridget. At the celebration dinnner which followed, Derby planned a second race for three-year-old colts and fillies, to be named after himself. On 4 May 1780 the first Derby took place – and a great English tradition was born. Both races continue to run, with The Oaks taking place the day before the Derby.

During its 201-year history the race has had more than its fair share of dramatic occurrences. In 1913 the suffragette, Emily Davison, was killed when she threw herself in front of the King's horse, a deliberate act of martyrdom designed to generate maximum publicity. More recently, in 1981, the crowds thrilled

to the most dramatic Derby win ever, when the legendary colt Shergar, ridden by Walter Swinburn, won effortlessly by a clear 10 lengths. Two years later Shergar was kidnapped from the Aga Khan's stud in Ireland, and to this day his fate remains a mystery.

From a racing point of view, the course over the Epsom Downs is supremely challenging. Run early in the season when the going can be heavy, the undulating and twisting 1½mile (2.4km) course requires great stamina. Rising 150ft (46m) in the first four furlongs, it then falls 100ft (30.5m) in varying gradients to the famous Tattenham Corner, before rising again towards the finishing post. The difficulties of winning such an event make the Derby a true test of equine greatness.

Tickets for the Derby and Oaks may be obtained by ringing 01372 470047. 'Derby Experience' tours of the racecourse (tel: 01372 726311) are available throughout the year.

Entries are cross referenced by number to the maps on pages 176–177

449 Avonmore Hotel ◆◆◆◆

66 Avonmore Road, Kensington, London W14 8RS **Tel:** (020) 7603 3121 or (020) 7603 4296 **Fax:** (020) 7603 4035
Web: http://www.dspace.dial.pipex.com/avonmore.hotel/ **E-mail:** avonmore.hotel@dial.pipex.com

Avonmore Hotel is the winner of a national award for the best private hotel in London. Refurbished to the highest standards with all in-room facilities – hairdryer, minibar with drinks, tea and coffee making facilities, colour television, telephone and a large bathroom with bath and shower! We are situated in Kensington in a quiet street, yet just a short walk from West Kensington station and buses. Avonmore Hotel is small enough to provide that personal touch where we look after our clients with care and courtesy.

Bed & Breakfast per night: single room from £58.00–£85.00; double room from £80.00–£95.00

Bedrooms: 1 single, 2 double, 3 twin, 3 triple
Bathrooms: 7 en-suite, 1 public
Cards accepted: Mastercard, Visa, Switch/Delta, Amex, Diners, Eurocard, JCB

450 Hotel Number Sixteen ◆◆◆◆◆ Gold Award

16 Sumner Place, London SW7 3EG **Tel:** (020) 7589 5232 **Fax:** (020) 7584 8615
Web: http://www.numbersixteenhotel.co.uk **E-mail:** reservations@numbersixteenhotel.co.uk

Situated in South Kensington, Number Sixteen has been created from four Victorian town houses. Offering style, elegance and seclusion, guests are encouraged to make themselves at home. There is a relaxed informality about the drawing room and the library, where everyone is invited to pour themselves a drink from the honour bar. The conservatory opens onto an award-winning garden. The comfortable well-appointed bedrooms are individually decorated with a combination of antique and traditional furnishings.

Bed & Breakfast per night: single room from £95.00–£130.00; double room from £170.00–£195.00

Bedrooms: 9 single, 23 double, 4 triple
Bathrooms: 32 en-suite, 2 private, 1 public
Cards accepted: Mastercard, Visa, Switch/Delta, Amex, Diners, Eurocard

451 Cavendish Guest House ◆◆◆◆

24 Cavendish Road, London NW6 7XP **Tel:** (020) 8451 3249 **Fax:** (020) 8451 3249

Small, friendly Victorian family house in a quiet residential conservation area. Five minutes' walk from Kilburn underground station (Jubilee line), with 15 minutes' travelling time to the West End. Easy access to Wembley Stadium, Heathrow, Gatwick and Luton. Ten minutes from the M1. Shops, restaurants, theatres and pubs nearby. Free parking. Special emphasis is given to cleanliness and hospitality. Multi-lingual.

Bed & Breakfast per night: single room from £30.00–£45.00; double room from £48.00–£54.00

Bedrooms: 2 single, 1 double, 1 twin, 2 triple
Bathrooms: 3 en-suite, 2 public
Parking: 4 spaces

At-a-glance symbols are explained on the flap inside the back cover

452 Aucklands

◆◆◆◆ Silver Award

25 Eglington Road, North Chingford, London E4 7AN **Tel:** (020) 8529 1140 **Fax:** (020) 8529 9288

Comfortable Edwardian family home on the edge of London, where an open fire and caring owners welcome guests as friends. Within easy reach of Stansted and London City airports, just five minutes' walk to the station (lifts offered), 25 minutes to Liverpool Street station, and 35 minutes to Oxford Circus. We are right on the edge of Epping Forest, where you can enjoy relaxing walks or play a game of golf at the local course. We have one king-size double room, one twin, and a super bathroom. Enjoy our secluded garden with its small pool (May to September). We serve good food and offer lunches by arrangement. The resident cat will tolerate guide-dogs only.

Bed & Breakfast per night: single occupancy from £32.50–£40.00; double room from £65.00–£80.00
Dinner, Bed & Breakfast per person, per night: £50.00–£57.50
Lunch available: 1130–1430 (or packed lunch)

Evening meal: 1700 (last orders 2300)
Bedrooms: 1 double, 1 twin
Bathrooms: 1 public

453 Oak Lodge Hotel

★★ Silver Award

80 Village Road, Bush Hill Park, Enfield, Middlesex EN1 2EU **Tel:** (020) 8360 7082

Exclusive country-style hotel with exquisite restaurant overlooking evergreen gardens. With good central London access, it is just 45 minutes from four of London's airports. With its warm ambience and charm, Oak Lodge has a reputation for being the director's choice and, at weekends, a family favourite for wedding guests and honeymooners. The university town of Cambridge, the cathedral and Roman amphitheatre of St. Albans' and the old fishing port of Leigh-on-Sea are all within an hour's drive.

Bed & Breakfast per night: single occupancy from £79.50–£93.50; double room from £89.50–£130.00
Dinner, Bed & Breakfast per person, per night: £75.00–£120.00
Evening meal: 1950 (last orders 2100)

Bedrooms: 4 double, 2 twin, 1 family room
Bathrooms: 6 en-suite, 1 private
Parking: 6 spaces
Cards accepted: Mastercard, Visa, Switch/Delta, Amex, Diners, Eurocard

Key to Symbols

For ease of use, the key to symbols appears on the back of the cover flap and can be folded out while consulting individual entries. The symbols are designed to enable you to see at a glance what's on offer, and whether any particular requirements you have can be met. Most of the symbols are clear, simple icons and few require any further explanation, but the following points may be useful:

Alcoholic drinks: Alcoholic drinks are available at all types of accommodation listed in the guide unless the symbol [UL] (unlicensed) appears. However, even in licensed premises there may be some restrictions on the serving of drinks, such as being available to diners only.

Smoking: Some establishments prefer not to accommodate smokers, and if this is the case it will be indicated by the symbol ⚟. Other establishments may offer facilities for non-smokers such as no smoking bedrooms and parts of communal rooms set aside for non-smokers. Please check at the time of booking if the non-smoking symbol does not appear.

Pets: The symbol 🐕 is used to show that dogs are not accepted in any circumstances. Some establishments will accept pets, but we advise you to check this at the time of booking and to enquire as to whether any additional charge will be made to accommodate them.

Entries are cross referenced by number to the maps on pages 176–177

Useful Information

Symbols

For ease of use, the key to symbols appears on the back of the cover flap and can be folded out while consulting individual entries. The symbols which appear at the end of each entry are designed to enable you to see at a glance what's on offer, and whether any particular requirements you have can be met. Most of the symbols are clear, simple icons and few require any further explanation, but the following points may be useful:

Alcoholic drinks

Alcoholic drinks are available at all types of accommodation listed in the guide unless the symbol [UL] (unlicensed) appears. However, even in licensed premises there may be some restrictions on the serving of drinks, such as being available to diners only. You may wish to check this in advance.

Smoking

Some establishments prefer not to accommodate smokers, and if this is the case it will be indicated by the symbol ⊁. Other establishments may offer facilities for non-smokers such as no smoking bedrooms and parts of communal rooms set aside for non-smokers. Please check at the time of booking if the non-smoking symbol does not appear.

Pets

The symbol 🐕 is used to show that dogs are not accepted in any circumstances. Some establishments will accept pets, but we advise you to check this at the time of booking and to enquire as to whether any additional charge will be made to accommodate them.

Booking checklist

When enquiring about accommodation remember to state your requirements clearly and precisely. It may be necessary or helpful to discuss some or all of the following points:

- Your intended arrival and departure dates.
- The type of accommodation you require. For example, a twin-bedded room, a private bath and WC, whether the room has a view or not.
- The terms you require, such as room only; bed & breakfast; bed, breakfast and evening meal (half board); bed, breakfast, lunch and evening meal (full board).
- If you have any children travelling with you, say how old they are and state their accommodation requirements, such as a cot, and whether they will share your room.
- Any particular requirements, such as a special diet or a ground-floor room.
- If you think you are likely to arrive late in the evening, mention this when you book. Similarly, if you are delayed on your journey a telephone call to inform the management may well help avoid any problems on your arrival.
- If you are asked for a deposit or the number of your credit card, find out what the proprietor's policy is if, for whatever reason, you can't turn up as planned – see 'cancellations' overleaf.
- Exactly how the establishment's charges are levied – see opposite.

Misunderstandings can easily occur over the telephone, so it is advisable to confirm in writing all bookings, together with special requirements. Please mention that you learnt of the establishment through *Somewhere Special*. Remember to include your name and address, and please enclose a stamped, addressed envelope – or an international reply coupon if writing from outside Britain. Please note that the English Tourism Council does not make reservations; you should address your enquiry directly to the establishment.

Prices

The prices given throughout this publication will serve as a general guide, but you should always check them at the time of booking. The following information may prove useful when determining how much a trip may cost:

- Prices were supplied during the autumn of 1999 and changes may have occurred since publication.
- Prices include VAT where applicable.
- You should check whether or not a service charge is included in the published price.
- Prices for double rooms assume occupancy by two people; you will need to check whether there is a single person supplement if a single occupancy rate is not shown.
- Half board means the price for the room, breakfast and evening meal per person per day.
- A full English breakfast may not always be included in the quoted price; you may be given a continental breakfast unless you are prepared to pay more.
- Establishments with at least four bedrooms or eight beds are obliged to display in the reception area or at the entrance overnight accommodation charges.
- Reduced prices may apply for children; check exactly how these reductions are calculated, including the maximum age for the child.
- Prices are often much cheaper for off-peak holidays; check to see whether special off-season packages are available.

Deposits and advance payments

For reservations made weeks or months ahead a deposit is usually payable which will be deducted from the total bill at the end of your stay.

Some establishments, particularly the larger hotels in big towns, now require payment for the room upon arrival if a prior reservation has not been made. Regrettably this practice has become necessary because of the number of guests who have left without settling their bills. If you are asked to pay in advance, it is sensible to see your room before payment is made to ensure that it meets your requirements.

If you book by telephone and are asked for your credit card number, you should note that the proprietor may charge your credit card account even if you subsequently cancel the booking. Ask the owner what his or her usual practice is.

Credit/charge cards

Any credit/charge cards that are accepted by the establishment are indicated at the end of the written description. If you intend to pay by either credit or charge card you are advised to confirm this at the time of booking.

Please note that when paying by credit card, you may sometimes be charged a higher rate for your accommodation in order to cover the percentage paid by the proprietor to the credit card company. Again find this out in advance.

When making a booking, you may be asked for your credit card number as 'confirmation'. The proprietor may then charge your credit card account if you have to cancel the booking, but if this is the policy, it must be made clear to you at the time of booking – see overleaf.

Cancellations

When you accept offered accommodation, including over the telephone, you are entering into a legally binding contract with the proprietor. This means that if you cancel a reservation or fail to take up all or part of the accommodation booked, the proprietor may be entitled to compensation if the accommodation cannot be re-let for all or a good part of the booked period. If you have paid a deposit, you will probably forfeit this, and further payment may well be asked for.

However, no such claim can be made by the proprietor until after the booked period, during which time every effort should be made to re-let the accommodation. It is therefore in your interests to advise the management immediately in writing if you have to cancel or curtail a booking. Travel or holiday insurance, available quite cheaply from travel agents and some hotels, will safeguard you if you have to cancel or curtail your stay.

And remember, if you book by telephone and are asked for your credit card number, you should check whether the proprietor intends charging your account should you later cancel your reservation. A proprietor should not be able to charge for a cancellation unless he or she has made this clear at the time of your booking and you have agreed. However, to avoid later disputes, we suggest you check whether he or she intends to make such a charge.

Service charges and tipping

Some establishments levy a service charge automatically, and, if so, must state this clearly in the offer of accommodation at the time of booking. If the offer is accepted by you, the service charge becomes part of the contract. If service is included in your bill, there is no need for you to give tips to the staff unless some particular or exceptional service has been rendered. In the case of meals, the usual tip is 10% of the total bill.

Telephone call charges

There is no restriction on the charges that can be made by hotels for telephone calls made from their premises. Unit charges are frequently considerably higher than telephone companies' standard charges in order to defray the costs of providing the service. It is a condition of the National Rating Scheme that unit charges are displayed by the telephone or with the room information. But in practice it is not always easy to compare these charges with standard telephone rates. Before using a hotel telephone, particularly for long-distance calls, it is advisable to ask how the charges compare.

Security of valuables

It is advisable to deposit any valuables for safe-keeping with the management of the establishment in which you are staying. If the management accept custody of your property they become wholly liable for its loss or damage. They can however restrict their liability for items brought on to the premises and not placed in their special custody to the minimum amounts imposed by the Hotel Proprietors Act, 1956. These are the sum of £50 in respect of one article and a total of £100 in the case of one guest. In order to restrict their liability the management must display a notice in the form required by the Act in a prominent position in the reception area or main entrance of the premises. Without this notice, the proprietor is liable for the full value of the loss or damage to any property (other than a motor car or its contents) of a guest who has booked overnight accommodation.

Feedback

Let us know about your break or holiday. We welcome suggestions about how the guide itself may be enhanced or improved and you will find our addresses on page 4 of the guide.

Details listed were believed correct at time of going to press (December 1999), but we advise telephoning in advance to check that details have not altered and to discuss any specific requirements.

Most establishments welcome feedback. Please let the proprietor know if you particularly enjoyed your stay. We sincerely hope that you have no cause for complaint, but should you be dissatisfied or have any problems, make your complaint to the management at the time of the incident so that immediate action may be taken.

In certain circumstances the English Tourism Council may look into complaints. However, the Council has no statutory control over establishments or their methods of operating. The Council cannot become involved in legal or contractual matters.

If you do have problems that have not been resolved by the proprietor and which you would like to bring to our attention, please write to:
Quality Standards Department
English Tourism Council
Thames Tower
Black's Road
Hammersmith
London W6 9EL

Code of Conduct

All establishments appearing in this guide have agreed to observe the following Code of Conduct:

1 To ensure high standards of courtesy and cleanliness; catering and service appropriate to the type of establishment.

2 To describe fairly to all visitors and prospective visitors the amenities, facilities and services provided by the establishment, whether by advertisement, brochure, word of mouth or any other means. To allow visitors to see accommodation, if requested, before booking.

3 To make clear to visitors exactly what is included in all prices quoted for accommodation, meals and refreshments, including service charges, taxes and other surcharges. Details of charges, if any, for heating or for additional services or facilities available should also be made clear.

4 To adhere to, and not to exceed, prices current at time of occupation for accommodation or other services.

5 To advise visitors at the time of booking, and subsequently, of any change, if the accommodation offered is in an unconnected annexe, or similar, or by boarding out, and to indicate the location of such accommodation and any difference in comfort and amenities from accommodation in the main establishment.

6 To give each visitor, on request, details of payments due and a receipt if required.

7 To deal promptly and courteously with all enquiries, requests, reservations, correspondence and complaints from visitors.

8 To allow an English Tourism Council representative reasonable access to the establishment, on request, to confirm that the Code of Conduct is being observed.

Index

Abbey House and Coach House, Maxey, Peterborough 108
The Acer Hotel, York 53
Adelaide Hotel, Brighton, East Sussex 198
The Albynes, Nordley, Bridgnorth, Shropshire 79
Alden Cottage, Stonyhurst, Clitheroe, Lancashire 61
The Alderley Edge Hotel, Alderley Edge, Cheshire 59
Amberfold, Heyshott, Midhurst, West Sussex 194
Ambleside Lodge, Ambleside, Cumbria 28
Appleby Manor Country House Hotel, Appleby-in-Westmorland, Cumbria 25
Ashbourne House Hotel, York 52
Ashcroft, Haltwhistle, Northumberland 38
Ashdown Park Hotel, Wych Cross, Forest Row, East Sussex 200
Aston House, Moreton-in-Marsh, Gloucestershire 96
Aucklands, London E4 214
Avalon Barn, Lower Godney, Glastonbury, Somerset 162
Aviary Court Hotel, Illogan, Redruth, Cornwall 139
Avonmore Hotel, London W14 213
Bank House, Oakamoor, Stoke-on-Trent, Staffordshire 76
Bankfield Bed and Breakfast, Luddendenfoot, Halifax, West Yorkshire 58
Barff Lodge, Brayton, Selby, North Yorkshire 55
Barnsdale Lodge Hotel, Exton, Oakham, Leicestershire 108
Bay Lodge, Weymouth, Dorset 158
Beaumont, Windermere, Cumbria 34
Beechleas Hotel and Restaurant, Wimborne Minster, Dorset 187
Beechworth Lawn Hotel, Cheltenham, Gloucestershire 92
Berkeleys of St James, Plymouth, Devon 144
Beryl, Wells, Somerset 163
Bessemer Thatch Hotel and Restaurant, Berrynarbor, Devon 133
Bethersden Old Barn, Bethersden, Ashford, Kent 205
The Bishop's Table Hotel & Restaurant, Farnham, Surrey 185
Bishops Hotel, York 53
Bissick Old Mill, Ladock, Truro, Cornwall 139
The Black Swan Inn, Culgaith, Penrith, Cumbria 24
Blackmore Farm, Cannington, Bridgwater, Somerset 152
Bloomfield House, Bath 167
Blue Haze Hotel, Torquay, Devon 154
The Boar's Head Country Hotel, Ripley Castle Estate, Harrogate, North Yorkshire 45
Bokiddick Farm, Lanivet, Bodmin, Cornwall 139
Borwick Lodge, Hawkshead, Ambleside, Cumbria 31
Bowling Green Hotel, Plymouth, Devon 145
Bowlish House, Shepton Mallet, Somerset 163
Bracken House Country Hotel, Bratton Fleming, Barnstaple, Devon 135

Bradiford Cottage, Bradiford, Barnstaple, Devon 135
Braeside Hotel, Weston-super-Mare 164
Bridge House, Sedbergh, Cumbria 34
Britannia Lodge Hotel, Harrogate, North Yorkshire 45
Britmead House, Bridport, Dorset 158
Brockencote Hall, Chaddesley Corbett, Kidderminster, Worcestershire 82
Bromfield Manor, Bromfield, Ludlow, Shropshire 82
Brook Farm, Beyton, Bury St Edmunds, Suffolk 119
Broom House, Egton Bridge, Whitby, North Yorkshire 47
Broomshaw Hill Farm, Haltwhistle, Northumberland 37
Broxwood Court, Broxwood, Leominster, Herefordshire 84
Brunswick House, Middleton-in-Teesdale, Barnard Castle, County Durham 40
Buckle Yeat Guest House, Near Sawrey, Ambleside, Cumbria 30
Burford House Hotel, Burford, Oxfordshire 179
Burnt House Farm, West Cranmore, Shepton Mallet, Somerset 163
Burpham Country House Hotel, Arundel, West Sussex 196
Burtree House Farm, Hutton Sessay, Thirsk, North Yorkshire 50
Butcombe Farm, Butcombe, Bristol 164
Buxton View, Buxton, Derbyshire 71
Cairn Grove, Fenny Bentley, Ashbourne, Derbyshire 74
Cathedral House, Ely, Cambridgeshire 121
Cavendish Guest House, London NW6 213
Chadstone, Aston Munslow, Craven Arms, Shropshire 81
Channel House Hotel, Minehead, Somerset 151
Chapter House, Roade, Northampton, Northamptonshire 106
Charlton Kings Hotel, Charlton Kings, Cheltenham, Gloucestershire 92
The Chase Hotel, Ross-on-Wye, Herefordshire 89
Chequers Hotel, Pulborough, West Sussex 196
Chimney Farmhouse, Aston, Bampton, Oxfordshire 180
Chippenhall Hall, Fressingfield, Eye, Suffolk 113
The Churchill, Dover, Kent 208
City Guest House, York 52
Cleff House, Iwerne Minster, Blandford Forum, Dorset 188
Cliff Head Hotel Limited, Carlyon Bay, St Austell, Cornwall 142
Clive House, Corbridge, Northumberland 38
Cloud High, Eggleston, Barnard Castle, County Durham 40
The Coach House, Crookham, Cornhill-on-Tweed, Northumberland 35
Coalbrookdale Villa, Ironbridge, Telford, Shropshire 79
Combe House Hotel, Holford, Bridgwater, Somerset 152
Coningsby, Buxton, Derbyshire 71
Coombe House, Bourton-on-the-Water, Gloucestershire 95
Corfield House, Sporle, Swaffham, Norfolk 109

Corkickle Guest House, Whitehaven, Cumbria 22

Cornerstones, Sale, Cheshire 58

The Cornmill, Kirkbymoorside, York, North Yorkshire 49

The Cottage in the Wood Hotel, Malvern Wells, Worcestershire 87

Coulsdon Manor Hotel, Coulsdon, Croydon, Surrey 211

County Hotel, Bath 166

Court Barn Country House Hotel, Clawton, Holsworthy, Devon 136

Courtlands, Shipton-under-Wychwood, Oxfordshire 179

Crabwall Manor Hotel and Restaurant, Mollington, Chester, Cheshire 60

Craigside House, Grasmere, Ambleside, Cumbria 27

Cressbrook Hall, Cressbrook, Buxton, Derbyshire 71

The Cretingham Bell, Cretingham, Woodbridge, Suffolk 115

Cross Lanes Guest House, Bledlow, Aylesbury, Buckinghamshire 182

D'isney Place Hotel, Lincoln, Lincolnshire 107

Dairy House Farm, Wix, Manningtree, Essex 117

The Dairy, Moreton, Thame, Oxfordshire 182

Dale Head Hall Lakeside Hotel, Thirlmere, Keswick, Cumbria 26

Dalton Hall, Dalton, Richmond, North Yorkshire 41

Danesfield House, Marlow-on-Thames, Buckinghamshire 183

Denmark House, Cottenham, Cambridge, Cambridgeshire 122

Derwent Cottage, Portinscale, Keswick, Cumbria 22

Ditch House, Chelmorton, Buxton, Derbyshire 72

Dormy House, Broadway, Worcestershire 99

The Dower House, Padstow, Cornwall 138

The Drunken Duck Inn, Barngates, Ambleside, Cumbria 29

Earsham Park Farm, Earsham, Bungay, Suffolk 112

Eastwell Manor Hotel, Boughton Lees, Ashford, Kent 206

Eckington House, Ripe, Lewes, East Sussex 199

Eden Grove House, Bolton, Appleby-in-Westmorland, Cumbria 24

Edge Hall, Hadleigh, Ipswich, Suffolk 118

Edgemoor Hotel, Bovey Tracey, Devon 148

Efford Cottage, Everton, Lymington, Hampshire 192

Ermewood House Hotel, Ermington, Ivybridge, Devon 146

Eversley, Westward Ho!, Bideford, Devon 136

The Falcon Hotel, Bude, Cornwall 137

Farncombe, Clapton, Bourton-on-the-Water, Gloucestershire 95

Feathers Hotel, Ledbury, Herefordshire 89

Felbrigg Lodge, Aylmerton, Aylmerton, Norfolk 109

Felton House, Felton, Hereford 85

Fern Cottage, Nr Porlock, Exmoor National Park, Somerset 151

Ferncliffe Country Guest House, Ingleton, via Carnforth, North Yorkshire 62

Fieldhead Hotel, West Looe, Cornwall 143

Fieldway Bed & Breakfast, Framlingham, Woodbridge, Suffolk 115

Fir Trees, Windermere, Cumbria 34

The Firs Bed and Breakfast, North Woodchester, Stroud, Gloucestershire 92

Five Rise Locks Hotel, Bingley, West Yorkshire 58

Folly Farm Cottage, Ilmington, Shipston-on-Stour, Warwickshire 101

Ford Side House, Buxton, Derbyshire 70

Forest Edge, Lea, Ross-on-Wye, Herefordshire 89

Forest Pines Hotel, Broughton, Brigg, Scunthorpe, South Humberside 55

Gainsborough Hotel, Bath 165

Gate Cottage, Sutton Benger, Chippenham, Wiltshire 169

Georgian House, Sutterton, Boston, Lincolnshire 107

Gilpin Lodge Country House Hotel and Restaurant, Windermere, Cumbria 33

Glebe Cottage Farm, Ashmore, Dorset 169

Glebe Farm, Benniworth, Market Rasen, Lincolnshire 107

Glebe Farm, Bolton Percy, York, North Yorkshire 54

Glebe Farm, Loxley, Warwickshire 102

Glen Tor Hotel, Ilfracombe, Devon 133

Glydwish Place, Burwash, East Sussex 200

The Golden Lion Inn of Easenhall, Easenhall, Rugby, Warwickshire 105

The Grand Hotel, Eastbourne, East Sussex 201

The Grange, Long Marston, Stratford-upon-Avon, Warwickshire 101

The Grange, West Burton, Leyburn, North Yorkshire 42

Grapevine Hotel, Stow-on-the-Wold, Gloucestershire 97

The Great House Restaurant and Hotel, Lavenham, Sudbury, Suffolk 120

Green Lawns Hotel, Falmouth, Cornwall 141

Greenbank, Borrowdale, Keswick, Cumbria 26

Grendon Guesthouse, Buxton, Derbyshire 70

Grey Friar Lodge Country House Hotel, Clappersgate, Ambleside, Cumbria 28

Greycroft, Alston, Cumbria 20

Grove House, Maidstone, Kent 211

Guiting Guesthouse, Guiting Power, Cheltenham, Gloucestershire 97

Ha'penny House, Milford-on-Sea, Lymington, Hampshire 192

Hampers End, Storrington, Pulborough, West Sussex 197

Harbourside Bed and Breakfast Hotel, Folkestone, Kent 207

Hardicot Guest House, Walmer, Deal, Kent 208

Harmony Country Lodge, Burniston, Scarborough, North Yorkshire 47

Hawkhill Farmhouse, Lesbury, Alnwick, Northumberland 36

Hazel Bank, Borrowdale, Keswick, Cumbria 26

The Hazelwood, York 53

Heatherly Cottage, Gastard, Corsham, Wiltshire 168

Helliers Farm, Aveton Gifford, Kingsbridge, Devon 146

Helm, Askrigg, Leyburn, North Yorkshire 41

Heron House Hotel, Thurlestone Sands, Salcombe, Devon 147

Hidelow House, Acton Beauchamp, Worcester, Worcestershire 86

High Buston Hall, High Buston, Alnmouth, Northumberland 36

High Farm, Cropton, Pickering, North Yorkshire 48

High House, Rowington, Warwick, Warwickshire 104

Highfield, Leominster, Herefordshire 83

Highfield Farm, Sandy, Bedfordshire 124

Highfield Guest House, London SE6 — 212

Highfield House Country Hotel, Hawkshead Hill, Ambleside, Cumbria — 28

Highlands, Nailsworth, Stroud, Gloucestershire — 93

The Hillsman House, Lymington, Hampshire — 193

Holbeck Ghyll Country House Hotel, Windermere, Cumbria — 32

Holcombe Hotel & Restaurant, Deddington, Banbury, Oxfordshire — 178

Holdfast Cottage Hotel, Little Malvern, Worcestershire — 88

Holly Cottage, Corton, Lowestoft, Suffolk — 112

Holly Lodge, Bath — 167

Holly Park House, Windermere, Cumbria — 33

Holmhead Guest House, Greenhead, via Carlisle — 37

Holmwood, Binfield Heath, Henley-on-Thames, Oxfordshire — 183

Holmwood House Hotel, York — 54

Holyleas House, Buckland Newton, Dorchester, Dorset — 159

Home Farm, Biddestone, Chippenham, Wiltshire — 169

Home Farm, Great Witley, Worcester, Worcestershire — 83

The Homestead, Burgess Hill, West Sussex — 198

Honeyholes, Hackthorn, Lincoln, Lincolnshire — 106

Hope Lodge Hotel, Shanklin, Isle of Wight — 193

Horizon House, Carlyon Bay, St Austell, Cornwall — 142

Hotel Number Sixteen, London SW7 — 213

Hotel on the Park, Cheltenham, Gloucestershire — 91

Hucklesbrook Farm, South Gorley, Fordingbridge, Hampshire — 187

The Hundred House Hotel, Ruan Highlanes, near Truro, Cornwall — 141

Hunters Way Guest House, Keswick, Cumbria — 23

The Hurtwood Inn Hotel, Peaslake, Guildford, Surrey — 196

The Hythe Imperial, Hythe, Kent — 206

Ilex Cottage, Worth, Deal, Kent — 210

Ing Hill Lodge, Kirkby Stephen, Cumbria — 35

Isbourne Manor House, Winchcombe, Cheltenham, Gloucestershire — 97

Island House, Lavenham, Sudbury, Suffolk — 120

Iwood B&B, Heathfield, East Sussex — 200

Jeake's House, Rye, East Sussex — 203

Kenora Private Hotel, Weymouth, Dorset — 158

Kingford House, Lynton, Devon — 134

The Kings at Ivy House, Biggin-by-Hartington, Buxton, Derbyshire — 74

Kings Head Inn and Restaurant, Bledington, Gloucestershire — 96

Knock Hundred Cottage, Clungunford, Craven Arms, Shropshire — 81

The Knoll, Shiplake, Henley-on-Thames, Oxfordshire — 183

Knottside Farm, Pateley Bridge, Harrogate, North Yorkshire — 44

Knowle Farm, Rattery, Nr Totnes, Devon — 147

Lains Cottage, Quarley, Andover, Hampshire — 185

Lake Isle Hotel, Uppingham, Oakham, Leicestershire — 106

The Lansdown Grove, Bath — 167

Lansdowne Hotel, Eastbourne, East Sussex — 201

Lansdowne House, Bourton-on-the-Water, Gloucestershire — 95

Lavenham Priory, Lavenham, Sudbury, Suffolk — 119

Lea Hill Hotel, Membury, Axminster, Devon — 157

Lee House Farm, Waterhouses, Stoke-on-Trent, Staffordshire — 76

Ley Fields Farm, Cheadle, Stoke-on-Trent, Staffordshire — 77

Limetree Farm, Grewelthorpe, Ripon, North Yorkshire — 43

Linden Hall Hotel, Health Spa & Golf Course, Longhorsley, Morpeth, Northumberland — 37

Lindeth Fell Country House Hotel, Windermere, Cumbria — 33

Linthwaite House Hotel, Windermere, Cumbria — 30

Little Brendon Hill Farm, Wheddon Cross, Exmoor, Somerset — 150

Little Holtby, Leeming Bar, Northallerton, North Yorkshire — 43

Little Orchard House, Rye, East Sussex — 205

Little Silver Country Hotel, St Michaels, Tenterden, Kent — 205

Littlegarth, Ebberston, Scarborough, North Yorkshire — 48

Low Dover Beadnell Bay, Beadnell, Chathill, Northumberland — 36

Lower Farm, Kingweston, Somerton, Somerset — 161

Lower House, Leintwardine, Craven Arms, Shropshire — 81

Lower Nichols Nymet Farm, North Tawton, Devon — 150

Lowerfield Farm, Willersey, Broadway, Worcestershire — 100

Lowfell, Bowness-on-Windermere, Cumbria — 29

Loxley Farm, Loxley, Warwickshire — 101

The Lygon Arms, Broadway, Worcestershire — 98

Lynwood House, Keswick, Cumbria — 23

Lyth Hill House, Shrewsbury, Shropshire — 78

M'Dina Courtyard, Chipping Campden, Gloucestershire — 100

Mallard Grange, nr Fountains Abbey, Ripon, North Yorkshire — 44

The Manor Country House, York — 54

Manor Farm, Acton Bridge, Northwich, Cheshire — 59

Manor Farm Oast, Icklesham, Winchelsea, East Sussex — 203

Manor House Farm, Great Ayton, Cleveland — 47

Marina Hotel, Fowey, Cornwall — 142

The Marlborough at Ipswich, Ipswich, Suffolk — 116

Marriott Hollins Hall Hotel & Country Club, Baildon, Shipley, West Yorkshire — 57

Marygreen Manor Hotel, Brentwood, Essex — 124

May Cottage, Thruxton, Andover, Hampshire — 185

Maynard Arms Hotel, Grindleford, Derbyshire — 73

The Meadow House, Burwell, Cambridge, Cambridgeshire — 121

Meadowland, Bath — 168

Middleton Lodge, Middleton Priors, Bridgnorth, Shropshire — 80

Mile Hill Barn, Kelsale, Saxmundham, Suffolk — 115

The Mill Arms, Dunbridge, Romsey, Hampshire — 186

The Mill at Harvington, Harvington, Evesham, Worcestershire — 99

Mill Common House, Ridlington, North Walsham, Norfolk — 109

Mill End Hotel, Chagford, Devon — 148

Mill Orchard, Kingstone, Hereford — 85

Millstream Hotel and Restaurant, Bosham, Chichester, West Sussex — 194

Milton House, Londonderry, Northallerton, North Yorkshire — 43

Molehills, Bladbean, Canterbury, Kent — 207

Monkshill, Monkton Combe, Bath 168

Moor Farm, Holyport, Maidenhead, Berkshire 184

Mortons House Hotel, Corfe Castle, Wareham, Dorset 188

Mount House, Goudhurst, Cranbrook, Kent 201

Muchelney Ham Farm, Muchelney, Langport, Somerset 160

Nailcote Hall Hotel and Restaurant, Berkswell, West Midlands 104

New Barn Cottage, West Chiltington, Pulborough, West Sussex 197

New Capernwray Farm, Capernwray, Carnforth, Lancashire 61

Newton Farm House, Salisbury, Wiltshire 170

North End Barns, Bletsoe, Bedford, Bedfordshire 123

North Lodge, Saxmundham, Suffolk 114

Northcote Manor, Langho, Blackburn, Lancashire 61

Northcourt, Shorwell, Newport, Isle of Wight 193

Northleigh House, Hatton, Warwick, Warwickshire 104

Norton House, Whitchurch, Ross-on-Wye, Herefordshire 90

Number Eighty Eight, Salisbury, Wiltshire 170

Number Nine, Stow-on-the-Wold, Gloucestershire 96

Number Twenty Eight, Ludlow, Shropshire 82

The Nurse's Cottage, Sway, Lymington, Hampshire 191

Oak Lodge Hotel, Bush Hill Park, Enfield, Middlesex 214

Oak Tree Farm, Hopwas, Tamworth, Staffordshire 105

Oakbank House, Bowness-on-Windermere, Cumbria 29

October House, Swarkestone, Derby, Derbyshire 75

The Old Bell Foundry, Burford, Oxford, Oxfordshire 179

The Old Cowshed, Bromyard, Herefordshire 86

The Old Deanery, Ripon, North Yorkshire 44

The Old Forge at Totnes, Totnes, Devon 148

The Old House, Eyke, Woodbridge, Suffolk 116

The Old Manse, Chatton, Alnwick, Northumberland 35

The Old Pump House, Aylsham, Norwich, Norfolk 111

The Old Rectory, Didmarton, Gloucestershire 93

The Old Rectory, Harborough Magna, Rugby, Warwickshire 105

The Old Rectory, Hope Mansell, Ross-on-Wye, Herefordshire 90

The Old Rectory, Winterbourne Steepleton, Dorchester, Dorset 159

The Old School House, Alton, Stoke-on-Trent, Staffordshire 76

The Old Tollgate Restaurant & Hotel, Bramber, Steyning,
West Sussex 197

The Old Vicarage, Brooke, Norwich, Norfolk 112

The Old Vicarage, Easingwold, York, North Yorkshire 51

The Old Vicarage, Hougham, Dover, Kent 207

The Old Vicarage, Lorton, Cumbria 22

The Old Vicarage, Milborne Port, Sherborne, Dorset 160

The Old Vicarage, Vowchurch, Hereford 85

Old Vicarage Hotel, Worfield, Bridgnorth, Shropshire 80

Ye Olde Cop Shop, Washington Village, Sunderland,
Tyne and Wear 39

The Olde House on the Green, Fulford, Stoke-on-Trent 77

Oldstead Grange, Coxwold, York, North Yorkshire 50

Omnia Somnia, Ashbourne, Derbyshire 75

Osborne Hotel & Langtry's Restaurant, Torquay, Devon 154

The Paddock, Shobdon, Leominster, Herefordshire 83

Parsonage Farm, Iddesleigh, Winkleigh, Devon 150

Partway House, Swalcliffe, Banbury, Oxfordshire 178

Payton Hotel, Stratford-upon-Avon, Warwickshire 103

Pembroke House, Oxford 181

Pen-y-Dyffryn Country Hotel, Rhyd-y-Croesau, Oswestry,
Shropshire 77

Penryn, East Lambrook, South Petherton, Somerset 160

The Pheasant Inn (by Kielder Water), Stannersburn,
Hexham, Northumberland 20

Pinkhill Cottage, Standlake, Witney, Oxfordshire 180

Pipwell Manor, Holbeach, Spalding, Lincolnshire 108

Playden Cottage Guesthouse, Rye, East Sussex 203

Poplar Hall, Frostenden, Wangford, Suffolk 113

Porlock Vale House, Porlock Weir, Somerset 151

Port William Inn, Trebarwith Strand, Tintagel, Cornwall 138

Preston Lea, Faversham, Kent 210

Prince of Wales, Hilton, Huntingdon, Cambridgeshire 122

Ravenstone Lodge, Bassenthwaite, Keswick, Cumbria 21

Red House Farm, Haughley, Stowmarket, Suffolk 118

The Red House, Lavenham, Sudbury, Suffolk 119

The Red House, Roundswell, Barnstaple, Devon 135

Red Lion House, Kirkbymoorside, York, North Yorkshire 49

Redlands, Combe Florey, Taunton, Somerset 152

Reevsmoor, Hollington, Ashbourne, Derbyshire 75

Regency Guesthouse, Neatishead, Norwich, Norfolk 110

Regency Park Hotel, Thatcham, Newbury, Berkshire 184

Riber Hall, Matlock, Derbyshire 74

Ring O' Roses, Holcombe, Bath, Somerset 164

The Ringlestone Inn & Farmhouse Hotel, Harrietsham,
Maidstone, Kent 211

Riverside Lodge, Rothay Bridge, Ambleside, Cumbria 27

Rockley Farmhouse, Brayford, Barnstaple, Devon 134

Rockvale Hotel, Lynton, Devon 134

Rombalds Hotel and Restaurant, Ilkley, West Yorkshire 56

Rookhurst Country House Hotel, Gayle, Hawes,
North Yorkshire 41

Rose Farm, Middleton, Saxmundham, Suffolk 113

Rosefield House, Lymington, Hampshire 192

Roundham House Hotel, Bridport, Dorset 157

Royal Castle Hotel, Dartmouth, Devon 155

Royal Spring Farm, Longhope, Gloucestershire 90

Royal York and Faulkner Hotel, Sidmouth, Devon 155

Rufus House Hotel, Lyndhurst, Hampshire 191

Ruskin Hotel and Restaurant, Harrogate, North Yorkshire 46

Rye Hill Farm, Slaley, Hexham, Northumberland 38

Rye Lodge Hotel, Rye, East Sussex 204

St Edmund's, Colyford, Colyton, Devon 155

Sambourne Hall Farm, Sambourne, Redditch, Worcestershire 103

Sandalwood House, Chipping Campden, Gloucestershire 100

Sawrey House Country Hotel, Near Sawrey, Ambleside,
Cumbria 31

Sayang House, Hope Bowdler, Church Stretton, Shropshire 80

Scagglethorpe Manor, Scagglethorpe, Malton, North Yorkshire 52

Seawood Hotel, Lynton, Devon 133

Seckford Hall Hotel, Woodbridge, Suffolk 116

Sevenford House, Rosedale Abbey, Pickering, North Yorkshire 48

Shallowdale House, Ampleforth, York, North Yorkshire 50

Shelleys Hotel, Lewes, East Sussex 198

Shipton Glebe, Woodstock, Oxfordshire 180

Shortgate Manor Farm, Halland, Lewes, East Sussex 199

Siena Hotel, Bath 165

Skiddaw Hotel, Keswick, Cumbria 23

South Paddock, Maresfield Park, Uckfield, East Sussex 199

Southlands Bed and Breakfast, Huntington, York 51

The Sportsman, Sholden, Deal, Kent 209

Sproxton Hall, Sproxton, Helmsley, North Yorkshire 49

Staddlestones, Thorndon Cross, Okehampton, Devon 149

Stafford Barton, Broadhembury, Honiton, Devon 153

Staggs Cottage, Brisco, Carlisle, Cumbria 20

Stangray House, Keinton Mandeville, Somerton, Somerset 161

Stanneylands Hotel, Wilmslow, Cheshire 59

The Steppes, Ullingswick, Hereford 86

Still Cottage, Somerton, Somerset 161

Stour Valley House, Chilham, Canterbury, Kent 210

Stratford Victoria, Stratford-upon-Avon, Warwickshire 103

Stretton Lodge Hotel, Cheltenham, Gloucestershire 91

The Stud Farm Countryside Bed and Breakfast, Pilsley, Chesterfield, Derbyshire 73

Studley Priory Hotel, Horton cum Studley, Oxfordshire 182

Sudeley Hill Farm, Winchcombe, Cheltenham, Gloucestershire 98

Suite Dreams Hotel, Maidencombe, Torquay, Devon 153

Swaledale Watch, Caldbeck, Cumbria 21

Swallows Eaves Hotel, Colyford, Colyton, Devon 156

The Swan Hotel, Bibury, Gloucestershire 94

Swan Inn, Sturminster Newton, Dorset 188

Talland Bay Hotel, Talland Bay, Looe, Cornwall 143

Tatnam Farm, Poole, Dorset 190

Tavern House, Willesley, Tetbury, Gloucestershire 93

Thatch Lodge Hotel, Charmouth, near Lyme Regis, Dorset 157

Thomas Luny House, Teignmouth, Devon 153

The Three Lions, Stuckton, Fordingbridge, Hampshire 187

Throstle Gill Farm, Dalton, Richmond, North Yorkshire 40

Thurlestone Hotel, Kingsbridge, Devon 146

Tides Reach Hotel, Salcombe, Devon 147

Tor Cottage, Chillaton, Lifton, Devon 145

Tregildry Hotel, Manaccan, Helston, Cornwall 140

Trehellas House, Washaway, Bodmin, Cornwall 138

Trenderway Farm, Pelynt, Polperro, Cornwall 143

Trevinhurst Lodge, Eastbourne, East Sussex 202

Tudor Cottage, Albury, Ware, Hertfordshire 124

Tudor Terrace Guest House, Cleethorpes, North East Lincolnshire 55

Tye Rock Country House Hotel, Porthleven, Helston, Cornwall 141

Tylney Hall Hotel, Rotherwick, Basingstoke, Hampshire 184

Uppaton Country Guest House, Buckland Monachorum, Yelverton, Devon 145

Valley Hotel, Harrogate, North Yorkshire 45

Villa Magdala Hotel, Bath 165

Village Farm Holidays, Newton-on-Ouse, York, North Yorkshire 51

Villiers Hotel, Buckingham, Buckinghamshire 178

Wallett's Court Country House Hotel & Restaurant, St-Margarets-at-Cliffe, Dover, Kent 208

Wallis Farm, Hardwick, Cambridge, Cambridgeshire 122

Wateredge Hotel, Waterhead Bay, Ambleside, Cumbria 30

Waterside Guest House, Dymchurch, Romney Marsh, Kent 206

Watersmeet Hotel, Mortehoe, Woolacombe, Devon 132

Weavers, Hadleigh, Ipswich, Suffolk 118

Welland Court, Upton-upon-Severn, Worcestershire 87

The Wenlock Edge Inn, Wenlock Edge, Shropshire 79

Wentbridge House Hotel, Wentbridge, Pontefract, West Yorkshire 56

Westwood Barn, Wood Dalling, Norwich, Norfolk 111

White Horse Inn, Sutton, Pulborough, West Sussex 195

White Horse Inn, Withersfield, Haverhill, Suffolk 120

The White House, Clifton, Penrith, Cumbria 24

The White House, Highcliffe, Christchurch, Dorset 190

White Lodge Hotel, Swanage, Dorset 189

Whiteacres Guesthouse, Broadway, Worcestershire 99

Whitley Hall Hotel, Grenoside, Sheffield 56

Whitley Ridge Country House Hotel, Brockenhurst, Hampshire 191

Willowfield Hotel, Arnside, Cumbria 62

Wind in the Willows Hotel, Glossop, Derbyshire 70

Wings Cottage, Kemerton, Tewkesbury, Gloucestershire 98

Winter Dene Hotel, Bournemouth 190

Witch Hazel, Wicklewood, Wymondham, Norfolk 111

Woodacre, Fontwell, Arundel, West Sussex 194

Woodland Crag Guest House, Grasmere, Ambleside, Cumbria 27

Woodlands, Grindleford, Derbyshire 73

Woodlands Country House, Ireby, Cumbria 21

Wyche Keep Country House, Malvern, Worcestershire 87

Wyndham Arms, Clearwell, Coleford, Gloucestershire 91

Wynncroft Hotel, Paignton, Devon 154

Yalbury Cottage Hotel and Restaurant, Lower Bockhampton, Dorchester, Dorset 159

Yardley's, Hadstock, Cambridge 121

Yeoldon Country House Hotel and Restaurant, Northam, Bideford, Devon 136

Yewfield Vegetarian Guest House, Hawkshead Hill, Ambleside, Cumbria 31